The origins of the modern idea of religion can be traced to the Enlightenment. This study shows how the concepts 'religion' and 'the religions' arose out of controversies in seventeenth- and eighteenth-century England. The birth of 'the religions', conceived to be sets of beliefs and practices, enabled the establishment of a new science of religion in which the various 'religions' were studied and impartially compared. Dr Harrison thus offers a detailed historical picture of the emergence of comparative religion as an academic discipline.

'RELIGION' AND THE RELIGIONS IN THE ENGLISH ENLIGHTENMENT

'RELIGION' AND THE RELIGIONS IN THE ENGLISH ENLIGHTENMENT

PETER HARRISON

Assistant Professor of Philosophy,
Bond University, Queensland

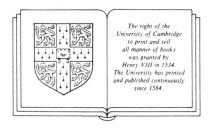

CAMBRIDGE UNIVERSITY PRESS

Cambridge
New York   Port Chester
Melbourne   Sydney

To my parents,
Jean and Duncan

Published by the Press Syndicate of the University of Cambridge
The Pitt Building, Trumpington Street, Cambridge CB2 IRP
40 West 20th Street, New York, NY 10011, USA
10 Stamford Road, Oakleigh, Melbourne 3166, Australia

First published 1990

Printed in Great Britain by The Bath Press, Avon

British Library cataloguing in publication data
Harrison, Peter *1955*–
'Religion' and the religions in the English Enlightenment
1. England. Religious movements, history
1. Title
291'.0942

Library of Congress cataloguing in publication data
'Religion' and the religions in the English Enlightenment / Peter
Harrison.
p.   cm.
Includes bibliographical references.
ISBN 0 521 38530 X
1. Religion – Study and teaching – England – History – 17th century.
2. Religion – Study and teaching – England – History – 18th century.
3. Enlightenment. 4. England – Intellectual life – 17th century.
5. England – Intellectual life – 18th century. 6. England –
Religion – 17th century. 7. England – Religion – 18th century.
1. Title.
BL41 H37   1990   89–77292
291 – dc20   CIP
ISBN 0 521 38530 X hardback

BS

CONTENTS

ACKNOWLEDGEMENTS

For much of my academic life the Department of Studies in Religion of the University of Queensland has provided a congenial and stimulating environment for research and discussion. To all of the Department there I give my thanks. I owe a particular debt of gratitude to Philip Almond for his many valuable comments on the various drafts of this work. I have also benefited from the advice of David Pailin and Richard Popkin, whose special knowledge of this period has proved most helpful. Eric Sharpe, too, made a number of useful observations on an earlier version of this book. Finally I should thank Narelle Mallett who has painstakingly proof-read the typescript.

INTRODUCTION

And such is the deplorable Condition of our Age, that a Man dares not openly and directly own what he thinks in Divine Matters, tho it be never so true and beneficial... and yet a Man may not only make new Discoveries and Improvements in Law or Physick, and in the other Arts and Sciences impunibly, but also for so doing be deservedly encourag'd and rewarded.

John Toland, *Christianity not Mysterious*, Preface

That there exist in the world such entities as 'the religions' is an uncontroversial claim. There may be discussion about whether the beliefs and practices which are said to constitute the various religions are legitimate or 'true', but few would deny that these systems exist. So too, the term 'religion', as a generic description of what the plural 'religions' are about, is part of everyday discourse and is used with some precision by scholars. However, it was not always so. The concepts 'religion' and 'the religions', as we presently understand them, emerged quite late in Western thought, during the Enlightenment. Between them, these two notions provided a new framework for classifying particular aspects of human life. The task of this study is a twofold one: first, to examine the emergence of the twin concepts 'religion' and 'the religions'; and second, to give an account of the new science of religion which they made possible.

The first part of this project owes much to Wilfred Cantwell Smith's classic *The Meaning and End of Religion.* It is Smith's contention that during the age of reason the name 'religion' was given to external aspects of the religious life, to systems of practices. Whereas in the Middle Ages the concern of the Christian West had been with faith – a 'dynamic of the heart' – in the seventeenth-century attention shifted to the impersonal and objective 'religion'. Increasingly this term came to be an outsider's description of a dubious theological enterprise. Along with 'religion' came the plural 'religions' – 'the Protestant Religion', 'the Catholic Religion', 'Mahometanism', 'heathen Religion', and so on. These too were abstracted, depersonalised systems which were intended to represent in propositional terms the sum

I

total of the religious lives of other peoples (a task which, incidentally, Smith believes the concepts were inadequate to perform).[1] In the present work I shall be examining in more detail this process of the objectification of religious faith, focussing particularly on the English contribution to the ideation of 'religion' and 'the religions'. In the course of this examination I shall be paying particular attention to the unique contributions of Protestant scholastics, Platonists, and those rationalists generally referred to as 'deists'.

The second theme of this book is rather more neglected. Most accounts of the history of comparative religion or of *Religionswissenschaft* have the 'dispassionate' study of the religions beginning in the nineteenth century with such figures as Max Müller and C. P. Tiele.[2] Yet for a number of reasons the science of religion had to begin earlier. In the first instance, it would be rather curious if in the seventeenth century – the age of developing natural science – attempts were not made to place the study of religion on a similar footing. This was the projected discipline which that champion of free thought John Toland urged upon his more conservative contemporaries. It was an undertaking made all the more urgent by a crisis of authority within Christendom which highlighted the need for an honest and unbiassed appraisal of the competing forms of Christianity and, for the most thoroughgoing thinkers, of the claims of other 'religions'. The great revolutions in science and religion which took place in the sixteenth and seventeenth centuries thus paved the way for the development of a secular study of the religions, and equally importantly, of a concept 'religion' which could link together and relate the apparently disparate religious beliefs and practices found in the empirical 'religions'.

Another reason we would expect the 'scientific' study of 'religion' to begin at this time is to do with the process of ideation itself. Paradoxical though it may sound, it is evident from the philosophy of science that objects of study are shaped to a large degree by the techniques which are used to investigate them. If we apply this principle to the history of 'religion', it can be said that the very methods of the embryonic science of religion determined to a large extent what 'religion' was to be. It would be expected that 'religion' and the strategies for its elucidation would develop in tandem. For this reason 'religion' was constructed along essentially rationalist lines, for it was created in the image of the prevailing rationalist methods of investigation: 'religion' was cut to fit the new and much-vaunted scientific method. In this manner, 'religion' entered the realm of the intelligible. It lay open to rational investigation while its specific forms – 'the religions' – could be measured against each other, or against some intellectualist criterion of truth. As we shall see, inquiry into the religion of a people became a matter of asking what was believed, and if it was true. The emergence of the idea of religion thus entailed tests of religious truth, theories of religion, comparisons of 'religions', in short, a whole set of rules which governed the manner in which the nascent concept was to be deployed. Toland's wish had come true, though perhaps not in the way he would have liked.

If the time of the appearance of this new interpretative framework was the late seventeenth and early eighteenth centuries, then the place was England. Of course, England was not the only country in the Western world where a secular approach to the religions was evolving. The *philosophes* of the eighteenth-century French Enlightenment have some claim to be considered as co-pioneers of comparative religion.[3] Yet it was in England, in the previous century, that the groundwork was laid down. Here the Enlightenment first dawned in an historically tangible way. The religious upheavals of the sixteenth and seventeenth centuries meant that Englishmen enjoyed a freedom of religious expression which was matched nowhere in Europe, with the possible exception of the Netherlands. The early Enlightenment in England is attested by a body of literature, by controversies, and by certain figures in a way that is not true of France, or anywhere else.[4] Most importantly, England, during the time-frame of this study, underwent considerable changes in religious orientation. As Locke put it, the kings and queens of post-Reformation England had been 'of such different minds in point of religion, and enjoined thereupon such different things', that no 'sincere and upright worshipper of God could, with a safe conscience, obey their several decrees'.[5] Not only did this diachronic pluralism contribute greatly to secularisation, but it led also to the comparison of the various forms of Christianity with each other, and shaped to a significant extent the way in which the English were to view other 'religions'. The whole comparative approach to religion was directly related to confessional disputes within Christianity. As we shall discover, these confessional conflicts were the single most important factor in the development of comparative religion.

Another reason that England was the setting for the emergence of these new ideas of religion was that it was here that historical criticism of the Bible got under way in earnest. While within Christendom, religious pluralism had provided the impetus for the comparison of 'religions', from without, discoveries in the New World and the Pacific were calling into question biblical views of human history. This challenge to sacred history, reinforced by the writings of such thinkers as Spinoza, La Peyrère, and Hobbes, was to set the more radical of the rationalising theologians on the path of biblical criticism.[6] 'Religions' thus came to be credited with a natural, rather than a sacred history.

It remains only to indicate something of the plan of this book. After a brief examination of the backgrounds of Enlightenment ideas of religion, we shall move, in the second chapter, to a consideration of the rise of the idea of religion in theological controversy. Two countervailing tendencies will be examined: Calvinism, in which 'genuine religion' is construed as 'saving knowledge', and Platonism, in which 'religion' is deemed to be 'natural'. In the third chapter we shall see how in a creative combination these two tendencies, the so-called deists modified 'religion' to make it a natural object constituted primarily by propositional knowledge. These two chapters thus describe how religious ideas of religion were secularised. In the final two chapters, we see how the history of 'religion', once thought to be exhausted in biblical accounts of idolatry and apostasy, came to be credited with its own, non-sacred or natural history. Thus, just as the theology of 'religion' was secularised, so the sacred history of 'religion', became simply the history of 'the religions'.

We turn now to antecedents – the reformers, Renaissance Platonists, and classical atheists who were important precursors of, respectively, the seventeenth-century Calvinists, the English Platonists, and the 'deists'.

ONE

ANTECEDENTS

Nor think, in NATURE'S STATE they blindly trod;
The state of nature was the reign of God . . .

Take Nature's path, and mad Opinions leave
All States can reach it, and all heads conceive;
Obvious her goods, in no extreme they dwell,
There needs but thinking right, and meaning well;
And mourn our various portions as we please,
Equal is common sense, and common ease.
Pope, An Essay on Man. III.247–8, IV.29–34

The concept 'religion' involved the relocation of religious faith into a new sphere, a sphere in which the presumed substance of religion could serve as an object of rational investigation. The new context for 'religion' was the realm of nature. In much the same way that the world became the object of scientific enquiry in the sixteenth and seventeenth centuries through a process of desacralisation, so too, religious practices (initially those of other people) were demystified by the imposition of *natural* laws. As the physical world ceased to be a theatre in which the drama of creation was constantly re-directed by divine interventions, human expressions of religious faith came increasingly to be seen as outcomes of natural processes rather than the work of God or of Satan and his legions. For both scientists and students of the new-found 'religion', most of whom maintained religious convictions, it remained to be determined what role could be found for God in the natural world. This in turn hinged upon what was meant by 'nature' and 'natural'.

In the seventeenth and eighteenth centuries the term 'nature' had taken on a variety of meanings. This polyvalence is reflected in the variety of evaluations of natural religion.[1] In the treatment of religion, three quite distinct understandings of 'nature' developed, from which there arose three discrete interpretations of religion and the religions. These three positions between them delimit the range of seventeenth-century notions of religion. According to the most conservative interpretation, the natural order is opposed to the supernatural. In this scheme of things 'natural' religion is the result of human sin and stands in opposition to 'revealed' or supernaturally based religion. While this distinction did not originate with the Reformers, it was they who fashioned it into a sharp dichotomy, damning those who presumed to construct a religion based on reason. Protestant Christianity remained within the ambit of divine operation: Papism and all other forms of piety were regarded as the degenerate products of a fallen nature.

Such a view of nature was not acceptable to more enquiring minds in the seventeenth century. In opposing the *Scientia inflat* of divines of the reformed tradition, Francis Bacon put forward two quite different understandings of nature. The 'light of nature', he said, 'is used in two several senses':

> the one, that which springeth from reason, sense, induction, argument, according to the laws of heaven and earth; the other, that which is imprinted upon the spirit of man by an inward instinct, according to the law of conscience, which is a sparkle of purity of his first estate; in which latter sense only he is participant of some light and discerning touching the perfection of the moral law.[2]

Bacon here spells out the two views of nature which were to dominate the intellectual landscape for almost two centuries. Kant was eventually to label them 'pure reason' and 'practical reason'. The latter, Bacon's 'inward instinct', is derived from Renaissance thought and has deeper roots in Stoic philosophy. 'Nature', according to this view, is simply another mode of divine operation. Here the natural is not opposed to the supernatural, but rather complements it. Nature participates in original divine essence because the divine power pervades nature itself.[3] In their reaction against the Reformers, the seventeenth-century Platonists were to adopt this view of nature, proposing that natural religion, in its most perfect expression, was a legitimate, and indeed *the* legitimate form of religion. In theory, this potentially universal religion of morality should not differ from revealed religion, for both issue from a common source – God.

As the Enlightenment progressed, a third view of nature – Bacon's 'reason, sense, induction, argument' – came into prominence. The 'light of nature' in this scheme has to do with 'the laws of heaven and earth'. An inchoate natural *order* was invested with its own laws of operation and ultimately came to admit investigation without any reference to the divine. 'Religion' was similarly constituted as something that was amenable to rational investigation, or more importantly, to rational justification. The laws of heaven pertaining to 'religion' were not less mutable than those which described the physical universe. In what amounted to a victory of the natural over the supernatural, reason, in this last sense, came to be a criterion of revelation. Equally important was the perceived contrast between the independent operation of a lawful nature and the human social realm of 'convention'. This orientation harks back to the ancient sophists' distinction between nature and convention. English free-thinkers were eventually to collapse putative revelations into the category of human conventions, for what is truly natural is universal. The diversity and incompatibility of beliefs supposedly based on revelations automatically placed positive 'religions' outside the ordered realm of nature and into the category of arbitrary human conventions. The classical age provided free-thinkers with not only the nature – convention distinction, but also more specific theories about the origin and maintenance of diverse religious conventions.

The chief ideological sources for the seventeenth-century construction of 'religion' were then the Reformation, the Renaissance, and the Classical Age. The importance of these sources is difficult to overestimate, for in the seventeenth century, if not the eighteenth, the superiority of ancient learning was virtually unquestioned. In one sense, seventeenth-century religious disputes were about which ancient authorities were to be normative – the New Testament and the Church Fathers, Plato and his interpreters, or the 'atheists' of the classical period. [4]

THE REFORMATION

It is a commonplace that the Reformation established the material conditions which led to secularisation, and consequently to the growth of secular views of religion.[5] Our concern here, however, is not to retell the story of how those conditions were established, but rather to isolate those ideologies of the reformers which led more directly to the 'naturalisation' of matters of faith. Of these, the most important was the sharp distinction drawn between natural and revealed knowledge of God.[6] This distinction had been fully worked out by Medieval theologians, although significantly, the term 'natural *religion*' is a seventeenth-century one.[7] Thinkers of the Middle Ages generally maintained that through the exercise of human reason alone man can come to a knowledge of the existence of God in his works, to a knowledge of the human soul with its attributes of freedom and immortality, and can discover Natural Law. This view found its way into traditional Catholic theology.[8] According to the medieval synthesis, two types of knowledge of God, the natural and the revealed, complete each other.

For the reformers, however, these two kinds of knowledge – natural and revealed – were fundamentally opposed. Following Augustine's lead, Luther and Calvin had stressed the negative consequences of the Fall, arguing that it had resulted in the corruption of human reason. Since natural theology resulted from the exercise of fallen human powers of speculation, it became for the reformers a highly suspect enterprise, which, viewed in the light of the cardinal doctrine of justification by grace, was no more than man's arrogant attempt to storm the ramparts of heaven. Thus John Calvin conceded a natural knowledge of God, but claimed that this knowledge had been corrupted by the warped minds of men, and served only to render them without excuse.[9] Since all non-christian religious beliefs were thought to be based on this dubious foundation of natural knowledge, it followed that all the forms of heathenism were bereft of truth, and that no salvation was to be found within them.[10] This stance was further reinforced by Calvin's view of the nature of salvation. Only to 'the elect' – those predestined by God for salvation – is saving knowledge of Christ given. The elect, from the time of the advent of Christianity seem implicitly to be confined to, though not identified with, the visible church. Calvin could thus endorse the traditional formula 'extra ecclesiam nulla salus' (no salvation outside the Church).[11]

Luther also conceded that there was 'universal knowledge of God among all heathen' and that 'this light cannot be subdued or extinguished'.[12] But he qualified this judgement with the insistence that this 'God' cannot be properly identified: 'reason never finds the true God, but it finds the devil or its own concept of God, ruled by the devil'.[13] This illusory God of reason was not only the object of heathen worship, but was also the God of 'the papists and the religious', and of 'the Jews during Christ's sojourn on earth'.[14] Followers of the heresiarch Muhammad were similarly deluded by their natural inclinations. Muhammad's law, Luther insisted, teaches 'only what human wit and reason can bear'.[15] Luther was thus left with the conclusion that all of these religious forms, while superficially different, shared a common essence:

> Jews, Turks, papists, radicals abound everywhere ... Even if they do not all pursue the same course, but one chooses this way, another that way, resulting in a variety of forms, they nonetheless all have the same intent and ultimate goal, namely, by means of their own deeds they want to manage to become God's people.[16]

Jews, Turks and papists also shared the characteristic of 'hard-heartedness'.[17] All erroneously believed that they would be saved by works;[18] all their holy writings were human fabrications.[19]

There is an important element to Luther's treatment of other faiths which is almost entirely absent in Calvin, and which has far-reaching implications for the development of 'the religions' in the following centuries. Luther, at the vanguard of the Reformation, was far more involved in controversy than Calvin. The heathen, the Turks, and the Jews are most often discussed in the context of anti-Catholic polemic. Norman Daniel has ably demonstrated that there was for the medieval polemicist a ready-made 'image' of Islam which could be appropriated to bolster the claims of Western Christianity.[20] Luther appropriated this image but deployed it in an entirely new context – that of confessional conflict within Christendom – to show that papism was simply another form of paganism.[21] This utilisation of other religions to serve particular religious exigencies was also to become normative. Catholicism, or any creed substantially different from one's own, could be subjected to criticism by virtue of its purported affinity with heathen religion. In the seventeenth and eighteenth centuries, this strategy which came to be known as 'paganopapism' played a major role in the rhetoric of sectarian disputes.[22]

The Reformation both set up the conditions of religious pluralism which provided the predominant focus for theological disputes in the seventeenth century and furnished a model for the treatment of religious forms, first by positing that other faiths were simply different manifestations of natural religion, and second by giving the non-Christian 'religions' a negative role in parochial conflicts within Christendom. As the religious rites and beliefs of other peoples were discovered, and indeed, as information on the cults of antiquity came to light, the possible scope for comparison continued to increase. As Edward Said has pointed out with regard to 'the Orient', exotic locations and peoples provided for the modern West a backdrop against which could be projected images designed to serve some domestic ideological function.[23] In matters of religion, in the centuries immediately following the Reformation, the exigency which made the most urgent demands in England was to do with the truth of competing Christian factions. Accordingly, the 'religions' of the 'Orient', of the Pacific and the Americas, of ancient Greece and Rome were pressed into the service of the religious interests of the West. They became heresies which were formally equivalent to some undesirable version of Christianity, be it papism, Calvinism, Arminianism, or any other of the myriads of Protestant sects.

Controversy and apologetic thus led to the comparison of 'religions', which in turn became the discipline of comparative religion. But more importantly, the rhetorical technique of paganopapism eroded the privileged status of Christian religion, for the continual assertion of fancied parallels between this or that creed of Christianity and types of heathenism led in time to the view that all forms of Christianity had something in common with the other religions. The Christian faith inevitably came to be seen as different only in degree from other creeds. Equally momentous was the fact that Christendom came to be viewed as a microcosm of the world. In the projection of the West's religious fragmentation onto the whole world was created the intellectual problem of global religious pluralism.

In fine, the significance of the Reformation transcends mere theological controversy. This enormous upheaval contributed to the establishment of social and political conditions which in turn enabled quite new ways of thinking. By freeing both states and individuals from the shackles of a central religious authority it set in motion steps towards religious liberty. Indeed, it established in principle the right for individuals to make up their own minds in matters of religion. Such religious freedom, was, of course, far from the minds of the reformers themselves. Nonetheless, it was largely because of their efforts that there flourished in succeeding centuries a profusion of religious sects. These made the question of religious authority quite acute, for the claims of sectaries to have sole access to divine truths could no longer be judged by an appeal to a central institutional authority, and wounded reason could not be relied upon to distinguish spurious from genuine religion. This crisis of religious authority accounts in large measure for the resurgence of Christian Platonism – a seventeenth-century movement which sought to re-establish the respectability of nature by healing the breach between revelation and reason. These English Platonists were forced to circumvent the previous century of religious thought, and put down roots in the rich soil of the Italian Renaissance.

RENAISSANCE PLATONISM

While the inevitable legacy of the Reformation was a fragmented Christendom, the reformers' strategies for coping with the pluralism were not accepted with the same inevitability. For those thinkers with a less parochial vision and a more generous spirit the idea that religious pluralism was the historical consequence of the secret determination of God to save but a fortunate few was preposterous. Particularly repugnant to many seventeenth-century minds was the picture of an arbitrary God which Calvinism seemed to promote. If God's universe operated in accordance with immutable and rational laws as the new science seemed to suggest, why should the divine legislator resort to such an arbitrary system of salvation as predestination? If the book of nature bespoke a creator who had followed a rational and predictable pattern in the creation, why should not that same creator offer a reasonable scheme of redemption? By the same token, how could one make sense of human freedom, or of the essential goodness of a God who, according to the ascendent theology, had created millions of souls with a view to condemning the bulk of them to an eternity of torment in hell? Such questions were foremost in the minds of the English Platonists. These men resisted the growing tide of predestinarian theology in the seventeenth century, and

abjuring their Reformation heritage, harked back to the Renaissance Platonists, and even further back to Plotinus and Plato for solutions to the problems facing their age.

In a consideration of the development of the seventeenth-century idea
of 'religion', the Renaissance Platonists have a double significance. Not
only did they serve as a conduit for Platonic (or more correctly Neoplatonic)
theology, but they also took the first steps towards redefining the medieval
notion of 'religion'. For the Church of the Middle Ages, the word which
dominated theological discussion was 'faith'. 'Religion', by way of contrast,
had a restricted and technical use, referring to 'the state of life bound by
monastic vows'.[24] Thus to speak of the 'religions of England' in the fifteenth
century was to refer to the various monastic orders. (This usage survives
as part of current Roman Catholic vocabulary, according to which one is
said to 'enter religion'.[25] In two leading Renaissance thinkers – Nicholas
of Cusa (1401–64) and Marsilio Ficino (1433–99) – we encounter both
modifications of this concept 'religion' and attempts to bring other faiths
within the rubric of a universal 'Christian religion'.

Nicholas of Cusa, a German Cardinal with an abiding interest in religious
unity, was an important precursor of English Platonism.[26] Max Müller bestowed upon him the honour of having been 'the first to study non-christian
religions in the independent spirit of a scholar and an historian'.[27] Cusanus
believed that the apparent contradictions between the claims of various traditions could be ameliorated by locating the whole discussion of religious
diversity within the larger context of epistemology. Accordingly, his theological reflection began not with the traditional question of God's nature, but
rather with an inquiry into the possibility of knowledge of God. Different
modes of faith, for Cusanus, were not the result of different objects of
worship, but of the conditions of human knowledge. Religious diversity
was a welcome, if inevitable, consequence of epistemic limitations. This
was for two reasons. First, the relationship between each individual and
God is unique, and it is to be expected that expressions of the divine
encounter will differ. Second, on account of the chasm between finite and
infinite, all 'objective' descriptions of divine reality will only be relatively
true.[28] Paradoxically then, the very multiplicity of religious beliefs and practices serves as a guarantee that a single, infinite reality lies behind the heterogeneous religious expressions. Nicholas, though a stalwart of the Church,
claimed no special privilege for Christian dogma. All divine truth, unknow-
able in itself, could be expressed only as 'other': 'the ungraspable unity
of truth is known in conjectural otherness'.[29] In the religious epistemology
of Cusanus all orthodoxy is conjecture.

It may strike us as remarkable that a medieval Cardinal was prepared
to demote theology to the level of conjecture. But this is balanced by a

corresponding emphasis on 'faith'. For Cusanus, the Jewish patriarch Abraham was the great exemplar of faith, who served as a paradigm for all faithful peoples, be they Jews, Arabs, Christians, or even polytheists. The conjectural nature of religious doctrines is irrelevant in light of the fact that no form of faith, however perverted its appearance, is inefficacious. This is because the object of faith, the ultimate source of faith, is immutable. The flux of religious forms and institutions is of little moment while that upon which they all focus remains the same. Thus the symbols may change, but what they signify does not.[30]

While asserting the primacy of faith in the religious life, Nicholas nevertheless contributed to the development of the concept 'religion'. In *De pace fidei*, he set forth a scenario in which representatives of all cultures and faiths gather to petition God to settle once and for all the religious differences which divide the world. It is here that we find him speaking of 'one religion in the multiplicity of rites':

> Therefore, hide yourself no longer, Lord. Have mercy, show your face, and all peoples shall be saved ... If you deign to hear our plea, the sword, hate, envy, and all evil will vanish, and all shall know that there is but one religion in the multiplicity of rites. If this diversity of rites cannot be given up, or if it does not seem good to do away with it – since the differences themselves may become a spur to piety, bringing each land to cultivate its own customs with even greater zeal as those most pleasing to God – let there at least be one religion, and one worship, even as you are One.[31]

Now it is clear that Cusanus does not mean one 'religion' in the modern sense, for that would imply an end to the 'diversity of rites'. Yet neither is he using the term in the limited sense of 'monastic rule'. Instead, he seeks to promote the view that diverse religious customs (the accidents of 'religion', if you will) conceal a true or ideal 'religion'. This *'una religio'* is the unattainable truth about God – the Platonic ideal of which all existing belief systems are but shadowy reflections. The faithful of all nations and creeds should persevere in their particular expressions of piety in the firm belief that the one true 'religion' is the basis of them all.

The concept 'religion' took a slightly different turn in the writings of Marsilio Ficino. Ficino was even more enamoured with Plato and the Neoplatonists than Cusanus. This zeal for Plato led him to produce the first complete translation of the Dialogues in Latin. Ficino was also the translator of the highly regarded *Corpus Hermeticum* – that collection of works attributed to Hermes Trismegistus. As founder of the Florentine Academy, and as a figure more central to the Italian Renaissance than Nicholas, he had a more direct influence on seventeenth-century English Platonists.

Ficino was as conscious of the multiform expressions of the religious life (*ritus adorationis*) as was his predecessor, and was equally concerned to give some account of them. In *De Christiana Religione* (1474), he proposed that *religio*, despite appearances, was at all times and in all places the same thing – namely, a universal property of humanity, a distinguishing characteristic, and the one thing which made humanity human: 'The worship of god is as natural to men, as is neighing to horses or barking to dogs.'[32] We should not be deceived by the *appearances* of multiformity, urged Ficino, for: 'All human opinions, all responses, all customs, change – except religion.'[33]

Ficino's '*religio*' differed somewhat from the concept of Nicholas, in that he identified it as a universal human propensity. '*Religio*' remained an ideal, though now it was to be found in the human heart, where it issued in the diverse *ritus adorationis*. Yet both insisted on the ideal nature of true *religio*, and neither sought to denigrate its historical manifestations. Cusanus thought a healthy competition between religious traditions would be a 'spur to piety'; Ficino salvaged the traditions by invoking that Platonic favourite – the principle of plenitude:

> Divine providence ... at different times and in different places, permits various modes of divine worship. In truth, perhaps variety of this kind, divinely ordained, decorates the world with a kind of marvellous beauty.[34]

There is another aspect of Ficino's use of 'religion' which is novel. He spoke of *De Christiana Religione*, literally 'Christian religion', not '*the* Christian Religion'. What then, given Ficino's framing of 'religion', does the adjective '*Christiana*' contribute? If religion is a common human property, what is '*Christian* religion'? For Ficino, 'Christian religion' was simply the kind of religion exemplified by Jesus. Christ, he says, 'is the archetype and model of virtue'.[35] One practises Christian religion when one lives a life oriented towards truth and goodness. Imitation of Christ's life is the best form of Christian worship. That such a life is possible without any connexion with historical Christianity hardly needs to be stated.[36] In Ficino's eyes, then, any religion may qualify as 'Christian' religion: 'Every religion has something good in it; as long as it is directed towards God, the creator of all things, it is a true Christian religion.'[37]

The apparently 'liberal' views of Cusanus and Ficino sit rather oddly with other ideas of their age. There seems to be a great gulf between lofty talk of the efficacy of all faiths on the one hand, and the grisly practice of burning heretics at the stake on the other. We may reduce this gulf somewhat by realising that the threat of the heretic lay not primarily in his heterodox conjectures, but in the possibility of schism. The heretic was a threat to social order and ecclesiastical authority. For this reason, heresy (which often involved beliefs scarcely distinguishable from orthodoxy) was a far more serious matter than mere heathenism.[38] But more importantly, when there is no *propositional* 'religion' supposedly at the heart of the religious life, and when there are no 'religions' construed as mutually contradictory sets of propositions, then the modern problem of 'conflicting religious truth claims' cannot come into play. The concessions which Cusanus and Ficino made to other peoples were made on the basis of an assumed common piety, which for them was the primary element of the religious life.

For all this, the writings of these Platonists signal a change in the use of 'religion'. 'Religion' had become for the first time a generic something which allowed a variety of historical expressions. Moreover, in Ficino's 'Christian religion' lay the inchoate 'religions'. The stage was now set for the modern concepts to appear.

CLASSICAL THEORIES OF RELIGION

The appearance of 'religion' as a natural object coincided with the development of a *Religionswissenschaft* which both defined its object and explicated it. In other words, the intellectual construct 'religion' is to a large measure constituted by the methods which are supposed to elucidate it. 'Religion' is not therefore antecedent to 'theories of religion', for the development of each is dialectically related. The classical canon was to play a prominent role in the provision of ready-made theories of religion. Although, as we have been at pains to stress, 'religion' did not exist in antiquity, there were nonetheless theories about the origins of the various modes of worship of different peoples. In the early modern period, these were seized upon with considerable enthusiasm, particularly by the deists, and applied to the new-found object 'religion'.

The European Enlightenment has always been recognised as the era of modern history which has closest affinities with classical antiquity. Peter Gay thus describes the first stage of Enlightenment as 'the rise of modern paganism', with its predominant element being 'the appeal to antiquity'.[39] The more restricted description 'Augustan Age' for English culture and letters in the early seventeenth century is also evocative. Neither are these labels totally retrospective. The *philosophes* themselves subscribed to a four-fold division of history: first were the civilisations of the ancient Near East; then Greece and Rome; followed by the Christian millennium; and finally, commencing with the Renaissance, was the modern era. The first and third epochs were regarded as ages of myth and superstition, while the second and fourth were periods in which reason and science flourished.[40] Small wonder, then, that the classical canon served as a veritable encyclopaedia of 'scientific' theories of religion.

In many respects, the fancied parallels between the classical age and the age of Enlightenment were not far wide of the mark. Certainly, the intellectual climate of Greece in the fourth and fifth centuries BC had a number of features in common with that of Augustan England. At the dawn of the classical age in Greece, wandering sophists in the course of their travels had become aware that human conventions differed from place to place. Like their Enlightenment counterparts they were faced with a plurality of beliefs and customs, not least those relating to the gods. The sophists concluded that many beliefs and rituals concerning the gods were not integral to human nature, but were mere conventions. At the same time, the growth of natural science was demystifying nature in the course of the search for naturalistic explanations. This combination of factors opened up, perhaps for the first time in history, the possibility of giving non-religious explanations of the origin of human piety. Plato thus complained that the naturalistic explanations of the Ionian scientists combined with the relativism of the sophists had led to a climate of religious scepticism.[41] Once it had been established that the gods had but conventional status, it became possible to offer natural explanations of religious customs. Over the next two hundred years there arose accounts of religious beliefs involving projection, fear, daemons, imposture, euhemerism, and even linguistic theories.[42] Each of these theories was to have its champions during the Enlightenment, and it is instructive to see how they developed in their original forms.

The oldest known 'theory of religion' is the 'fear theory'. Sextus Empiricus credits the atomist Democritus with the authorship of this hypothesis. Democritus is said to have suggested that men became frightened when the sky thundered, imagining gods to be the causes of such phenomena.[43] Correlated with this theory was the corollary that the study of nature disabuses man of his erroneous beliefs concerning the causes of various natural phenomena.[44] So it was that as the heavens were demystified, explanations of the movement of the celestial bodies which had relied upon the operation of personal agents were no longer deemed necessary. All that remained was to establish the reason for the original attribution of personal agency to these phenomena. The answer of Democritus was simple – human fear and ignorance.

The fear theory did not play a major role in subsequent Greek thought. It receives mention in Cleanthes, Epicurus, Lucretius, Cicero and Lactantius, but, more importantly for us, became central in accounts of primitive religion in Hobbes, Vico, and Hume.[45]

Democritus, it should be noted, did not explain away the gods entirely, but only insofar as they usurped the place of rational explanation. According to Sextus, Democritus cherished the belief that 'there exist in the circumambient gigantic images of human shape' which 'impinge on men'.[46] These beings, neither fully mortal nor yet immortal, were the 'daemons' of traditional belief, to whose status the gods of Greek polytheism were later demoted.[47] Thus Democritus actually had two different theories about the origins of theistic beliefs. This second 'daemonology' theory was seized upon enthusiastically by the fathers of the Church, who by placing a purely negative construction on 'daemon' provided an explanation of paganism which persisted through the Middle Ages.[48] It was, however, a supernatural explanation, and therefore one of the few classical 'theories of religion' to fall from favour during the seventeenth century.

If natural scientists were wont to see their domain – the phenomena of nature – playing a role in the explanation of the origin of religious beliefs, then it was no less true of the sophists, who sought explanations in the sphere of human affairs. The most important theory of the origin of religious beliefs in the fifth century was the imposture theory proposed by the sophist Critias.[49] He placed this speech in the mouth of his character Sisyphus:

> A time there was when anarchy did rule
> The lives of men, which then were like the beasts'. . .
> Some shrewd man first, a man in counsel wise,
> Discovered unto man the fear of Gods,
> Thereby to frighten sinners should they sin
> E'en secretly in deed, or word, or thought.
> Hence was it that he brought in Deity.[50]

As we shall see, the imposture theory was the most popular of all seventeenth and eighteenth century accounts of religion. Its great strength as a theory lay in the fact that it could take a variety of forms and be combined with other explanations of religion. It could account for the origin of religion, the maintenance of religion, or as in this example, both. Moreover it meshed neatly with the very closely related theories of the twofold philosophy and priestcraft. According to the twofold philosophy, the philosophers, priests and rulers of every age had a vested interest in keeping the populace deceived by religious fictions to which they themselves did not subscribe. Thus Plato thought that his philosopher-kings would 'have to make considerable use of falsehood and deception for the benefit of their subjects'.[51] For both Greek and Roman writers, Plato's 'noble lie' became a favourite justification of the necessity of some of the more absurd elements of popular religious cults.[52] Most free-thinkers in England justified their 'deistic' beliefs on similar grounds, claiming that the more supernaturalistic elements of Christianity were merely fables perpetuated for the civil control of the vulgar.

One other fifth-century figure is of importance to us. Prodicus of Ceos was a famous sophist who argued that men came to believe in gods through the deification of objects which were useful to them.[53] Prodicus was renowned for his ability as a grammarian, and appears occasionally in the dialogues of Plato as one skilled in making fine distinctions between syno-nyms.[54] It would be surprising if his theory did not reflect his linguistic skills, and we might venture the suggestion that Prodicus supposed that the mechanism by which useful objects became hypostasised was through an inappropriate use of language. Thus people named useful objects and fell into the error of using the names as proper names. The use of a proper name for an object thus led to the misconception that an object was in fact an acting being – in short, a god.[55] This thesis seems all the more likely when we consider the great stress placed on the origin of certain words and on the link between word and object which was so characteristic of the period.[56] Etymological speculations, however fanciful they seem to us, at least show how some of the ancients believed that the names of the gods rose from attributing agency to inanimate natural phenomena.[57] If it can be surmised from this treatment of the names of the gods that there was amongst the sophists a 'linguistic' account of the origins of theism, then we have here a remarkable anticipation of seventeenth- and eighteenth-century linguistic accounts of religion.

There is one final theory – a late development of the Daemon theory – which is of importance for this study. The Epicurean and Stoic schools had both reduced the distance between the gods and men.[58] Even before them, Plato had already suggested that the existence of daemons was linked to the apotheosis of heroes: 'every wise man who happens to be a good man is more than human (*daimonion*) both in life and death, and is rightly called a daemon'.[59] Thus while the gods were being reduced to the level of daemons, humans were being elevated to the same status; the gap between mortals and gods was narrowing. This tendency reached its logical conclu-sion in Euhemerus.

Around the year 300 BC, Euhemerus composed a story in which it was implied that the Olympian gods and goddesses had simply been men and women who on account of their being benevolent rulers were worshipped, and who after their deaths continued to be objects of worship.[60] Sextus sums up the story as follows:

> And Euhemerus, nick-named 'the Atheist' says – 'When the life of mankind was without order, those who so far excelled the rest in strength and intelligence that all men lived subservient to their commands, being intent to gain for themselves more admiration and veneration, invented for themselves a kind of superhuman and divine authority, and in consequence were by the populace accounted Gods.[61]

As we have seen, many of the elements of this theory were already present in Greek culture. In fact Hecataeus of Miletus had already in the fifth century propounded a kind of euhemerism in the context of a story similar to that of Euhemerus. However Euhemerus' account received considerable impetus and was given much credence by the conquests of Alexander. In Alexander we have a clear paradigm of the process of the deification of a ruler. Euhemerus doubtless reasoned that if Alexander was a ruler who had come to be considered a god, then it was reasonable to assume that all the anthropomorphic gods of tradition had attained divine status in much the same way.

This view of the origin of the gods was received by the Church fathers with considerable eagerness. While Euhemerus had not in all probability intended to deny the genuine divinity of the heroes, Christian apologists, while allowing that the ancient gods had once been men, denied that they had in any real sense become gods. Thus were the pagans considered to have worshipped dead men.[62]

The classics proved to be an invaluable source of naturalistic explanations of religious phenomena for those researchers of the modern age who wished to stress the non-supernatural basis of religion. There was also the added bonus of the authority of the classical writers themselves which lent credibility to these theories, even though they were some two-thousand-years old. While some of the latter-day historians of religion were able to derive from sacred history more novel views of the development of religion, in certain circles – amongst the deists in particular – the ancient theories of fear, imposture and euhemerism served as the sole explanations of religious beliefs and practices. The very first steps towards the adoption of such theories did not take place in deist circles however, but in the more theologically-con-servative writings of the English Platonists.

TWO

'RELIGION', REVELATION, AND THE LIGHT OF NATURE: PROTESTANTS AND PLATONISTS

Reason discovers, what is Natural; and Reason receives, what is Supernatural.

Whichcote, *Aphorisms*, 99

RELIGION AS KNOWLEDGE: PROTESTANT SCHOLASTICISM

The Protestant theology which came to dominate English thought in the post-Reformation era had a number of important implications. The sharp distinction between two sources of religious truth – revelation and nature – not only provided the ideological basis for the separation of the sacred realm from the secular, but also spawned two discrete species of the newly ideated 'religion' – 'natural religion' and 'revealed religion'. Along with the dual forms of religion came an increasing emphasis upon knowledge and correct belief. There are a number of reasons for this unfortunate preoccupation. Calvin, in his *Institutes*, had fired a broadside against the 'Popish fiction' of implicit faith. On account of the complexity of such cardinal doctrines as the Trinity, medieval school men had conceded that not all members of the Church could aspire to explicit knowledge of and therefore belief in more esoteric and subtle dogmas. Those of modest intellect were therefore encouraged to have 'implicit faith' in these abstruse formulas, 'implicit faith' being essentially the belief that the doctors of the Church had got it right. It was, in short, faith in the faith of the theologians. This concession, in Calvin's view, was 'the surest precipice to destruction'. 'Faith', he insisted, 'consists in the knowledge of God and Christ (John xvii.3), not in reverence for the Church.'[1] As we shall see, in actual practice Calvinist 'faith' amounted to little more than assenting to the appropriate creeds and confessions, for it was here that correct knowledge of God, or true religion, was to be found.

In the highly-charged atmosphere of post-Reformation controversy, creeds were statements in which expression was given not only to what was thought to be central to Christian belief, but also to those beliefs which distinguished this or that branch of Christianity from other heretical or erroneous forms. The perceived need for explicit knowledge together with the reframing of articles of belief led to the publication of numerous summaries and catechisms based on the Protestant confessions. These were essentially pedagogical tools designed to instil into the believer the essence of 'the Christian Religion'.[2] Salvation was intimately linked to teaching, knowing and believing. The charter of the Church of England, the Thirty-Nine Articles, was thus described in a highly-regarded commentary as 'a Brief of that Religion, which amongst themselves was taught and beleeved, and whereby through the mercy of God in Christ they did hope to be saved.'[3]

The new role which creeds and catechisms played in the religious lives of English Protestants shows how 'religion', now imagined to be a set of beliefs, came to displace 'faith' and 'piety'. The actual contents of these creeds, however, give an even more direct indication of the perceived necessity of correct belief. In addressing the question of religious truth, confessional statements from the English Reformation onwards were in complete unanimity: God is known through his self-revelation, witnessed in scripture. In line with Calvin's original teaching, the possibility of saving knowledge of God in nature or through reason was emphatically rejected. Thus the Scotch Creed of 1560, one of Britain's earliest post-Reformation confessions:

> for of nature we are so dead, so blind, and so perverse, that nether can we feill when we ar pricked, see the licht when it shines, nor assent to the will of God when it is reveiled, unles the Spirit of the Lord *Jesus* quicken that quhilk is dead, remove the darnesse from our myndes, and bow our stubborn hearts to the obedience of his blessed will.[4]

The Confession stresses that nothing of value can be known of God through nature, for the unaided mind is incapable of discovering religious truth. Not even revealed truths can be embraced without divine assistance.

More influential than the Scotch Creed, though slightly less Calvinistic, were the Thirty-Nine Articles (1563). These were promulgated during the reign of Elizabeth and remain in use to this day. They, too, deny efficacious knowledge of God in nature:

> They also are to be had accursed that presume to say, That every man shall be saved by the Law or Sect which he professeth, so that he be diligent to frame his life according to that Law, and the light of Nature[5]

This extract also gives a hint of what was later to become quite explicit, namely the view that salvation is correlated with, and may even depend upon knowledge. This incipient tendency came to full flower in the Westminster Confession.

The Westminster Confession (1647) was drawn up at the height of the

Puritan Revolution and represents the acme of Protestant Scholasticism in England. According to the Westminster divines, the light of nature, along with works of creation and providence, 'manifest the goodness, wisdom and power of God' and thus leave men without excuse. However, while this natural knowledge leaves men 'inexcusable', it is 'not sufficient to give that knowledge of God, and of his will, which is necessary unto salvation.'[6] The connexion between salvation and knowledge is quite clear. 'Nature' alone cannot provide the knowledge necessary for salvation. Salvation, by implication, is related to what one knows, to the propositions which go to make up one's 'religion'. As if to emphasise this point, a popular edition of the Confession appeared in 1652 which included a synopsis entitled 'The Sum of Saving Knowledge'.[7] The essence of the Confession of *Faith* thus came to be understood as 'saving *knowledge*'.

Of course, within the tradition of reformed theology, at some ideal level, the fundamental principle of salvation was always 'by grace, through faith'. But at a more practical level, the gift of faith was seen to be accompanied by, or to reside in, knowledge of a special kind, to which those unfamiliar with the truths of 'revealed religion' could not be privy. The tendency to equate the assurance of salvation with correct belief was further complicated by another formula which went into the soteriological equation: that most notorious aspect of Calvin's thought – predestination.[8]

In the Thirty-Nine Articles, the doctrine of election, most closely associated with Calvinism in the popular mind, is presented with subtle ambiguity:

> Predestination to Life is the everlasting purpose of God, whereby (before the foundations of the world were laid) he hath constantly decreed by his counsel secret to us, to deliver from curse and damnation those whom he has chosen in Christ out of mankind, and to bring them by Christ to everlasting salvation.[9]

The apparent severity of this standard is mitigated somewhat by the absence of any mention of double decree (that is, of persons predestined to damnation). This slight ambiguity enabled Archbishop Laud and others to give an Arminian interpretation to the Articles.[10]

The Lambeth Articles (1595) have no such ambiguity. While they share the prestige of neither the Thirty-Nine Articles nor the Westminster Confession, they show, on the one hand, the ascendancy of a doctrinaire Calvinism in England, and on the other, the kind of resistance with which extreme predestinarianism was met. In the closing decades of the sixteenth century, Cambridge had become the stronghold of Calvinism. At this time a French refugee named Peter Baro was elevated to the Lady Margaret Chair of Divinity. He put forward the view (later known as 'Arminianism') that God had predestined all men to eternal life, conditional upon their faith.[11] To settle the resulting controversy, representatives of the University met with the Archbishop and formulated the nine Lambeth Articles. These deal solely with the issue of predestination and give a blunt statement of double predestination: 'God from eternity hath predestinated certain men unto life; certain men he hath reprobated.'[12]

At Westminster, some fifty years after the Lambeth Articles, the assembly of divines reiterated this dogma. 'Some men and angels', reads the third section of chapter three, 'are predestinated unto everlasting life, and others foreordained to everlasting death.'[13] While the elect in this scheme do not correlate exactly with the visible Church, it nonetheless seems clear that no-one outside the Church will be saved. Certainly, following the light of nature avails nothing:

> Others, not elected, although they may be called by the ministry of the Word, and may have some common operations of the Spirit, yet they never truly come unto Christ, and therefore cannot be saved: much less can men, not professing the Christian religion, be saved in any other way whatsoever, be they never so diligent to frame their lives according to the light of nature and the law of that religion they do profess.[14]

The phrase 'any *other* way' might lead one to suspect that the heathen, in spite of their beliefs, might nevertheless be part of the elect, and be saved through Jesus Christ. This gains some plausibility from the preceding article (x.iii) which informs us that there are elect persons 'incapable of being outwardly called by the ministry of the word'. While such an interpretation is possible, the Confession seems never to have been so interpreted.[15]

The apparently conflicting 'causes' of salvation in Calvinistic thought – saving knowledge and divine election – are not as contradictory as they might first appear. God gives only to the elect knowledge of his nature and, crucially, knowledge of his will. Saving knowledge does not of itself bring about salvation, but rather is correlated with it. Because this knowledge is not to be found in nature, those with no historical connexion to revealed religion are *ipso facto* excluded from salvation. Even those who hear the gospel may not be given the gift of faith. God may 'harden their hearts', thereby consigning them to the reprobate.

While there is a certain logic in this relation of knowledge and salvation, it is not hard to see why the unfortunate conjunction 'saving knowledge' led to considerable misunderstanding. Calvinists did not mean (or should not have meant) 'knowledge' in any objective sense. 'Knowledge unto salvation' was not, originally at least, a set of propositions the acceptance of which conferred automatic membership of the elect. The 'knowledge' to which the Calvinists referred was rather knowledge of God's *will*, the assurance of salvation, the 'resting on Christ and his righteousness', made possible by the gift of faith.[16] In time, however, this expression came to denote a body of objective truths, which when presented to a prospective believer required only voluntary assent or dissent. This misconstruction was part of that more general objectifying tendency which characterised the age of reason. Added impetus for this inept interpretation came from the emergence of a new soteriology, one more in tune with Enlightenment principles, and one which was opposed to the deterministic strictures of the Calvinists. This was the doctrine of Jacobius Arminius and his followers.

One of the chief objections to Calvinism was that if God predetermines those who are to be saved, then free will plays no role whatsoever in salvation. Human moral responsibility is downplayed, and God must assume much of the burden for moral evils – not only the evil in the world, but also that great evil of predestining people to hell. Calvinists, in other words, would seem to run into contradictions in affirming the essential goodness and justice of God while at the same time advocating predestination. The other stumbling block of Calvinism was its denial of the universality of Christ's atonement. While the New Testament states directly that Christ died for all, the followers of Calvin were committed to the view that he died only for the elect. Arminianism promised a way out of these quandaries, and the idea of 'saving knowledge' was to play an integral part in the solution which Arminianism offered.

The Arminian controversy began in the Netherlands towards the end of the sixteenth century. Jacobius Arminius (1560–1609), with the backing of such powerful figures as Hugo Grotius, proposed 'conditional predestination' as an alternative to strict Calvinism. According to this view, it was God's eternal purpose to save those who believed in Jesus Christ, and who persevered in their belief. The dilemma for Arminius was to allow human agents to play a role in their salvation while avoiding any suggestion that salvation had been earned. (Salvation by works was the Pelagian heresy of which the Protestants had accused the papists.) Arminius solved the problem by allotting to human agents the almost imperceptible intellectual act of saying 'I believe' to certain formulas. God was thereby relieved of the necessity of having to predestine individuals to hell, while no *moral* acts (which could be construed as 'works') were required on the part of those who were saved as a pre-requisite for salvation.

Conditional predestination and four other anti-Calvinist doctrines were codified in the 'Five Articles', compiled in 1610 after the death of Arminius. The Synod of Dort, which met in 1619 to resolve the matter, decided in favour of the Calvinists, but despite this setback Arminianism continued to have great influence in Europe. In England, as early as 1580, Peter Baro at Cambridge had been espousing what were to become Arminian ideals. From that time onward, Arminianism and Calvinism shared an uneasy coexistence until the Restoration, when Calvinism, on account of its link with the revolutionary movement, began to lose ground to Arminianism.[17]

Of the Five Arminian Articles, the first is of most concern to us. It states simply that God determined to save those who chose to believe in Jesus Christ.[18] This deceptively bland declaration has a significance which goes well beyond the theological controversy it engendered. For now, effectively, the whole business of salvation no longer falls under divine jurisdiction. From the inaccessible reaches of the inscrutable will of God, it enters the realm of human affairs, of objective knowledge and human assent. Saving knowledge does not now exist merely in some occult, divinely-initiated transaction between God and members of the elect, but like other kinds of knowledge is available to be discussed, to be denied or accepted, to be promulgated. In short, the rise of Arminianism signals a new phase in the conception of religious truth. Certainly, the Calvinist emphasis on saving knowledge set the process in motion, but in removing the safeguard of divine initiative, in lifting the veil from the incomprehensible divine will, Arminianism had unwittingly transformed the divinely imparted saving knowledge into just another species of information. God's place as the object of faith had been subtly usurped by a set of doctrines. Faith was no longer a precarious balancing act between *assensus* and *fiducia*: assent had triumphed over trust. Saving knowledge had begun a descent from the heavens to take its place in human discourse.

The final stage of the process took place when 'saving knowledge' was aligned with 'revealed religion'. Up until the middle of the seventeenth century, the truth of revelation was contrasted with the light of nature. Almost from the moment of its birth, the propositional 'religion' was divided into two types, based on the two modes of divine knowledge. The 'religion' witnessed to by Scripture became 'revealed religion', a mode of religion which was contrasted with 'natural religion'.[19] Following the emergence of the two kinds of religion there ensued a debate over which form was superior. Strict reformed orthodoxy posited a fundamental opposition between the two, claiming the superiority of revealed religion in all respects. At the other extreme, 'deism' asserted the sufficiency and universality of natural religion. Between these poles were the Cambridge Platonists and 'Latitudinarian' divines who were willing to concede that natural religion, though deficient, was a necessary preparation for revealed religion.[20]

Not only did the dimorphic 'religion' set the agenda for the religious disputes of an age, but it also led to a radical new understanding of divine revelation. This revised estimate of revelation is of more immediate importance. What was now revealed through revelation was an objective 'religion', presumably a religion consisting of saving knowledge. This was quite new, for the traditional view had been that in the process of revelation God reveals himself. Now God reveals saving knowledge, similar in kind (if different in content) to knowledge of God in nature. 'Christianity', declared Nathaniel Crouch in 1683, 'is the Doctrine of Salvation, delivered to Man by *Christ Jesus*'.[21]

The literature of the seventeenth century bears witness to these remarkable changes in the perception of the Christian faith. A profusion of books, pamphlets and broadsheets appeared attempting to encapsulate in propositional form the essence of 'the Christian Religion', 'the Protestant Religion', 'the true Catholic Religion', or just simply 'Religion'. In 1658 for example, another edition of Thomas Rogers' *English Creed* appeared bearing the title *The Faith, Doctrin and Religion Professed in this Realme of England.* This commentary on the Thirty-Nine Articles presents the faith, doctrine and religion of England as articles 'analised into Propositions'.[22] The new title of this work is indicative of the new status of credal statements. In 1585, its original title had been simply *The English Creed*. In the seventeenth century, however, it was no longer merely 'the English Creed', but the sum total of the faith, doctrine and religion of England. In the same year (1658), Calvinist tract writer Richard Younge published his *Short and Sure Way to Grace and Salvation*. Younge serves as an example of how the concept of religion (or of 'a religion') was thought to simplify and clarify matters for prospective believers. Younge set out 'three fundamental principles of Christian Religion' as a minimal statement of what should be believed. If 'well learned', Mr. Younge earnestly declared, these three principles 'would keep millions out of Hell that blindly throng thither'.[23] Almost thirty years later, attempts of this sort culminated in Nicholas Gibbon's *Theology Real, and Truly Scientifical*. Here the ambitious Gibbon set forth the sum of the Christian religion in a 'scheme or diagram' which occupied a single printed page.[24] Literally hundreds of seventeenth-century works, most of them dating from the time of the Westminster Assembly, claim similarly to present the sum, the substance, the ground, the body, or the system of 'the Christian Religion'.[25] Almost without exception, they present as the substance of Christianity articles of belief.

Some voices, admittedly, were raised against this reduction of Christian piety into a propositional religion. As early as 1645, Robert Harris, a staunch puritan and member of the Westminster Assembly, pleaded for a return to 'true religion *in the old way*', by which he meant the way of faith and love. Harris was clearly conscious that a significant change had taken place in the meaning of 'religion'.[26] Others, like Richard Allestree and Richard Baxter, also decried the elevation of knowledge over duty,[27] while on a larger scale, the Platonists and after them the Methodists attempted to counter the general trend of Protestant Scholasticism. Yet even these dissenting voices accepted the centrality of the idea of religion.

The creation of a propositional religion enabled discussions of the merits of other 'religions', conceived to exist similarly as sets of beliefs. The religions so constructed could then be impartially examined and compared with each other, and evidence for or against their truth could be accumulated. Titles of religious works published in the last decades of the 1600s thus abound with such terms as 'impartial view', 'comparison', 'evidences', 'grounds and reasons'.[28] The truth or falsity of a religion had become a function of the truth or falsity of the propositions which constituted it. True religion was not genuine piety, but a body of certain knowledge. 'False religion' in this intellectualist conception of things, was equated with ignorance, incredulity, or error. Richard Younge, in 1648, thus set out to determine the cause of 'Ignorance, error, enmity, atheism and prophaness', that he might thereby provide 'a hopeful and speedy way to salvation'.[29] A major cause of atheism, according to the diagnosis of John Edwards, was ignorance of common notions.[30] In a similar study Jean Le Clerc sought to find those 'causes of incredulity' which he believed 'dispose unbelievers to reject the Christian Religion'.[31] Even the theological category 'sin' was recast. No longer was it primarily rebellion against God, or moral turpitude, but nescience. In his discourse on mental errors, John Flavell informs us that sin is primarily to do with deviations in opinions and judgements. He goes on to point out that because the highest form of knowledge is 'knowledge of saving truths revealed by Christ in the Scriptures', those 'Errors [are] always the worst, which are committed against the most important truths revealed in the Gospel'.[32] The unforgivable sin was now erroneous belief.

Calvinism and Arminianism between them delimit the range of Protestant orthodoxy during the Enlightenment. Both contributed to the reification of religious faith and to the construction of the object 'religion'. But while 'revealed religion' remained entrenched in the theological vocabulary of the seventeenth and eighteenth centuries, there could not be an all-encompassing science of religion. For this to occur, the various forms of religion needed to be placed on the same footing. Revealed religion, admittedly, consisted of propositions which could be objectively appraised. Yet their veracity was primarily to do with their source – God – and their truth dependent upon such 'external' evidences as miracles and prophecy. The mutually exclusive claims of revealed religions, all of which claimed the relevant external evidences, could not easily be adjudicated. Despite 'impartial' considerations of the religions, despite 'scientifical theologies', there was not the kind of scientific treatment of religion which Toland advocated. For this to take place, revealed religion had to come into a more positive relation with natural religion. More specifically, the contents of revealed religion had to be subjected to the same tests as natural religion.

The bringing together of the two forms of religion was a response to the perceived theological inadequacies of the dominant theologies. Neither Arminianism nor Calvinism allowed a saving knowledge which was accessible independent of special revelation. Arminianism, admittedly, made the Christian Religion in principle available to all, yet even this concession was not altogether satisfactory. If, for example, there was no opportunity to hear the Gospel, then clearly there could not be an appropriate response. Grace is not efficacious in the absence of belief, and without conscious knowledge of the Gospel, there can be no belief in it. Salvation then became in large measure a function of accidents of birth. Those living in remote corners of the earth were at a decided disadvantage, having to rely for their salvation on the missionary zeal of the right branch of the Christian Church. The result was that for both Arminians and Calvinists, salvation is a lottery.

For those thinkers blessed with both theological acumen and a broadness of perspective, neither the arbitrary and inscrutable decree of God, nor geographical considerations provided a satisfactory basis for salvation. True, it was possible to build epicycles into these soteriologies to make them more commensurate with the demands of natural justice. Many Latitudinarian divines came to acknowledge the value of pure 'natural religion'. Other charitable souls were to suggest that a post-mortem experience of God would place the unevangelised heathen on a similar footing to those who in their earthly lives had heard the gospel. (But this prompted the question as to the necessity of the Christian revelation in the first place.) Another suggestion, popular amongst the Platonists, was that actions in a previous state determined the circumstances of our terrestrial lives. To be born into a tribe of benighted savages was a sure indication of a trespass committed in a pre-terrestrial existence. It was their own fault that such savages never heard the gospel. But as the Ptolemaic universe eventually collapsed under the accumulated weight of its epicycles, so too these kinds of *ad hoc* proposals were only to underline the inadequacies of the dominant soteriologies. The paradigmatic revolution which was called for involved the adoption of that very possibility which both the Thirty-Nine Articles and the Westminster Confession explicitly rejected, namely, the assertion of a genuine religion of nature.

Herbert of Cherbury and the Cambridge Platonists were, in their own ways, to develop Ficino's inchoate 'natural religion' as a means of coping with the scandal of particularity of the Christian revelation and as a means of choosing between competing 'revealed religions'. Lord Herbert has close affinities with both Platonism and 'deism', and we shall discuss him under the latter head in due course. The Platonists, more than Herbert, were concerned to develop the idea of 'religion' or 'natural religion' as it came to be known, from within the theological enterprise. Indeed, in the estimation of one commentator, the work of the Cambridge Platonists represents 'the highest expression of Christian theology in England'.[33] Certainly, they, more than any other group, developed a theology of religion which they subsequently applied to 'the religions'. In so doing, they incorporated the intractable category 'revealed religion' into nature, and inadvertently paved the way for the evacuation of supernatural elements from the concept 'religion'.

NATURAL AND REVEALED THEOLOGY

The religious pluralism which sprang up in the wake of the English Reformation raised the question of authority in an acute way. The problem was not simply the kind of intellectual quandary which the conflicting truth claims of the world religions give the modern philosopher of religion. At this time even the most trivial religious differences could lead to considerable civil instability and much blood-letting. As Swift expressed it in his inimitable fashion:

> Difference in opinion hath cost many lives; for instance, whether *flesh* be *bread*, or *bread* be *flesh*; whether the juice of a certain *berry* be *blood* or *wine*; whether *whistling* be a vice or a virtue; whether it be better to *kiss a post*, or throw it into the fire; what is the best colour for a *coat*, whether *black*, *white*, *red*, or *grey*; and whether it should be *long* or *short*, *narrow* or *wide*, *dirty* or *clean*, with many more. Neither are any wars so furious and bloody, or of so long continuance, as those occasioned by differences in opinion especially if it be in things indifferent.[34]

Perhaps religious differences were not all as inane or indifferent as Swift suggests, but the effects of these differences is accurately portrayed. Hobbes' proposed solution – that religious peace could be achieved through the imposition of the will of a supreme sovereign – proved, in the light of the civil war, to be quite the opposite of what was actually the case; the religious faction which wielded most power could determine who ruled England. As this became more apparent, advocates of opposing religious dogmas came to press their claims more stridently. It is against this background that we need to understand the attempts of such diverse groups as the Cambridge Platonists and the English deists to establish some final court of appeal on matters of religious doctrine.

   The Cambridge Platonists were a group of seventeenth-century English theologians and philosophers who were distinguished by their veneration of Plato and Plotinus, their opposition to religious fanaticism, and their preaching of a reasonable religion of holiness. The major figures in the school were Benjamin Whichcote, Ralph Cudworth, Henry More, Nathaniel Culverwel, Peter Sterry, and John Smith. George Rust, John Worthington, Simon Patrick and Richard Cumberland were lesser lights. All of the major figures in the group were educated at Emmanuel College, Cambridge, although Platonism also had its disciples at that traditional stronghold of Aristotelianism, Oxford. There, Joseph Glanvill, and to a lesser extent, John Norris were strongly influenced by the movement.[35] Like their Renaissance forebears, the English Platonists became involved in the question of religious epistemology. How, they asked, can one attain certain knowledge in religious matters? For the Platonists (as for Descartes who found early favour with the group), one way to ground religious belief was to ignore institutional authority in favour of the certitude of the mind itself. Accordingly, the Cambridge school came to rely upon 'innate ideas', 'common notions' – those ideas which received universal assent – and *a priori* or self-evident logical truths. While the distinction between these three noetic sources is not always observed, they flow into Western thought from quite separate tributaries and should be carefully differentiated. 'Innate ideas' had always been an integral part of the Platonic tradition: Plato's 'reminiscence' found its way into Medieval and Renaissance thought largely due to the influence of such luminaries as Origen and Augustine. 'Common notions' were derived from the Stoic notion of universal reason: 'De quo autem omnium natura consentit, id verum esse nesesse est.'[36] Self-evident logical truths had risen to prominence through the influence of Descartes, who had revived the *a priori* arguments of Anselm.[37]

The appeal to these internal authorities in religious matters amounted to a virtual denial of the orthodox denigration of 'the light of nature'. Calvin and his followers might have acknowledged some natural or innate idea of God, but they also insisted that this knowledge was subsequently corrupted through ignorance or malice, and thus served no useful end.[38] For the Cambridge Platonists, this natural knowledge could not be corrupted, though through differences in breeding and education, it could admit of different expressions. One of the first tasks of the Cambridge Platonists, then, was to clarify the relationship between this intuitive knowledge of God and the Christian revelation.

Another important task concerned the vital question of salvation. If the Cambridge Platonists denied the Calvinist view of natural religion, they were even less eager to affirm the dark doctrine of double predestination. With one or two notable exceptions, the Cambridge divines rejected the notion that God's will alone determined those who would be saved, and those who would be damned. In the true spirit of Plato, they insisted that God's goodness is not different in kind to human goodness. What, after all, was human goodness ultimately but participation in the divine nature itself? The double decree, repugnant to reasonable notions of goodness, could not be explained away by the claim that God's goodness is different from our own, or that his goodness is subordinate to his will. As Glanvill put it:

> For the first Errour, which is the ground of the rest, is, that things are good and just, because God Wills them so to be; and if that be granted, we are disabled from using the arguments taken from *natural Notions*, and the Attributes and Perfections of the Divine nature, against the blackest and most blasphemous Opinions that ever were entertained concerning Gods procedings with the Sons of Men. If there be no settled Good and Evil, independent upon any Will of Understanding, then God may have made his reasonable creatures on purpose to damn them for ever.[39]

In their understanding of salvation, the Cambridge Platonists tended towards Arminianism or Universalism.

Apart from the appeal to Platonic ideals, the Platonists had another ally in their battle against exclusive predestinarianism. Although their mystical rationalism tended to set them against the growing tendency towards empiricism in England, on the question of the nature of divine will, the Cambridge Platonists were able to turn to account the findings of empirical science. It was apparent from the discoveries of science that the world was governed by a ruler who operated in a lawful fashion, not capriciously or arbitrarily. As the judicious Hooker had observed some time earlier:

> They erre, therefore who thinke that the will of God to do this or that, there is no Reason beside his Will ... Let no man doubt, but that every thing is well done, because the world is ruled by so good a Guide, as transgresseth not his owne law: then which, nothing can be more absolute, perfect and just.[40]

The Cambridge Platonists, particularly Rust and Glanvill, developed this notion further. Rust declared that the order of the universe cannot be a 'mere casual issue of absolute independent will'. Even salvation, he argued, had to be based on moral laws which were not dependent on divine will alone.[41] For Rust, and indeed the whole of the Cambridge school, knowledge and salvation together were placed under the dominion of that same Reason which permeated nature.

Benjamin Whichcote is generally regarded as the father of the Cambridge Platonists.[42] In his thought we find one of the more comprehensive treatments of the relationship between natural and revealed knowledge. Unlike many of his contemporaries, he believed that the heart of religion was simple and non-dogmatic. For him, the 'summary of all necessary divinity' was encapsulated in these words from the book of Titus: 'For the grace of God hath appeared, bringing salvation to all men, instructing us, to the intent that, denying ungodliness and worldly lusts, we should live soberly and righteously and godly in this present world.' (Titus 2.12) The essence of religion for Whichcote and his school, as for Ficino, had more to do with leading an upright life than with assenting to correct doctrines. Christ was but a means to bring about moral perfection; a saved state was a state of moral rectitude. There is a universalistic emphasis in this New Testament passage which is also characteristic of the Cambridge Platonists to varying degrees. Affirmation of the universality of saving knowledge entails a denial of the sharp dichotomy between the light of nature, and revelation.[43]

According to Whichcote, the 'light of creation' is an essential preparation for the more complete communication which follows. Nature prepares the way for revelation. The 'truth' of religion, Whichcote insisted, cannot be divided up according to its content, but only 'in way of descent to us'.[44] Thus, reason and revelation are merely different vehicles of the same truth.[45] In Whichcote's theology, the different means of communication give us the distinction between truths of 'first inscription' and those of 'after revelation'.[46] Truths of first inscription, that is, natural truths, are grasped by reason, and provide the basis of natural theology.

It is not always easy to discern exactly what Whichcote or his circle meant by 'reason'. But it is helpful to distinguish 'reason' as used by the Platonists, from 'reason' as it came to be used by the 'deists' and by Enlightenment rationalists in general.[47] Plato taught that reason is man's highest faculty, for it corresponds to divine reason (*Nous*). Divine reason knows things as they are in themselves; it knows the pure 'ideas' which give form and substance to all phenomena. Human reason too, can attain to this kind of knowledge by transcending the evils of the material world through intellectual and moral discipline. Yet in a certain sense, true knowledge resides in the mind of God, and is available to man only through divine dispensation.[48] For the Cambridge Platonists reason was, therefore, never merely a human faculty. It was at least as much a participation in divine Reason as the exercise of a purely natural attribute. It included that domain which Kant was later to designate 'practical reason' – the ethical. It was the incorruptible image of God in man. As an authority, it was to take that place which the Reformers had given to scripture, as the voice of God in man, it was the equivalent of the Holy Spirit. Richard Baxter was therefore substantially correct when he indignantly declared of the Cambridge Platonists that they 'thinke yt Reason must know more of the Divine Being than Scripture'.[49]

In Whichcote's thought we find that 'reason' involves both the process of reasoning and the ability to apprehend self-evident truths. More than just a property of the functioning mind, reason is both the voice of God in the human soul, and that which enables the soul to distinguish and recognise God's voice as communicating what is good and true.[50] Whichcote suggests, in other words, that this internal *vox Dei* 'recognises' genuine revelation. In making this innocent claim, Whichcote unwittingly laid the foundation for both rational theology and for the more radical 'deist' interpretations of revelation which were to follow. 'Reason' drifted from its original Platonic and Stoic moorings, and, taking on a more restricted meaning, came to be seen as a means of settling the competing claims of various revelations and interpretations of revelations. In short, reason became the criterion and judge of revelation. Thus, at the turn of the century, we find Locke announcing that 'Whatever God hath revealed is certainly true... but whether it be *divine* revelation or no, reason must judge.'[51] This elevation of reason to the status of the judge of revelation, was to become the catch-cry of 'deism' and 'free-thought'.[52]

Whichcote, for his part, had never intended to promote human reason above revelation. He thought only to correlate two valid kinds of knowledge which he believed derived ultimately from the same source. Reason, for the Platonist, was always bound up in religion and did not constitute an *independent* court of appeal. Says Whichcote:

> in the state of religion, spirituals and naturals join in and mingle in their subjects; so that if a man be once in a true state of religion, he cannot distinguish between religion and the reason of his mind; so that his religion is the reason of his mind, and the reason of his mind is his religion.[53]

The faculty of reason has an integral role in the apprehension of the 'truths of first inscription'. These truths are 'connatural to man', they are 'the light of God's creation', they are 'immutable and indispensable', and receive 'universal acknowledgement'.[54]

To a large degree, Whichcote's assumptions about the universal acknowledgement of natural truths went untested. 'Natural light', in his view, should have been expressed in the first instance in some natural and common moral notions which should correspond, more or less, to the contents of the Decalogue. Whichcote, however, did not proceed beyond *a priori* reasoning to establish his thesis in any strong way. This task was undertaken by his Cambridge colleague Ralph Cudworth.

Cudworth entered Emmanuel College in 1632, where he soon came under the influence of Whichcote. From the time he took his degree in 1639, he was recognised as an apologist for Whichcote's Platonic theology. (His degree was actually a defence of his teacher's doctrine of 'the good', which had drawn severe criticism from the Calvinists.) In 1678, Cudworth published his great bulwark against atheism – *The True Intellectual System of the Universe*.[55] It was the burden of this prolix work to demonstrate that all men tend naturally to believe in the one God and can, through the exercise of reason, attain even to those truths which have been argued to be the sole preserve of revealed religion. Cudworth, in other words, sought historical verification for the views of his school. So convinced was Cudworth of the essential unity of natural and revealed knowledge that he claimed a natural knowledge of the most esoteric religious doctrines to be possible, and in fact demonstrable. Traditionally it had been accepted that natural knowledge was to do with God's existence, his attributes (omnipotence, omnipresence, omnibenevolence) his moral demands, and a future life with rewards and punishments. Cudworth went far beyond this to maintain that even the 'exclusively Christian' dogma of the Trinity could be found in the theology of many of the pagans. His reading of the sources indicated that trinitarian theology could be found in Orpheus, Pythagoras and Plato, and in the arcane theology of the Egyptians, Persians, and Romans.[56]

At first Cudworth seems to be leaning towards the common Enlightenment thesis of plagiarism – since the notion of a threefold Godhead was a revealed notion and could not be known naturally, it must have been communicated from the Hebrews to those other nations whose theology contains it.[57] He then goes on, however, to make the apparently contradictory claim that the existence of a form of trinity in the Platonists (in fact, mainly Plotinus), refutes those who would deny the trinity and cling to a natural religion of 'Theism':

> Whereas bold and conceited wits precipitantly condemning the doctrine of the trinity for nonsense, absolute repugnancy to human faculties, and impossibility, have thereupon some of them quite shaken off Christianity, and all revealed religion, professing only theism; others have frustrated the design thereof, by paganising it into creature worship or idolatry; this ignorant and conceited confidence of both may be returned, and confuted from hence, because the most ingenious and acute of all the Pagan philosophers, the Platonists and the Pythagoreans, who had no bias at all impose upon their faculties, but followed free sentiments and dictates of their own minds, did notwithstanding not only entertain this trinity of divine hypostases eternal and uncreated, but were also fond of the hypothesis, and made it a fundamental of their theology.[58]

Cudworth had two aims in mind here: first, to provide historical evidence of the dubious nature of the division of religious knowledge into 'natural' and 'revealed'; second, to show that dogmas denigrated as irrational by such groups as the 'deists' and socinians had in the past been held on rational grounds alone, without the aid of supernatural revelation.

Cudworth's speculations serve to remind us of the different uses of the term 'natural'. Not even Cudworth believed that the Christian dogma of the trinity was, in some literal way, lodged in the minds of all men. That particular belief was not common enough to warrant such an extravagant hypothesis. Belief in a triune Godhead was 'natural' in two senses: it was known without the help of revelation; it was arrived at through the application of the natural faculty of reason. Cudworth's painstaking investigations thus served to erode further the distinction between natural knowledge and revealed knowledge. Equally, he had shown that there were more general truths which had received universal assent throughout history. These beliefs many Cambridge Platonists held to be 'natural' in a stronger sense than belief in the Trinity. These more general truths were regarded as 'connatural' or 'innate'.

THE RELIGIOUS *A PRIORI* AND INNATE IDEAS

For many apologists in the seventeenth century the innateness of the idea of God constituted incontrovertible proof of God's existence. Henry More, for instance, in his *Antidote Against Atheisme* (1659), placed in the forefront of his attacks on atheism the argument for 'the Existency of the God-head from the naturall *Idea* of God, inseparably and immutably residing in the Soul of Man'.[59] Now it may seem that the innateness of an idea is no guarantee of its veracity. As Shaftesbury was to point out to an age which invested nature with the same authority as ours is prone to grant to science, a notion may be innate, and yet be vain.[60] But the apparent fault in the argument based on innate belief lies not so much in the careless logic of More and his fellow apologists, but in the assumptions of their interpreters about what is meant by 'atheism' and 'innate'.

'Atheism' in the seventeenth century had retained many of the connotations which it had acquired in classical antiquity. Atheists in both eras included those who denied the force of arguments which were regarded as supporting theism, or who proposed non-religious theories of the origins of religion. In antiquity, Democritus, Euhemerus, and Critias were all accounted atheists, not because of their denial of the existence of God or the gods, but because they espoused naturalistic theories of the origin of religious mores, or were materialists.[61] In the seventeenth century, particularly amongst the Platonists, 'atheism' denoted primarily the materialistic and 'Epicurean' metaphysic of Hobbes, which was seen to entail the denial of spiritual reality. (Bruno and Spinoza were atheists of second rank.) Hobbes and others also adopted such theories as the fear theory from the ancient atheists to account for the origin of religious beliefs.

The term 'innate', by current standards, had a similarly idiosyncratic use. It could mean (1) literally congenital, (2) logically necessary, (3) universally acknowledged, or (4) the end result of the natural workings of some innate capacity. Critics of the doctrine of innate ideas from Locke onwards have often failed to appreciate the polyvalence of the term, and as a result much of their criticism has been misdirected. Hume, with his usual perspicuity, went to the nub of the problem, observing that: 'If by innate be meant, contemporary to our birth, the dispute [about innate ideas] seems frivolous'. In his opinion, Locke's whole critique of innate ideas missed its mark because Locke had been 'betrayed into this question by schoolmen, who, making use of undefined terms, draw out their disputes into a tedious length, without ever touching the point in question'.[62]

Rarely, if at all, was 'innate' used in the first sense.[63] It could reasonably be claimed that many of the truths of 'practical reason' were innate in this sense, but this amounted to little more than an insistence that all men had a conscience, and that there was a broad consensus about what was right and what was wrong. To say that moral sense was innate was really just another way of speaking of the *imago dei*. That there were certain religious propositions congenitally lodged in the mind was a claim of quite a different kind. Of the English Platonists, Joseph Glanvill seems to be the one who came closest to adopting this position.

Glanvill's philosophy is an intriguing and sometimes puzzling amalgam of empiricism, scepticism and Platonism. His empiricism anticipates that of Locke and Hume in important respects, while his Platonism is redolent of Cusanus and shows signs of the influence of Henry More. Glanvill's religious epistemology, though it contains much that is original, has much in common with that of Cambridge Platonists. According to Glanvill there are two principles in religion – those which are fundamental and essential, and those which are accessory and assisting. The fundamental principles concern the existence of God and his commonly-acknowledged attributes, the difference between good and evil, God's inclination to pardon those who repent, and future rewards and punishments.[64] These principles, said Glanvill, have been 'more clearly and explicitly reveal'd to the Christian Church', but in some measure are 'owned also by the Gentiles'.[65] The essence of religion, for Glanvill, lay in these propositions of natural theology. He called them 'the sum of the religion of mankind', and insisted that they alone were a sufficient basis for salvation. Thus, 'though our Church require our assent to *more* propositions; yet these are only *Articles of communion*, not doctrines absolutely necessary to salvation'.[66] These notions, Glanvill seems to suggest, are innate, or at least 'imbred'. They are, he says:

> imbred *Fundamental Notices*, that God hath implanted in our Souls; such as arise not from external objects, nor particular Humours or imaginations, but are immediately lodged in our Minds; independent upon other Principles or Deductions; commanding a sudden assent; and acknowledged by all sober mankind.[67]

Glanvill insists that the fundamental principles 'may be mistaken, but cannot be corrupted'.[68]

Glanvill's analysis of natural knowledge of God is noteworthy not only on account of the broad claims which he makes for it, but also because of its epistemological implications. Innate religiosity is described in terms which were to become the hallmarks of later *a priori* approaches to religion as 'immediate' and 'independent'. The notion of God and his attributes receives universal acknowledgement, and neither arises out of empirical knowledge, nor begins with external perception. This, in part, is the anti-atheistic thrust of *a priori* theories of religious knowledge. On this view, such reductive explanations of theistic belief as the fear theory must be wrong because they assume that religion begins with the experience of certain fearful events, rather than arising out of a natural disposition.

There remains a difficulty, however, in attaching any meaning to Glanvill's ambitious hypothesis that the fundamentals of religion are 'imbred'. He could hardly be claiming that these fundamentals are, in Hume's turn of phrase, 'contemporary to our birth'. Glanvill clarifies the matter by grouping together certain propositions which he regards as 'instinctive'. These include: 'That God is a Being of all Perfection, That nothing hath no attributes, That a Thing cannot be, and not be, That the Whole is greater than any of its Parts.'[69] The fundamentals of religion fall into the same category as those *a priori* rational truths which constitute the basis of our reasoning faculty. 'God exists' is thus of the order of the principle of contradiction. We can no more reasonably deny the former than the latter, and while we do not encounter infants reciting the law of contradiction, there is a certain sense in which that law is built into the structure of the rational mind and is biologically inherited. It is not itself deduced, but provides the basis of all deduction. The claim that certain kinds of religious truths are of this kind might be contentious, but at least it is meaningful, and most probably it was this claim which Glanvill intended to advance.

The theory of innate religious principles was supported in different ways by most of the Cambridge Platonists. Henry More argued for the connate God-idea on the dual grounds of its logical necessity and universality:

> Now for the *Adoration* of *Religious Worship* it is as universall as mankind, there being no other Nation under the Cope of heaven that does not do divine worship to something or other, and in it to God as they conceive; wherefore according to the ordinary *naturall light* that is in all men, there is a God.
>
> And therefore if there were any Nations that were destitute of the knowledge of a *God*, as they may be it is likely of the Rudiments of *Geometry*, so long as they will admit of the knowledge of one as well as of the other, upon due and fit proposall; the acknowledgement of a *God* is as well to be said to be according to the *light of nature*, as the knowledge of *Geometry* which they thus receive.[70]

Cudworth similarly stressed universal acknowledgement. There is, he said, a 'connate idea and prolepsis of God in the minds of men', as evidenced by the fact that:

> amongst the most barbarian Pagans at this day, there is hardly any nation

to be found without an acknowledgement of a sovereign Deity, as appears
from all those discoveries which have been made of them since the improvement
of navigation.[71]

These views of the nature of religious knowledge mesh with a more general
epistemological rationalism, which the Platonists shared to a degree with
Descartes. Glanvill, More and Cudworth each insisted upon the *a priori*
nature of fundamental religious beliefs, and indeed of all knowledge. Descartes' defence of his own understanding of the innate idea of God serves
just as well for the Cambridge Platonists:

> I never wrote or concluded that the mind required innate ideas which were
> in some sort different from its faculty of thinking; but I observed the existence
> of certain thoughts which proceeded, not from extraneous objects nor from
> the determination of my will, but solely from the faculty of thinking that
> is within me, then, that I might distinguish the ideas or notions (which are
> the forms of thought) from other thoughts ADVENTITIOUS or FACTITIOUS, I
> termed them INNATE. In the same sense we say that in some families generosity
> is innate, in other certain diseases like gout or gravel, not that on this account
> the babes of these families suffer from these diseases in their mother's womb,
> but because they are born with a certain disposition or propensity for contract-
> ing them.[72]

The influence of Descartes, however, was not more than that of Plato,
and it is to the influence of Plato's distrust of the material world that we
must attribute much of the *a priori* epistemology of the Cambridge school.
This influence is unmistakable in John Smith: 'The *Mental faculty* and power
whereby we Judge and Discern things ... must *retract* and *withdraw* it self
from all *Bodily operation* whensoever it will nakedly *discern* Truth.'[73] In the
view of the Cambridge Platonists, and Smith in particular, religious error
arose when the mind, which was spiritual in nature, could not sufficiently
extricate itself from its bodily housing, or from objects in the external world.
In this dualistic scheme of things, religious blunders occur when '*Melancholy*
and Turgent Phancies', from the lower and more material realms of mind
swamp the rational faculty.[74] Atheism and idolatry result from the victory
of the material over the spiritual: 'Atheism most commonly lurks ... when
the Mindes of men begin to draw these gross earthly vapours of sensuall
and material speculations.'[75]

Henry More reiterated Smith's view. The first mistake of the human
race, he said, was to 'acknowledge no God but this Visible or Sensible
world'.[76] Idolatry, accordingly, was 'a very sore a grievous Disease of the
Soul, vilely debasing her and sinking her into *Sensuality* and *materiality*,
keeping her at a distance from the true sense and right knowledge of God'.[77]
For the most Platonic of the Platonists then, in every human being there

resided in the *a priori* structures of the mind irreducible religious truths which in principle were always recoverable, even by the most benighted savages. Conspicuous instances of atheism and impiety arose because of the evil and pervasive nature of the material world. Certainty and unanimity in religion, as in geometry, lay in an introspection untroubled by the intrusion of the empirical realm.

The other aspect of Platonism which is pertinent to this whole discussion is the notion of 'reminiscence'. On the whole, the Cambridge Platonists regarded this doctrine with some suspicion, in part, because of its connexion with the doctrine of pre-existence, although there were some who relied upon this heterodox opinion in their explanations of religious pluralism. But if the seventeenth-century Platonists were ambivalent in their attitudes to *anamnesis*, generally they welcomed its epistemological implications. Cudworth is again typical, cautioning that learning is not merely 'remembrance of what the soul once before actually understood, in a pre-existent state, as Plato would somewhere have it'. But he continues:

> Yet is all human teaching but maieutical, or obstetritious; and not the filling of the soul as a vessel, merely by pouring into it from without, but the kindling of it from within; or helping it so as to excite and awaken, compare and compound, its own notions.[78]

Two of the group, however, disparaged both Platonic reminiscence and innate religious ideas. Nathaniel Culverwel sits rather oddly with the rest of the Cambridge circle, not only on account of his denial of innate ideas, but also because he was an unabashed Calvinist. According to him, the doctrine of innate notions was a disreputable legacy of the 'Platonical fiction' of pre-existence of souls. One could not hold the former, he seemed to imply, without assenting also to the latter. 'Do but analyze your own thoughts', orders Culverwel, 'do but consult your own breasts ... Had you such notions as these when you first peep'd into being? ... Had you these connate species in the cradle?'[79] To be sure, Culverwel, like Locke, had mistakenly assumed that innate ideas were in a literal sense congenital, but there were nonetheless significant differences between his epistemology and that of his fellows.[80] Culverwel preferred to accord a much greater significance to the role of the external world in the knowing process. The mind evinces that the true rise of knowledge is from 'the observing and comparing of objects, and from thence extracting the quintessence of some such principles as are worthy of all acceptation'.[81]

Another, more marginal member of the group, Richard Cumberland, suggested that on the question of natural knowledge, his Cambridge confrères had taken the soft option: 'The *Platonists* indeed, clear up this Difficulty in an easier manner, by the Supposition of *innate ideas*.' Cumberland sarcastically remarks that he had 'not been so happy to learn of the Laws of Nature in so short a way'.[82] But whatever their views on the mechanisms of natural knowledge, both Culverwel and Cumberland were convinced that religious principles, if not religious propositions, were natural to humanity. Culverwel insisted that there were 'some cleare and indelible Principles' which are 'stampt and printed upon the being of man'. These principles, he said, must first be 'put together' before they spell out the law of nature.[83] Cumberland, in the end, was happy to accept any explanation of how religious principles came to be universal. 'Such ideas', he admits, 'might be both *born with us*, and *afterwards impress'd* upon us from without.'[84]

It is not unreasonable to conclude that the Cambridge Platonists' belief in innate religiosity would be better termed belief in a religious *a priori*. They proposed, in other words, that each of us possesses an independent mental capacity which tends naturally to develop certain concepts of deity and morality. Despite minor differences on the epistemological significance of empirical input, the Cambridge Platonists were united in their belief that certain religious principles were an irreducible part of the structure of the human mind. Whether this religious *a priori* consisted of a moral disposition, or a variety of divine truths, and whether such natural religion could be placed on a par with Christianity, was something which will become apparent when we consider the application of the Cambridge Platonists' broad view of religion to the specific religions.

'INNATE RELIGION' AND 'THE RELIGIONS'

The modern expression 'the religions' found its way into English vocabulary at about the same time as 'religion'. The earliest occurrence is in Hooker's *Lawes of Ecclesiastical Politie* (1593), where we find the following usage: 'The church of Rome, they say ... did almost out of all religions take whatsoever had any fair and gorgeous show.'[85] With the publication, twenty years later, of the first edition of Edward Brerewood's *Enquiries Touching the Diversity of Languages and Religions through the Chief Parts of the World,*[86] the plural expression entered common usage. In his preface, Brerwood explains that there are 'four sorts of Sects of Religion' – Christianity, Mahometanism, Judaism and paganism, making it clear that these 'religions' are species of the generic 'religion'. This fourfold classification of religion was to hold for the rest of the century.[87] It was generally agreed that the first three were religions of revelation (or at least laid claim to a special revelation), while paganism or heathenism were forms, albeit corrupt forms, of natural religion.[88]

The appearance of the religions in the seventeenth century meant that in coming to terms with other faiths the English Platonists had fewer options than their Renaissance predecessors. In the absence of discrete religions (now construed as mutually exclusive sets of beliefs and practices), Ficino could assert that any system of worship could be Christian religion. The arrival of *the* Christian Religion ruled out this possibility, for by definition heathen religions could in no sense be identified with the Christian religion. There remained to Cambridge Platonists, however, that appeal to the limitations of the human mind which had provided the key to Cusanus' theodicy of religious pluralism. This meant that differences between the four types of religion were not considered to be the result of different sources of knowledge – be it natural knowledge or different revelations – but were seen rather as resulting from the conditions of knowledge. Religious pluralism reflected not different sources of knowledge but rather the way in which different minds expressed the same truth in different ways. More pejoratively, the religions could be accounted for by custom and education, or by arguing that *a priori* religious ideas had been contaminated by 'material', or empirical factors.

There is no easy equation from an acceptance of the validity of natural knowledge to a positive evaluation of the religions. The Platonists tended to view Christianity as the one religion in which the truths of revelation coincided with the truths of reason. But if they denied that the Fall had irreparably damaged reason, Adam's transgression was nonetheless credited with having set important limits to human knowledge. Crucially, they held revealed knowledge to be no less susceptible to error than natural knowledge. The finitude and fallenness of the human condition together determined the conditions of all forms of knowledge – putative revelations included. While this understanding did not of necessity enhance the status of non-Christian knowledge of God, at the very least it ameliorated some of the more absolutist claims of Christianity, and led towards tolerance and a mild relativism.

The writings of Peter Sterry (1613?-1672) show him to be, of all the Platonists, the most gracious and tolerant. He was both puritan and Platonist. As a puritan, he had sat in the Westminster Assembly and had served as sometime chaplain to Oliver Cromwell. His mystical Platonism is evidenced in his insistence on the circumscribed nature of our knowledge of God. 'All our notions and Opinions can be but broken Things', he wrote, 'we can have in them but Pieces, but bits of Spiritual Truth, and but little, very little of Spiritual Glory.'[89] These fragments of divine knowledge cannot always be easily pieced together to form a coherent picture, for 'the same Truth may appear under contrary Notions and in contradictory Opinions'.[90] This was a remarkable statement for its time, when for many, truth was to be encapsulated in dogmatic propositions. Sterry obviously realised that any attempt to identify a common source of religious experience would run up against the problem of 'conflicting truth claims'. The solution to this conundrum lay, for Sterry, in the circumscribed nature of all human knowledge, and in the adaptability of divine truths:

> This is the Glory of Spiritual Things, that they can cloth themselves with all manner of Earthly Shapes. It is the Greatness and Majesty of Jesus Christ, that he passes thro' all Forms and Conditions; and yet still is the same in the midst of them all.[91]

That the limits of human knowledge necessarily issue in pluralism of belief was an axiom of the Renaissance Platonists which found wide acceptance amongst their heirs at Cambridge. Cudworth informed his readers that all the pagan deities were 'nothing else but so many several names and notions of that one Numen, divine force and power, which runs through the whole world, multiformly displaying itself therein'.[92] The epistemological premise upon which this thesis was based was at root the same as Sterry's, but with a Platonic flavour. 'Truths', averred Cudworth, 'are not multiplied by the Diversity of Minds that apprehend them, because they are all but Ectypal Participations of one and the same Original or Archetypal Mind and Truth.'[93]

Of the Cambridge men however, neither Sterry nor Cudworth gave the kind of attention to this problem as did Nathaniel Culverwel. In his rather presumptuously entitled *Elegant and Learned Treatise of the Light of Nature*, Culverwel provided the most extensive statement of pluralism as a necessary condition of natural knowledge. Following Cusanus and Ficino, he adopted the thesis that the light of nature shone in all of the nations of the world, and that despite superficial discrepancies, all religious traditions derive from knowledge of the one God:

> When you see so many Rayes of the same light, Shooting themselves into the several corners of the world, you presently look up to the Sun, as the glorious original of them all.[94]

The variety of different expressions of natural truth did not concern Culverwel. The operation of the light of nature was, for him, something like the operation of the spirit at Pentecost – a common experience was expressed in a number of different idioms:

> You may hear every man in his own Language, in his own dialect, and Idiom speaking the same works of *Nature*: Parthians, and Medes, and Elamites, and the dwellers in *Mesopotamia* ... you may hear them speak in their Tongues the wonderful works of God and *Nature*.[95]

Variety in belief was not, for Culverwel, as for many others, the result of the corruption of a pure original intuition. Instead, variety was regarded by him as a vital part of nature itself.[96] As for Cusanus, pluralism was a necessary condition of natural knowledge. Culverwel enjoined Christians not to emulate the Jews, who, he said, attempted to deny the benefits of the light of nature to the Gentiles. We cannot, he insisted, 'strip them of Nature, plunder them of the essences, rob them of their first principles and Common Notions'. For God did not leave any bereft of witnesses to himself: 'He himself has took care of them, and has made better provision for them.'[97]

Culverwel speaks highly of the theological achievements of those nations bereft of any special revelation. Even more than this, he claims that it is in the most primitive nations of all that we find the most natural belief. The noble savage can tell us more of the religion of nature than anyone from Western civilisation:

> But the famous *Salmasius* in his late Tractate *De Coma* ... tells us that he had rather search for Nature's Law in a naked Indian; then in a spruce Athenian, in a rude American, rather then in a gallant Roman; in a mere Pagan, rather then in a Jew or Christian.[98]

There is, in other words, much of value in the beliefs of the heathen nations, and these beliefs should not be disparaged. Here, Nature can be observed ungilded and unadorned, and the light of revelation can be mingled with the light of nature:

> let the Testimonies of Gentiles be esteem'd somewhat more than the barking of dogs. Me thinks if they were meere Cyphers, yet the Jews going before them, they might amount to somewhat. Let the prints of Nature in them be accounted sacred: a Pearle in the head of a Heathen, some Jewels hid in the rubbish of Nations, let them be esteem'd precious. Whatsoever remains of God's image upon them, let it be lov'd and acknowledg'd. Their darknesses and misery is great enough, let not us aggravate it, and make it more. To mix the light of their Candle, with that light which comes shining from the Candle of an Heathen, is no disparagement to Jew nor Christian.[99]

But even in these optimistic views of religious diversity was an acknowledgement that variety of belief might spring from other sources. Sterry, Cudworth and Culverwel might stress the natural basis of pluralism, and yet not exclude other external factors from the equation. Geography, custom and habit were most commonly touted as ways in which innate religion could be shaped or even distorted. Whichcote, for example, had spoken of verbal differences and differences of 'habitude':

> truth, and that which follows upon truth, is the self-same thing materially, only called by several denominations in respect to different habitudes and distinct functions and purposes; as the sea which is one and the same, is one where called the *Mediterranean*, in another place the *German ocean*, and the like.[100]

Recognition of the determining influence of environment, or 'habitude', as Whichcote would have it, necessarily leads to toleration and a kind of relativism. Said Sterry:

> Had my Education, my Acquaintance, the several Circumstances and Concurrences been the same to me, as to this person from whom I now Dissent, that which is now his sense and state, might have been mine.[101]

The influence of social and physical environment was not always adjudged benign, however. Glanvill, unlike his peers, adopted a negative view of diversity, admitting the influences mentioned by Sterry and Whichcote, but regarding them as being far from indifferent. 'We contract', he said, 'an obstinate adherence to the conceits in which we were bred, and a resolv'd contempt for all other Doctrines.'[102] According to Glanvill, this obstinacy was nowhere more apparent than in the religious sphere. He pointed out that there existed whole nations of idolaters for whom 'the impressions of a barbarous *education*' triumph over 'nature'.[103] It was not only barbarous education which usurped the place of nature, however, but any kind of education at all. Judaism, Islam, and even Christianity were religions which for the majority of adherents were grounded in neither reason nor revelation, but custom:

> *Education* hath so rooted these misbelievers [Turks and Jews] in their ungrounded *faith*, that they may assoon [sic] be pluck'd from themselves as from their obstinate adherences ... And 'tis to be feared, that *Christianity* it self by most, that have espoused it is not held by any better tenure.[104]

In Glanvill's view, Christian and non-Christian alike smother the light of nature through custom and education. No clear distinction between Christianity and the other religions could be made on the basis of reason or revelation. Christianity resembles paganism, if not in the substance of its beliefs, then in the manner in which those beliefs are held to be true. Religious conflict is born out of this stubborn clinging to the prejudices in which one was raised. 'This immodest obstinacy in opinions', said Glanvill, 'Hath made the world a Babel; and given birth to disorders like those of the Chaos.'[105] Glanvill shows how discourse about other religions was almost always implicitly discourse about Christianity as well. Glanvill's 'paganopapism' lay in his belief that the *grounds* of the non-Christian religions are the same as those of many forms of Christianity as well – stubborn prejudice. Truths about the other religions could be arrived at simply by examining the various factions of Christianity.

Glanvill had a special category for religion based not on reason but on opinion. Such religion he termed 'animal religion':

> For the generality of men are tempted into *Schism* and *Parties*, not so much

by the *arguments* of *dissenters*, as by the *opinion* of their *Godliness*, which opinion
is grounded upon things which may arise from the *meer Animal Religion*, and
very commonly do so.[106]

'Animal religion', or 'low religion', to use Smith's term, is an important,
if neglected, category in the theology of the Cambridge Platonists. It forms
the basis of some of the more negative evaluations of the other religions.
While the Cambridge school extolled the virtues of natural religion, this
would only result in a positive assessment of other religions if it was also
held that those religions were based on natural religion. It has to be borne
in mind that the Platonists developed natural religion in response to a crisis
of authority which had been precipitated by the Reformation. Natural religion
was salvaged in the first instance to provide Christianity with a more sound
epistemological basis of a reason which correlated with revelation, and as
an aid to help discern the necessary fundamentals of religious belief. If
it happened that other religions also were based on natural knowledge of
God, this was only an interesting corollary to the main thesis. Some Cambridge Platonists did not even go this far. The notion that other religions
were based on natural religion was, after all, a Reformation idea, and was
quite independent of any upgrading of the status of natural religion. Henry
More, Joseph Glanvill, and to a lesser extent, John Smith, developed the
category of 'animal religion' which was in large measure comparable to
the 'natural religion' of the Reformers in that it was regarded as providing
the basis of false religions.

'Animal religion' must be understood in the context of a Platonic interpretation of the Fall. For the Platonists, the Fall meant primarily a fall into
the material world of sensuality. As More put it, '*Adam's* Soul descended
into the prepared Matter of the earth', and he 'appeared clothed in the
skin of beasts'. Because of the Fall, 'he became a down-right *Terrestrial
Animal*'.[107] Reason, which was essentially spiritual in nature, could survive
the Fall intact only to the extent that it was not subjugated to lower material
desires. When that spiritual, religious faculty was overcome by the material,
animal religion was the result. The Cambridge group, or at least some of
them, could therefore agree with the reformers that the Fall had been the
ultimate cause of religious diversity, without being committed to the view
that fallen *reason*, and natural theology based on that reason, were at the
heart of false religion. Reason for them was the remedy and not the cause
of religious error.

More's understanding of animal religion was quite literal. He suggested
that higher forms of animal life exhibit rudimentary religious behaviour.
Apes and elephants, he maintained, at times show 'a strange kind of Sense
or impress' at the sight of the sun or moon. Their behaviour, More thought,

showed that these animals experienced '*Love, Fear* and *Wonderment*, near to that *Passion* which in us is called *Veneration*'.[108] The human worship of the sun and moon may accordingly be attributed to 'animal life' which has usurped the place of rational human nature: '*Idolatry* may be the *proper fruit of the Animal life*, as is handsomely discovered in the Worship of the Sun and Moon. For what the *Apes* and those *Elephants* in *Mauritania* do, the same is done by the *Idolaters* of the *East-Indies*.'[109] The category of 'animal religion' demonstrates that a positive view of the religions does not necessarily flow from a positive view of natural religion.

It may be concluded that despite their consensus on the validity and universality of natural knowledge of God, the Cambridge Platonists were by no means agreed upon the extent to which that knowledge of God was expressed in the religions. Sterry, and to a lesser extent, Whichcote and Culverwel, carried through the position of the Renaissance Platonists, according to whom religious diversity was the natural result of epistemological limitations. However, they did not proceed to an all-embracing relativism, for the truth which appeared in many different guises in the world religions was still the truth of Christianity. As we saw, Sterry's 'Forms and Conditions' of spiritual knowledge ultimately did not shroud some impenetrable mystery, but could be interpreted (with the benefit of a Christian perspective) as expressing the 'Greatness and Majesty of Jesus Christ'. Closer to the spirit of Enlightenment rationalism, Glanvill espoused the view, later to become a central tenet of deism, that education and custom thwart natural religious development. He, along with More and Smith, thought that material elements could easily override *a priori* religious tendencies to produce animal religion. Significantly, however, animal religion was an ever-present component of all religions, and was not postulated as providing an absolute basis for distinguishing Christianity from other religions.

The Platonists' views of knowledge within the religions show that they were, on the whole, reluctant to invest the newly created category 'the religions' with much significance. If, on the positive side, knowledge of God was to be found in all religions, and if, on the negative side, animal religion could also be found in all the religions, then in the things that really counted, 'the religions' were entities with little more than a superficial significance. However, our picture is not yet complete, for we have yet to see whether for the Platonists, salvation also was no respecter of the arbitrary boundaries of 'the religions'.

THEODICY AND SALVATION IN THE RELIGIONS

The approach of the Cambridge Platonists to the problem of salvation was almost completely determined by their desire to safeguard the justice of

God. The currently available soteriological alternatives of Calvinism and Arminianism each had their difficulties. Calvinism was problematic because from a human standpoint it seemed to impugn the righteousness of God who arbitrarily saves the elect, while damning the reprobate. This view of salvation, said More, 'free Spirits will think the worst news and most mischievous that ever was communicated to the World'.[110] Arminianism, however, was only slightly less problematic, because it required human assent to God's plan of salvation, and the godless heathen in obscure corners of the globe had little hope of hearing the gospel, far less assenting to it. The Cambridge Platonists had to develop an understanding of divine redemption which seemed fair to everybody. In consequence, the general direction of their soteriology is determined more by notions of natural justice than by Pauline and Augustinian predestinarianism: soteriology was bound up with theodicy. Amongst the various alternatives considered by the Cambridge Platonists were Pelagianism (God saves those who, by the light of conscience, lead morally upright lives), and Universalism (God eventually saves everybody).

Whenever emphasis is removed from correct belief to correct behaviour, there is a tendency towards a Pelagian understanding of salvation. Of the Platonists, Benjamin Whichcote most conspicuously displays this leaning. Whichcote emphasised the validity of natural knowledge of God, but stressed that the content of this natural knowledge was not propositional, but moral. Natural truths, he declared, are fundamentally to do with 'Man's observance of God in all instances of morality'.[111] More specifically, natural truth means 'to do justly, to love mercy and walk humbly with God... to live godly, righteously and soberly in this present world'.[112]

Whichcote's insistence on the primacy of morality in natural knowledge of God is closely linked to his Platonic understanding of God as *the first and chiefest good*. 'His prime perfection is goodness', says Whichcote, 'and our truest notion of him is, that he is *almighty goodness*.'[113] The true natural knowledge of God is God's self-communication of his own divine goodness – it is a knowledge of the divine nature, a nature which is the 'form of the good', and is only genuinely communicated when it results in the living of a morally upright life. If the moral requirements of our natural knowledge of God are satisfied, then doctrinal matters are irrelevant. 'Nothing is desperate in the condition of good men', Whichcote assures us, 'they will not live and die in any dangerous error.'[114] Whichcote's implicit soteriology involves an understanding of grace which appears to be quite Catholic. If there is good will on the part of an individual, and a genuine desire to please God, 'so ample and abundant is the grace of God, that it will supply all that is defective', by 'affording more strength', by 'candid reconstruction', or by 'free pardon'.[115] Such a pardon seems to be available even to the heathen, for Whichcote insisted that the piety of a heathen is to be preferred to the false zeal of a Christian.[116]

This emphasis on practical morality, as opposed to a theoretical knowledge of the divine attributes, had other important consequences for Whichcote's view of the non-Christian world. From the premise that the truths of first inscription are universally acknowledged, it follows that the heathen also may be acquainted with God's moral attributes. In fact the universality of broad moral principles constitutes clear evidence for the validity of Whichcote's general case about natural truths. These truths:

> are concurrent with the sense of heathens and strangers, who do agree with us in all the instances of morality; in these we cannot speak beyond them, they speak and act so as to shame us: for how many of us do act below them in these particulars? And as to many things of the new testament concerning Christ, we have great testimony from them as was shew'd.[117]

Whichcote did not commit himself to the view that all men in all times have explicitly acknowledged the natural truths about the divine nature. Universal acknowledgement means that all those who 'have attained to any reformation, either the improvement of their intellectuals, or the refinement of their morals', concur with the 'immutable and indispensable virtues'.[118]

What then, can be said of the variety of religious conceptions held by the nations throughout history? Some are undoubtedly wrong, for as Whichcote observes, 'there have been in the world several persons that have grossly neglected the materials of natural knowledge'.[119] Muhammad was such a person. On the other hand, Whichcote thought that many differences in religious matters were not about any 'necessary and indispensable truth, nor any thing that is declared plainly in any text of scripture'. Instead disagreements were either 'in points of very curious and nice speculation', or 'in arbitrary modes of worship'.[120] To some degree, then, religious pluralism was acceptable and even inevitable. But on what grounds could it be decided that a religion or creed flew in the face of 'necessary and indispensable truth'? For Whichcote the grounds were primarily moral. Islam was a false religion because of the immorality of its founder.[121] Whichcote's discussion of Islam is of particular interest because he states the conditions under which it could be regarded as a true religion.

> Now if God had given testimony to his [Muhammad's] religion, it would have been in a way of reason, and most agreeable to the understandings of men, and not in a way of debauchery and stupid ignorance; but in some way of worth, perfection, and excellency, purity, and holiness, in such a way as might challenge the greatest opposers to find anything contrary to those principles of reason and understanding which he hath planted in man's mind.[122]

Here we find an enlargement of the criteria of true religion: true religion must accord with those principles of reason which are the natural possession of man (remembering, of course, that man's natural reason is primarily to do with living a morally correct life). Any religion, is the implication, may be true if it is morally edifying.

The elevation of the moral aspect of natural knowledge over its theoretical component is taken up again by Whichcote in a later discourse. 'Knowledge', he says, is not content simply to remain as knowledge and understanding alone, but ultimately comes to rest in 'will and affections'. It should become goodness, for 'we begin in knowledge, and end in practice'.[123] In a passage reminiscent of Cusanus, Whichcote explained that theoretical knowledge can be expressed verbally in a variety of modes, but it should issue in a way of life which is at all times the same. 'Truth' he says, is 'knowledge in respect of the understanding, goodness in a man's heart, etc.' Truth does not serve a theoretical, but a practical function: 'the understanding is not finally enlightened for itself; but is as the eyes which receive light for the use and service, guidance and direction of the body'.[124] Specific dogmatic expressions are, in consequence, quite secondary to living a life of holiness. If pluralism of belief does not result in pluralism of practice, then Whichcote is happy to dismiss the significance of the former. The important thing for Whichcote was not, in the parlance of modern philosophy of religion, conflict in 'truth claims', but concord in 'practice claims'.

For all this, Whichcote differed from the Renaissance Platonists and Cusanus in particular in failing to take seriously enough moral and cultic differences between cultures. While Nicholas accepted that not even moral pluralism need constitute an insurmountable barrier to the establishment of a universal religion, it is at precisely this point that Whichcote baulked. On the one hand, he asserted a universal agreement in matters of morality, yet on the other, condemned Islam as a religion contrary to reason on account of its moral precepts. Ironically, he seemed to demand that all mankind should comply with a particular moral code, (ostensibly that 'natural' one which is universally acknowledged, but in fact one closely bound to the Judaeo-Christian tradition) and in so doing placed himself in a comparable position to those who demanded uniformity of belief. To be kind to Which-cote, his moral parochialism was unintended, and resulted from the mistaken assumption of a universal morality. Had he been less inclined to insist on this *a priori* presumption, and more open to the gradual accumulation of empirical evidence which was making this supposition quite suspect, he might have arrived at a quite different result. As it was, while his scheme in principle promised an open evaluation of religious traditions, it resulted in an outright dismissal of Islam and Catholicism.[125] On a more positive note, Whichcote had a far broader conception of religion than many of his cavilling contemporaries. He avoided those fruitless debates based on positive authorities, and had his Platonic presuppositions been well-founded, he would have ended up with a promising solution to the problem of religious pluralism.

Most other Cambridge Platonists agreed with Whichcote's rejection of Calvin's predestinarianism, embracing instead a kind of Pelagianism which offered some hope for pious and virtuous pagans. Seldom, however, do we find a commitment to any particular mechanism of salvation. More, for instance, attempted to establish a median position between Calvinism and Arminianism. Some, he said, are predestined to salvation, while others determine their own fate through the exercise of free choice.[126] What does this mean for those beyond the pale? More did not commit himself, but concentrated instead on the proper attitude of Christians to those of other religions. The case for the truth of Christianity is not enhanced, he warned, by 'villifying and reproaching all other Religions' nor by 'damning the very best and most conscientious *Turks, Jews*, and *Pagans* to the pit of Hell, and then to double lock the door upon them, or to stand there to watch with long poles to beat them down again, if any of them should offer to emerge and endeavour to crawl out'. On the contrary, it is 'more becoming to the Spirit of the Gospel, to admit and commend what is praiseworthy and in either *Judaisme, Turkisme* or *Paganisme*'.[127] More, in fact, granted far more to the non-Christian religions than to Catholicism. In his *Antidote Against Idolatry*, he distinguishes pagan from Catholic idolatry, ranking the latter well beneath the former. 'We cannot say', he concludes, 'that every Idolatrous Heathen must perish eternally', but 'we have no warrant ... to think or declare any of the *Popish* Religion, so long as they continue so, to be in the state of Salvation'.[128] The salvation of noble pagans was a view which the majority of the Cambridge Platonists found quite congenial – whatever their formal theological commitments. More serves to show us how such a view might be compatible with Arminianism. Nathaniel Culverwel reached a similar conclusion from a Calvinist perspective.

Culverwel's Platonist credentials, as we have seen, were always questionable. He denied innate ideas because he considered them undesirable relics of Platonism. When we examine his soteriology, we discover that he was an unabashed Calvinist, and thus was rather an odd bedfellow for the rest of the Cambridge group.[129] While he was prepared to grant genuine knowledge of God to the heathen, he was exceedingly reluctant to grant them salvation. He conceded that no nation utterly neglects their natural knowledge of God, but nonetheless declares that ''tis the condemning sin of the Heathen; that so many of them imprison this natural light, and extinguish this *Candle of the Lord*'.[130] In consequence, the heathens shall be held accountable for 'resisting those relics of primitive light that shined out so strongly upon them'.[131]

There are then, limits to the value of natural knowledge of God. Culverwel admits the damage wrought by the Fall, for although he insists that God has communicated 'several Resemblances' of himself through various 'looking glasses', he maintains that we would see more clearly through the glass had it not been for the Fall.[132] Moreover, while we might gain some intelligence of God and his workings through nature, we gain no inkling of 'the whole plot of the Gospel', or of 'the treasures of free grace and infinite mercy'.[133] Culverwel thus echoed the Reformers in stressing the negative consequences of the Fall, the culpability of the heathen because of their natural knowledge of God, and the necessity of the saving knowledge of the Gospel.

Yet there is hope for virtuous heathen. Culverwel's clearest statement on the possibility of salvation for the heathen in general, and 'noble pagans' in particular, appears in chapter eight of *The Light of Nature*. In a lengthy passage, he explains that despite all benefits of the light of nature, human knowledge and effort alone are insufficient for salvation:

> Yet a creature cannot come to heaven by all those improvements which are built upon Natures foundation; for if it should accurately and punctually observe every jot and tittle of Natures Law, yet this natural obedience would not be at all correspondent or commensurate to a supernatural happinesse.[134]

Culverwel adds a disclaimer, however, insisting that those sentimental favourites in the salvation stakes – the noble pagans – should not be condemned out of hand. It is not our part to stand in judgement over such men. Their salvation is possible, but it would be a salvation through Jesus Christ, and would not be effected through their own good deeds:

> Yet notwithstanding their censure is too harsh and rigid, who as if they were Judges of eternal life and death, damne *Plato* and *Aristotle* without any question, without any delay at all; and do as confidently pronounce that they are in hell, as if they saw them flaming there. Whereas the infinite goodnesse and wisdom of God might for ought we know finde out several wayes of saving such by the Pleonasmes of his love in Jesus Christ ... But ... you must be sure not to entertain such a thought as this, that the excellency of their intellectuals and morals did move and prevail with the goodnesse of God to save them more then others of the Heathen, as if these were *dispositiones de congruo merentes salutem aeternam*, this indeed were nothing but Pelagianisme as little disguised.[135]

Despite this show of sympathy, Culverwel rejects a universal salvation.

> Yet I am farre from the minde of those Patrons of Universal grace, that make all men in an equal propinquity to salvation, whether Jewes, or Pagans, or Christians ... For if the *remedium salutiferum* be equally applied to all by God himself, and happinesse depends only upon mens regulating and compos-

ing their faculties; how then comes a Christian to be nearer to the Kingdome of Heaven then an Indian? Is there no advantage by the light of the Gospel shining among men with healing in its wings? Surely though the free grace of God may possibly pick and choose an Heathen sometimes, yet certainly he does there more frequently pour his goodnesse into the soul where he lets it streame out more clearly and conspicuously in external manifestations. 'Tis an evident sign that God intends more salvation there, where he affords more means of salvation; if then God do chose and call an heathen, 'tis not by universal, but by distinguishing grace.[136]

Culverwel's position might be termed 'benevolent' Calvinism. Unlike most of his fellow Platonists, he held to the doctrine of election. Unlike most of the Calvinists, he was prepared to make the most of the loopholes left by the doctrine. He strongly rejected the suggestion of salvation on the basis of personal merit, insisting that salvation always occurs through Jesus Christ. At the same time he asserted that God may afford means of salvation through Jesus Christ of which we know nothing. More than any of his contemporaries he made explicit the principle which usually lay dormant within the doctrine of the absolute decree, namely, that God can choose whomever he pleases to be in the body of the elect, and is not restricted by the boundaries of Christianity or the visible church. Yet he distances himself from universalists, maintaining that no special significance can be attached to the gospel if all are to be saved,[137] and also argues the standard Calvinist line that election is accompanied by such 'external manifestations' as are found within the Christian Church. The salvation of a heathen is an extra-ordinary demonstration of divine grace; it is the exception rather than the rule.

Culverwel was quite unembarrassed by the notion of God's arbitrary decree – that single aspect of Calvin's thought which constituted such a stumbling block for his platonising contemporaries. He tells the Christian that God 'planted thee in a place of light, when he shut up and imprison'd the world in palpable darknesse'. The Gospel, he says, 'shines out but upon a little spot of ground which God hath enclos'd for himself'.[138] Yet, the intellectual problem associated with the arbitrary and exclusive operation of the Gospel did not go unnoticed by Culverwel. 'Give a reason if thou canst', he challenges the Christian, 'why thou wert not plac'd in some obscure corner of *America*, and left only to the weak and glimmering light of nature?' He further questions: 'Hath God dealt so with every Nation, or have the Heathen knowledge of this Law?'[139] For Culverwel, no reason can be given and no explanation is offered. The point he wishes to make is that God's free grace must simply be accepted thankfully and uncritically. As a concession to the apparent injustice of condemning noble and ignoble pagans alike to the same fate, Culverwel refers to differing degrees of temporal reward and to a post-mortem hierarchy of punishments. He assures us that the actions of such men as Aristides, Solon, Lycurgus, Numa Pompilius, Cato, Scipio, Fabius, Cicero, to name a few, will merit some temporal reward.[140] Not only here, but also in the afterlife, the punishment of these men will be less severe than that of their more depraved counterparts:

> *Socrates* shall taste a milder cup of wrath, when as *Aristophanes* shall drink up the dregs of fury; if divine justice shall whip *Cicero* with rods, 'twill whip Catiline with Scorpions. An easier and gentle worm shall feed upon *Augustus*, a more fierce and cruel one shall prey upon *Tiberius*.[141]

The worst torment of all is reserved for those who specifically reject the offer of divine grace. Culverwel warns the would-be apostate of his fate in hell: 'O how fain would'st thou then change places in hell with a Turk, or an Infidel, and be ambitious of ordinary damnation.'[142] Small comfort to Socrates perhaps, but at least this speculation shows some sensitivity to the demands of natural justice, and given Culverwel's commitment to the basic precepts of Calvinism, this was probably as far as he could go. For others in Culverwel's circle, however, this solution was far from satisfactory.

The Cambridge Platonists met the conundrum presented by particular Revelation with the postulate of an equally viable revelation in nature, which was universal in its scope. Some took the further step of asserting that there was a salvation which was as universal in its operation as was natural knowledge of God. Peter Sterry was one.

Sterry was both a universalist and a Calvinist. At one level, universalism and Calvinism seem diametrically opposed. At a deeper level, however, they can be seen to be based on similar assumptions. Universalism is in fact a 'limit case' of double predestination, in which the number of the reprobate is reduced to nil and the elect includes everyone. Consequently there is no great inconsistency in asserting both universalism and predestination, and this is precisely what Peter Sterry did. Only universalism, he argued, could solve the riddle of redemption without doing violence to the goodness of God:

> Universal Grace doth no longer thrust out his Special and Peculiar Favour. Reprobation here will be found combining with Election, yea Damnation it self with Salvation, here all those knots which other systems of Divinity have hitherto tied faster, are in great Measure loosened.[143]

Only within a Calvinistic framework, however, could God's prevenient grace be similarly preserved. Sterry's 'Calvinist' universalism involved a denial of that view which Sterry's Cambridge colleagues found so attractive. Arminianism, for Sterry, was an over-reaction to Calvinism, which conceded 'a Freedom of Will absolute and independent as to those Acts relating to a future State'.[144] This concession to human freedom could only mean an erosion of God's sovereign power, for it placed into the hands of men the right to determine the future course of events. This, Sterry, like his fellow Calvinists, was unwilling to do.

Sterry's universalism was not simply a theological form of wishful thinking. His understanding of salvation was thoroughly conditioned by his theological anthropology. We must look upon mankind as our brothers, he says, even though they may exhibit 'the greatest Deformities and Defilements', for all men are bound together by a 'Double Consanguinity':

1. *All men are made of the same blood in* Adam
2. *All men are redeemed by the same blood of the Lord Jesus, who has given himself a Ransom for all, to be testified, en (kai) rois idiois,* in the proper times. Each person which hath his part in this Ransom, hath its proper time for its discovery in him. Thine may be now sooner.[145]

Sterry's view of salvation is quite obvious in this passage. He asserts a universal redemption of mankind, but points out that the discovery of this redemption is communicated sooner to some than to others. Moreover, there may be no obvious signs that redemption has in fact been accomplished. Sterry goes on to develop his christocentric anthropology still further, pointing out its implications for the traditional distinction between nature and grace:

Look upon every person through this *two-fold Glass, the Blood,* and *Beauties* of *Christ. Christ hath died for all.* The *natural being* of *every person* hath his *Root* in the *Grave of Christ,* and is watered with his blood. *Christ lives in all.* His *Resurrection* is the *life* of the *whole Creation.* He is the *Wisdom,* the *Power,* the *Righteousness* of God in every work of *Nature* as well as of *Grace.* He is the *Root* out of which every *natural,* as well as every *spiritual,* Plant springs, which brings forth himself through every natural existence, and brings forth himself out of it, as the *flower,* the *brightness of the Glory of God.*[146]

Christ's work, according to Sterry, was a cosmic redemption, in which the whole of nature was rehabilitated to a state of grace.[147] Thus the revelation of God in nature cannot be separated from his revelation in Jesus Christ.

God, e.g., is manifested in 'Outward providence', and uses human reason to communicate something of himself. 'Another man is *Rational,* and Philosophical, led, by inclination, and study to trace the hidden ways of Nature, to search the first springs, and continued course of Things. The Lord Jesus works Himself into the Reason, and speculation of this Man ... Now Jesus Christ is the *Reason of* his *Reason,* and the only *Reason* to it. Now *Jesus Christ* is all his *Philosophy,* and *Study.*'[148]

This in turn implies no exclusive saving knowledge independent of the knowledge given in creation.

Sterry was left with an obvious dilemma. On the one hand, he claimed that all have access to genuine knowledge of God; he claimed a universal redemption of human nature; he claimed that the mark of true belief is holiness. On the other hand, he could hardly deny the existence of evil men in the world, nor could he ignore more blatant examples of superstition and ignorance. The empirical facts clearly contradicted his theological speculations. Three aspects of Sterry's thought help overcome this apparent inconsistency. First, with regard to clear instances of ignorance and superstition, Sterry pleads the relative and circumscribed nature of all human knowledge.[149] No single tradition has the whole truth, and the truth may appear in different guises – even in contradictory assertions.

Second, Sterry admits that though Christ has won victory over the powers of evil with his death, the heavenly image which is born in man as a result, is subject to 'various Clouds, and Storms'. He observes that:

> the Law of Sin, which is the Spirit of this World, where Death, Hell and the Devil have their place, and their Throne, is still manifest and Powerful in thy members, in thy outward Man. What wonder then, if thine inward Man... be discerned by thee very weakly.[150]

The objective work accomplished by Christ's death does not completely destroy the subjective experience of evil. Such is the pervasive nature of this evil that consciousness of redemption may not occur at all. Many of the redeemed may therefore remain 'anonymous' – not only to themselves, but to the world as well. This accords to some extent with the Calvinist view that the elect are not identified with any visible institution.

Finally, Sterry was able to maintain his moral view of the essence of religion by conceding that there are wicked men in the world (presumably not just outwardly wicked men), and that these wicked men are in some sense objectively different from others. For this reason the body and soul of sinners at death are sent to a kind of hell, while those of the saints proceed directly into the presence of God. This hell of Sterry's is not the traditional place of everlasting damnation however. Rather, hell is the 'Light of Heaven' as it is perceived by sinners. Here, the wicked experience 'a sense of their losse, restlesse desyres, and pursuites, perpetuall frustrations & disappointments with the feares, cares, anguishes & torments that accompany these'. This is not primarily a punitive, but a purgative state. Eventually, when the cleansing process is complete, 'the seed of God immediately puts forth itselfe into them' and they are redeemed 'through suffering into Rest & Glory'. Sterry is at pains to stress that it is not through their own sufferings *per se* that the wicked are eventually redeemed, but through participating in the sufferings of Christ.[151]

Without wishing to labour the obvious, it can be said that Sterry's universalism allows for the salvation of non-Christians. It is interesting to speculate as to whether his distinction between saint and sinner, for the purposes of determining who goes directly to heaven and who is to spend time in purgatory, corresponds to the distinction between Christians and non-Christians. Given his anthropology, and his view of the Nature–Grace distinction, I suspect not, but it remains a possibility.

Much of Sterry's case about the 'hidden nature' of universal redemption relies upon his notion that the knowledge of God manifests itself in many different guises. If men are holy, then their knowledge is guaranteed as genuine. Accordingly, toleration is needed in all discussions between dissenting parties. Sterry's pleas for tolerance and his understanding of the restricted nature of human knowledge of the divine are quite consonant with the views of the other Cambridge Platonists. It is his unambiguous commitment to a belief in universal redemption which distinguishes him from those we have so far considered. Sterry, however, was not alone in advocating this particular view of the atonement. 'Universalism', 'Origenism', sometimes (ambiguously) 'Arminianism', were labels for a view which had a small but committed following in England at this time.[152]

The revived interest in Origen's notion of *apokatastasis* dates from the Renaissance. Erasmus was reputed to have confided to Thomas More that he believed a single page of Origen 'taught more Christian philosophy than ten pages of Augustine'.[153] John Donne, too, made an even-handed assessment of Origen's theology, cautioning his listeners in a sermon lest they too readily judged the Greek father only on the evidence of his accusers.[154] This rekindling of interest in Origen resulted in the publication of a number of positive assessments of his views. The most celebrated of these – *A Letter of Resolution Concerning Origen and the Chief of his Opinions* – was published anonymously in 1661. There is little doubt that it was authored by George Rust, sometime fellow of Christ's College, Cambridge, and one closely associated with the Cambridge circle.[155]

At the heart of Rust's discussion of redemption lies a concern with reconciling divine goodness and justice with the observed state of the world. One of the questions which plagued Rust and others of his circle was: why does God allow most of the nations of the world to exist in a primitive and ignorant condition, beyond all hope of hearing and responding to the gospel? How, Rust wished to enquire, could these individuals be justly condemned to hell without having had the same opportunities of those in Christian lands? The Calvinist solution, which attributed it all to the obscure determinations of divine will, was an option unavailable to the Platonists, for it relied upon a nominalist view of the good which seemed to contradict all earthly understandings of justice. As Rust himself noted, the 'peremptory asserters of his *absolute Will and Power*... with very great ease and satisfaction of mind, resolve all into the *pleasure* and *sovereignty* of God, who being the Creator and Lord of all men, may (they say) dispose of them how and where he pleases'.[156] The Platonists, however, could hardly agree with such a view of divine justice. On the contrary, they were bound to insist with Socrates that the gods approve of those things which are inherently good and that acts do not become good by virtue of the gods' approval.[157] This commitment to the ideal of 'the good' made the particularity of the Christian revelation a genuine intellectual problem for the Cambridge Platonists. Fortunately, in the assertion of the immortality and pre-existence of human souls, they had the means by which they could construct a theodicy which went some way towards ameliorating the intellectual problem.

In his defence of Origen, Rust shows how some of the more obscure opinions of Origen are defensible, and indeed a necessary element of a proper understanding of the world. Why, you may ask, says Rust, does Providence so ordain it such that 'many whole nations both of old and at this present day were so overrun with all kinde of barbarity, ferity and bestial lust, so utterly estranged from the knowledge of God and the love of vertue'.[158] The placing of individuals in such unequal circumstances can only be just if it is somehow related to the activities of those individuals. This can only be so, Rust argues, if we allow the pre-existence of souls. '[A]ll those wretched souls,' says Rust, 'had of old by their long *revolt* from God and the laws of his righteous Kingdome highly deserv'd this Scourge'. As a result, these rebellious souls 'by choice and affection fell off to [sic] in other Regions of the World'.[159] The existence of barbarous nations and heathen religions with all their bizarre and cruel cultic acts, is only consonant with divine providence if the pre-existence of souls is upheld. This remarkable view had a small but enthusiastic following, some of whom even cautiously suggested a Christian doctrine of reincarnation.[160]

Rust does not neglect the other infamous aspect of Origen's teaching. This earthly situation is not the final word. For there is both the 'possibility and hope that the present sad part of the *Drama* may end' and that 'the Benignity of Providence may in due time be as illustrious as her justice hath been conspicuous'.[161] Rust shows us something of the strong link between Platonic philosophy and universalistic tendencies. The Platonic ideal of 'the good' was quite incompatible with the Calvinistic notion of the *decretum absolutum* and propelled Platonic thinkers in the direction of alternative understandings of atonement. When this impulse was combined with the doctrines of pre-existence and immortality of souls we obtain the more novel and liberal understandings of salvation that we find in the Cambridge Platonists.

Henry More, like Rust, places the problem of other religions within the ambit of theodicy. While More's most systematic discussion of other religions is given in *An Explanation of the Grand Mystery of Godliness*, his most imaginative writing on this topic is found in *Divine Dialogues* (1668).[162] In these dialogues a number of topics are discussed until one of the participants – Hylobares – professes that he has considerable difficulties in reconciling divine providence with 'the Manners and Religions of the *barbarous* Nations as they are described in History'.[163] Philotheus puts forward the standard response that this situation results from the fact that 'Mankinde is in a *lapsed* condition'.[164] But Philotheus is not entirely satisfied by his own response, acutely observing that the assertion of the squalid conditions of the barbarous nations implies 'a tacit concession that the *civilized parts* of the world are at least *passable*', and of the civilized parts, Christendom most passable of all.[165] The problem would dissolve, he claims, if it could be shown either that there is no real harm in the apparently base beliefs and brutal customs of these nations, or that the gulf between Christendom and those heathen nations was not as extensive as it appeared. With regard to the first point, Cuphophron sets out the familiar argument that the apparent polytheism and idolatry of the barbarous nations is simply the worship of different symbols and images of the one divinity.[166] With regard to the second matter, there follows a long comparison of aspects of heathen worship with the religious practices of Western Christianity. The idolatry of the heathen is regarded as less reprehensible than that of Rome, for the Romanists have a written law which proscribes the practice, whereas the heathen do not. Human sacrifices of a kind also were practised not only by savages, but also by 'that Bloudy Church of *Rome*', through its persecutions and inquisitions. The eating of human flesh is little different from the Romish doctrine of transubstantiation. Even the Mexican High Priest, who, according to Acosta, went by the name 'Papa', has his counterpart in the Roman Pontiff.[167]

Roman Catholicism is not the only religious institution of the West to suffer by comparison. Calvinism also comes in for its share of attention. The devil, who was reputedly worshipped by Peruvians and Mexicans, is little different to the God of the 'Superlapsarians':

> For the object of their [the superlapsarians] Worship is a God–Idol of their own framing, that acts merely according to *Will* and *Power*, sequestered from all respect to either *Justice* or *Goodness* ... which is the genuine *Idea* of a *Devil*.[168]

Moreover, the religion of these 'superlapsarians' is a good deal worse than that of the Mexicans, for they sacrifice not only human bodies, but human souls as well – 'arbitrarily tumbling them down into the pit of Hell, there to be eternally and inexpressibly tormented, for no other reason but because this dreadfull Idol will have it so.'[169]

Behind all this comparison is more than the kind of polemic which we find in Luther. It is true, of course, that More is able to score points off his Catholic and Calvinist opponents by means of this type of comparison. But at the heart of this dialogue remains a genuine concern with theodicy. Religious diversity does not automatically demand a hierarchy in which some religious forms are shown to be superior to others. Religious pluralism allows religions to 'become a mutual Theatre one to another', giving us the capacity of 'censuring what is evil in our selves by reflecting upon others; the Deformities which we espie in others being nothing else but a reprehensible Parable touching our selves'.[170] It is concluded that 'Providence lets such horrid Usages emerge in the World, that the more affrightfull face of Sin in some places might quite drive out all similitude and appearance of it in others'.[171] The appearance of evil then, is to bring about a greater good, God allowing creation to sink into a 'more palpable Darkness', so that 'a more glorious Light might succeed and emerge'.[172]

The whole theodicy is then reinforced by reference to the pre-existence and immortality of the soul in ways reminiscent of both Rust and Culverwel. While it has to be admitted that in heathen countries the opportunities for a happy life are somewhat limited, it is pointed out that the duration of our earthly life is nothing compared to that of the afterlife. Further, 'the present disadvantages of them that are *sincere* may prove Advantages to them in the other state'.[173] Indeed, those who have had no opportunity to hear the gospel do not die without hope, for there remains to them the possibility of post-mortem salvation through the redeeming work of Christ.[174] Like Rust, More also suggests that the activities of souls before they are placed into bodies may have a bearing on the conditions of earthly existence. A rebellious soul will warrant birth under deprived conditions.[175]

In all of this discussion More seems to imply that no individual is ever completely excluded from divine redemption. Because religion, or the capacity for religion, is vital to being human, all humans, by definition, have something of the divine life, or the capacity to attain it.[176]

We must be wary, however, of identifying More with any of the characters of his dialogue. In the more direct work, *An Antidote Against Idolatry*, More is quite uncompromising in his approach to Catholicism. Here, he outlines a definition of Idolatry which he describes as a pathological immersion in sensuality and materiality, with a view to showing that Catholicism exhibits all the features of idolatry in a way that not even the worst nations of idolaters could imitate. He concludes that 'we have abundantly demonstrated that the Church of *Rome* stands guilty of Gross Idolatry'.[177] The implications of this statement for the salvation of Catholics are far-reaching:

> And therefore we cannot say that every Idolatrous Heathen must perish eternally: But to speak no farther then we have commision, and according to the easy tenour of the Holy Scriptures, we must pronounce, though with

great sadness of heart, that we have no warrant therefrom to think or declare any of the *Popish* Religion, so long as they continue to do so, to be in the state of Salvation.[178]

Thus, the lesson of other religions is primarily to show Catholics the errors of their ways – errors which if not redressed, would lead directly to hell. More is clearly not a universalist like Sterry and Rust. He discusses the possibility, but dismisses it citing the appropriate articles of the Church and upholding God's 'absolute decree'.[179] More almost certainly means 'absolute decree' in the Arminian sense, viz., that God declared from the beginning of the world that those who believed in his son Jesus Christ would be saved. More is not easily categorised as Calvinist, Arminian or Universalist. In his more mystical and charitable moments he does hint at a kind of universalism: 'As much as the Light exceeds the Shadows, so much do the Regions of Happiness those of Sin and Misery.'[180] In other places, he outlines a confused combination of Arminianism and Calvinism, in which some are predestined to salvation, while others exercise their free choice.[181]

In sum, the Cambridge Platonists exhibited a variety of views about the salvation of the heathen, generally tending towards a charitable inclusivism. Their views represent virtually all of the options which have been presented in more recent times. Perhaps most interesting is the fact that despite their elevation of natural knowledge of God, on the whole their view of salvation remained Christocentric. In other words, natural knowledge did not suffice for salvation. To be sure, virtuous (and in some cases not so virtuous) pagans could be saved, but almost always through God's redemptive work in the person of Jesus Christ.

The Cambridge Platonists' attempts to find within their religious philosophy a place for those of other religious persuasions represented the most significant attempt in the West to that time to acknowledge and deal with global religious pluralism. It may be objected that their efforts were tainted with dubious philosophy and theological bias, but for all this it was their unique theological insights which paved the way for the more objective study of the religions. Four aspects of their thought were of prime importance in this process. First was their view that God's activity must be as lawful and universal in the religious realm as in the physical world. Second was their application of a reason unshackled by subservience to institutional or even biblical authority to the problem of religious pluralism. Third was their insistence on the validity of the religion of nature, along with that theory of innate religion which I have termed, somewhat anachronistically, the 'religious *a priori*'. Finally there was the recognition, in Cudworth's writings at least, that 'innate ideas' are bound to have an historical correlate, that the religious *a priori* issues in the positive data of 'common notions', making hypotheses about innate religiosity in principle verifiable in the pages of history, and in the religious practices and beliefs of the contemporary world. These changes meant that for the first time, the positive religions become important sources for Western theories of religion. Only after these foundations had been laid did the dispassionate study of religion become possible.

The development of a science of religion from this theological starting point was to begin with the desacralisation of nature itself. God was banished from the world and from naturalistic explanations. Nature became independent of divine fiat, and was considered lawful on its own account. It has been suggested in other quarters that the world view of seventeenth-century Platonists was a key middle phase in the transition from a providentially guided natural world to a secular, self-explanatory one. Platonist–scientist Thomas Burnet, for example, had extolled the virtues of a mechanistic account of the creation of the world. Divine providence was enhanced, he argued, by the 'exact and regular' course of nature.[182] But Burnet's mechanism was seized upon with considerable enthusiasm by deist Charles Blount who found that the mechanistic account worked quite well without any reference to providence at all.[183] In a similar fashion the deists secularised the Platonists' views of religion. Through their ministrations, reason ceased to be another mode of divine revelation, becoming instead a legitimate source of knowledge in its own right. Discussion of religion no longer required recourse to theology, as it had for the Platonists. Religion was to be understood as issuing from human nature and human reason.

THREE

THE RELIGIOUS INSTINCT AND PRIESTLY CORRUPTIONS: LORD HERBERT AND DEISM

For the Heathens hitherto had nothing to direct them, but common Notions imprinted in their Hearts. Afterwards a certain Sect of Men sprang up, who persuaded them to entertain Rites and Ceremonies.

Herbert of Cherbury, *The Antient Religion of the Gentiles*, pp. 11f

LORD HERBERT, DEISM AND RELIGIOUS FUNDAMENTALS

Like so many seventeenth-century figures, Edward, the first Lord Herbert of Cherbury was a man of contrasts.[1] He has been described variously as 'a blasphemous Atheist' (Thomas Halyburton), 'England's treasure' (Gassendi), 'the commander and Oracle of his time' (Charles Blount), 'Plato and Don Quixote' (Walpole), 'Bodalil-Kant' (Leslie Stephen).[2] Part of the paradox of Herbert is to do with his quixotic character, exemplified most conspicuously in the autobiography;[3] part is due to his uncertain place in the history of thought.

From those early commentators of deism – Thomas Halyburton and John Leland – comes the standard interpretation of Herbert as the father of deism. In his rather intemperate critique of the deist phenomenon, Halyburton labels Herbert 'the great Patron of Deism', claiming that Herbert first brought a recognisable form to the movement.[4] John Leland's more balanced assessment – *A View of the Principal Deistical Writers* (1745) – gives Herbert a far more sympathetic hearing, but still concludes that he was 'the first remarkable Deist in order of time'.[5] Despite these judgements, Charles Leslie, writing earlier than either Halyburton or Leland, identified Charles Blount as the leader of the movement.[6]

The vindication of Leslie's view relies not so much upon a direct comparison of the views of Herbert and the school he is supposed to have founded, but by comparing the attitudes and motives of Herbert with other writers of deistical bent. Herbert was most concerned with sectarianism and persecution which he saw as resulting from the elevation of religious authority over common sense or reason. As a result he was as much concerned with epistemology as with the idea of religion. If Protestant scholastics arrived at their notion of saving knowledge by way of a theory of salvation, Herbert came at his own version of saving knowledge from the other side, by way of a theory of knowledge. In this he differed from the free-thinkers of a later age. While the deists of the eighteenth century might give a nod in the direction of some theory of knowledge – Toland, for instance, makes a great show of subscribing to Locke's epistemology – they were, as a rule, more critical than constructive. They were individual malcontents, lacking the system of the Platonists, or of Herbert himself.

The problem of Herbert's relation to the deists is compounded by the difficulty in attaching any significant meaning to the term 'deism'. This label is notoriously difficult to define with any degree of precision.[7] For our purposes, 'deism' will represent the extreme manifestation of the rational-ising tendency within the religious thought of seventeenth- and early eight-eenth-century England. This tendency we have already observed in the Cambridge Platonists, and it was present also in more orthodox figures such as Stillingfleet, Chillingworth, and Tillotson. This desire to demon-strate the reasonableness of religion becomes deism when doubt is cast upon the adequacy of revelation as a medium of religious truth. Generally we can say therefore, that the deists parted company with orthodox religious thinkers when they were led to deny the necessity of revelation. Deism, then, was not a monolithic phenomenon which can be characterised by a single set of tenets.[8] Rather, the group was a diverse collection of free-thinkers, drawn from all strata of society, whose notions, to exploit a rather tired image, share only 'family resemblances'. The names most closely associated with deism in England are Herbert of Cherbury (1583–1648), Charles Blount (1654–93), John Toland (1670–1722), Anthony Collins (1676–1729), and Matthew Tindal (c. 1657–1733). Less prominent deists, or, in some cases, prominent men whose deism was less conspicuous, include Peter Annet, Henry St John (Viscount Bolingbroke), Thomas Chubb, Henry Dodwell jun., Bernard de Mandeville, Conyers Middleton, Thomas Mor-gan, Anthony Ashley Cooper (Third Earl of Shaftesbury), William Whiston, William Woolaston, and Thomas Woolston.

Whatever the similarities between Herbert's views and those of free-thinkers who came some fifty years later, it can be said that Herbert had much in common with that earlier group, the Cambridge Platonists.[9] As an older contemporary of the Platonists, Herbert sought solutions to the same kinds of questions which they faced. Not surprisingly, he too harked back to the Renaissance for the raw materials with which to forge his philoso-phical vision of Christianity. His hypothesis of a 'plastic nature', for example, echoes the Medieval and Renaissance synthesis of reason and religion, bringing together God and the world, postulating God as a vital ingredient in the causal nexus. Although, like Bacon, he decried reliance on authorities, he also derived many of his ideas from the ancients. Thus, his view of mind has elements of the Aristotelian *nous*, and even stronger affinities with the Stoic *logos*.[10] Yet Herbert's epistemology and his related view of religion illustrate considerable originality, and distinguish him from his Renaissance forebears and his Cambridge contemporaries. Whichcote and his peers had addressed the issue of religious pluralism by generating a theology which stressed the precedence of virtue over orthodox belief. Herbert embarked on a diverging course, plucking 'religion' from its theological context, and generating a rather more secular view of religion, which could equally be described a philosophy of religion or a science of religion. Herbert's idea of religion combines the Platonists' emphasis on religion as a natural human characteristic and the Calvinists' view of religion as a form of knowledge. Thus 'religion' for Herbert is a human propensity the positive manifestation of which is belief in certain propositions. These propositions Herbert enumerated as the 'five common notions concerning religion'.

Following the Reformation, the fragmentation of Christendom led to a change from an institutionally based understanding of exclusive salvation to a propositionally based understanding. Formerly it had been 'no salvation outside the Church'. Now, it had become 'no salvation without the profession of the "true religion"'. But which religion was the true religion? The proliferation of Protestant sects, which heresy hunter Thomas Edwards likened to the spreading of gangrene, had made the question exceedingly complex, for there were not simply two opposing Churches, but many. This situation placed critically-minded individuals in something of a quandary. Herbert was one such individual. 'What', he enquired, 'shall the layman, encompassed by the terrors of divers churches militant throughout the world, decide as to the best religion?' For, he continues, 'there is no church that does not breathe threats, none almost that does not deny the possibility of salvation outside its own pale'.[11] One solution would be to discover 'the fundamentals' of religion – those articles of belief substantial enough to ensure salvation, yet not so numerous or esoteric as to exclude all but a small circle of one's co-religionists. The innumerable confessions, catechisms, 'summes of divinity', and 'brief abstracts of the Christian religion', which English Protestants of the mid-1600s produced with a praiseworthy zeal, represent, in part, attempts to arrive at this solution. Sadly, it is a matter of record that even in 'the fundamentals', consensus could not be reached. The deist Matthew Tindal, reviewing two-hundred years of fruitless religious bickering from his vantage point in the eighteenth century, was to observe:

Tho' the Clergy have taken all possible Methods for a blind Submission, and a forc'd Uniformity, yet they have not been able to hinder *Christians* from being endlessly divided, even in what they call *Fundamentals*, and tho' no one Sect, as far as I can find, have ventured to give us a compleat set of their *Fundamentals*, yet all Sects unanimously own, that those Things which are necessary to Salvation of *Christians*, must be so plain, as that all *Christians*, even those of the meanest Capacities, may apprehend them.[12]

Herbert believed that his fundamentals – the 'common notions' – were the essence of true religion. (Tindal was later to agree.) They were 'saving knowledge', they were the true church: in his own words 'the only Catholic and uniform Church'. And Herbert insisted that 'it is only through this Church that salvation is possible'.[13] 'This Church', crucially, was not an institution, but a set of ideas.

Herbert's creed, as we shall soon see, was considerably shorter than the 'summes of divinitie' of his Calvinist counterparts, for it was designed to include rather than exclude. The incorporation of all religions (not just Christian 'religions') into such a statement required only a judicious abridgement of Christian fundamentals – specifically, deletion of any reference to the Incarnation and Trinity. Indeed if one wished to cast the net wide enough to enmesh even Christians of the most radical stripe – Socinians and Arians – articles concerned with Incarnation and the Trinity (as defined at Chalcedon and Constantinople) would have no place in a list of fundamentals. This omission would in turn allow for the inclusion of Turks and Jews, and if one's knowledge of the beliefs of other religions was a little sketchy, virtually anyone. Even if this extension should not take place – and it certainly did in the case of Herbert – the very attempt to arrive at a list of fundamentals could show how little difference there was between Christianity and other religions. Concern for fundamentals, sparked off by the pluralism which followed the Reformation, and further fuelled by the Protestant notion of saving knowledge, could bring Christianity into a closer relationship with other faiths. For while it is evident that the way of life within the positive institution of medieval Christendom was quite different from that of, say, the Ottoman Empire, when the notion of religion is evacuated of all connotations except those pertaining to belief, 'religions', propositionally conceived, may be brought into a proximity with each other which was previously impossible.[14] With the disintegration of Christendom, such expressions as 'the religion of the English' or 'the religion of the French' failed to reflect what had become important differences of belief in a way that the new expressions 'the Protestant Religion', or 'the Popish Religion' could. These new 'religions', of course, were sets of beliefs rather than integrated ways of life. The legacy of this view of 'the religions' is the modern problem of conflicting truth claims. But if the generic and universal 'religion' is given precedence over the heterogeneous 'religions', as it was by the Platonists and deists, a theoretical rapprochement could be reached which was not possible before. Herbert's 'five common notions' serve to show how an emphasis on the propositional aspects of the religious life can illustrate the common ground of apparently disparate religious groupings.

THE RELIGIOUS *A PRIORI* AND THE FIVE COMMON NOTIONS

The 'five common notions' make their first appearance in Herbert's principal work, *De Veritate, prout distinguitur a Revelatione, a Verisimili, a Possibili, et a Falso*, which appeared in Paris in 1624.[15] Despite this, it should not be thought that they are merely the offshoots of an elaborate theory of knowledge. Rather, the five common notions are the chief application of Herbert's theory of knowledge. Moreover, in the later work, *De Religione Gentilium* (1668), Herbert makes it clear that common notions were developed to address specific theological concerns. Here he points out that according to the divines of his age 'the far greatest part of mankind must be inevitably sentenced to eternal punishment'. This opinion he found 'too rigid and severe' to be consistent with the attributes of God. The common notions then, are proposed as a means of salvation for those beyond the pale of Christendom, and serve at the same time to preserve the goodness of God.

At any rate, it is in *De Veritate* that the common notions make their debut. Not only has posterity deemed this an important work, but even before it appeared in print, no less a scholar than Hugo Grotius praised it warmly, and, if we are to take Herbert's word for it, God himself sanctioned its publication.[16] It is the first work on metaphysics by an English philosopher, and placing it in its correct historical lineage, it appeared thirteen years before Descartes' *Discours de la Méthode*, sixty-six years before Locke's *Essay*, and 157 years before the first edition of Kant's *Kritik der reinen Vernunft*. While it may appear a humble work for such exalted company, *De Veritate* is an important precursor of each of these works. Like his older contemporary Francis Bacon, Herbert wished to promote the liberation of English thought from the shackles of scholastic philosophy. Unlike Bacon, however, who dealt mostly with the rules of empirical evidence, Herbert was more directly concerned with the conditions of knowledge, that is, with epistemology. Moreover, like Cusanus before him, and Sterry, Glanvill and Locke after him, he based his pleas for religious toleration on the conditions and limits of human knowledge.

Herbert's theory of perception, though novel, is not of primary importance to us.[17] It is worth looking at briefly, however, because it raises the issue of the *a priori* in religion. Kant, in his first *Critique*, located the fault of all previous metaphysics in the assumption that in the process of perception, cognitions conform to objects.[18] Kant's Copernican revolution was to assert precisely the contrary – that objects must conform to our cognitions. A third possibility, which Kant seems not to have entertained, is that objects undergo no change, but are received 'an sich' by *a priori* forms of the mind.[19] In this possibility lay Herbert's solution to the problem of perception.

Mental faculties are classified by Herbert into various categories – Natural Instinct, Internal Sense, External Sense and Discourse (reasoning). Of these, the first is the most important. Natural Instinct is that faculty which produces the 'common notions' which arise independent of external perceptions or the reasoning processes.[20] Herbert regards this faculty as 'the immediate instrument of universal divine Providence, some measure of which is imprinted on our minds'.[21] He further elaborates this in the following passage:

> Our mind, then, is the best image and specimen of divinity. Accordingly, whatever truth and goodness exist in us exist pre-eminently in God. And pursuing this view, I believe that the divine image is in turn imparted to the body. But just as the diffusion of light which, the wider it is cast, tends gradually to become fainter till it finally merges into shadows and darkness; so the divine image imparting itself fully to us when we are harmoniously alive and free, is reflected first in Natural Instinct or the general law of Providence, and next in an infinite number of faculties, internal and external, corresponding to their special objects, and fades at last into the shades of the body, so that it often seems to dissolve into matter itself.[22]

Herbert's articulation of the role played by the Natural Instinct in the apperception of the divine is nothing less than an insistence of the existence of a religious *a priori*. The primary function of the Natural Instinct is to act as a faculty which apprehends the divine immediately. It is here that we find the 'pure', undefiled image of the deity. Subsequently, the vision of the divine penetrates, with loss of intensity and purity, to the other internal and external faculties. The apprehension of the Common Notions is, as such, unimpeachable, for it is an unmediated apprehension. Error can only arise after mediation by conditions.[23] In this manner Herbert laid the epistemological foundations for his view of the essence of religion. Indeed, when we consider how much of Herbert's general epistemological speculation finds specific application to the issue of religious knowledge, it seems most probable that the principal aim of *De Veritate* was to provide the formal basis for conjectures about the essence of religion.[24] To put the matter succinctly, Herbert implies that positive forms of religion are expressions of that more obscure image of the deity which is manifested in the internal and external faculties. At the heart of Herbert's theory of religion is the view that if we wish to arrive at the pure essence of religion, we must recover the contents of the Natural Instinct, ignoring the 'material' elements which have become associated with the original communication of divine providence.

The significance of Herbert's religious epistemology is hard to over-emphasise. Introspection is elevated above authority and tradition, becoming the new bench-mark of truth. Just as Descartes was to rely upon the 'clear and distinct ideas' of the subject, so Herbert claimed that truth is determined by 'that *sensus* which I adduce in evidence on every possible occasion'. The criteria are internal. 'At every point', he says, 'I refer the reader to his own faculties.'[25] In specifying this subjective starting point for religious researches, Herbert was anticipating the *a priori* approach which was characteristic of Schleiermacher and Otto. If we are to discover the nature of religion, says Schleiermacher in his *Speeches*: 'The sense of the whole must first be found, chiefly within our own minds, and from thence transferred to corporeal nature.'[26] Likewise, Otto, before embarking on his exploration of the essence of religion, invites his reader to 'direct his mind to a moment of deeply felt religious experience, as little as possible qualified by other forms of religious consciousness'.[27] Equally important were the implications of this view for the history of religion. In allocating to religious experience a distinct faculty of the mind, Herbert laid the basis of the 'natural history of religion' genre. The natural predisposition to adhere to certain religious truths must have its historical correlate. We should expect that these innate beliefs will be manifested historically. Accordingly, the next step in Herbert's science of religion was to conduct an historical study to illustrate the truth of his epistemology. But before we consider that essay, we should first explore the specific content of his common notions.

Herbert introduces his chapter 'Common Notions Concerning Religion' with the observation that not all religion which proclaims a revelation is good. Thus he establishes the need for some 'standard of discrimination'.[28] It will not do, he continues, to discard human reason and heed the prescriptions of an infallible Church or its priesthood, for such authorities 'may be equally used to establish a false religion as to support a true one'.[29] As an alternative, Herbert urges reliance upon 'the teaching of Common Notions, or true Catholic Church, which has never erred, nor ever will err and in which alone the glory of Divine Universal Providence is displayed'.[30] The teaching of the true Catholic Church is contained in these five propositions.[31]

(1) That there is a supreme God. All religions in the past, and indeed all future religions, Herbert confidently announced, have acknowledged the existence of some sovereign deity. Admittedly, this God is known by different names, and in some instances is worshipped according to his attributes as many gods. Despite this, there is underlying agreement that a

supreme being exists, with such attributes as goodness, justice, wisdom and so on.

(2) That God is to be worshipped. Not only do humankind cherish in their hearts a belief in God, but everywhere their religious practices show that worship is offered to this God. To this purpose, says Herbert, prayers and sacrifices are offered, shrines and sanctuaries are built, and the sacerdotal order arises. This last development did not meet with Herbert's unqualified approval, for he says of these priests and pontiffs that 'they have often been a crafty and deceitful tribe, prone to avarice'.[32] Because of this, 'they have corrupted, defiled, and prostituted the pure name of religion'.[33] The anti-clerical tendency so typical of deism surfaces here for the first time.[34] It should not be seen as merely a subterfuge for criticising the clergy of Herbert's day, though it was certainly that. More importantly, it was a key element in the deists' view of the history of religion. The religion of the five notions is not only natural religion in the sense of being installed in the Natural Instinct. It is also natural in the sense of original – it was the basis of the first religion of mankind. The record of history is, accordingly, not the story of how natural religion has been universal in all times and in all places, but is rather the story of the corruption of a pure original religion by the priestly class. Herbert notes in passing the observation of 'an author of reputation' that in one remote region no religious practice can be observed. This evidence, which Locke was to find so telling against Herbert's common notions, is thrown off by Herbert with the explanation that the writer was ignorant of the language of that land.[35] Herbert concludes that it is religion (and not reason), that makes man, man.

(3) That virtue and piety are the most important part of religious practice. Herbert simply notes in this connexion that while there exists no general agreement concerning rites, ceremonies and traditions, it is universally acknowledged that virtue and piety should be cultivated. The chief threat to the development of piety is that our 'animal nature' will lure us into superstition and vice. Herbert again anticipates Glanvill and More, who spoke of 'animal religion'. Moreover, his understanding of the function of virtue is quite Platonic:

> Since Nature unceasingly labours to deliver the soul from its physical burden, so Nature itself instils men with its secret conviction that virtue constitutes the most effective means by which our mind may be gradually separated and released from the body, and enter into its lawful realm.[36]

(4) That we must repent our wickedness. In his discussion of repentance, Herbert makes it clear not only that there is universal agreement about the necessity for contrition, but also that this principle can be seriously proposed only if it is assumed that 'our crimes are washed away by true

penitence'.[37] This may seem a trivial point, but it has a twofold significance. Herbert ostensibly uses it as a launching pad for an attack upon Calvinism. Unless there is a 'universal source to which the wretched mass of men, crushed beneath the burden of sin, can turn to obtain grace and inward peace', then it seems that 'God has created and condemned certain men, in fact the larger part of the human race, not only without their desire, but without their knowledge'. But this counts against God's *universal* providence and impugns his righteousness. Herbert concludes that either through 'general providence' or through 'particular providence or Grace', God provides means of reconciliation.[38]

What is perhaps more important in this discussion, and what might easily be missed if we see these deliberations purely as an attack upon predestination, is that the assumption that repentance alone reconciles us to God obviates the need for a mediator. The whole drama of Incarnation and atonement is made quite superfluous by Herbert's insistence that God has given every man, without distinction, the necessary means by which to become acceptable to him. (This is Herbert's greatest difference with the Cambridge Platonists, none of whom were willing to dispense with the necessity of the Incarnation.) Herbert, with characteristic prudence, does not state his view explicitly, but hints at it when he mentions in passing that 'man is a finite animal, and therefore cannot do anything which is absolutely good or absolutely bad'.[39] This assertion is a direct contradiction of classical forensic theories of atonement, according to which human sin is infinite, and that because of this no human can make recompense for his own sin. If human sin is infinite, only God himself can satisfy divine justice, hence the necessity for the Incarnation.[40] Herbert's stress upon the sufficiency of repentance enabled him to sidestep the question of Incarnation. Those few of his contemporaries who read his work and later deist-hunters were quick to seize upon this as grounds for condemning Herbert's work as heterodox. In any case, it was clear from the outset that the Incarnation could have no place in a scheme which demanded universality as a criterion, and which to all intents and purposes excluded historical and empirical factors.

(5) That there is Reward or Punishment after this life. Herbert does not elaborate much on this point, beyond noting that there is considerable difference of opinion as to the 'nature, quality, extent and mode' of these rewards and punishments. As we would expect, he does not speculate on the nature of hell, as do several of the Cambridge Platonists, suggesting rather that there is no basis in the faculties of the mind which lend support to such fanciful constructions. His silence suggests that elaborate and detailed pictures of the hereafter are but 'superstitions'.

Having set out and expanded briefly on the five common notions, Herbert gives their application. First he clarifies the condition of universality: 'it is not what a large number of men assert, but what all men of *normal* mind believe, that I find important'.[41] This is an important qualification, for it allows for the development of a theory of religious pathology in which those who adhere to more extravagant forms of heathenism are not seen as counting against natural religion on account of their being insane or sick. Herbert, then, does not approve of all religions. Not every religion is good, he informs us, nor can we admit, he continues, that salvation is open to men in every religion.[42] By the same token it should not be assumed that all Christians will be saved either, for 'how can anyone who believes more than is necessary, but who does less than he ought, be saved?'[43] His point with regard to salvation then, is that once the universal notions are assented to, salvation is dependent upon the practical application of them, in the living of a virtuous life. True religion is therefore not simply a matter of believing in the necessity of leading a virtuous life, but of actually living it. In sum:

> The only Catholic and uniform Church is the doctrine of Common Notions which comprehends all places and all men. This Church alone reveals Divine and universal Providence, or the wisdom of Nature. This Church alone explains why God is appealed to as the common Father. And it is only through this Church that salvation is possible.[44]

A number of criticisms might be levelled at Herbert's common notions. Simply, it might be held that they are not innate or instinctual, that they are not common or universal, and that they are not sufficient for salvation. The first objection is the most common, and John Locke is its most celebrated spokesman.[45] As we saw with the Cambridge Platonists however, much of the sting of this criticism is removed when we clarify what was meant by 'innate'. Herbert did not mean to say that the common notions literally form the content of the Natural Instinct, but rather that the faculties of the Natural Instinct will, when in proper working order and in interaction with internal and external faculties, arrive at the common notions.[46] The common notions are not stamped upon the mind of every infant, but the infant's mind is predisposed to arrive at them when it begins to function. A related misconception involves the term 'natural'. As we saw earlier, Herbert considers the Natural Instinct to be informed by divine providence. 'Natural' does not at this stage connote absence of the supernatural – quite the contrary.[47] Implicit here is the ancient distinction between nature and convention, which, as we shall see, formed the basis of the natural history genre of which Herbert's *Antient Religion of the Gentiles* is one of the first examples. The Natural Instinct is therefore equivalent to the Aristotelian *nous*, or more accurately, I believe, to the Stoic *logos* which apprehends the working of the divine *Logos* in the world at large.[48]

The second criticism seems to have empirical evidence on its side. John Ogilvie, for example, made the unkind remark that 'so far from being universal characteristics', Herbert's *notitiae communes* 'are reprobated by his immediate successors in the same department'. He points out that Shaftesbury turns the doctrine of immortality into mere children's tales for the entertainment of the vulgar, and holds the notion of punishment to be inconsistent with the goodness of the deity.[49] Again, Locke drew attention to the historical reports of 'nations of atheists', anticipating the many difficulties which Theravada Buddhism was to provide for proponents of primitive Monotheism or some species of innate theism.[50] Yet this second criticism also rests to some extent upon another misconception – that the common notions were literally universal. Herbert had added the important disclaimer that the five notions would be found 'in men of normal mind'.[51] With an appropriate definition of normality, his common notions might yet be made 'universal'. Still further, he did not claim that his notions received universal assent, but rather that if they were not resisted or corrupted, they would emerge as conscious beliefs. If was left to his *Antient Religion of the Gentiles* to show that the common notions were behind all the varieties of pagan worship and belief. Thus, the commitment to a universal consensus upon religious truths brought with it a particular historical commitment. The diligent historian should be able, in theory, to break through the superficial layer of corrupted rituals and superstitions and uncover the common notions which lay at their basis. This historical method came to be known as natural history, and provided a means by which human conventions could be distinguished from Natural Instinct. To establish empirically the universality of common notions therefore, required the historian to distinguish what was natural from what was conventional, or to show how natural beliefs had been corrupted into human conventions. This procedure was later adopted by Herbert in the historical application of his metaphysical speculations.

The third criticism – that the common notions were not sufficient for salvation – is by nature theological and amounts to little more than a denial of the validity of Herbert's whole enterprise. There is little point in discussing it here, beyond noting that the success of such criticism will ultimately rely upon the provision of an alternative solution to the theological problem which Herbert was attempting to address.

The greatest fault of Herbert's scheme is implicit in criticisms of the first and second kind, and is simply this: the thesis is unfalsifiable. The claim that the five common notions are 'innate' (in Herbert's special sense) is supported by the appeals to universality and introspection. Yet if it is argued that these notions are not in fact literally universal, it is replied that they would be, had they not been 'shut out' or 'thwarted' and that this is what is meant by 'innate'. If the test of universality fails, so too must the test of introspection, for what only some believe intuitively to be true cannot be innate in all.[52] Like all such schemes which urge the essential religiousness of human nature, Herbert's was self-confirming, and represents chiefly a commitment to view the empirical evidence in a certain way.

It is clear that Herbert regarded the five notions as his most significant contribution to the thought of his age. He mentions them in no fewer than four of his works, and it seems likely that his chief motive for writing many of these was simply to vindicate his position concerning the common notions. Thus, *De Veritate* lays down the epistemological groundwork; *The Antient Religion of the Gentiles* demonstrates his point historically; *The Dialogue* shows their practical necessity.

If Herbert was not the first thinker to attempt to arrive at the lowest common denominators of religious belief, he was not the last. Hugo Grotius, having read *De Veritate* in manuscript and encouraged its publication, drew up a list of four fundamental religious beliefs in *De jure belli et pacis* (1625).[53] He argued, as had Cusanus before him, and Culverwel after him, that variety of belief disguises common, underlying fundamentals, but that variety was as much a part of nature as the fundamentals themselves. (This is in contrast to later deists and Schleiermacher. The former regarded all variety as corruption or elaboration of the fundamentals; Schleiermacher saw variety as resulting from different stages of religious development, or from different kinds of religious development.)[54] Herbert's notions also parallel the attempts of the Cambridge Platonists to arrive at some clear essence of religion, an attempt which shows most clearly in Glanvill's setting out of the 'essential principles of religion' and to a lesser extent, in the concern of some Puritans with the 'fundamentals'.

Any theory which proposes innate ideas must claim for those ideas antiquity and universality. Herbert's was no exception.[55] Yet the fact that nowhere on the earth in his age, nor in recorded history, had any substantial group held to the five notions and to them alone should have caused Herbert considerable embarrassment. We find, therefore, that when Herbert comes to the historical ramifications of his theory, he adds a corollary. From an historical perspective what seemed to be universal in the religions were certain structures and certain roles, the most basic of which was the priesthood–laity distinction. The gap between what was predicted by theory and what was actually the case could thus be accounted for by 'priestcraft'. The priests, who could be found in every religion, were seen as agents of corruption, thwarting the natural religious predispositions of the populace, and turning religion into a system from which they could derive profit. The 'great Defection from the Pure Worship of the *Supreme God*', says Herbert, may be justly attributed to 'the Sacerdotal Order'.[56]

The theory of priestly imposture provides the strongest link between Herbert and the deists. This view, significantly, is found in virtually all of those who were considered 'deists', and in none of the Cambridge Platonists. Indeed, even though there was widespread anti-clerical sentiment in England in the last decades of the seventeenth century, only in critical deism was this sentiment elevated into a full blown theory of religion.

IMPOSTURE

The deists did not share Herbert's epistemological and theological interests to any great degree. They tended rather to assume the antiquity of natural religion, and in their historical endeavours bent their efforts not towards establishing the universality of any set of beliefs, but rather the universality of priestcraft. They studied what they considered to be the most visible superstructure of religion. And this was not natural religion and common notions, but superstition and the deceits of the clergy.

Herbert's only self-acknowledged disciple was Charles Blount. Leslie, I believe, is substantially correct in identifying him as the chief deist of his age, for whatever rationalising tendencies existed in English theology prior to Blount's writing, with him there begins a more radical critique of revealed religion, and in his works we have the beginnings of the deist canon. In 'The Original of Idolatry' (1695), Blount introduces the thesis of a natural religion gone bad:

> Before Religion, that is to say, Sacrifices, Rites, Ceremonies, pretended Reve-
> lations, and the like, were invented amongst the Heathens, there was no worship
> of God but in a rational way, whereof the Philosophers pretending to be
> Masters, did to this end, not only teach Virtue and Piety, but were also them-
> selves great examples of it in their Lives and Conversations; whom the people
> chiefly follow'd till they were seduced by their crafty and covetous Sacerdotal
> Order who, instead of the said Virtue and Piety; introduced Fables and Fictions
> of their own.[57]

The two novelties in particular which were introduced by the priesthood to 'multiply their advantages' were polytheism and sacrifices.[58] The priests were not unabetted in their nefarious activities, for other fictions were foisted onto the masses by the civil powers. 'The Primitive Institution of Idolatry', says Blount, 'receiv'd its Birth from the Princes' and afterwards was 'Edu-cated by Ecclesiasticks', for there was need 'to abuse the people into any belief, that might relate to some publick good'.[59] This imposition by the temporal authorities concerned the area of rewards and punishments in the afterlife, for as Blount maintains in his letter 'Concerning the Immortality of the Soul', magistrates, knowing 'the proneness of Man to Evil ... estab-lish'd the Immortality of the Soul' in the hope that this would 'induce Men to Virtue'.[60] Imposture was not the only string to Blount's bow. He refers in passing to euhemerism and projection, but in each case these are linked to his primary thesis – priestly imposture.[61]

In all of this Blount was somewhat more careless than Herbert with the notion of the universality of belief in the supreme deity. Herbert had safeguarded his contention concerning the universality of monotheism by claiming that the supreme deity was worshipped in his earthly manifestations. While Blount in one place inclines towards this view,[62] his emphasis was far more upon the natural inclination to superstition, rather than religion. Corresponding to this emphasis, a much greater stress was placed on the culpability of the clergy. (The princes, for their part, only perpetrated imposture for the good of the state, not for personal gain.) These men were 'fanatical sellers of words, who are most quarrelsome with their Pulpits'.[63]

The reference to pulpits is a telling anachronism, for while Blount gave some concessions to the clergy of his native land, these were less than generous. His main contention regarding the development of idolatry, for example, is summed up thus: 'The general decay of Piety, hath in most religions whatsoever proceded from the exemplary viciousness of their Clergy; though perhaps less in ours than in others.'[64] This was small comfort to the occupants of pulpits round the country. Blount, in implicating Anglican clergymen in his imposture theory, was giving notice that in deist accounts of religion, Christianity was to lose its immunity from historical–critical investigation. For Blount, the imposture theory was virtually self-evident. Its proof derived from the fact that 'there be but three Laws' – of Moses, of Christ, and Muhammad. Blount surmised from this state of affairs that either all are false, 'and so the whole world is deceived'; or only two of them, 'and so the greater part is deceived'; but whatever the solution to the conundrum, it is patent that the majority of mankind are deceived in matters of religion.[65] Once this had been established, it was simply a matter of identifying the perpetrators of imposture, for in Blount's simple equation, a deceived populace required deceivers, and as we would expect, the priests were the most probable candidates. The fallacy in this syllogism is, of course, that pluralism implies deceit. Yet this fallacy was virtually axiomatic for the critics of revealed religion, who, by and large, were committed to the view that man, left to his own devices, would come to embrace the religion of nature. Only corrupting influences could sway him from his natural course, and hence some mechanism – for the deists, the fictions of the priesthood – had to be postulated in order to account for deviations from normal religious development. Pluralism was unnatural, and combined with intolerance, gave rise to untold human misery. The cure was to be a return to the unsullied religion of the *illud tempus* which would result in a universal worship of the one God, and bring an end to religious strife.

John Toland's excursion into the history of religion, like Blount's, came in the form of an essay on 'The Origin of Idolatry, and Reasons of Heathenism'.[66] The opening scenario is familiar. He speaks of 'the plain Easiness' of the religion of the ancient Egyptians, Persians, Romans, and Hebrews, which was 'most agreeable to Simplicity of the Divine Nature'. Then came the Fall: 'But tho *God did thus make Men upright, yet they found out ... many Inventions.*'[67] Toland stopped short of attributing the origin of idolatry directly to the priesthood. Instead, projection, euhemerism, and the ancients' preoccupation with astronomy combined to bring about the degradation of ancient religion. At first, men came to attribute human characteristics to God, having 'the same Conceptions of God himself, which they had before of their earthly Princes'. As a result, God was imagined to be jealous, vengeful and arbitrary, and was best placated, like earthly rulers, by approaches to his minions.[68] The perceived necessity for mediators soon led to henotheism. Subsequently, the study of the heavenly bodies came to play a role, with stars and planets being invested with human characteristics, and at length taking on the names of dead heroes or rulers.[69] For Toland, this kind of euhemerism was 'the first, the most natural, the most universal' basis of heathen religion.[70]

To the priests fell the honour, not of establishing heathenism, but of maintaining it, and of introducing its various rites. The modes of worship of the gods, says Toland, 'were afterwards manag'd by the Priests so as to make their imagin'd Intimacy with Heaven more valu'd, and to get Revenues settled on themselves'. 'Moreover', he adds, after the manner of Blount, 'there was not wanting sometimes a mutual Compact between the Prince and the Priest', which bound the priests to preach the absolute power of the prince and the fear of hell, to contribute to the stability of the state.[71] Toland concludes his essay with a summary of his case, given in the following piece of doggerel:

> Natural religion was easy first and plain,
> Tales made it mystery, offrings made it gain;
> Sacrifices and shows were at length prepar'd,
> The priests ate roast meat, and the people star'd.[72]

The most historically-sophisticated version of the priestcraft theory was articulated by the self-styled 'Christian deist', Thomas Morgan. Morgan refers to the historical religions as 'religions of hierarchy', thus formalising the deistic tendency to regard the priest–laity distinction as the common feature of all positive religions.[73] The task for the historian of religion was to determine how the religion of hierarchy came to replace the religion of nature.

Morgan, like most of the deists, extolled the virtues of the primitive golden age. In the 'first and purest Ages', he says, holy men followed natural religion, living a simple life of virtue and temperance.[74] Through an excess of piety, these men came to interpret any unusual occurrence in nature as 'the Voice and Monition of God', and while this was harmless enough in itself, 'yet when they carried it too far ... it ran into Enthusiasm and sometimes led them into Error'.[75] Morgan drew examples from sacred history to illustrate his theory. He shows, for example, that even the patriarch Abraham had episodes of extravagant fetishism, interpreting unusual natural events as divine communications. However, it was in Egypt that the corruption of the Jewish religion, and indeed all religion was to begin:

> But what at first had a very good moral Sense and Construction, and argued a pious and religious Trust in, and Dependence on God and Providence, came afterward to be turned into Superstition, Enthusiasm, and the most unnatural and incredible Accounts of God and Providence. This great Degeneracy, Inversion of Nature, and gross Corruption of Religion, happened afterward in *Egypt*, when *Joseph* had established an hereditary Priesthood there, endow'd with vast Revenues in Lands, and made independent on the Crown.[76]

The exact nature of the link between fetishism and priestcraft was never fully spelt out, but we can assume that the priests saw in these excesses of piety a means of exploiting the people. Moses, schooled in the magic of the Egyptians, thus formed a compact with Aaron, and together they imposed upon the people of Israel for 'their own Purposes and ambitious views'.[77] Moses' purported deceit was demonstrated beyond doubt through an application of Humphrey Prideaux's criteria of imposture. The Dean, in his *Letter to the Deists*, had urged against the charges of the deists that there was a 'Rule of Judgement', which would demonstrate beyond doubt that 'Mahometanism' was a religion founded on imposture, while Christianity was not. Unfortunately Prideaux cast his net too wide and, as Morgan pointed out with some satisfaction, had inadvertently enmeshed other fish.[78] Moses thus stood convicted of imposture on the basis of Prideaux's 'marks and characters of imposture'. A similar pattern of imposture was presumed to have taken place in all the religions. Once false religion had gained a foothold in Egypt, it was 'more and more corrupted, from Time to Time, by the Priests, and propagated from thence to other Countries, till at last it terminated in the grossest Idolatry of the Heathen Nations'.[79] The religion of the Jews rates chief mention because sacred history was able to flesh out in detail the stages of its corruption – stages which in other deist accounts of religion remained conjectural. Morgan was able to show that Prideaux's analysis of 'Mahometanism' fitted equally well what was known of the history of Judaism. By implication, if more was known of the history of other religions, they too could be shown to have arisen from similar instances of imposture. Morgan thus proffered genuine historical data to support the contention that imposture was the universal pattern of religious development.

Toland and Morgan were the most historically-minded of the deists, and, despite their naïvité and their tendency to project aspects of the present onto the past, they anticipated to a large extent later histories of religion. Other deists, who set forth no histories of religion, were not thereby deterred from embracing the thesis of imposture and priestcraft however, but added their voices to the refrain. The priests, Anthony Collins simply declared, were 'the chief Pretenders to be the Guides to others in matters of Religion'.[80] 'There was nothing too absurd to be receiv'd as divine', said Tindal, 'after People once gave themselves up to believe in their Priests'.[81] So Richard Bentley, summing up the *idée fixe* of these 'free thinkers', complained that 'dreaming and waking they have one perpetual theme, *Priestcraft*.'[82]

PRIESTCRAFT AND ANTICLERICALISM

The theory of priestly imposture was, of course, more than just a means of accounting for the perversion of primitive monotheism. Few of the deist writers in their attacks upon the race of priests bothered explicitly to exclude their own compatriots. This omission did not go unnoticed by contemporary divines who saw all too clearly that they were being lumped together with some of the most unsavory examples of religious imposture in the history of religion. Jonathan Swift, as we shall see, viewed this overt condemnation of all priests as a covert attack upon the clergy of England, and on them alone. This, perhaps, was to go too far, for deist histories of religion required some mechanism to account for the corruption of natural religion in remote antiquity. In laying the blame at the feet of the priests, the deists juggled the demands of both impartial history and polemic. On the other hand, there was not, in the seventeeth and eighteenth centuries, the relatively modern view that history should be a more or less objective elucidation of events which occurred in the past. On the contrary, the past was uncovered not for its own sake, nor simply for interest, but primarily because it could serve a didactic purpose.[83] The lesson of history for the deists was that the priests had been the original corruptors of religion, and given the assumption that human nature had not changed too much in the intervening years, continued to be the corruptors of religion.

While the deists made themselves few friends amongst 'the Light and Glory of present Christianity', as Bentley was wont to call the English clergy,[84] they must have struck a responsive note in the community at large. From about the middle of the seventeenth century to the first decades of the eighteenth, there was a gradual increase in anti-clerical sentiment in England.[85] It was expressed in many different quarters and for a variety of reasons. Moderate gentlemen, like Addison and Steele of *The Spectator*, confined themselves to making observations about how disproportionate the number of clergy were in the general population.[86] Others commented upon the decline in the education and breeding of men of the cloth. Such sentiments are found in John Eachard's *The Grounds and Occasions of the Contempt of the Clergy and Religion* (1670). Eachard set forth his theory boldly and simply: The clergy were held in contempt on account of 'the *Ignorance* of some, and the *Poverty* of others'.[87] The work proved to be quite popular and ran to many editions. It also seems to have provided the basis of Lord Macaulay's assessment of the clergy of this period. He was to maintain that 'the clergy were regarded, on the whole, as a plebeian class', and that the modest earnings of most clergymen had led to the degradation of the priestly character.[88] There is doubtless some truth in Macaulay's observation, although his view of the clergy of the late seventeenth century is by no means comprehensive.[89]

Eachard's provocative and mocking piece elicited several responses. Generally these apologies proposed either that the grounds for the contempt of the clergy were spurious, or that if the condition of the clergy was accurately portrayed, it should not serve as an occasion for their contempt.[90] Other criticisms were very close to those of the deists. Edmund Hickeringill used an inordinate amount of ink to put the case that the priests defile 'true Religion, making void the great Laws of God, and Nature, and of right Reason', establishing instead 'Pride, Cruelty, Avarice and Revenge'.[91] A fearful and ignorant humanity are easily duped by this class, whose deceitful ways could readily be exposed by free enquiry and a free press.[92] Hickeringill's 'deism' even extended to the view that the 'externals' of religion are insignificant compared with virtue, which is practised even by heathens who know nothing of the Gospel.[93]

Despite obvious links between the priestcraft theory and the anticlericalism of English society in general, the deists' view of the clergy fitted into a broader theory of religion in a way which was not true of the views of Addison, Eachard or even Hickeringill. Generally, anti-clerical feelings could be attributed to a decline in the status of the clergy. The deists, on the other hand, wished to argue that the English clergy were contemporary manifestations of a universal religious type – the priestly impostor.[94] The current unpopularity of the clergy is nonetheless significant here, for it illustrates how the apparently extreme attitude of deism would have gained some impetus from the general feeling in the community.

If highly-placed, scholarly clergymen could afford to ignore the cavills of an Eachard, the accusations of the deists were closer to home. For all their references to the priests of antiquity, there was no doubt that the deists meant to implicate the divines of England in their accusations of imposture. These were not simple charges of ignorance and poverty, but of massive fraud. The more lofty clergymen were not slow to realise this. Said Jonathan Swift of Collins' anti-clerical *Discourse of Free-Thinking*:

> The writer, when he speaks of priests, desires chiefly to be understood to mean the English Clergy, yet he includes all priests whatsoever, except the ancient and modern heathen, the Turks, Quakers and Socinians.[95]

William Warburton, Bishop of Gloucester, responded more directly, indignantly proclaiming that the clergy had had to bear the heaviest load of the deists' 'Calumny and Slander'. The priesthood in toto, he said, had been represented by the scurrilous free-thinkers as:

> debauched, avaricious, proud, vindictive, ambitious, deceitful, irreligious and incorrigible. *An order of Men profligate and abandoned to Wickedness, inconsistent with the Good of Society, irreconcilable Enemies to Reason, and Conspirators against the Liberty and Property of Mankind.*[96]

While the deist thesis of imposture might, with some plausibility, account for the origin and maintenance of positive religions in antiquity, the assumption that what applied in ancient times applied equally well to modern heathenism and modern Christendom could not be as easily sustained. It was not at all clear that the divines of England were purposely imposing some giant fraud upon the faithful in the same manner as the pagan priests of the past. Neither was it obvious that the priests had been duped by their own traditions, and were simply perpetuating age-old deceits. Still less likely was it that they stood to gain from the preaching of such doctrines as the deists found 'mysterious' and superstitious.[97] The ecclesiastical establishment was not slow to point this out, and the wrath and rhetoric of many highly-placed divines fell upon the hapless deists.

One of the more entertaining interludes of this present controversy took place between Anthony Collins and Jonathan Swift. Collins, in his *Discourse of Free-Thinking*, had made the unfortunate error of displaying his wit at the expense of Swift, Atterbury, and other divines, proposing that they be dispatched to foreign parts to propagate the gospel – if possible, as part of a religious exchange with a corresponding assembly of 'Talapoins' (Buddhist monks) from Siam. This, Collins maintained, would allow the Church to triumph abroad and bring an end to factions at home.[98] Swift was not amused by the prospect of this cultural exchange, and retaliated with his unique brand of irony in a 'three-penny pamphlet' entitled *Mr C—s's Discourse of Free-Thinking, put into plain English, by way of abstract for use of the Poor* (1713). The frontpiece of the parody adds with dark irony that the work is by 'a friend of the author'. What follows is a simplistic caricature of Collins' argument which exposes a number of non-sequiturs previously hidden in the verbiage. Amid the mockery Swift's main response emerges.

'The bulk of mankind', he pronounced, 'is as well qualified for flying as for thinking', and if every man took it upon himself to think freely and publish his thoughts abroad, 'it would make wild work in the world'.[99] Seizing upon Collins' unhappy analogy between thinking and seeing, Swift pressed home his point:

> Why may I be denied the liberty of free-seeing as well as freethinking? Yet nobody pretends that the first is unlawful, for a cat may look upon a king; though you may be near-sighted, or have sore eyes, or are blind, you may be a free-seer; you ought to see for yourself, and not trust to a guide to choose the colour of your stockings or save you from falling in a ditch.[100]

For Swift, the blindness of human reason meant that to advocate free-thinking was to invite anarchy. Here was a tacit recognition that the principle of liberty of conscience, established as a result of the Reformation, had given rise to 'the whole herd of Presbyterians, Independents, Atheists, Anabaptists, Deists, Quakers and Socinians'.[101] For all this, it seems that Swift did not take Collins too seriously, and his primary motivation in writing this piece may well have been political. Tindal, Toland, Collins, and 'all the Tribe of *Free-Thinkers*', were associated with the Whig party, towards which the more conservative Swift cherished an undisguised animosity. The Tory cause was well served by showing that a firm link existed between Whig politics and deism or 'atheism'.[102]

A more direct and less politically-motivated attack on Collins came in the form of Richard Bentley's *Remarks Upon a late Discourse of Free-Thinking*. Bentley was outraged that the Talapoins of Siam were 'put here upon a level with the whole *Clergy of England*'.[103] Bentley's critical acumen spent itself, for the most part, in taking Collins to task for his dubious attempts at scholarship. Much of the work is a merciless exposé of Collins' clumsy translations. Yet Bentley does make this substantive point. The right of free thought may, in principle, be desirable; that free thought tends uniformly towards deism, however, was highly doubtful.

The anti-clerical approach of the deists met with many other responses.[104] The clergy, it seemed, would not easily be forced into the villainous role which the deists wished them to play. As far as Swift and his peers were concerned, the accusations of imposture were unsubstantiated. Their accusers, they felt, were hardly the great minds of the age and in fact could really only be distinguished from the mindless mob by the unfortunate predilection for exposing their own ignorance and culpability. They were both stupid and profligate; they were not-so-mute testimonies to where freethinking would lead. Addison was to observe of these 'modern Infidels' that 'their Infidelity is but another Term for their Ignorance'.[105] Their theory implied, as Bentley put it, 'that there are but two sorts in Mankind, Deceivers and Deceiv'd, Cheats and Fools'.[106] In the clergy's own minds, they were not deceivers; nor is it likely that they were themselves deceived. In the conflict with the deists, virtue and sagacity were on the side of the divines. If any were to qualify as knaves, fools, or both, it was the deists, and the *ad hominem* arguments of Swift and Bentley were designed to show precisely this. For the deists' case to be acceptable, it required first a theory that could find niches for both themselves and clergy, and second, an historical theory which dealt specifically with Christianity, and showed how 'abuses' and 'superstitions' had been introduced into a tradition the content of which had originally been the same as natural religion.

Another reason that the criticisms of both Eachard and the Deists went wide of the mark was that both had failed to take into consideration the vast gulf between an eminent divine like Swift, and the average country parson. By and large, Eachard's complaints were true of the latter, but not the former.[107] Many a country curate fitted his picture of poverty and ignorance. The deists also had a point when they insisted that the clergy simply indoctrinated their charges with inherited religious prejudices, if by the clergy they meant the more bigoted and bucolic variety. There is ample evidence of the material and intellectual impoverishment of the country clergy. Macaulay reports that the Anglican priesthood at this time 'was divided into two sections, which in manners, and in social position, differed widely from each other'.[108] As a rule, the country parson, in addition to being poor and ignorant, was conservative to the core, brooked no tolerance of dissenters, and preached an uncritical subservience to the Crown. For all this, they were a power to be reckoned with, and in their pulpits were potent propagandists in the Tory cause.[109] Not surprisingly the deists, who were usually of the opposite political persuasion, despised them. The general nature of the priestcraft theory, however, did not allow them to be discriminating enough in their attacks on the clergy, and Collins' blunder in particular, in lampooning Swift and others, raised the ire of the most educated and eloquent men in England. Such was the reputation of these men that the priestcraft theory in its original form became untenable.

For all this, the theory was far too resilient simply to disappear completely. Instead it underwent a number of modifications. In one of the surviving forms of the priestcraft theory, less emphasis was placed on the culpability of the clergy, who came to be seen rather as unwitting pawns, manipulated by inexorable social forces: the blame for religious corruption lay not with any group or individual, but with the social institution of education. Religious diversity thus came to be seen as the result of the victory of convention over nature. For the deists, individual development paralleled the development of the human race, the primitive monotheism of earliest man having its counterpart in the idea of God which was thought to develop in the infant. A human mind with the requisite intelligence should, of its own accord, come to apprehend the truths of natural religion. But the same corrupting influences which originally warped religion were still operative, and the natural course of religious development continued to be thwarted by the pressures of education and prejudice. The officers presiding over this process were, of course, the clergy, who as of old, distorted religious development. This hypothesis lies at the heart of Toland's essay, 'The Origin and Force of Prejudices'.[110]

It is impossible, Toland states, for anyone not to be educated in error. Every person with whom a child comes in contact 'endeavours to deprave his reason from the very beginning ... so that not remembering when, or where, or how he came by many of his notions, he's tempted to believe that they proceed from Nature itself'.[111] School, he declares, serves only the communication of 'mutual Mistakes and vicious Habits', while University is 'the most fertile Nursery of Prejudices'.[112] (Toland's education, we might project, was less than ideal.) The most important role in this process was reserved for the clergy: 'the bulk of mankind', Toland contended, 'are retain'd in their Mistakes by the Priests'.[113]

Toland was covering somewhat familiar ground. Milton had declared some half a century earlier that 'of all teachers and masters that have ever taught', custom 'hath drawn the most disciples'; and further, that 'error supports custom' and 'custom countenances error'.[114] Applying this sentiment to religion, the Platonist Glanvill observed of 'idolaters' that 'the impressions of a barbarous *education* are stronger in them than *nature*'. Jews and Turks as well, were rooted in their 'ungrounded faith' by education.[115] Charles Blount's brother, Sir Thomas (of similar sceptical cast to his younger sibling), in his *Essays on Several Subjects*, treated in turn 'popery and priestcraft', the 'great mischief and prejudice of learning', and 'education and custom'. He quite literally echoed Glanvill when he declared:

> there's nothing so absurd, to which *education* cannot force our tender Youth:
> it can turn us into Shapes more Monstrous then those of *Africk* ... The
> *Half Moon* or *Cross* is indifferent to us; and with the same ease can we Write
> on the *Rasa Tabula*, TURK or CHRISTIAN.[116]

Tindal also complained that education had usurped the place of nature: 'Education is justly esteem'd a second Nature, and its force is so strong, that few can shake off its Prejudices'. Again the fault was laid at the feet of the Clergy, for according to Tindal the education of the young was committed to men 'devoted to the Interest of their own Order', and that upon which it depends – '*The Good of the Church*'.[117]

These sentiments make the charge of priestcraft far more plausible, for according to this view the crime of the clergy was more a matter of maintaining traditional beliefs or, as the deists would have it, 'prejudices', rather than originating some giant fraud. The priests were no less the great corruptors of religion, but in a more restricted sense than those ancient originators of superstition. They may not have been guilty of conscious deceit, but they nonetheless diverted the mind from its true course, corrupting an originally pure religious instinct. This is the presumed link between free-thinkers (those who have liberated themselves from corrupting influences) and natural religion. Here also is an explanation of why the priests could still be regarded as sources of corruption, even though it was clear that few ever introduced novelties of their own.

In light of this we may re-assess the deists' charge of priestcraft, and distinguish it from that of imposture. The latter is to do with the authorship of fraud, the former with its perpetuation. The deist theory of priestcraft was not so much concerned with the origin of religion, as with the formal characteristics possessed by all religions. Nature and innate religion could account for the origins of religion. What was required were explanations of the corruption of natural religion. Those few deists who did not subscribe to primitive monotheism relied on other theories – projection, euhemerism, the fear theory – to account for the origin of religion and superstition.[118] Priestcraft was most commonly used to account for the remarkable and unnatural persistence of religious follies. According to the deists, all religions had priests, and in all religions they performed a similar function – that of maintaining the vulgar in their ignorance.

Evidence for the formal similarity of all religions came not only from the comparison of the religions of antiquity with those of the modern age, but from the observation of Britain's own turbulent history in the sixteenth and seventeenth centuries, and of the bloody religious conflicts which occurred then. The misanthropic Swift described the seventeenth century as 'a heap of conspiracies, rebellions, murders, massacres, revolutions, banishments'.[119] From this history it could be concluded that there was little to choose between the excesses of Catholicism and those of Protestantism. Through the consecutive eras of Bloody Mary's Catholic reign, the Elizabethan settlement, the Puritan Revolution, the Restoration, and the Bloodless revolution, each with its concomitant religious changes, came the realisation, right or wrong, that despite superficial differences Catholic religion and the various forms of Protestant religion were all formally similar. It is in this recognition that we find the reason for the general application of the priestcraft theory.

The roots of late seventeenth-century anti-clericalism lie in Reformation polemics against monks, priests and popes, and in the humanistic reaction against medieval ecclesiastical hierarchy. Both of these tendencies emerge in the writings of William Tyndale (c. 1495–1536). In *The Practyse of Prelates*

(1530), is found Tyndale's outspoken condemnation of hierarchical church government, backed, as in deist histories of religion, by a particular historical view. Tyndale uses the humanistic vision of a pristine primal period, arguing that the New Testament presents a picture of the ideal Church, and that the beginnings of the corruption of that pure Church coincided with the rise of the priesthood.[120] Throughout history, the papacy was seen to have served as a source of idolatry, aided by the bishops.[121] This view was formed quite independent of Reformation ideology although it was closely linked with it. 'Popery' and 'priestcraft' were not exclusively bound to Reformation polemic, and could as easily be applied to the episcopal structure of Anglicanism. Such an adaptation was made by William Turner in *The Huntyng and Fyndyng out of the Romish Foxe* (1534). The prelates of the recently-formed Church of England, Turner claimed, were merely perpetuating corrupt Catholicism, despite their outward profession of the new creed. Again, reference was made to the earliest Church as representing the perfect paradigm: 'But in Christes tyme and the Apostles tyme and in the tymes of the holy martyres was the most perfit chirch.'[122]

There is ample evidence that this view persisted until well into the next century. In John Milton's writings, we find outspoken criticism of the highly-placed Anglican clergy. 'They live like earls', he charges, 'sending herds of souls starving to hell, while they feast and riot upon the labours of hireling curates'. We must, he urges, 'take that course which ... Luther took against the pope and monks'.[123] Even at this stage, however, Milton's *Apology* was not anticlerical simpliciter. It had in fact been composed in defence of five Presbyterian clergymen.[124] This was soon to change, however, for following the ascendency of the Puritans in the parliament, Milton came to realise that the 'obdurate clergy' of Presbyterianism were little better than the prelates of Laud's High Church party.[125] Thus it was held in some quarters that, as one writer expressed it, the Protestant clergy (Presbyterians included), had merely 'found out a plausible way to be *Papists*'.[126]

England, we have said, was unique in Europe, having experienced within the span of a single century officially condoned clergymen from the whole spectrum of Christianity, from the Catholic priesthood through to the Puritan ministers. The deists, like Milton, concluded from this experience that similar functions were performed by the clergy, irrespective of their professed creeds. Even John Locke pointedly noted that 'in the reigns of Henry VIII, Edward VI, Mary, and Elizabeth, how easily and smoothly the clergy changed their decrees, their articules of faith, their form of worships, everything according to the inclination of those kings and queens'.[127] The dexterity with which many clergymen were able to adapt themselves to the religious predispositions of the ruling party no doubt aided the deists in their indictments of the clergy, no less than fancied parallels with classical culture.

The deist charges of priestcraft, then, had their origins in humanistic anti-clericalism, expressed initially as anti-Catholic polemic, but which was subsequently adapted to a more general purpose. Like so many weapons originally forged to advance the claims of one Christian faction or other, priestcraft, in the hands of the deists, became a blunderbuss levelled against all forms of religion. Equally important is the fact that the deists also subscribed to the humanist conception of an uncorrupted *illud tempus*, but instead of locating it in the age of the earliest Church, pushed it further back into the era of the birth of mankind. Thus all positive manifestations of Christianity came to represent corruptions, even the earliest, New Testament forms. The reformers, in the eyes of the deists, simply had not been radical enough in retreating to primitive Christianity – they should have returned to primitive religion itself, which for the constructive deists was 'genuine' Christianity.

For the deists this more sophisticated, sociological version of the priestcraft theory came to be a fundamental axiom of religious development. The priests of all positive religions performed similar functions – perpetuating human conventions which were but perverted forms of natural religion. The chief limitation of this view, however, was that it would never prove acceptable to the powerful ecclesiastical establishment. For this reason it was to undergo one final metamorphosis and find new life as the twofold philosophy – perhaps the most widely held theory of religion in seventeenth-century England. The twofold philosophy, while incorporating many elements of the priestcraft theory, had an appeal which went well beyond the circle of deism, and came to be applied not only in the sphere of religion, but in many other areas of learning as well. It fitted both contemporary and historical religious data equally well, and had the singular advantage, from the establishment point of view, of removing the blame for the development of superstition from the shoulders of the Clergy.

TWOFOLD PHILOSOPHY

To hold to a twofold philosophy is to divide philosophy (in its broadest sense) into two aspects – as Toland put it – '*External* or popular and depraved', and '*Internal*, or pure and genuine'.[128] In the religious sphere this amounts to a division between popular 'superstition' and esoteric 'religion'. The human race is divided into two groups, not cheats and cheated as in the imposture theory, but into the credulous, superstitious mob and the intellectual elite. The twofold philosophy has an ancient lineage, finding mention in classical and patristic literature. Strabo, Plutarch, Cicero, Clement of Alexandria, Origen, Lactantius, and Augustine all note of various ancient religions that there existed two distinct theologies – one for the intellectuals or rulers, the other for the great ignorant masses.[129] Some of the fathers, most notably Origen and Basil the Great, had suggested that this double structure was also characteristic of Christianity.[130] In the Middle Ages the twofold philosophy was formalised into the doctrine of the 'double truth', commonly attributed to Averroës and some of the medieval school men. According to this view, a proposition might be true theologically, yet false philosophically.[131] 'Double truth' so conceived provided the philosopher–scientist of the Middle Ages with a convenient means of 'reconciling' intractable revealed truths with the results of philosophical investigations. Closer to home, Francis Bacon, his opposition to scholastic philosophy notwithstanding, suggested that the truth is twofold – truths of religion being different from, and possibly even opposed to, truths of reason.[132] Perhaps the strongest links of the twofold philosophy, however, are with the thesis of the ancient theology, of which the former is a secular version.

We shall be dealing with the ancient theology in a later chapter. For the moment, if we cast our minds back to Herbert of Cherbury, we shall recall his insistence that beneath the plethora of religious beliefs and rites was a common, natural religion. While the acknowledged existence of the manifold forms of heathenism made this view difficult to sustain, Herbert proposed that polytheistic heathenism was 'symbolic' worship of God, or worship of God in his attributes. Later deists retreated from this view, granting that the majority seldom rose above superstition in their efforts to be religious, while insisting that in all ages there had been an exclusive group of philosophical bent who had believed no more and no less than the principles of natural theology. ''Tis confest', says Blount, 'that whole Nations have never follow'd our Opinion: but how many of a nation ever consider to the bottom of any Religion!' What was important was that thinking men of every age had subscribed to natural religion: 'Heathen philosophers and Poets', Blount avers, and indeed 'many men of all Religions at this day, have centr'd in the Opinion of Natural Religion'.[133] Following Blount's lead, the deists of the eighteenth century opted for exclusive but explicit belief in natural religion rather than the universal and implicit belief which Herbert proposed. Herbert, admittedly, had flirted briefly with the twofold philosophy, arguing that Socrates, Plato and Aristotle were monotheists who hid their real views from 'the ignorant multitude'.[134] Yet he was astute enough to realise that he could not at the same time uphold both the universality of belief in the 'five common notions' and a twofold philosophy. Blount and his successors, probably because of Locke's penetrating criticisms of innate ideas, were quite willing to abandon the former in favour of the latter.

Of the deists it was Toland and Collins who made the most of this theory. In his early writings Toland made scattered references to the existence of the twofold philosophy amongst the ancients.[135] Later in life, however, he was to make considerably more of it, devoting two complete works to it – *Clidophorus: or Of the Exoteric and Esoteric Philosophy*, and the enigmatic *Pantheisticon*.[136] *Clidophorus* is mostly historical, and weaves together the themes of twofold philosophy, priestcraft and imposture, showing how the priests of all religions could justify their impostures by use of the twofold philosophy. The theme of the work is that which Toland identifies as the motto of the sacerdotal order in all epochs: 'the Ignorance of the Laity is the Revenue of the Clergy'.[137]

Pantheisticon is a more intriguing work. It focusses upon Toland's own age, purporting to be a description of the beliefs and rites of a modern group called 'Pantheists' or the 'Socratic Society'. It contains a 'liturgy' of the society in which is expounded the morals and axioms of the brotherhood, their deity and philosophy, and their liberty and law. The main body of the text is preceded by 'a discourse upon the ancient and modern societies of the learned', and is followed by 'a short dissertation on the twofold philosophy'. From the outset it is clear that Toland is no longer the propagandist he used to be. With his first major work, *Christianity not Mysterious* (1696), he had openly sought to reform Christianity, to purge it of the mysteries which he considered to have crept in from paganism. The work certainly excited a number of responses, but almost without exception, they were negative. The book was condemned by both English and Irish parliaments and Toland was declared *persona non grata* in his own birthplace – Ireland.[138] Toland, the would-be reformer, enjoyed little public success. Nor did it seem likely that the open espousal of natural religion would meet with any response other than harsh censure. Toland had already complained in this work 'that a Man dares not openly and directly own what he thinks in Divine Matters, tho it be never so true and beneficial'.[139] Despite these complaints, the situation was not to improve. In 1697, the year following the publication of *Christianity not Mysterious*, new blasphemy laws were enacted. Writers had to be more circumspect than before, and not a few of the deists courted arrest and imprisonment for their writings. 'If ever a man deserved to be denied the common benefits of air and water', observed the usually mild-mannered Steele in *The Guardian*, 'it is the author of "A Discourse of Free-Thinking"'.[140] The author in question – Anthony Collins – took the point and prudently sailed for the Netherlands, relieving the courts of the responsibility of having to decide whether Mr Steele's view was correct. The addle-brained Woolston had less foresight, and died while in prison, having been incarcerated on blasphemy charges arising from his *Discourses on the Miracles of our Saviour*.[141] As late as the latter half of the eighteenth century, the schoolmaster Peter Annet was pilloried for his *Free Enquirer*.[142] It was realised very quickly that deist reforms, if they were to come, would need to flourish first in secret. There could not be at this time a *deism populi*. The early accusations levelled at Toland, that he 'openly affected to be the head of a sect',[143] may originally have had an element of truth – certainly his acquaintances were known as 'Tolandists' – but there was nothing public or popular in the sect which is spoken of in *Pantheisticon*. The strategy had changed, and a twofold philosophy had replaced outspoken criticism of revealed religion.

The pantheist, Toland warns, 'shall not make the Wicked, nor the Ignorant, nor any, except the Brethren alone, or other ingenious, upright and learned Men, Partakers of *Esoterics*'[144] 'Thus it necessarily must happen', he declares in another place, '*That one Thing should be in the Heart, and in a private Meeting; and another Thing Abroad, and in public Assemblies*'. 'This maxim', he continues, 'has often greatly been in Vogue, and practised not by the Antients alone; for to declare the Truth, it is more in Use among the Moderns, although they profess it is less allowed'.[145] This latter claim – that the practice of twofold philosophy was prevalent amongst Toland's contemporaries – raises a number of perplexing questions about the role of clandestine organisations. Was Toland's *Pantheisticon* merely a mockery of High Church or Masonic practices? Did groups of 'pantheists' as described by Toland exist in the seventeenth and eighteenth centuries? Or was this work a manifesto for future groups?[146] Toland himself seems to have anticipated these questions, for he insists that there were 'undoubtedly, in several places' pantheistic cabals, which met in 'private assemblies and Societies'. They are to be met with, he tells us, in Paris, Venice, in all the cities of Holland and at the court of Rome; but they abound in London, which is 'the Citadel of their Sect'.[147]

There is a considerable amount of indirect evidence which supports Toland's contention. There existed in Europe a long tradition of religious scepticism, including many who subscribed to doctrines similar to those of the 'pantheists'. The Huguenot La Noue, in the late sixteenth century, maintained that the French religious wars had created a million 'Epicureans and Libertines'.[148] Père Mersenne was to estimate in 1623 that there were over fifty-thousand 'atheists' in Paris.[149] Voltaire, in the following century, reckoned on one-million deists in the whole of Europe.[150] Even if these figures are gross exaggerations, it is quite probable that there were groups who met in private to discuss their heterodox religious views.[151] Given the fear of persecution and the consequent necessity for secrecy in continental Europe, we should not expect that there would be much in the way of written evidence for the existence of such groups, or at least any more evidence than the kind which Toland provides.

In England as well, there was general agreement amongst more pious authors that the present age was one of conspicuous infidelity. Gassendi's disciple Walter Charleton declared in 1659 that England had lately produced more swarms of 'Atheisticall Monsters' than any other age or nation.[152] 'Such is the degeneracy of the Age we live in', lamented Anthony Horneck, D.D., 'that the very Fundamentals of Religion are shuck at'.[153] Jean Gailhard likewise railed against the 'blasphemous *Socinianism* attended by Atheism, Deism, Prophaneness, Immorality, yea and Idolatry' which 'doth bare and brazen-faced walk in our Streets.'[154] Given the prevalence of such views, and the current fad of Clubs of one kind or another, it is highly likely that there were 'Socratic Societies' of the kind described by Toland.[155] Certainly, it was common knowledge that Toland, Collins, and kindred spirits frequented the Grecian Coffee House where they would discuss Bruno's *Spaccio de la Bestia Trionfante* (London, 1584). (Toland is said to have owned a manuscript copy of this infamous work, and certainly *Pantheisticon* shows evidence of Bruno's influence.)[156]

More direct evidence of Toland's involvement with underground free-thinking sodalities has recently been brought to light by the researches of Margaret Jacob.[157] Jacob argues for a strong link between Toland's covert activities and the establishment of the earliest masonic lodges. In the 1690s, a proto-masonic lodge was formed in London under the leadership of Sir Robert Clayton – a London merchant with republican leanings. Although little is known of this lodge it probably included prominent members of a Whig faction of that period known as 'the college'. John Locke, along with his friends Edward Clarke and John Freke, were involved in the latter group which was subsequently joined by Tindal and Toland. Toland also seems to have played a role in a similar group which was constituted in The Hague. The 'Chapitre General des Chevaliers de la Jubilation', as it is referred to in Toland's manuscripts, drew its membership from French Protestants and expatriate Whigs. Jacob suggests that the liturgy of *Pantheisticon* was trialled at one of the meetings of these Knights of Jubilation.[158] But this remains only a possibility, and Toland's role in the organisation is far from clear.[159] The knights, at any rate, seem to have played a major role in the dissemination of heterodox literature, and, with the help of avaricious Dutch publishers and sympathetic postal officials, managed to escape the attention of the Continental censors.

The upshot of all this is that the twofold philosophy was not simply a description of a past religious situation, but was, as Toland had said, 'more in use among the moderns' than it had ever been in antiquity. There is a curious irony in the fact that the man who originally would banish all mystery from Christianity ended his career advocating the practice of mysteries. Like Bruno, one hundred years before, Toland had sought to establish an all-embracing religion, a literal pan-theism, which fused together elements of a new science with a religious naturalism. But his emulation of the martyred Bruno could only proceed so far. Toland was prepared to postpone his vision of a universal religion of reason until such time as the pantheists attained 'full Liberty to think as they please and speak as they think'.[160] The twofold philosophy was therefore held to be a wide-spread practice, while at the same time serving as a stop-gap measure, effective only until freedom of expression had been won. The eschaton, in Toland's theology of rationalism, would be that day in which speech and thought would be shackled only by the limits of reason.

Toland, we have seen, envisaged a bipartite division of all religion. So far, we have only considered the formal or social basis of this division. Yet Toland wished to say more than this, and make the further claim that there was some substantive continuity and consensus in the esoteric philosophy. Admittedly, he placed no great store upon the necessity of subscribing to a body of dogma, however minimal. Rather more emphasis was placed on the use of reason, liberty of thought, and virtue. The Socratic Society is concerned, says Toland, with 'not only the cultivating of Modesty, Continence, Justice, and all Kinds of Virtues themselves, but also of exciting others, as well by Words as Example to their practice'. 'You may perceive', he adds, 'that their Religion is simple, clear, easy without Blemish, and freely bestowed, not painted over, not intricate, embarrassed, incomprehensible, or mercenary.'[161] But what was the credal content of this simple religion? Toland could not be expected to set out common notions à la Lord Herbert. The very technique of the twofold philosophy forbade such forthrightness. What we do find in *Pantheisticon* is the rather confused cosmology to which the pantheists subscribed.

The view of the universe professed by members of the Socratic Society has strong affinities with the pantheism of Bruno.[162] But it is not this 'pantheism' which constitutes the religious kernel of esoteric philosophy.[163] The closest we get to an affirmation of religious belief comes in the statement that 'Reason is the true and first Law, The Light and Splendor of Life'.[164] From this it follows that 'the same Law, eternal and immortal, has and shall contain all Times and Nations'. Correspondingly, there is one 'common Master and Ruler of All, that GOD, the inventor, Umpire and Giver of this Law'. The pantheists' religion consisted in being governed by this law, and not by the 'lying and superstitious fictions of men' which are 'neither clear nor universal'.[165] Toland did not articulate any more specific content to his religion than this. It seems more a methodological commitment than a set of beliefs – literally a religion of Reason. Yet we should also bear in mind that Toland still felt that he could not speak directly on such matters. His silence on this point reflects one of the major difficulties faced by the champions of natural religion – a difficulty which even Herbert had to face – namely, that the reasonable men of every age could not be shown conclusively to have shared a common set of beliefs. The twofold philosophy compounded the problem, for the philosophers succeeded not only in keeping their private beliefs hidden from the vulgar, but also from posterity. The twofold philosophy, as a general theory of religion, thus tended to degenerate into a truism, asserting only that rational men in all ages were rational men who resisted superstition.

The difficulty of assigning any specific content to the esoteric philosophy is particularly apparent in Anthony Collins' *Discourse of Free-Thinking*. Collins' great catalogue of 'free-thinkers' is supposed to be a list of all those who throughout history had resisted superstition and putative revelations, cleaving instead to natural religion. The list includes Socrates, Plato, Epicurus, Varro, Cato, Cicero, Seneca, Solomon, the Old Testament prophets, Josephus, Origen, Minutius Felix, Synesius, Francis Bacon, Thomas Hobbes, Archbishop Tillotson and many others.[166] Yet in a way, the very extent of the list is Collins' undoing, for the most superficial comparison of the thinkers involved will make it evident that there is little consensus amongst them on matters of religion. On the face of it, Archbishop Tillotson and Epicurus, for example, would find few areas of agreement, and certainly fewer than Tillotson and, say, Swift or Atterbury. This would be of little import if the deists had wished to argue only that the enlightened of all ages had supported freedom of thought and attacked superstition where they encountered it. However they seemed to imply as well that these 'free-thinkers' were united not only in what they denied, but also in what they affirmed – natural religion. As Bentley pointed out, there was little to support this view, and much against it. Only by making assumptions based on what ancient philosophers had not said could such a hypothesis be entertained.

In arguing for the existence of an enduring esoteric philosophy, the deists had deployed the twofold philosophy in quite a new way. The classical writers and the fathers had restricted themselves to the observation that there existed a discontinuity between the beliefs of the vulgar and those of the wise. Even when this difference was acknowledged to be between superstition and religion, it was not maintained that the content of the latter had always been the same. To say with Origen that in Christianity, as in pagan religion, there were two or more discrete levels of understanding, was not to say that esoteric Christianity was the same as exoteric paganism. At best, the traditional twofold philosophy could excuse a favoured philosopher's quiescent acceptance of the follies of pagan superstition.[167] Thus the fathers – with the exception of proponents of the ancient theology – did not rely on the twofold philosophy as a description of the structure of pagan religion, but used it as an apologetic or polemical tool to point out the excesses of popular superstition and the abnegation of responsibility on the part of those philosophers who allowed the masses to continue in their idolatrous ways.[168] Some, particularly in the East, had gone further, exploiting the principle in a more fundamental way for their theological and hermeneutical speculations. Origen's system of Biblical interpretation, for example, is firmly grounded in the twofold philosophy.[169] Moreover, Origen responded to Celsus' charge that Christianity is only for the ignorant and stupid by invoking the twofold philosophy. Celsus, he claimed, had not penetrated to the esoteric aspects of Christianity, and thus his criticism applied only to misinterpretations of the superficial doctrines of the religion.[170] The twofold philosophy, then, tended naturally to lead to talk of a hidden essence of religion. Schleiermacher was to utilise the same procedure as Origen when attempting to recommend religion to its cultured despisers. Religion was criticised, he maintained, because its critics had been satisfied to 'juggle with its trappings', and were not able to discern the inner core.[171] The deists, for their part, followed the lead of Origen, seeing in the twofold philosophy more than just a simple description of the structure of pagan religions. Like Origen, they self-consciously set out to exploit this principle in their theorising about the nature of religion. What Origen had shown was that both major 'world religions' – for him, Christianity and paganism – had a bipartite structure. The deists merely extended this to all religion, suggesting as a universal feature of religion a positive or superstitious cortex which shrouded a central core of natural religion. The original contribution of the deists lay in their insistence that beyond this formal similarity of religions, there was a substantial agreement in esoteric content.

Bentley, as we have seen, subjected this view to searching criticism, and his objections are for the most part well founded. The difficulty of the deists' position was that they wished to establish, by an appeal to history, a content of belief which their thesis committed them to believing had been secret and therefore historically invisible. Putting the matter simply, their historical thesis was self-defeating, for if the ancients had acted as the theory suggested, and remained silent about what they really believed, it could never be shown that they had subscribed to the tenets of natural religion. As Toland put it, all wise men are of the one religion, but if asked of what their religion consists, wise men never tell.[172] For better or worse, the deists' main contention about religion could never be historically verified. Like most subsequent attempts to find some universal characteristic of all the empirical religions, the deists' efforts proved to be both unscientific and unhistorical.

DEIST HISTORIOGRAPHY

To understand why the deists were so confident that they shared the beliefs of the ancient philosophers in the face of a dearth of historical evidence on that very point, we must look to eighteenth-century historiography. While it was true that at this time appeals to history had obvious advantages over appeals to authorities or to supposed revelations, yet the historical vision of this age was unfortunately myopic. One of the chief shortcomings of the historical enterprises of the period was the widespread belief that human nature was at all times and in all places the same – in the time-worn words of Hume: 'Mankind are so much the same, in all times and places, that history informs us of nothing new or strange in this particular.'[173] In religious terms, this axiom amounts to what Toland had observed some forty-four years earlier. 'In all times', he said, 'superstition is the same, however the names may vary.'[174] It was this kind of thinking which enabled the deists to see in the philosophers of antiquity mirror images of themselves. Religion in its twofold form had appeared in many guises throughout history, but always this form had remained. If human nature remained constant, so too had superstition and its esoteric counterpart – natural religion. It was this static understanding of history which gave to the deists their faith in the relevance of thousand-year-old theories of religion, and which led them unblushingly to apply them in their own era. The deists did not really succeed in freeing themselves from the tyranny of human authorities, but to a large extent substituted one set for another. Their reliance upon classical writings, particularly works of those whom they regarded as kindred spirits, was virtually slavish. This is nowhere more obvious than in their plagiarism of ancient theories of religion. The originality of the deists lay not in the formulation of new theories of religion, but in the fact that they rejected theological interpretations of other religions and replaced them with those theories of religion which can be found in the pages of Xenophanes, Plato, Sextus, Cicero, and Plutarch.

In view of this, we must be wary of confusing originality with subservience to different authorities. In this regard the deists were not unlike the Cambridge Platonists, who seem quite innovative in their context, yet were actually deriving their thought from an ancient tradition. The Cambridge school, we should recall, also subscribed to the novel and impious Copernican view of the solar system, but again, more as a result of their reverence for a Hermetic tradition in which solar symbolism played a dominant role, than of their scientific rigour. So pervasive was this confidence in ancient authorities that it extended even into the sphere of the physical sciences. Isaac Newton is commonly regarded as one of the fathers of modern science, a man whose empiricism triumphed over the stifling reliance upon outmoded Aristotelian science. Yet Newton's 'classical' Scholia[175] show that he was as concerned to find evidence for his theory of gravitation in the writings of the ancients as in the empirical world. Just as the deists maintained that they were contemporary proponents of an esoteric philosophy to which more elevated ancients had subscribed, so Newton argued that atomic theory, the Copernican view of the universe, and the law of gravitation were all known to certain of the ancients, but that they kept this knowledge from the vulgar.[176] He thus subscribed to a twofold philosophy as well, applying it in the field of natural science:

> But the Philosophers loved so to mitigate their mystical discourses that in the presence of the vulgar they foolishly propounded vulgar matters for the sake of ridicule, and hid the truth beneath discourses of this kind.[177]

This combination of the twofold philosophy with a static view of history exemplifies the widespread seventeenth-century assumption that all investigations – religious or scientific – could at best rediscover hidden truths from an ancient past.

This curious state of affairs serves to highlight the tension which existed in the late seventeenth and early eighteenth centuries between the idea of progress and more static views of history. In the 1690s this tension surfaced with the publication of Sir William Temple's *Essay upon the Ancient and Modern Learning* (1690), in which he propounded a cyclical view of history and argued the superiority of the ancients in most areas of learning. Four years later, William Wotton responded with *Reflections on Ancient and Modern Learning*, in which he granted the ancients an advantage in literature, but denied their superiority in natural philosophy.[178] The deists were unhappily caught in this conflict, for while they remained loyal to those 'free-thinkers' of antiquity and were resigned to the inevitability of superstition (through their belief in the immutability of the human condition), they agitated for change and cherished in their more optimistic moments a vision of a future universal religion of reason. Why is it, the idealistic Toland lamented, that we have advances in the sciences, but none in divinity?[179] While concern for their personal liberty may have come to dampen the deists' zeal for proselytising, there remained in deist writings of a more positive kind an awkward tension between a description of a religious situation which would never change and a prescription for improvement.[180] This tension runs through *Pantheisticon* and adds to its obscurity. Although this difficulty is alleviated somewhat by the fact that 'progress' for the deists was more a matter of recovery of original innocence than of building on tradition, there remains, nonetheless, this ambivalent element in the theories of religion of the deists. Like the Cambridge Platonists and Isaac Newton, the deists had not escaped the pervasive influence of the Italian Renaissance. The prevailing ethos of this movement was not originality, but 'rebirth' or 'rediscovery'. The Renaissance meant the circumvention of more immediate tradition in order to rediscover a more original, ancient and pristine one. The deists inherited something of this ethos and we see this both in their attempts to re-establish what they considered to be the religion of the earliest times, and in their adoption of classical theories of the origin of paganism.

The deists' reverence for these Greek and Roman thinkers accounts in part for their preoccupation with imposture and priestcraft. Of all the theories which are encountered in the ancient sources – the fear theory, euhemerism, projection, the utility theory of Prodicus – imposture was the only one which could easily be adapted to the contemporary situation, for it accounted for the maintenance of religious traditions, while others were more relevant to the question of origins.[181] The deists were concerned to illuminate not so much the origins of religion, but the means by which corruptions were introduced and maintained. This was in part because the Gospel records seemed to provide an accurate record of the beginnings of Christianity, and if the deists were to avoid direct historical criticism of the Bible, they had to show that Christianity had somehow deviated from its original path.[182] In their general discussions of religion, this was only hinted at, but individuals like Toland, Tindal, and Morgan, were to develop specific historical theories about Christianity.

The twofold philosophy, however, had much more to commend it. First, it did not require the deists to relinquish the thesis of priestcraft, but could be combined with it, so that the priests were seen to practise a kind of benign imposture. More importantly, however, it enjoyed an acceptance in the intellectual community which the priestcraft theory could never have achieved. Isaac Newton, as we have seen, was one who believed in the twofold philosophy. The Platonist Cudworth was another.[183] Yet 'pantheists', deists, and latitude men were not the only ones to accept the twofold philosophy as an historical theory. No less a defender of orthodoxy than Bishop Warburton, in his ponderous counter-attack on deism, finished up agreeing with this fundamental platform of deist theory.[184] Even more committed to the theory was Thomas Burnet, author of *The Sacred Theory of the Earth*, and disciple of the Cambridge Platonists. Though more theologically conservative than the free-thinkers, he insisted that there were doctrinal speculations which should be concealed from the masses of his day. Thus, he went beyond an espousal of the twofold philosophy as an historical fact, and consciously adopted it as a practice. In his determinations about the eternity of hell, he echoes the warning of the fathers: 'That whatever you decide, in your own Breast of these Eternal Punishments, the people, too easily prone to Vice and easily terrified from Evil must have the commonly received Doctrine.'[185] Burnet clearly was committed to the view that the masses required traditional, if erroneous religious beliefs to keep them from straying from the path of virtue.

In advocating secrecy, the deists and like-minded individuals were thus not only protecting themselves from prosecution, but were, in their own eyes, ensuring social stability by maintaining those religious sanctions which traditional religion provided. 'A *Devil* and a *Hell* may prevail, where a *Jail* and a *Gallows* are thought insufficient', said Shaftesbury.[186] There was an unspoken understanding amongst the upper classes that the orthodox faith (in particular those aspects which concerned hell and eternal punishment, or which enjoined submission to temporal authority) was a most important mechanism for the social control of the lower classes. As a result, much of the mischief of the proselytising deists was perceived to lie not in their personal beliefs, but in their publication of them to all and sundry. Addison attacked the deists on account of their naive and open admissions of infidelity. Deism, he maintained, had served to 'unsettle the Minds of the Ignorant, disturb the publick Peace, and throw all things into Confusion and Disorder'. Even the atheists of antiquity, said Addison, 'though the being of a God was entirely repugnant to their Schemes', kept silence 'because they would not shock the common Belief of Mankind, and the Religion of their Country'.[187] The present-day deists, he implied, should do as much.[188] Establishment reaction against the deists was therefore fuelled by more than righteous indignation. There was a genuine fear that existing social structures would be at risk if deistic notions gained wide currency. Already we have noted the Whig tendencies of the major deists. In the eyes of many an English gentleman it was almost as if the deists were representatives of the masses who had discovered the secret beliefs of the ruling class and were now going to let the cat out of the bag.

It is evident that the twofold philosophy presented a far more accurate picture of the state of religion in England at this time than did the imposture theory. Unlike that theory, it could find support not only in the pages of history, but also in contemporary intellectual life. It further confirmed that notion of the static condition of human nature, as well as reflecting the class structure of seventeenth- and eighteenth-century Britain.[189] The twofold philosophy, then, was more than a theory of religion. It was an axiom which related social structure to the content of belief, and which could be applied not only in the sphere of religion, but in the area of natural philosophy as well. If there was a *prisca theologia*, then there was a *prisca scientia* as well. The further ramifications of this view for a theory of history are patent. The human condition does not improve, thus any change must be for the worse. Knowledge gradually becomes corrupted. Progress in learning can only occur through the rediscovery of primal truths. This does not necessarily mean that all research is historical, but it does mean that modern discoveries should correlate with ancient and arcane truths.

Such a view had obvious implications for religions which claimed to be based on revelation. Implicit in the concept of historical revelation is a linear view of history, in which received knowledge is added to and made more complete. The deists, of course, wished to argue to the contrary that revelation, or at least some revelations, were communications (generally adapted to the capacities of the vulgar), in which God sought merely to re-establish the original religion of nature. Only in this way could such figures as Moses, and more importantly, Jesus, be acquitted from the charge of imposture.

To sum up, in the deistic approach to religion we witness a shift of attention from religious beliefs to religious forms. Herbert's quest for a substantive essence of religion encapsulated in five propositions broke down simply for want of evidence. The deists, instead of resolving all religious beliefs into common notions, concentrated instead on what they considered to be the empirical aspects of religion – its common structures and forms. To this extent they relied less on *a priori* assumptions about religion. Their proposed bipartite structure of religion, originally conceived as the priesthood–laity distinction and subsequently refined into the twofold philosophy, better fitted the available facts. Yet in a sense this view was merely a secular version of the supernatural and empirically transparent distinction between the reprobate and the elect, and to a large extent it shared the problems of that theological doctrine. For just as the distinction between those predestined to hell and those predestined to heaven was thought by Calvinists to be based only on God's arbitrary will, so the upper echelons of the social hierarchy were distinguished from the multitude not by any readily identifiable common beliefs, but by accidents of birth. The argument that vulgar superstitions were substantially the same throughout time and across cultures was no more convincing than the view that free-thinkers of all ages had cherished identical religious beliefs, albeit in secret. In short, while the deists might have correctly identified universal religious types, at the same time they glossed over the diversity of actual religious beliefs and were blind to any suggestions of religious development. This lack of a proper sense of history in the deist accounts of religion was owing in large measure to their rejection of revelation. Belief in historical revelation carries with it some notion of progress: the recipients of the divine Word must in some sense be better informed about religious truths than they were previously. Yet it was precisely this kind of religious progress that the deists denied as ever having taken place. Sacred history originally provided a genuinely historical perspective for the study of religion – a vital element which, with one or two exceptions, was missing from the deists' attempts to place the study of religion on a systematic basis. It was the absence of this historical perspective which severely limited the deists' views of religion.

In the preceding two chapters we have seen something of how 'religion' was constructed in theological discourse, in phenomenological discussions of the religious *a priori*, and now in an early 'sociological' grammar of religious types and social divisions. The historical study of religion, or more correctly the retrospective insertion of the object 'religion' into the stream of history, began with sacred history – the Judeo–Christian record of divine revelation. This narrative account of Jewish religious development provided the chronological basis which was crucial to an understanding of religious development in general. And if events of universal history tended to be somewhat constrained by the tribal records of the ancient Jews, the biblical record nonetheless provided the historical element which was lacking in deist accounts of religion, and served as the starting point for what is arguably the most fruitful approach to the study of religious phenomena – the history of religions.

FOUR

SACRED HISTORY AND RELIGIOUS DIVERSITY

For Scripture, which proves the truth of its historical statements by the accomplishment of its prophecies, gives no false information.

Augustine, *City of God*, XVI.9

In the early seventeenth century it was regarded as self-evident that the Bible provided the key to a proper understanding of history. So much was this taken for granted that it was rarely stated explicitly. While there was some reluctance to find in the pages of holy writ specific reference to contemporary historical events, there was through most of the seventeenth century an unspoken agreement that in the sphere of ancient history, Scripture was the pre-eminent source. At the close of the sixteenth century, Henry Smith could confidently declare that the antiquity and accuracy of Hebrew history was acknowledged even by the heathen, and therefore did not stand in need of proof.[1] By the end of the next century, however, some apologists found it necessary to take that very step which Smith had considered superfluous. The beginnings of biblical criticism, the development of comparative chronology, and the revival of polygenetic theories of human origins had together challenged the privileged status of the Scriptures, which now required some defence. Thomas Hearne argued parochially that Christians ought to give deference to their own holy writings. 'Nothing', he said, 'ought to weigh more with Christians than the authority of Holy Scripture.' Moses, he insisted, was 'without dispute' a writer more ancient than the other contenders – Homer, Thales and Pythagoras – who had gained 'so great a reputation in the world'.[2] Timothy Nourse likewise found it necessary to specify why Scripture was to be preferred above all others as an historical source. The Mosaic account of history, he said, had advantages over all other writings on account of its antiquity, its plain style, the unbiased manner of its writing, and the fact that it served as a source for other ancient chronologies.[3] David Collyer flatly denied that any other source could compete with Scripture on its own ground, asserting that the first six chapters of Genesis contain 'all we know of the History of the World, for above sixteen hundred years'.[4] Many other divines added their voices in support of the veracity and antiquity of the Mosaic history, and for the most part, historians concurred.[5]

In one sphere of history in particular – the history of religion – the Bible was most highly regarded.[6] It would be a mistake, however, to think that the Bible served merely as some pre-eminent source of narrative history. To be sure it was that, but even more, it was thought to contain timeless and recurring patterns of human religious development. These patterns were accompanied by theological explanations which, severed from their anchorage in the mists of antiquity, could serve as ready-made explanations of contemporary religious phenomena. In the Mosaic history of the beginnings of the world were three stories in particular which informed sacred histories of religion and the religions: the Fall, the Deluge and Babel.

HUMAN FRAILTY AND THE WORK OF THE DEVIL

To historians of the seventeenth century it was self-evident that, had it not been for the Fall, all peoples would be worshipping the same God in the same way. Implicit in the story of Adam's lapse was the view that the activities of the devil and the infirmity of human nature were together the irreducible causes of false religion. Of all human failings to arise from the devil's seduction of Adam and Eve, neglect of the worship of the true God was the greatest. 'The First and most Fundamental mistake of *Lapsed Mankind*', declared Henry More, 'is that they make *Body* or *Matter* the only true *Jehovah* ... and acknowledge no God but this Visible or sensible world.'[7] This 'Stratonician presumption', so antipathetic to the Platonism of More, occasioned the first instance of idolatry – the most pervasive consequence of the Fall.[8] Few writers of this era would have disagreed with More. Robert South declared:

> What prodigious, monstrous, mishapen births has the Reason of faln man produced! It is now almost six thousand years, that far the greatest part of the World has had no other Religion but Idolatry. And Idolatry certainly is the first-born of Folly, the great and leading paradox; nay the very abridgement and sum total of all absurdities.[9]

Sir Thomas Browne, in his exhaustive work on the aetiology of human error, endorsed South's sentiments, identifying as the 'First and Father-cause of Common Error' that human infirmity which had been born in Adam's transgression.[10] Nor was the original author of the evil denied a place. 'There is an invisible Agent, and secret promoter without us, whose activity is undiscerned, and lais in the dark upon us', said Browne, 'and that is the first contriver of Error, and professed opposer of Truth, the Devil', who deceives in matters of religion by means of 'pretended revelations or predictions'.[11] More found a similar role for the devil. In his scheme of things, God himself established the Jewish religion, while angels or 'the *better sort of Lapsed Spirits*, or *crafty Political men*, or *impure and malicious Devils*' instituted paganism.[12] The patristic theory of the daemonic origin of false religions was also favoured by Robert Burton. The devil, according to Burton, was the '*primum mobile*' of all superstition who, 'in a thousand several shapes, after divers fashions, with several engines, illusions, and by several names hath deceived the inhabitants of the earth, and in several places and Countries, [is] still rejoycing at their falls'.[13]

As theories which accounted for the various forms of corrupt religion which existed then and had existed in the past, the Fall and demonology were true but trivial. Like faith in the authority of Scripture, they were more assumptions than conclusions – the starting point of a theory of religion rather than the finishing point. More sophisticated theorising involved the location in Scripture of reasons for human diversity in general, which could then be applied to the more specific issue of religious pluralism. A number of closely related factors could be found in the biblical history of earliest times which explained human diversity – degeneration, admixture, and travel.[14]

THE FALL AND THE DEGENERATION OF THE WORLD

While the Fall and the invisible activities of the devil could be regarded as events of great significance in history, they were more theological axioms than historical explanations. Once the Fall was posited as the original cause of religious corruption, or less pejoratively, religious diversity, there remained the issue of how, in the course of history, this corruption came about. As in the realm of science, where attention had become focussed upon secondary causes, so too, in the sphere of history, theological explanations were regarded as incomplete. Bishop Warburton exemplified this shift in the approach to religious history with his observation that while the fathers may have been correct in asserting 'that the Devil had a great Share in the Introduction and Support of Pagan Revelations', his own approach was 'to enquire into the *natural* Causes of Paganism'.[15]

Such investigations were begun some time before Warburton's rambling *Divine Legation of Moses* appeared on the scene. In keeping with the enquiring spirit of his age, Burton, for instance, was driven to identify specific 'instruments' and 'engines' of the devil. The instruments of Satan, he concluded, were politicians, priests, heretics and blind guides, and his engines, fasting, solitariness, hope and fear.[16] Walter Raleigh had likewise identified three ways in which the devil could seduce men from the truth; first, 'by moving the cogitation and affections of men'; second, by his 'exquisite knowledge of Nature'; and third, by 'deceit, illusion, and false semblance'.[17]

The first step in the development of such natural explanations came with recognition that the Fall had had natural consequences which in turn determined the course of human history. Adam's lapse entailed not only such theological truths as the necessity for redemption, but gave important clues about the state of the world – specifically that change and diversity were ever to be man's lot. From biblical history, then, could be extrapolated a theory or theories of diversity which in turn could be brought to bear on the issue of religious diversity. In this manner, the question of the existence of the different religions could be subsumed under the broad question of human diversity.

The Bible served as the source of a number of theories of diversity which varied in their ability to exist independently as naturalistic explanations. Of the more theological kind we have the simple equation of sin and diversity, or the more obscure flights of Platonic interpretation. In the third century, for example, Origen had suggested that the 'great diversity in the world' resulted from 'the variety and diversity of the motions and declensions of those who fell away from the original unity and harmony in which they were at first created by God'. These beings, he said, were 'tossed about by the diverse motions and desires of their souls' and were thus changed from 'the one undivided goodness of their original nature'.[18] Origen went so far as to say that even diversity in the animal world sprang from the apostasy of angelic beings.[19] While this explanation was revived by Henry More and other Cambridge Platonists, it was one of the less popular accounts of diversity.[20]

More important for our purposes was the development of a broad theory of degeneration, revived during the Renaissance, and reaching its zenith in the seventeenth century.[21] This view had its sources in both classical and biblical literature. The predominant Judaeo-Christian sources, apart from the Bible, were the apocryphal Esdras and St Cyprian, while on the classical side its chief representatives were Lucretius and Ovid.[22] The revival of this doctrine can be attributed in part to the negative anthropology of the Reformation. More significant, however, were the advances in astronomy and the discovery of new civilizations. The dethroning of the earth from its place in the centre of the universe and the discovery of new stars in what had once been thought to be the unchangeable and incorruptible regions of the heavens weighed heavily upon seventeenth-century minds.[23]

It is particularly important to note that change – not only in the further reaches of the universe, but in human affairs as well – was always assumed to be change for the worse. It was for this reason that the seemingly indifferent discoveries of super-novae, sunspots, and comets (once thought to be phenomena of the earth's atmosphere) supported the belief in the decay of the universe. So too, travel literature spread the message of a humanity which was more religiously diverse than had hitherto been thought possible. As the Earth had been removed from the centre of the universe, now Christian Europe came to be seen as numerically and geographically insignificant when compared with Asia and the Americas. For the first time, geographers were to compute the percentage of the human race who embraced Christianity in some shape or form, finding that at best one sixth of the human race was Christian, while the vast bulk of the remainder had sunken into barbarism and idolatry.[24] It was patent that in most corners of the earth the pure worship of God, originally communicated to Adam and re-established by Noah, had degenerated to such an extent as to be almost unrecognisable as religion. This mood of pessimism which had prevailed since the Renaissance was only challenged by the hesitant optimism of the dawning Enlightenment in the late seventeenth century. For most of that century, however, it was axiomatic that any change was necessarily for the worse, any novelty in thought, decadent. *Mutatio in deterius* was the guiding principle of world history.[25]

Expressions of this belief in universal decay abound in early seventeenth-century literature. 'The world is runne quite out of square', lamented Spenser, and 'being once amisse grows daily worse and worse'.[26] Humanity and the physical world were seen to be gradually winding down in tandem, microcosm bound up with macrocosm. 'But man which is the lesser world declineth,' pronounced John Dove, 'and it followeth therefore as a good consequent, that the greater worlde also doth decline, and where there is declination there is also corruption and death'.[27]

There was, of course, biblical warrant for the suggestion that the moral fall was a direct cause of the decay of the physical world. A consequence of the human fall was the fall of nature. 'The ground is cursed because of you', the Lord tells Adam.[28] Cosmologists of the seventeenth and eighteenth centuries reinforced this theological point with fanciful geological speculations of their own. In *The Sacred Theory of the Earth* (1684), Thomas Burnet, one of the last and most articulate champions of the degeneration theory, reminded his readers of this causal link between human failings and the state of the physical world. The present 'deformity and incommodiousness' of the world, he said, was not original, for 'the first order of things is regular and simple, according as the Divine Nature is; and continues so till there is some degeneracy in the moral World'.[29] The eccentric William

Whiston, who disagreed with Burnet's geological speculations on almost
every point, agreed that 'by our own wilful Rebellion', we had made it
necessary for God to place us in 'a short, a vicious, in an uneasie and
vexatious world'.[30] Thomas Pope Blount epitomised the view of his age
when he confidently declared in the last decade of the seventeenth century
that the daily degeneration of the world 'is an Opinion so *Universally* Believ'd,
that whoever goes about to defend the Contrary, presently shall be thought
to maintain a Paradox'.[31]

In sum, it was taken for granted for much of the seventeenth century
that the original, created order bespoke a uniformity and perfection in both
physical and human spheres. The Fall had irrevocably altered this, setting
in motion a process of change, the bitter fruits of which were blemishes
in the physical world and moral decay within human society. Equally important for us, the Fall meant that man's condition had become, in Donne's
words, 'variable, and therefore miserable'. 'From this mutabilitie and inconstancy of man's will', said Meric Casaubon, 'we may deduce *Variety* of
fashions and *customes*'.[32] Inconstancy and variability thus contained the seeds
of diversity, which at that time could only be viewed in the worst possible
light. Religious diversity, in this scheme of things, was but one unfortunate
result of a process of universal degeneration which was manifested not only
in every sphere of human endeavour, but was evident even in the physical
constitution of the universe.

The theory of degeneration, as we might expect, fared less well in the
century which followed. George Hakewill had already suggested that melancholy views about the course of history were little more than 'vulgar errors'
based upon outmoded authorities.[33] In addition, the 'battle of the books'
controversy at the close of the seventeenth century made it evident that
there were some who believed that in the sciences at least, considerable
advances upon the knowledge of the ancients had been made.[34] It followed
from the conspicuous successes of the new 'scientific method' that the gradual process of corruption was not as pervasive as once thought. Indeed
it is a commonplace that the general mood of the age of Enlightenment
(among the intelligentsia at least) was one not of nostalgic pessimism but
of visionary optimism. In any case, the theory of degeneration, while it
enjoyed the patronage of biblical and classical writers, as an explanation
of diversity lacked two vital elements. Its status as a secondary, or 'natural'
explanation remained highly questionable, and it did not specifically identify
any human agents who might bring historical credence to a theory of gradual
religious corruption. Consequently, two other hypotheses came into play,
both related to the biblical tradition, but which could be employed quite
independently of any commitment to the veracity of the scriptural account
of history. These were the mechanisms of admixture and travel.

ADMIXTURE AND TRAVEL

As we have seen, the tendency to move away from supernatural explanations of religious pluralism led such figures as Burton and Raleigh to speak of the role of human agency in the development of the various religions. To those even more fastidious about matters of historical detail fell the task of identifying the specific individuals in whom the kinds of religious pathology and gullibility identified by Burton and Raleigh had been most conspicuously manifested. Such was the power still exercised by the biblical world view, however, that again it was the pages of scripture which provided the *dramatis personae* from which such figures could be identified.

If Adam was the first sinner, to his son Cain fell the more dubious honour of being the first murderer and apostate from true religion. Cain, the Genesis account tells us, slew his brother and was sentenced to remain for the rest of his life an outcast and a wanderer. Josephus further reports that 'the descendants of Cain went to the depths of depravity and, inheriting and imitating one another's vices, each ended worse than the last'.[35] Philo likewise depicts Cain as the originator of heresy and the father of all heretics: 'Those who assert that everything that is involved in thought or perception or speech is a free gift of their own soul, seeing that they introduce an impious and atheistic opinion, must be assigned to the race of Cain.'[36] So firmly established was this tradition that in the seventeenth-century historical imagination it was the vagabond Cain who first established false religion. Henry More made the curious observation that 'the most Fundamental mistake of the Soul lapsed is the birth of Cain', from which also sprang 'the vanity of pagan Idolatry'.[37] Cain, according to Charles Leslie, instituted pagan sacrifices, which were then practised by his posterity.[38] Dionisius Petavius was more expansive:

> And for this cause *Cain* burning with wrath and envy, murthered his innocent brother; and in revenge of this his murther, being a fugitive and vagabond on the Earth, he begat children like unto himself, namely rebels and enemies of God; and he built a City, and called it by the name of his son *Enoch*: but *Seth*, a while after *Abel's* death, being born to *Adam*, began a posterity contrary to that, namely godly and religious; whose son *Enos* is said to have begun to call upon the name of the Lord; because as the opinion is, he did publickly re-establish that worship of God, which had been blotted out by *Cain's* children.[39]

The true worship of God was soon to suffer another blow, for as Petavius explains, Cain's progeny began to intermarry with those of more pure stock:

> [Enoch's] posterity, whom the Scripture calls, The sons of God, being grown worse, and degenerated from their good manners, joyned themselves in marriage with *Cain's* posterity, out of whose mixture and commerce were Gyants

brought forth. Then mortal men, addicting themselves to all sorts of wickedness, did turn and draw God's wrath upon themselves.[40]

God's wrath descended in the form of the Deluge.

Petavius' account identifies some of the principles in the story of the
decline of genuine religion, while highlighting two further agents in the
degeneration process – admixture[41] and travel.

As Petavius tells the story, Cain was a 'fugitive and a vagabond', and
the physical mixing of his progeny with those of pure stock gave rise to
all manner of religious perversions. Raleigh similarly stressed that Cain
was a wanderer and noted that the 'land of Nod', where Cain was supposed
to have settled, signified 'wandering or no set place of habitation'. In fact
Raleigh himself believed that the real significance of Cain's nomadic status
was that he was 'a Vagabond or Wanderer in his cogitations'.[42] This restless-
ness of mind first occasioned idolatry. Admixture too, played its role in
Raleigh's history. He pointed out that 'the children and sons of God (or
of the godly) were corrupted and misled by their idolatrous wives, the
daughters of *Cain*'.[43]

In terms of the lineage of various religions, the story of Cain might seem
irrelevant, for the Deluge brought an abrupt end to the corrupt religion
of Cain's offspring. The reason this story retained significance is that it
provided the pattern for subsequent accounts of human apostasy in post-
diluvian times which again illustrate the corrupting power of wandering
and admixture. For these theories the focus was shifted to the story of Noah.[44]

According to biblical lore, Noah was a righteous man who practised the
true worship of God. Since he and his progeny were the only survivors
of the Flood, it was reasoned that religious degeneration must have found
its way back into history through Noah's line. A long-standing tradition
had it that religious corruption re-emerged in the sons of Noah, and in
particular in the person of Ham, 'who it's likely', said Bishop Simon Patrick,
'carried much of the Spirit of *Cain* with him into the Ark'.[45] Soon Ham's
offspring were to manifest the symptoms of their hereditary affliction. Genesis informs us that Ham's son Canaan was cursed by Noah, and also that
Ham was the ancestor of Nimrod, founder of Babylon, a city noted for
its depravity.[46] Moreover, Ham's descendants were reported to have colonised Egypt, a country identified in both classical and Christian sources
as the birthplace of idolatry.[47]

Augustine, patron saint of sacred history, had elaborated this tradition,
proposing that Ham prefigured the heretics, while Noah's other two sons,
Shem and Japheth, represented the Jews and Greeks respectively.[48] The
medieval historian Gregory of Tours reiterated this view in his work of
the late sixth century, *The History of the Franks*. He wrote that: 'Chus was

the first child of Ham: by the inspiration of the Devil he was the first inventor of idolatry and of the whole art of magic. He was encouraged by the Devil to be the first to set up an image to be worshipped.'[49] The sixteenth-century collector Joannes Boemus similarly noted that Ham, 'by the reason of his naughty demeanour towarde his father' was constrained to move to Arabia:

> Wher of it came to passe, that when in the processe of tyme they ware increased to to many for that londe: being sent out as it ware, swarme aftre swarme into other habitations, and skatered at length into sondry partes of the worlde (for this banyshed progeny grewe aboue measure) some fel into errours wherout thei could neuer vnsnarle themselues. The tongue gan to altre & the knowledge of the true God and all godlie worshippe vanished out of mind. Inso muche that some liued so wildely ... that it ware hard to discerne a difference betwirte them and the beastes of the felde.[50]

Boemus concludes: 'So great a mischief did the untymely banishements of one manne, bring to the whole.'[51]

British sacred historians, as we might expect, became heirs to this tradition. Sir Walter Raleigh linked the Fall, the Augustinian view of the transmission of its effects, and the origins of idolatry:

> Hence it was that ... the same defection hath continuance in the very generation and nature of mankind. Yea even among the few sons of *Noah*, there were found strong effects of the former poyson. For as the children of *Sem* did inherit the virtues of *Seth*, *Enoch*, and *Noah*; so the sonnes of *Cham* did possess the vices of the sons of *Cain*, and of those wicked Giants of the first Age. Whence the Chaldeans began soon after the Floud to ascribe divine power and honour to the Creature, which was onely due to the Creatour. First, they worshipped the Sun, and then the Fire. So the Egyptians and Phoenicians did not onely learn to leave the true God, but created twelve several gods and divine powers, whom thay worshipped, and unto whom they built Altars and Temples ... But as men once fallen away from undoubted truth, do then after wander for evermore in vices unknown and daily travail towards their eternal perdition: so did these gross and blinde Idolaters every Age after other descend lower and lower, and shrink and slide downwards from the knowledge of one true and very God.[52]

This extract presents in summary the salient features of the history of early religion according to seventeenth-century sacred historians. We should note not only the connexion between the original religious corruption of Cain and the subsequent infidelities of Ham and his offspring, but also the nature of the link. By Raleigh's account, the tendency towards idolatry was inherited physically or biologically, and not culturally. For this reason the destruction of the idolaters of the first Age did not solve the problem of idolatry, for this tendency lay dormant in Noah's seed, to be expressed subsequently in one particular blood line. Idolatry had, in modern parlance, a genetic basis, and as a result was characteristic of certain races – those races which descended from Ham.

Others were more inclined to spread the blame, making mention of the culpability of Japheth's children while maintaining agreement in other details. Dryden, for example, rehearsed Raleigh's thesis, but implicated Japheth's heirs in the spreading of irreligion:

> Truly I am apt to think, that the revealed religion which was taught by Noah to all his sons, might continue for some ages in the whole posterity. That afterwards it was included wholly in the family of Shem, is manifest: but when the progenies of Cham and Japhet swarmed into colonies, and those colonies were subdivided into many others, in process of time their descendants lost, by little and little, the primitive and purer rites of divine worship, retaining only the notion of Deity; to which succeeding generations added others.[53]

For the most part, however, to Ham alone was given the dubious honour of being father of all heathens. The Platonist Glanvill even went as far as to say that Ham had fathered, not a race of idolaters, but 'those *Mimick Animals*', the apes.[54] This judgement seems somewhat severe, but it is more than just an amusing eddy in the stream of historical thought about religion, for it again highlights the tendency to see sin and its first offspring – idolatry – as having a biological and inherited basis. Sin results in degeneracy. The ultimate degeneracy results in the loss of humanity.[55] Neither does Glanvill's view seem so far-fetched in the light of discussions about whether the American natives were human or not. We shall consider this later. For the moment there is one other important ramification of the equation of travel with degeneracy.

Once it was granted that travel was one of the chief mechanisms of corruption, it followed that those who were found farthest from the Ark's presumed resting place had the most corrupt religion, and were most probably the descendants of that profligate wanderer Ham. Equally important was the assumption that the most pure religion would be found adjacent to Noah's point of disembarkation. This latter assumption occasioned considerable debate about the Ark's final resting place, and about the status of the religions in the near vicinity. One thing at least was certain – that the Ark had landed somewhere in Eurasia. This meant that the inhabitants of the New World were as remote from the cradle of religion as they could be, and thus were most probably the worst idolaters amongst Ham's undistinguished line. (Little was known of the Antipodes at this time.) This *a priori* line of reasoning meshed neatly with the empirical facts of American religious customs. William Strachey maintained that the natives of the New World, because of their remoteness and their heathenism, must have descended from the biblical heresiarch:

Yt is observed that Cham, and his famely, were the only far Travellors, and Straglers into divers unknowne countries, searching, exploring and sitting downe in the same: as also yt is said of his famely, that what country soever the Children of Cham happened to possesse, there beganne both the Ignorance of true godliness ... and that no inhabited Countryes cast forth greater multy-tudes, to raunge and stray into divers remote regions.[56]

Wherever this line settled, he said, they brought with them 'the Ignorance of the true worship of God' along with 'the Inventions of Hethenisme, and the adoration of falce godes, and the Devill'.[57]

Strachey's speculations serve to illustrate the impact which the discovery of the New World had upon interpretation of the biblical story of human dispersion, and indeed upon biblical interpretation in general. While Jose-phus and the early Church historians had been concerned to assign to the progeny of Noah the paternity of this or that nation, generally their construc-tions were not too fanciful and involved only Shem, Ham and Japheth, or their immediate offspring.[58] With Columbus' discovery of the Americas, however, renewed speculation broke out as to which nations had descended from which of Noah's progeny.[59]

The growth of European nationalism meant that the focus was not only upon the peoples of newly discovered lands, but upon the origins of the nations of Europe as well.[60] Many writers attempted to trace their own ethnic origins, usually back as far as one of Noah's children (though not Ham, for obvious reasons). British historian George Harry thus constructed the ancestry of James I right back to Noah himself.[61] With comparable industry, Robert Sheringham established the likelihood that the pious Japheth (or at least one of his sons) settled the British Isles, while Edmund Campion argued that Ireland was settled by Bastolenus, again, one of Japheth's sons.[62]

When imaginations had run their course in establishing the purity of national blood-lines, attention was paid to other nationalities and other reli-gions. It was not always the case that the relation between Ham and the adherents of other religions was seen to reside only in biology. This was particularly so for the non-heathen, yet non-Christian religions of Judaism and Islam. The application of the stories of Cain and Ham to these religions involved a more complex, yet widely accepted hermeneutic. Pre-critical bibli-cal interpretation involved more than a simple acceptance of the historical veracity of the Bible stories. Of equal importance was the fact that the events presented by the Bible 'prefigured' subsequent happenings in history.[63] As we have already seen, such a typological link could be seen to exist between the stories of Cain and Ham. Certainly one of the chief uses of figurative interpretation was to harmonise various narratives within the Bible itself, in particular between events in the Old Testament and those in the New. For the interpretation of history, what is significant in this is that scriptural narratives could also be seen as prefiguring events of more recent history. Thus, as patterns of apostasy, the stories of Cain and Ham had abiding significance in explanations of other religions. The apostasy and wanderings of Cain prefigured not only the activities of Ham and his descendants, but also gave clues as to the significance of other religions. Raleigh applied the story of Cain to the situation of contemporary Judaism. The modern Jews, he observed, were a wandering people – 'Runnagates' with no 'certain Estate, Common-weale, or Prince of their own upon the Earth'. Clearly, said Raleigh, Cain and Abel were figures of the Jews and Christ respectively. As Cain had murdered Abel, so the Jews had murdered Christ. Both male-factors suffered a similar fate.[64]

Other lessons with a modern application could be learned from scriptural history as well. If it was the case that admixture and travel had in the past resulted in novel and erroneous religious traditions, then it was likely that new religions of more recent times were similarly formed. It was generally believed that admixture was the key ingredient of heresy – the pollution of Christianity had occurred through contamination of pagan philosophy or religion. Theophilus Gale maintained along these lines that 'all *pestiferous*, and *noxious Heresie*, and *Idolatries*' arose through the admixture of 'vain philosophy' with an originally pure tradition.[65] Much of Gale's energy was spent in showing that the religion of Rome was nothing but an ungodly mixture of various elements of pagan religion.

That other great 'heresy' – the religion of Muhammad – was another example of the unfortunate consequences of admixture, for according to the traditional Western view it had been formed through the mixing of two previously existing religious traditions – idolatry and Judaism, or even Nestorian Christianity and Judaism. Boemus, in his *Fardle of Façions* (1555), noted Muhammad's mixed parentage – specifically that his father was an idolater, and his mother a kind of Jew. This, averred Boemus, 'printed in hym such a doubtful belief, y when he came to age he cleaved to neither', but rather propagated a religion patched together 'with peces of all maner of sects'.[66] The tradition according to which Islam was a 'mixt and patched religion'[67] persisted until well into the Enlightenment. According to Humphrey Prideaux's popular account of Muhammad's imposture, Islam was 'made up of three parts, whereof one was borrowed from the *Jews*, another from the *Christians*, and the third from the *Heathen Arabs*'.[68] Robert Burton puts the matter somewhat less judiciously:

> *Mahometans* are a compound of *gentiles*, *Jews*, and *Christians*, and so absurd in their ceremonies, as if they had taken that which is most sottish out of every one of them, full of idle fables in the superstitious law, their *Alcoran* is itself a gallimaufry of lies, tales, ceremonies, traditions, precepts, stole from

other sects, and confusedly heaped up to delude a company of rude and barbarous clowns.[69]

Not all commentators agreed that the religion of Muhammad was the result of admixture. That Enlightenment apologist for Islam, Henri Boulainvilliers, accepted the premise that admixture causes corruption, but denied that it had occurred in the case of Islam. He praised the 'solitude' of the Arabians, maintaining that it isolated them from 'the irregular imaginations of other nations', thereby exempting them from the 'numberless superstitions' which plagued other religions. He concluded that the isolation of the Arabs 'preserved among them the natural notion of the true GOD for a length of ages, and that with little adulteration'.[70] Boulainvilliers, however, could hardly be said to reflect the views of his contemporaries. Interestingly, his fellow countryman Louis Le Roy had sometime previously made just this point about the Arabs. Their success in the world, he said, could only be attributed to the fact that they 'neuer mingled with others' and 'still preserued and kept entier the nobility of their blood'.[71] Le Roy therefore attributed their patent religious perversity not to admixture, but travel. The Arabs since the coming of Muhammad, he said, were 'a vagabond people'.[72] Again, like the wandering Cain, they had walked away from the true worship of God.

Because Islam was the only religion, apart from Judaism and Christianity, the historical origins of which were known in any significant detail, it could serve as a relatively recent example of how false religions might have originated in antiquity, being formed by various combinations of 'elemental' religions which themselves had developed as a result of human wanderings.[73] The religion of Muhammad could thus be forced into the biblical pattern of admixture and corruption, and once this tradition became firmly entrenched in the Western imagination it could in turn support the scriptural view, and indeed the view that all false religions had arisen in a similar way. Thus the biblical traditions about Cain and Ham, and the medieval image of Islam as a corrupt mixture of religious traditions were mutually confirming.

The biblical description of human origins could thus be adapted to explain something of the origin and significance of all three kinds of non-Christian religion – Judaism, Islam and Idolatry or Heathenism. For some, however, considerably more could be done with the bare facts of the Genesis stories. One of the intermediate stages between sacred and secular history involved supplementing the details of the biblical account with 'scientific' explanations. Theories of this type attempted to explain further the link between travel and idolatry. Why, it was asked, did travel bring about loss of knowledge of the true God? At one level, it could be argued that with loss of contact with the original tradition, correct beliefs were simply forgotten.

A different kind of explanation, however, suggested that environment was a major determinant of physical and psychological characteristics in the human race, and that it was not travel as such, but travel into *different environments* which produced religious diversity.

The theory that geographic environment influences physical and psychological traits has a long and varied history.[74] In the Hippocratic work *Airs, Waters, Places* is first articulated the view that regional character is determined by climate. This view rested upon the Hippocratic physiology of the four humours: climate influences the relative proportions of the humours, and certain physical and psychological attributes result.[75] Hippocrates suggests, for instance, that people who live in meadow-like hollows, where hot winds prevail, will tend to be 'broad, fleshy, and dark haired ... less subject to phlegm than to bile'. 'Bravery and endurance', he further notes, 'are not by nature part of their character'. By way of contrast, those who live in more rugged terrains subject to seasonal fluctuations will have large physiques and be strong and courageous.[76] Environmental theories of this nature also had Medieval and Renaissance proponents in such figures as Albertus Magnus and Jean Bodin.[77] Bodin, for example, divided the world into three climatic zones – hot, cold and temperate – the same regions referred to by Aristotle in the *Politics*. The climate of each zone tended to produce certain characteristics. The people of the south, Bodin observed, were predisposed to contemplation, religion and the occult sciences. From these races came the best philosophers, mathematicians and prophets.[78] Yet these abilities were offset by deficiencies in strength and courage.[79] Those of the northern regions were courageous, hearty and possessed of technical skill, but were slow-witted and lacked the ability to rule themselves.[80] Only the populations of the temperate regions enjoyed the happy medium, having more intellectual ability than their dim-witted northerly neighbours, as well as the courage and strength which was lacking in the timorous southern peoples.[81]

Theories of climatic influence such as that of Bodin attracted considerable interest in England from Elizabethan times until well into the eighteenth century – not least because the English were most often classified with the dull and politically-naive northerners.[82] The work of Louis le Roy, *De la Vicissitude des Choses* (1579), was translated and appeared in England in 1594. Le Roy here presented a positive account of diversity, proposing that the variety of things results from differences in climate and place, and that such differences are divinely ordained, variation between the parts contributing to the unified workings of the whole. Human diversity in particular was portrayed in a favourable light, human differences ensuring that 'the one hauing neede of the other, they might communicate togither, & succour each other'.[83]

Giovanni Botero's *Relations of the Most Famous Kingdomes and Commonweales thorough the World* (1630) was another popular book which ran to several editions in the seventeenth century.[84] In its introduction Botero rehearsed in some detail Bodin's views about climatic influence, including the suggestion that the English were possessed of the typical characters of the Northerners. English writers themselves were to take up these views, most notably Peter Heylyn and Nathaniel Carpenter. In his lectures at Oxford, Heylyn boasted of a 'new method' for joining history and cosmography, suggesting that the actions and attributes of men and nations could be explained by reference to their environments.[85] In fact, Heylyn's 'new method' of demonstrating the influence of geography on historical events was virtually indistinguishable from Bodin's geographico-historical approach. Heylyn is nonetheless a significant writer, not only because he acted as a medium for these ideas, but because he specifically applied them to the biblical account of human dispersion. Remarking on the dispersion of the descendants of Noah, Heylyn informed his readers that: 'Men thus one by originall, are of diuerse complexions of body, and conditions of mind, according to the diuerse climates of the Earth'.[86] Yet, despite a promise to examine various religions, dispositions and customs, Heylyn nowhere closely correlates climate and religion.

Carpenter's *Geographie* (1625) went further, bringing together elements of virtually all previous environmental theories. According to Carpenter, diversity is a function of three inter-related groups of variables – site, soil, and origin/culture. Site was further divided into two dimensions: the classical three zones – equatorial, middle, polar – and hemisphere. Carpenter followed the usual pattern in ascribing characteristics to inhabitants of the traditional three zones. However he overlaid this pattern with a theory of the negative consequences of dispersion. 'The people of the *Northerne Hemispheare*', said Carpenter, 'aswell in riches and magnificance, as vallour, science, and ciuill government, farre surpasse the people of the South Hemisphere'.[87] To this assertion was added a second 'theoreme', that 'people of the *Easterne* Hemispheare, in *Science, Religion, Ciuility, Magnificence*, and almost everything else, are far superiour to the inhabitants of the Westerne'.[88] According to Carpenter, these marked differences between Eurasians and the rest of the world were owing to soil and to the 'originall' of the various peoples. The populations of the south and west lived farthest from Noah's original landing place and hence had experienced most the deleterious effects of transplantation: 'Colonies transplanted from one region into another', said Carpenter, 'decline and suffer alteration'. Such changes have been observed, he continues, 'in the *Danes, Saxons and Angles*, comming into *Brittany*, who partly by the *Climate*, partly by *mixture* with them ... became more *ciuill*'.[89] Admixture would likewise have played a role in the degeneration of the inhabitants of the most remote colonies.[90]

Such views served to underline the common assumption that the diffusion of humanity which took place after Noah and his family disembarked must have had a corrupting effect. The modern heathen religions were simply vestiges of these ancient corruptions of Noachic religion. Again, these views can be seen to be closely related to the common opinion that the world was in a state of gradual decline.

It is worth bearing in mind that the acceptance of environmentalism did not necessitate the adoption of a negative interpretation of diffusion and diversity. French thinkers like Le Roy and Sieur Du Bartas (1544–1590) both stressed the positive aspects of variation. Le Roy, as mentioned earlier, placed stress on the divinely-ordained nature of diversity in the world. Du Bartas, whose writings influenced Milton and Heylyn,[91] stated that the dispersion and resulting diversity of mankind were in accordance with the divine plan, God wishing to lead his children away from the scenes of the crimes of their ancestors.[92] The Englishman William Wotton agreed with Du Bartas, proposing that the events which took place at Babel and the diversity which resulted from them should not be interpreted negatively.[93]

A minority of English writers had already urged a positive view of variety on the grounds that diversity and mutability were both part of the original divine plan. George Walker, for example, argued that 'as all this World is mutable and inconstant; so the mutability and inconstancy of all visible and naturall things in this World, is a thing which God purposed and foreshewed in the creation of them'.[94] The premise of Walker's argument which was not generally accepted was that God had ever intended mutability in his creatures. Mutability, as we have seen, was almost invariably regarded as an unfortunate consequence of the Fall. The idea that God might originally have intended a variety which extended even to religious worship was therefore always a minority view, and one which implicitly appealed to the principle of plenitude. According to this tenet of Platonism, the creator could not deny existence to any entity which could conceivably exist, and thus actuality was conferred upon all ideal possibilities.[95]

The principle of plenitude places diversity in a far more positive light because it assumes that differences result not from deterioration, but are divinely ordained. It is for this reason that the Italian Platonists viewed religious diversity more favourably. There is no explicit application of this principle in the Cambridge Platonists, however. This is probably because the principle was thought to apply to variation *of* species and not variation *within* species. One possible compromise was to affirm the variety of the original creation as good, while conceding that the Fall had brought about a less happy diversification. Meric Casaubon adopted this position, acknowledging both that human wilfulness had resulted in diversity, and that *natural* diversity of the earth had caused variety as well:

> For it is not possible for many reasons, that men that live under different clymates, should all live after one fashion: nor that the inhabitants of one place (the state of things altering often as it doth:) should alwaies live after one sort ... The consideration of this *varietie* affords, as unto the Naturalists, matter of speculation, how even herein nature delights in *varietie* ... I shall here onely observe the power and providence of Almighty God, who as hee can out of darknesse bring forth light, so can turne these wretched effects (in themselves:) of mans frailtie and corruption, to be the meanes, in part, of his happiness.[96]

Some variety therefore, is divinely ordained, and is good. Some, however, results from human sin, and is undesirable. The difficulty lay in distinguishing between the two.

What these differences of opinion signify is that within the ambit of the theological interpretations of history, there could still be disagreement about whether dispersion was a *felix culpa* or not. For sacred historians it was a delicate matter of balancing the implications of divine providence and physico-theology with the results of human sin. To what extent, in other words, was God to be held responsible for the physical and moral state of the world, and how much could be attributed to human failings? To the more theologically-conservative, the answer was clear. Religious diversity was linked with physical diversity and dispersion. If only one religion was true and all others false, then diversity could not have been part of God's original plan, and therefore should be attributed to human sin. But if climatic differences gave rise to religious pluralism, then however much human sin had led to dispersion into areas with differing climates, God, having established the earth with its separate climatic zones, could still be expected to bear some of the responsibility for religious variation. Indeed it might be argued that God had intended that there be different religions for different geographical regions. Against this, the negative view of religious diversity could be further reinforced if it was held not only that dispersion was the result of human sin but that climatic differences themselves also were caused by human sin.

Late seventeeth-century England produced a number of 'geological' works which managed to combine in a most curious fashion elements of biblical and scientific cosmologies. A number of these paid special attention to the link between the Fall and climatic variations. Thomas Burnet, sometime pupil of Tillotson and friend of Cudworth, devoted his *Sacred Theory of the Earth* to the thesis that the degeneracy of man had led to the transformation of the world from its original perfection to its present 'rude and ragged' state. Before divine judgement was handed down in the visitation of the Deluge, the earth stood upright on its axis, thus enjoying '*perpetual Æquinox* and unity of the seasons in the Year'.[97] William Whiston's cosmology differed greatly from Burnet's, but he nonetheless agreed that before the Flood, climatic variation was minimal. 'The Temperature of the *Antediluvian* Air', he said, 'was more equitable as to its different Climates, and its different Seasons'. Thus before the great inundation, the earth was 'without the scorching of a *Torrid Zone*, and of burning summers; or the freezing of the *Frigid Zones*, and of piercing winters'.[98] 'In this equitable State', observed Whiston, 'The *Polar* inhabitants might with little danger cut the *Line*, and the *Ethiopians* visit the *Frigid Zones*'.[99] In Whiston's scheme of things it was therefore possible for Antediluvian man to spread to the four corners of the earth (as in fact Whiston believed he had) without suffering the religious degeneration so evident in the post-diluvian world.

Sin and diversity – whether geographical or human – were so closely bound together that only the introduction of some non-biblical premise (such as the principle of plenitude) into the whole logical equation could yield a result where diversity was viewed in a kindly light. Few thinkers took that step, and throughout the seventeenth century theories of climatic influence served to bolster the sacred history of religious origins.

By the close of the century, environmentalism was proving to be something of a two-edged sword. While generally deployed to support a biblical view of things, it could also stand independently as an alternative, non-supernatural explanation of religious diversity. More ominously, it could also explain away putative revelations as being merely the result of climatic differences. Environmentalism had in the past, and could again, stand quite independent of Christian interpretations of history. Thus whereas religious truths, and in particular the Fall, had at one time been used to account for geographical differences, now geographical factors were being used to account for religious differences. An intermediate step in this reversal occurred with the combination of environmentalism with other theories of religion such as the imposture theory. This conjunction was to become a popular explanation of the success of the impostor Muhammad. Humphrey Prideaux, in his widely read anti-deist work, *The True Nature of Imposture* (1697), proposed that the prophet tailored his religion to suit his would-be converts. Muhammad's promises, Prideaux observed, were chiefly of Paradise, which he 'cunningly framed to the gust of the *Arabians*'. The 'gust' of the Arabians, he explains, was determined by their climate, for 'they being within the *Torrid Zone*, were through the nature of the *Clime*, as well as the excessive corruption of their Manners, exceedingly given to the love of Women'.[100] Paradise involved not only satisfaction of carnal lusts, but also a need even more basic to the desert nomad. The heaven of the Muslims was to have abundant and extravagant supplies of water, for according to Prideaux's reckoning, 'the scorching heat and dryness of the Countrey' made 'rivers of Water, cooling Drinks, shaded Gardens, and pleasant Fruits, most refreshing and delightful unto them'.[101] In short, they could hardly resist the blandishments which Muhammad held out to them. Prideaux's was a view which enjoyed considerable vogue amongst thinkers of widely differing opinions and it persisted for quite some time.[102] A century after Prideaux, the physico-theologian William Paley, who admittedly had a peculiar talent for expounding dated and unoriginal points of view, was still proposing that Muhammad's climatic concessions were a far cry from the 'unaccomodating purity of the Gospel'.[103]

Climatic theories, incidentally, seemed almost never to have been applied to that other great monotheistic religion, Judaism, for the Diaspora made nonsense of claim of climatic influence. As it turned out, this was of little account, for if the adherents of a religion were spread across a number of climatic zones, then their religious degeneration could always be accounted for by travel. This, as we have seen, was exactly what happened in the case of Judaism.

We encounter other applications of environmental theories, however. Herbert of Cherbury, rather than argue that environment physically affects human dispositions, suggested that certain environments are conducive to certain activities, which will in turn reflect on religious practices. Thus, worship of the planets originated in Egypt, because there the air is exceptionally clear.[104] Similarly, the Indians and Brazilians have access to spices and drugs which clear the mind and lengthen life (or so Herbert thought). Their religions accordingly resulted from lengthy meditation and cogitation.[105] The third Earl of Shaftesbury followed Herbert in attributing the fertility of the Egyptian religious imagination to their environment:

> Their solitary idle life whilst shut up in their houses by the regular inundations of the Nile; the unwholesome vapours arising from the new mud and slimy relicts of their river exposed to the hot suns; their various meteors and phenomena, with the long vacancy they had to observe and comment on them; the necessity withal, which, on account of their navigation and the measure of their yearly drowned lands, compelled them to promote the studies of astronomy and the other sciences, of which their priesthood could make good advantages – all these mauy be reckoned as additional causes of the immense growth of superstition, and the enormous increase of the priesthood in this fertile land.[106]

The idolaters of the East were no less influenced by their climate. David Collyer explained that the geography of an area, even if it has no direct effect on the physical disposition of the local inhabitants, nonetheless shapes their religious practices. The '*Eastern* Idolaters', he maintained, 'were wont to plant *Groves* around their Altars, which made the place shady and delightful in those hot Countries'. The shade so produced also struck the worshippers with 'a kind of Horror and awful Reverence' as well as making the shrine a more fit place for 'the impure and lewd Practices of the Idolaters'.[107]

Such analyses, while they are in principle independent of sacred history, do not really contain a comprehensive theory of religion based on climatic influence. It was left to the French thinker Montesquieu to give a thoroughgoing account of religious diversity in climatic terms. In book XIV of his *De l'Esprit des Loix*, Montesquieu observed that the Buddha had simply reinforced the effects of a 'lazy climate' in enjoining his followers to adopt a passive life.[108] A responsible religious leader, according to Montesquieu, should attempt to counter the effects of climate and not aggravate them. Such was the case in China, where the leaders of the nation had enforced practical laws which stressed appropriate duties.[109] Montesquieu also made mention of Islam, and Muhammad's sanctioning of polygamy. Again he attributed this feature of the religion to climate, pointing to the success of Islam in Asia, and the failure of Christianity there as evidence for the link between climate and religious precepts.[110]

As Montesquieu's observations imply, any substantial reliance upon environmental theories of religious diversity could threaten the exclusiveness and truth of the Christian revelation and its many forms. Even before Montesquieu had addressed what he called the 'immutability' of the religions and customs of the Eastern countries, Thomas Pope Blount, at the close of the seventeenth century in England, had come very close to proposing religious relativism on the grounds of climatic determination. Blount deployed the theory with no specific reference to the stories of Adam and Noah. To the basic thesis of Heylyn, he added the observations of the great physiologist Harvey, to the effect that: 'Those who are of a different Diet, are generally observed to be of different Opinions'.[111] Blount summed up his speculations on the diversity of human opinions (which he elaborated with a view to discussing religious diversity) with the following judgement:

> it plainly appears, That the great Variety of Mens Actions and Opinions cannot proceed from the Diversity of their Souls, which are accounted all equal, but from that of the Bodies; wherein according to the various Tempers thereof, the soul produces that variety of Manners. Let us not then any longer wonder, to find so great a Diversity of opinions in the World; since it is a thing wholly impossible for all Men to be of the same mind; For so long as Mens Organs are of several makes, and we live under divers Climats, we must necessarily have different Sentiments, and Apprehensions of things.[112]

Blount wished to argue for pluralism and a healthy scepticism by making it clear that once the influence of climate and diet is allowed, it must be considered universal if it is to be meaningful. Thus, *all* beliefs are only relatively true because all are subject to the vicissitudes of environment. His conclusion: 'How unreasonable are those Men, who are so positive and dogmatical in their own Opinions, that rather than admit of the least Contradiction, chuse to make the whole World an *Aceldama* and a *Babel?*'[113] Here Blount goes far beyond giving a simple explanation of the basis of different opinions and the need for mutual tolerance: he actually denies the validity of an exclusive revelation, and asserts a kind of relativism. This was an inevitable consequence of a theory which asserted that opinions were determined by natural causes. Environmental theories should logically lead to a tolerance of the excesses of certain peoples, for those who are unduly influenced by climate could not be fully responsible for their beliefs. Furthermore, God's control (or the devil's) was bound to be less if environmental influences were taken into consideration.

The tendency to attribute religious differences to natural causes is already present to some degree in Bodin's writings.[114] In Blount it is quite explicit. Others of Blount's period also stressed the relativism which seems necessarily to follow from any rigorous application of environmentalism. Of particular interest is 'Abdulla Mahumed Omar's'[115] refutation of Prideaux's contentions concerning Muhammad's teachings and their link with climate. In his *Defence of Mahomet*, Omar turns the tables on Prideaux by showing that if theories of climatic influence are to be admitted, they must be admitted across the board:

> This author (Prideaux) is born in a cold country and because the Laws and Customs of that place oblige the husband to have but one Wife, he attributes the more to a sinful Lust, tho' it has always been a Use in most of the hotter countries, to have a plurality of Wives; and Nature itself seems to have established this; for whereas there are more Males than Females born in a colder Climate, there are more Females than Males born in those regions nearer the Sun.[116]

Speculation along the lines developed by Blount and Omar serves to show that environmentalism, when sundered from biblical accounts of dispersion and the origin of idolatry, could provide explanations which competed with the biblical view, and which could lead to relativism and scepticism in religious matters. Once climate was posited as a determinant of religious ideas, only a seemingly *ad hoc* insistence on divine revelation and providential guidance could render the Christian Religion immune from the charges of corruption laid against other religions. In fact, some were to argue not only that Christianity had been given an exclusive revelation, but that divine providence had shielded the tradition from the tainting effects of environment, dispersion, and the passing of time. Just as Milton, despairing that his circumstances placed him in 'an age to late' and in a 'cold climate', was driven to the conclusion that his poetical genius had to be the result of divine inspiration and not natural circumstance,[117] so too, Christian apologists were forced to conclude that while all other religions might be determined in many of their fundamentals by various accidents, Christianity, for reasons which went beyond naturalistic explanation, was not.[118]

The attempt to place Christianity beyond the reach of naturalistic explanations proved unsatisfactory for a number of reasons. It threatened to reopen the gulf between natural and revealed religion, doing away with the common innate basis of all religions. Christianity would thus lose its status as the perfect manifestation of natural religion (albeit a natural religion whose content corresponded exactly with divine revelation). More awkward was the fact that, at an individual level, it was difficult to see how Christianity might be rendered immune from the influences of such natural forces as climate. These geographical variables were thought to work upon the humours of the individual, predisposing him or her to certain kinds of thoughts and activities. To assert that God had isolated all those of the true faith from these influences was a view, which, like Descartes' 'occasionalism', was quite foreign to these otherwise 'scientific' explanations.

For those who wished still to elevate Christianity above the other religions and yet remain within the sphere of naturalistic explanation, a solution suggested itself. From the realm of nature came the model of health and disease. The ravages of disease produce an undesirable state, and yet disease is natural. So too, health is a natural state. The relationship between Christianity and the other religions might conceivably be understood in terms of the two natural states of health and sickness.

THE PATHOLOGY OF RELIGION

The tendency towards secondary explanations resulted in the view that religious dispositions were affected, and indeed determined, by variables of the *external* environment, both physical and social. The model of religious pathology suggested that religious dispositions could also be determined by variables of the *internal* environment. The notion that the false religions result from different forms of religious pathology can, like other explanations of religion, be derived from the biblical stories of human origins. In our present age, in which a Darwinian view of the influence of heredity and environment is taken for granted, we tend to forget that, prior to the nineteenth century, belief in the inheritance of acquired characteristics was widespread.[119] The commission of *the* original sin, in this 'Lamarkian' scheme of things, was not simply a moral Fall which had dire theological consequences, but was an event which had pervasive physical consequences

– both for the world, as we have seen, and for the physical constitution of humanity. *Original* sin was thus *inherited* sin.[120] The most common hereditary religious affliction was idolatry – that 'grievous Disease of the Soul' as More would say. In our 'Lapsed state', he explains, we are '*naturally* prone to so mischievous a Disease, as both History and daily experience do abundantly witnesse'.[121]

Religious errors, then, had not only a social component, which was to do with political and priestly imposture, the twofold philosophy, custom and education, but a related physical component which underlined the effect of these social variables. As More again put it, 'what *Custome* and *Education* doth by degrees, distempered *Phancy* may doe in a shorter time'.[122] The whole history of human apostasy might therefore be compressed and manifested in the religious formation of the individual. The victim of religious distemper is a microcosm of the world. As in other explanations of religious error, the key was again *variation*. Sin resulted in climatic variation, variation of social mores, and now variation in individual physiology. In this physiological variation lay the seeds of all pathological conditions, including not only simple heathenism or idolatry, but also those religious maladies which had infected both agents and patients of imposture in the historical religions.

Robert Burton credited himself with being the first to investigate 'religious melancholy' as a discrete condition. 'No Physician', he announced, 'hath as yet distinctly written of it ... all acknowledge it a most notable Symptom; some a cause, but few a species or kind'.[123] As a natural, and independent human faculty, the religious propensity has its own distinct pathology. Its general pattern however, was similar to that of other infirmities. Because Burton subscribed to the classical view of health as equilibrium, he thought religious disorders to be of two types, resulting from opposite extremes. The healthy religious condition was thus bounded by these two poles – the 'extreames of *Excess* and *Defect*, Impiety and Superstition, Idolatry and Atheism'.[124] Those suffering from excess were 'all superstitious idolaters, Ethnicks, Mahometans, Jews, Hereticks, Enthusiasts, Divinators, Prophets, Sectaries, and Schismaticks'. Also included were 'many other curious persons, Monks and Heremites etc.', along with 'those rude Idiots and infinite swarms of people that are seduced by them'.[125] At the other end of the scale were 'those impious Epicures, Libertines, Atheists, Hypocrites, Infidels ... that attribute all to natural causes, that will acknowledge no supreme power'.[126] As a theory which accounts for the origin of false religions, religious pathology was often deployed in conjunction with an imposture theory. Both impostors and their followers were thought to be afflicted with similar mental symptoms. Both ignore reason, uncritically accepting whatever is presented to their imaginations, the difference between them being that in the case of the impostor, the presentation to the imagination derives from the unstable mind itself, while the duped disciples receive the presentation from the impostor himself, or from tradition.

While identifying the physiological basis of all non-Christian religions (and many Christian sects as well), Burton was extremely reluctant to jettison supernatural explanation. To do so would be to move perilously close to 'Epicureanism'. He admitted, for instance, that the brain 'is the part affected of Superstition', but at the same time insisted that it was the devil who remained the chief cause of extremes of religious melancholy.[127] Burton's religious pathology thus hovered uncomfortably between natural and supernatural explanation, and although it stressed the biological aspects of religious diversity, it still fell short of seeing this biological sphere of operation as devoid of supernatural influence.

No such ambivalence can be found in the writings of Meric Casaubon and Henry More. Casaubon's *Treatise Concerning Enthusiasme* (1655) appeared some thirty years after Burton's *Anatomy* and is perhaps the most systematic approach to religious pathology of that period. In it, the various kinds of enthusiasm are fitted into a typology:

> *Enthusiasme*, say I, is either naturall, or supernaturall. By supernatural, I understand a true and reall possession of some extrinsical superior power, whether divine, diabolical, producing effects and operations altogether supernatural: as some kind of divination... speaking strange languages, temporary learning, and the like. By natural *Enthusiasme*, I understand an extraordinary, transcendent, but natural fervency, or pregnancy of the soul, spirits or brain, producing strange effects, apt to be mistaken for supernatural.[128]

Of natural enthusiasm, said Casaubon, there are four kinds – 'Contemplative and Philosophical', 'Rhetorical', 'Poeticall', and 'Precatory'. Each of these types, according to Casaubon, was commonly confused with the supernatural type, the result being that 'some men ... through mere ignorance of natural causes have been seduced by supposed raptures and Enthusiasmes, and make shipwreck of the true faith'.[129] Casaubon thus seemed to deny that heretical or heathen enthusiasm results from demonic agency. These symptoms of enthusiasm are natural, and consequently innocent, if erroneous. Heresies and false religions thus result from the behaviour of impostors who have produced 'some extraordinary though not supernatural effects; really, not hypocritically, but yet falsely and erroneously, to seem themselves divinely inspired'.[130]

Henry More's pamphlet *Enthusiasmus Triumphatus* (1662) endorsed the sentiments of Casaubon. Like other Cambridge Platonists, More was concerned to combat the dual and related errors of atheism and enthusiasm.[131] '*Atheism* and *Enthusiasm*', he informs us, 'are commonly entertain'd, though successively, in the same Complexion'. Both are religious fancies, which 'vary and change with the weather and present temper of the body'. More continues:

> So those that have onely a fiery *Enthusiastick* acknowledgement of God; change of diet, feculent old age, or some present damps of *Melancholy*, will as confidently represent to their *Phancy* that there is no God, as ever it was represented that there is one.[132]

According to More, the chief cause of enthusiasm was the imagination, which in turn was influenced by the weather, 'various tempers of the Aire', diet and disease.[133] These were all instances of 'that mighty power there is in *naturall Causes* to work upon and unavoidably to change our *Imagination*'.[134]

One natural cause of enthusiasm to which More gave particular attention was melancholy, for it was this 'pertinacious and religious complexion', he believed, which had led to the majority of cases of religious imposture.[135] Religious melancholy led to such movements of the mind that the subject was sorely tempted to believe that he was genuinely possessed of the divine spirit, as were those in his company. More sceptically observed that whatever flights of fancy overtake the melancholic enthusiast, 'there is nothing better then *Nature* in it':

> the *Spirit* then, that wings the *Enthusiast* in such wonderful manner, is nothing else but that *Flatulency* which is *Melancholy* complexion, and rises out of the *Hypocondriacal* humour upon some occasional heat, as *Winde* out of an *Æolipila* applied to the fire.[136]

Amongst these purveyors of hot air, More listed Montanus, Manes, Muhammad, the Anabaptists, Quakers, Theosophists and Chymists.[137]

More, like the rest of his circle, always took care to ensure that he did not fall into 'sadducism' – the materialistic denial of the reality of spirits. The dilemma which he faced here was that in denying satanic involvement in religious imposture, he was reducing the extent of the spiritual world. Conscious of this dilemma, More hastened to assure his readers that his attitude toward the Devil was but a methodological agnosticism:

> his *Causality* is more vagrant, more lax and general then to be brought in here, where my aim was to indigitate the more proper and constant causes of that *Disease*. I might add also less philosophical for this present search, which was only into the *natural* principles of the said Distemper.[138]

The issue of causality had another component. A conundrum faced by all exponents of naturalistic explanations was that if the various religions came about through the operation of natural laws, then there could be no culpability in falling prey to heresies or false religions. If, as Casaubon maintained, neither the impostor nor his followers act hypocritically, how then could blame accrue to them as a result of what had been physically determined? More negotiated the difficulty by claiming that religious malady can be consciously resisted: 'the *Enthusiast*, though he be necessarily assaulted by his own Complexion, yet not irresistably; and ... therefore the guilt of his own extravagancies lies at his own door'.[139] Burton, perhaps more realistically, suggested that only a miracle could overcome the forces of religious melancholy. His cure called for 'some monster-taming *Hercules*, a divine *Æsculapius* or CHRIST himself to come in his own person'.[140] Failing this, toleration was a solution.[141] It seems reasonable, although Burton does not concede this, to tolerate what was, after all, a physical sickness.[142] The only other possibility would be a physical or psychological cure. This, I suspect, was Burton's preferred option, for in his conclusion he recommends for the victims of religious melancholy, with characteristic lack of bedside manner, that 'the most compendious cure for some of them at least, had been in Bedlam'.[143] Burton's views notwithstanding, it can again be seen, as in the case of climatic theories of religion, that when physiological accounts of false religion are put forward, toleration and relativism are not far away.

An equally intransigent, and not unrelated difficulty, lay in the need to establish criteria to distinguish real (supernatural) from false (perverted-natural) inspiration. For Burton, the symptoms – albeit ideological rather than physical ones – spoke for themselves. Those who professed forms of religion other than Protestantism had evidently fallen prey to religious distemper. By the middle of the seventeenth century in England, however, this method of diagnosis became problematic, for it was no longer clear that one particular form of Protestantism was the hallmark of all religious truth, nor was its profession the sole sign of psychological well-being.

Henry More adopted a different strategy, and true to the Cambridge tradition, appealed to the impartial light of reason. He likened the enthusiast's state of consciousness to a dreaming state in which the imagination presented images to the soul as if they were external perceptions.[144] These religious delusions are received as true because human reason, wounded in the Fall, is too weak to resist them:

> Wherefore it is the enormous strength of the *Imagination* (which is yet the Soul's weaknesse or unwieldinesse, whereby she so far sinks into Phantasmes that she cannot recover her self into the use of her more free Faculties of *Reason* and *Understanding*) that thus peremptorily engages a man to believe a lie.[145]

Religious fancies are perpetuated in much the same way, but by use and custom, for 'the case in both is much like that in *Dreams*, where that which is represented is necessarily taken for true, because nothing stronger enervates the perception'.[146] For More, cultural and biological factors thus combined to perpetuate false religions.

It was only after the turn of the century that anyone bothered to distinguish, to any significant degree, ideological symptoms from physiological. The third Earl of Shaftesbury maintained that if the physiological and behavioural symptoms of religious enthusiasm are observed in an impartial manner, it is evident that all forms of religion are blighted with enthusiasm. Thus religious pathology is not directly correlated with non-Protestant religion, but is manifested in all religions, the Protestant included:

> whether the matter of apparition be true or false, the symptoms are the same, and the passion of equal force in the person who is vision struck ... All nations have their lymphatics of some kind or another; and all churches, heathen as well as Christian, have had their complaints against fanaticism.[147]

Shaftesbury, by placing Christianity on the same footing as the other religions, effectively did away with religious pathology as an explanation of the various religions. Equally, he made it difficult to use pathology to account for the origin of religions, for he claimed that it was characteristic of them all – presumably both true and false.

The final stage in the development of the disease-model of religion came with the view that any form of positive religion is a pathology of the human condition. While freethinkers had tended to stress the un-natural quality of the empirical religions, this was generally with a view to establishing some positive form of natural religion. In the deists' view, all positive religions were distortions of natural religion. The extreme tendency of this position is the claim that religion is not a natural propensity which is attacked by disease and degenerates into heathenism, but is itself a disease of the psyche. *All* religious sentiments are then considered pathological. John Trenchard proposed this in his *Natural History of Superstition* (1709), in which he identifies a universal and innate propensity for superstition.[148] He rehearses the familiar physiological arguments of Burton, Casaubon, and More, but regards the symptoms of the religious malady to have been of epidemic proportions in all ages and in all religions.[149] David Hume took a similar stance in his *Natural History of Religion* (1757). We shall be examining both of these works in some detail in the chapter which follows. Suffice it at this point to cite Hume's conclusion that 'the religious principles, which have, in fact, prevailed in the world' are nothing but 'sick men's dreams'.[150] For both Hume and Trenchard, the non-pathological golden mean was not Christianity, or any positive religion, but rather 'the temperate and the moderate', the 'calm, though obscure, regions of philosophy'.[151] The insight that religion in general is a pathological state clearly involves the denial of the naturalness of religion. Religion in this view must be derived from the perversion of some other elemental faculties. This contribution of Trenchard and Hume was to be one of the more enduring religious theories of the eighteenth century, finding more complete expression in Baron d'Holbach and his school, and later still in Marx and Freud.[152]

Both climatic and pathological theories of religion have somewhat tenuous links with sacred history. Certainly, they could lay some claim to having a biblical basis, but they are easily severed from these biblical roots, and could be employed quite independent of any commitment to the biblical story. Even more importantly, they threatened to place Christianity on the level of the other religions, subjecting it to the vicissitudes of nature, and calling into question its revelatory basis. Added to this, the privileged status of Christianity was gradually being eroded on another front, and indeed the whole edifice of sacred history was crumbling. The biblical record itself was being subjected to increasing criticism.

THE DECLINE OF SACRED HISTORY

In an unfortunate paragraph in Book sixteen of *The City of God*, Augustine states with characteristic forthrightness that the fable of the Antipodes is 'on no ground credible', that 'it is too absurd to suppose that some men might have taken ship and traversed the whole wide ocean', and that Scripture is never wrong.[153] By the seventeenth century it had become apparent to all that he was mistaken on the first count, and if correct on the second, then wrong on the third. In short, the father of sacred history was indisputably in error, and it was quite possible that the Scripture which he had enlisted in support of his contentions was similarly fallible.[154] The discovery of the New World in particular had created difficulties for the biblical record, and the full import of these difficulties was only beginning to be fully realised. With the benefit of a two-hundred year perspective, Abbé Corneille de Pauw was able to state that:

> No event is more memorable for the human race than the discovery of America. Looking back from the present to the most remote ages, we see no event that can be compared with it; and indeed it is an impressive and terrible spectacle to see one-half of this globe so ill favoured by nature that all it contains is either degenerate or monstrous.[155]

One of the difficulties which America created for the biblical account of human origins was, as de Pauw observed, the sheer 'degeneracy' of the American natives. How could they possibly have descended from Noah, the common father of all? Equally problematic was the remoteness of America. How could such a primitive people have colonised the New World from the Old, without, as Strachey had put it, 'furniture of shipping'?[156] A range of possibilities suggested themselves. Peter Heylyn argued that some knowledge of shipbuilding had persisted in Europe from the time of Noah, enabling some of the Tartars to negotiate the 'very small Strait' between Tartary and the New World.[157] Dionisius Petavius and Simon Patrick favoured the thesis that a land bridge had once existed between the West and the Americas.[158] Hale happily entertained both theories.[159] Thomas Burnet, that adventurous exegete, daringly proposed that Adam's immediate progeny had settled the whole world, there being in antediluvian times no oceans to impede their migration. During the Deluge, God had preserved some of these remote outposts.[160]

While these proposals for the most part left sacred history untouched and explained how the American natives got there, they did not account for the obvious differences in culture and constitution. So great were these differences that many early explorers thought the Americans not human at all, but rather an advanced kind of ape. This proposal (pace Glanvill) also had the advantage of obviating the necessity of establishing their descent from Noah. As de Pauw related:

> At first Americans were not thought to be men, but rather orang-utangs, or large monkeys, that could be destroyed without remorse and without reproach. Finally, to add the ridiculous to the calamities of that era, a certain pope issued a bull in which he decreed that, as he wished to establish dioceses in the richest regions of America, it pleased him and the Holy Spirit to recognise Americans as true men. Thus, without this decision made by an Italian, the inhabitants of the New World would still today be, in the eyes of the faithful, a race of dubious animals.[161]

The Pope was perhaps wiser than he knew, for it was conceivable that Noah's descendants might somehow have crossed the seas after the Deluge, bringing beast and fowl with them. That a menagerie could have organised their own migration was less likely.[162] Likelihood, however, did not figure largely in theories about the origin of the American Indians. Bishop Francis Goodwin toyed with the notion that the natives of the New World were of extraterrestrial origin, being the flawed rejects of a Utopian Lunar civilisation.[163] Goodwin's view, in fact, is merely the demythologised explanation of the Platonists. The savages of the New World, contended More and Rust, were bodies inhabited by souls which had committed some offence in a previous existence. They had fallen, not from the moon, but from grace.[164]

It is hardly surprising, given these attempts to reconcile empirical fact with sacred history, that aspects of the Genesis stories began to be stretched beyond credibility. Even so slavish a follower of the biblical account as Peter Heylyn was to remark that the differences between the various races of the world were so marked that 'it might seem they had been made at first out of severall Principles, and not at all derived from one common Parent'.[165] Less inhibited thinkers had already taken the plunge, and freeing themselves of the strait-jacket of sacred history denied that all mankind descended from Noah or Adam. Paracelsus, Bruno, and Vanini had all given notice that they no longer strictly adhered to the traditional view.[166] But it was left to Isaac de la Peyrère to articulate the most systematic and most infamous alternative to the monogenetic theory. His *Preadamitae* and *Systema Theologicum ex Preadamitarium Hypothesi* were both published in 1655 and appeared in Britain in the following year as the single work, *Men before Adam*. Here La Peyrère proposed, on exegetical grounds, that there were men who existed before Adam, and who fathered all races except the Jewish. The significance of the biblical account, he claimed, was that *sacred* history began with the creation of the first Jew – Adam.

While La Peyrère enjoyed only brief notoriety – he was publicly to recant in 1656 – his thesis proved less susceptible to the powers of persuasion of the ecclesiastical rulers. Despite condemnation from official sources, 'pre-Adamism' remained a threat to the Christian understanding of the nature and destiny of man. According to Richard Popkin, from the middle of the seventeenth century onward, pre-Adamism was 'the most fundamental challenge to the Judeo-Christian tradition to arise from the "new science" and the "new philosophy"'.[167] It is evident that if a 'preadamite' theory is embraced, a very different picture of the history of religion will emerge.[168] At one level, it implies that diversity does not result from corruption, and that pluralism in whatever form, need not be seen as an evil. At a deeper level however, the polygenetic alternative challenged the whole drama of redemption portrayed in the Scriptures. If Adam was not a common ancestor of all humanity, then serious questions could be raised about the Fall and the legacy of original sin. Did the races which did not spring from Adam have their corresponding falls? If not, how did they inherit the 'poyson' of original sin; or did they remain in a 'natural' state – practising natural religion?[169] Difficulties were also raised for the Pauline understanding of Christ as the 'second Adam' (Romans 5). As Paul expressed the symmetry of redemption, sin entered the world through the act of one man and the world was redeemed by the act of one man. Yet if the first premise is denied, what becomes of the second? If Adam is not unique, then neither is Christ – if Adam is not our patriarch, then neither is Christ our redeemer.

Yet another problem came from speculation about 'new worlds' on other planets, for the discovery of the Americas, combined with the Copernican theory of the solar system, led to theorising about the possibility of extra-terrestrial life. As Francis Goodwin expressed it: 'That there should be *Antipodes* was once thought as great a *Paradox* as now that the *Moon* should be habitable.'[170] Bernard Fontenelle's celebrated *Conversations on the Plurality of Worlds* (1686) also drew a number of parallels between the newly discovered tribes of the New World and hypothetical beings on other planets.[171] English writers had similarly pondered these weighty questions – the Platonists More and Cudworth, along with their friend Burnet, Burton, the astronomer–cleric Derham, Hale, and even more popular writers like Addison – and many of them well before the appearance of Fontenelle's *Plurality of Worlds*.[172] Creatures inhabiting such worlds could scarcely have descended from Adam and thus many questions could be asked about whether these aliens had fallen, and if provision had been made for their redemption. Bishop Wilkins, in his *Discovery of the New World* (1684), asks of his men in the moon 'whether they are of the seed of *Adam*, whether they are there in blessed Estate, or else what means there may be for their Salvation?'[173] The conclusion which could most readily be drawn from such exercises of the imagination was that Christianity was not in the most complete sense a universal religion, and that if inhabitants of new worlds on other planets had their own valid systems of religion, why could not inhabitants of the terrestrial New World be similarly blessed? Polygenetic theories, in short, called into question the whole drama of Fall and Redemption and the uniqueness of Jesus Christ.

Many other factors contributed to the general erosion of biblical authority – the growth of natural science,[174] the development of an historical–critical method,[175] the acceptance of the supremacy of extra-biblical sources in some spheres of history, and not least, substantial disagreements amongst sacred historians themselves.[176] The Bible remained an authority, but increasingly it was interpreted so as to conform to secular history and science rather than determining the agenda of those disciplines. Hans Frei, I believe, correctly characterises the different role which biblical history was to assume in the eighteenth century, when he observes that:

> It is no exaggeration to say that all across the theological spectrum the great reversal had taken place; interpretation was a matter of fitting the biblical story into another world with another story rather than incorporating that world into the biblical story.[177]

FIVE

FROM SACRED HISTORY TO NATURAL HISTORY

What is now called Christian religion, has existed among the ancients, and was not absent from the beginning of the human race, until Christ came in the flesh: from which time true religion, which existed already, began to be called Christian.

Augustine, *Retractions*, 1.13

It would be a mistake to think that with the growth of biblical criticism came a whole new field of 'secular' history. What in fact took place was the development of a number of hybrid histories in which biblical material was supplemented with historical information drawn from other sources. Augustine himself had made the admission that 'it is difficult to discover from Scripture, whether, after the deluge, traces of the holy city are continuous, or are ... interrupted'.[1] Augustine, in other words, could insist on the historical accuracy of the Bible without pressing the further claim that it gave full information about the history of true piety; and if the 'City of God' did not have a continuous history written out in the pages of Scripture, still less could it be claimed that the Bible gave a full historical account of manifold forms of religious error. In view of this, it is not surprising that the Catholic biblical scholar Richard Simon hardly aroused a ripple when in 1680 he declared that the Bible, by itself, is an insufficient basis for a universal history.[2]

In any case, there were Christian thinkers in every period who had admitted that the Bible was not the sole repository of God's revelation. The seventeenth and eighteenth centuries were no exception, and a number of sacred histories incorporated what were thought to be extra-biblical sources of revealed truth. Some of the Christian Platonists, for example, held that Moses had fathered an oral tradition which was transmitted as Cabbala. Others of the group believed that there were a number of pre-Mosaic writings which contained important truths which had been omitted from a much-condensed Pentateuch.[3]

All of this meant that there was considerable latitude for those who might wish to augment the biblical record with additional material – an activity which in itself posed no major threat to biblical authority, but which often meant a tacit acceptance of the supremacy of some other sources in matters of historical detail not directly addressed in Scripture. Two approaches fell into this category – 'ancient theology' and comparative mythology. Both initially involved the harmonising of biblical and non-biblical source materials, or more correctly, the alignment of other sources with the biblical record. Both were based upon the premise that Judaic civilisation was the parent of all gentile cultures, and that all other histories were derived and elaborated from the original and true history of the Jews. According to this 'single-source' view, every aspect of pagan culture, including religion, had its rise in age-old Jewish traditions.

In England, it was the hermetic-cabbalist Robert Fludd who propounded the single-source theory most forcefully. 'The true Sophia or wisdom', he announced,

> is the ground of all Arts; and therefore it being revealed or discovered unto man, he may be taught and instructed by it, as by the onely wise and essential school-mistress in all science and knowledge.[4]

This 'true wisdom', according to Fludd, had been revealed by God to Moses, who in turn was the source of all human knowledge. 'The wisest amongst those Pagan Naturalists', said Fludd, 'did steal and derive their main grounds or principles, from the true and sacred philosopher *Moses*, whose philosophy was originally delineated by the finger of God'.[5] Here Fludd had in mind not simply the principles of natural religion, but literally all arts and sciences. Arithmetic, geometry, rhetoric, the making of clothing and jewelry, carpentry, moral doctrine and politics are but some of the enterprises which, according to Fludd, a virtuosic Moses gave to the ancient world.[6]

This single-source theory is, of course, nothing more than a strict, and perhaps extreme, application to human culture of the monogenetic view of human origins. Most often, in the seventeenth century, this single-source theory was applied to the history of philosophy and religion. In this more restricted form, it was closely allied with the thesis of the 'ancient theology'.[7]

ANCIENT THEOLOGY

If the single-source view of history involved the somewhat chauvinistic assumption that all civilisations had their rise in what was to develop into Judaeo-Christian culture, 'ancient theology' merely focussed upon one implication of this view – that the religion of all lands must originally have been that of the parent culture. This belief in primitive monotheism went virtually unchallenged for the sixteenth and much of the seventeenth century and was an implication not only of sacred history, but also of such related and often unspoken assumptions as 'truth is more ancient than error'.[8] Proponents of the ancient theology, while accepting primitive monotheism as an axiom, made the further claim that true religion had been preserved intact in many pagan countries for a considerable time – albeit by a sophisticated few. The textual evidence for this view came from such writings as the *Hermetica, Orphica*, and the *Sibylline Oracles*, in which vestiges of true religion – God, immortality, *creatio ex nihilo*, the Trinity – were to be found. These writings were presumed to have drawn upon the wisdom of the Jewish patriarchs and to have pre-dated Plato, who subsequently relied upon them for much of his theology. Plato, however, was not the only heir to this tradition. From the Jewish sources of Adam, Enoch, Noah and Abraham, Moses and David, the ancient theology was passed on to such varied figures as Zoroaster, Hermes Trismegistus, Brahmins and Druids, Orpheus, Pythagoras, Plato, and the Sibyls.[9] Of these pagan figures, the most important were Plato and the Egyptian theologian Hermes, who was reckoned to be the author of the *Hermetica*.[10]

Throughout the centuries, Christian Platonists in particular found the ancient theology a most congenial approach, for it enabled a happy marriage of Platonism and Christianity. But in any case such a view could be derived directly from the biblical record and was not, therefore, restricted to Platonists. All religions, however degenerate, developed out of the true religion. What happened at Babel was that as the human race was scattered abroad each language group took with them a different name for the same God. The fact that each country had different names or symbols for God did not mean that the symbols did not represent the same God; initially they must have. Those who proposed a continuity of the original tradition thus had a twofold focus: first, to show that certain individuals had preserved, practised, and even preached true religion in their pagan environments; and second, to investigate how amongst the vulgar the symbols and names for God gradually became dissociated from the proper object of worship.

The resurgence of ancient theology at this time is a little puzzling, particularly in view of the growing body of scholarship which cast grave doubts upon its textual basis. Amongst the Cambridge Platonists it granted a certain historical justification for deference to Plato, but its appeal was certainly wider than this group alone. Most probably the ancient theology was espoused to ameliorate the 'scandal of particularity'; namely, that it seemed unreasonable for an historical religion which has been revealed to a chosen few to advance the claim of an exclusive salvation. As Pope expressed it:

> Remember, Man, 'the Universal Cause
> Acts not by partial, but by general laws;'
> And makes what happiness we justly call
> Subsist not in the good of one, but all.[11]

Ancient theology showed that the deity had at least made an effort to make his worship universal.

The problem of universality was to provide the basis of Lessing's dictum which speaks of the problem of the relation of accidental truths of history to necessary truths of reason. It is not surprising that this problem should manifest itself at this time, albeit not in the clear terms in which Lessing was later to express it. Combined with a growing awareness of the global insignificance of Christianity (in numerical terms) was an ever increasing gulf between the universal religion of reason and the exclusive religion of revelation. Added to this was the ascendancy in England of a Calvinism which seemed to make the whole question of salvation even more restricted and arbitrary. There were three distinct responses to this problem. Some simply ignored it and affirmed some doctrine of election. (This proved popular amongst those who were fairly confident of their own election.) Others maintained that despite being a revealed religion, Judaism/Christianity had been propagated universally. This, of course, was what proponents of the ancient theology believed. Still others identified as genuine religion the religion of reason and nature (which was universally available) and attempted to relate 'revealed religions' to it in some way. More orthodox divines took the first course, Christian Platonists opted for the second, and deists or free-thinkers tended towards the last view.

In seventeenth-century England, the ancient theology was promoted by the Christian Platonists Henry More and Ralph Cudworth. In *Conjectura Cabbalistica* (1662), More proposed that God's revelation to Moses had three aspects – literal, philosophical and moral. The Pentateuch, of which Moses was author, contained the 'Literal Cabbala' while the 'Philosophical Cabbala' was an oral tradition, hidden from the vulgar: in More's words, it was 'a Doctrine received by *Moses* first, and then from him by *Joshua*, and *Joshua* by the seventy *Elders*, and so on'.[12] In places, More, like Fludd, simply lists various aspects of human knowledge – mathematics, atomical philosophy – which were plagiarised from the Jews.[13] Mostly, however, he gives attention to the dissemination of religious truths throughout the ancient world. 'There is', he insists, 'no knowledge of God but what *Moses* his Text set on foot in the world, or what is *Traditional*'.[14] The tradition to which More refers is, of course, the 'philosophical' or 'moral cabbala'. (More, incidentally, mentions elsewhere that Adam was also a source of ancient theology.)[15]

The most compelling evidence for the Mosaic origin of the religions of the ancients was thought to come from the appearance in their writings of doctrines which could not have been the result of rational speculation. In Plato and Pythagoras, for example, More found the specifically Christian doctrine of the Trinity, a doctrine which had never been a proposition of natural theology, and which More reasoned must have come to them indirectly through revelation.[16] It was, as the earliest Christian apologists had proposed:

> a special act of Providence that this hidden *Cabbala* came so seasonably to the knowledge of the *Gentiles*, that it might afore-hand fit them for the easier entertainment of the whole Mystery of Christianity, when in the fullness of time it should be more clearly revealed unto the world.[17]

If the truths revealed to Moses were passed on to Plato and Pythagoras, and subsequently brought out to Asia and Europe, it was nonetheless indisputable that most pagans had showed little evidence of familiarity with these truths. More, having explained how knowledge of God came to the more elevated pagans, proceeded to account for the manifold errors of the masses. First, he elaborated a standard twofold philosophy. The 'Mysterie of God', he says, 'lies not bare to false and adulterous eyes, but is hid and wrapped up in decent coverings from the sight of Vulgar and Carnal men'.[18] The vulgar were thus left to their own devices. To understand the development of their corrupt religion, we need to follow More's dualistic account of the Fall. As noted earlier, More views the Fall essentially as the victory of the material over the spiritual. In the *Conjectura Cabbalistica* this is represented by Adam's soul descending into the matter of the earth – 'he became a downright *Terrestrial Animal*'.[19] As the soul was now subjugated to the body, the religious instinct of man was expressed in 'animal religion' – a religion of the body and not the soul.[20] Accordingly, the sun and the moon became the first deities of pagan idolatry because of 'the *sensible* good they conferred upon hungry mankind'.[21] To these original deities were added a number of other gods (like Bacchus and Ceres) 'which could please or pleasure degenerate mankind in the Body'.[22] It was the atheist Prodicus of Ceos who had originally suggested that man worships those things from which he derives benefit – the sun and the moon primarily, but also rivers and springs, and gods of bread, wine, water and fire.[23] More adapted this classical theory, combining it with his Platonic reading of the first chapters of Genesis.

It is worth reminding ourselves at this point of the ever present relation of these histories of religion and the current religious situation. The question of the essence and origins of idolatry had, for More and others, an important bearing on aspects of Catholicism which were, according to the Protestant view, manifestations of heathenism or 'animal religion'. More's *Antidote*

Against Idolatry purports to demonstrate that Popish religion exhibits all the signs of the idolatry of ancient times. Worship of the Host, invocation of the Saints, and the veneration of Mary showed conclusively, said More, that Catholicism was the worst historical example of the 'sensuality and materiality' which result from the Fall.[24] It is no exaggeration to say that More's whole understanding of the role of idolatry in the history of religion is conditioned by his attitude towards Catholicism. This is borne out by the fact that (like Luther) he regarded Popish religion as the worst manifestation of heathenism. He concludes his 'antidote' with the remarkable observation that the 'Idolatrous Heathen' have a better chance of salvation than those 'of the *Popish* Religion'.[25]

The Platonist Joseph Glanvill similarly stressed the relevance of the events of religious history for the present. Whereas More placed emphasis on idolatry as the first-fruit of the Fall, now epitomised in Catholicism, Glanvill took a broader perspective, suggesting that 'animal religion' results in schism, and that ironically, 'Paganised, degenerated Christendom' is distinguished from the 'Heathen-world' only by its arguments and disputes.[26] Both men thus viewed the Fall and subsequent development of idolatry with their contemporary situation very much at the forefront of their minds.

Like his friend and Cambridge colleague More, Ralph Cudworth also grafted a classical theory of the origin of religion onto the trunk of ancient theology. He relied not upon a 'benefit' or 'utility' theory, but on the more widely accepted euhemerism. Cudworth began with the common assumption that all pagan worship orginated in Egypt. It followed that the names of the various gods of antiquity were simply variants of the names of the gods of Egypt. The Egyptian gods themselves ultimately derived from Ham and his kin, who had originally settled Egypt. Support for this claim came from a comparison of the names of the various gods. The Egyptian equivalent of Jupiter – 'Hammon' or 'Ammon' – is derived from Ham or Cham, whose descendants were known to have settled in Egypt.[27] It was also possible, Cudworth speculated, that the Greek Zeus was named after Ham.[28]

From this euhemeristic theory, with which he explained the origins of popular idolatry, Cudworth moved on to show the continuity of true religion. He informs us that the Egyptians, like the Persians, Syrians and Indians, as well as having a 'vulgar and fabulous theology', had an 'arcane and recondite theology'.[29] At the heart of all of these systems of theology was the revealed doctrine of the Trinity:

> the most ingenious and acute of all Pagan philosophers, the Platonists and Pythagoreans... did notwithstanding not only entertain this trinity of divine hypostases eternal and uncreated, but were also fond of the hypothesis, and made it a fundamental of their theology.[30]

Trinitarian theology was also to be found in the writings of Orpheus, Hermes Trismegistus, as well as that of the Romans and Persians.[31] The conclusion drawn by Cudworth was that there existed 'a theology of divine tradition or revelation, or a divine cabala' amongst the Hebrews which was 'from them afterwards communicated to the Egyptians and other nations'.[32]

The theory of the *prisca theologia*, as it was expounded in the eighteenth century, encountered a major stumbling block as a result of advances in textual scholarship. In 1614, the Greek scholar and Church historian Isaac Casaubon redated the *Hermetica*, placing it well within the Christian era.[33] While not denying the existence of Hermes Trismegistus, Casaubon disputed that he had had anything to do with the writings generally attributed to him, suggesting that they were probably Christian forgeries. Clearly if Casaubon's researches were taken seriously, the view that Egypt was the fountainhead of pagan wisdom would become highly suspect and the whole edifice of the ancient theology would threaten to come tumbling down. In fact, Casaubon's work produced varied reactions. Some, like Robert Fludd and Athanasius Kircher, continued to extol the virtues of the *Hermetica* as if there was no problem at all.[34]

More and Cudworth, however, were too acute simply to ignore Casaubon's findings.[35] Cudworth, while conceding a late date for the *Hermetica*, could still argue that its general acceptance in the Christian period meant that it accurately represented an ancient Hermaic tradition and was an authentic account of the doctrines of Hermes.[36] More noted the existence of non-Christian doctrines in the *Hermetica* and cited these as evidence that the Hermaic writings were not simply Christian forgeries.[37] Nonetheless he treated the appearance of the doctrine of the Trinity in the Hermetic writings with some scepticism, and his *Conjectura Cabbalistica* is virtually devoid of references to Hermes Trismegistus. Both men tended to divert importance from Hermes to Plato and Pythagoras. Despite devices of this sort, the hypothesis of the ancient theology, particularly while it relied upon Hermes Trismegistus as the main conduit of revealed knowledge from Jewish sources to the pagan world, seemed doomed to founder upon the rock of textual criticism. The sentiment behind the ancient theology, however, showed considerable resilience, and the belief that God's revelation to the Jews had found its way into all cultures was still cherished by many students of sacred history.

Robert Jenkin is a typical example of the pervasiveness of an attenuated ancient theology. 'In the first Ages of the world', he tells us, 'the revealed will of God was known to all Mankind'.[38] It was preserved in the antediluvian world because of the longevity of mankind, and the similarity of languages.[39] Following the dispersion which resulted from the confusion of languages, there remained the opportunity for nations to come to know God, for the Israelites had 'dealings' – trade – with the whole world, including the Americas.[40] Accordingly, there are 'footsteps to be found in Heathen Authors, of what the Scriptures deliver to us', and further, 'several Allusions and Representations in the Rites and Ceremonies of their Religions, expressing, though obscurely and confusedly, the chief points of the scripture story'.[41] Jenkin's concern in all of this was not merely to elaborate an historical thesis, but to show that at all times and in all places, individuals had had the opportunity to respond to divine revelation. This motivation can be seen most clearly in Jenkin's claim that not only were God's revelations to Adam, Noah, and Moses spread across the globe, but that Christianity itself, from its inception, had been preached throughout the entire world.[42]

In its weakest form, the central concept of the ancient theology survived as the view which we might term 'plagiarism'. Advocates of this view held simply that, in Nathaniel Culverwel's words, 'the whole generality of the Heathen went a gleaning in Jewish Fields'.[43] Plagiarism, in the Enlightenment and the preceding century, was virtually an axiom of historical research. There might be disagreements about whether the Jews had pilfered ancient learning from the Egyptians or whether the reverse had been the case, or even whether India or China had been the cradle of civilisation, but it was generally acknowledged that higher culture began in a single place, and was disseminated thence to other countries. It is not insignificant that after the ancient theology proper had reached its zenith in England, it enjoyed some success in France. But with the redating of the *Hermetica* and the waning of interest in the religions of dead civilisations, it had quite a new focus – the religion of China.

Robert Fludd, champion of the single-source theory, had a continental counterpart in the person of Daniel Huet, bishop of Avranches. Huet's *Demonstratio Evangelica* (1679) followed Fludd's agenda, tracing every aspect of human culture back to Moses. Its thoroughness and detail surpassed even Fludd's. All the gods and goddesses, all the myths of the classics, and even of Egypt, are shown to have originated in Mosaic history.[44] As in England, while few were prepared to go as far as Huet, many were willing to spell out the implications of such a view for the history of religion. The factor which was significantly different in France was the presence of Jesuit priests who had served time as missionaries in China. These men brought about a revival, or to use Walker's words, a 'survival', of ancient theology in late seventeenth-century France. The contentions of these individuals require our brief attention because in the seventeenth century they found their way back into England.[45]

The factor which gave fresh impetus to the theory of a *prisca theologia* on the continent was the view that traces of ancient theology could be found in the history and philosophy of ancient China, and in documents the antiquity of which was far more certain than that of the *Corpus Hermeticum* and *Orphica*. The general tendencies of the beliefs of the Jesuit missionaries concerning China are perhaps best seen in these six propositions which were condemned by the Sorbonne in 1700:

i.   During more than 2,000 years before the birth of Jesus Christ, China preserved the knowledge of the true God.

ii. It had the honour of sacrificing to him in the most ancient temple of the universe.

iii. It honoured him in a manner which was able to serve as an example even to the Christians.

iv. It practised a moral code as pure as religion.

v.   It had the faith, humility, interior and exterior cult, priesthood, sacrifices, sanctity, miracles, the spirit of God, and purest charity, which is the character and the perfection of true religion.

vi. Of all the nations of the world, China has been the most constantly favoured by the graces of God.[46]

These propositions are a summary of the views of Louis Le Comte, expressed in his *Noveaux Mémoirs sur l'état présent de la Chine* (1696).[47] Le Comte's work appeared in England in 1699, bearing the title *Memoirs and Observations ... Made in a Late Journey through the Empire of China*, and ran to several editions.[48] Le Comte, despite experience as a missionary in China, drew freely upon Phillipe Couplet's lengthy preface to the first Latin translation of Confucius.[49] Both Le Comte and Couplet expressed the view that the people of China had for some centuries possessed knowledge of the true God, from tradition as well as from nature.[50] Unlike pagan culture, where but a few enlightened philosophers adhered to the true faith, the Chinese populace as a whole had resisted the degeneration into superstition, and therein lay their particular merit.[51] The source of China's theology was, according to Le Comte and Couplet, of great antiquity, pre-dating even Moses. The most likely candidate was Noah's son Shem. Said Le Comte:

> The Children of *Noah*, who were scattered all over eastern parts of *Asia*, and in all probability founded this Empire, being themselves in the time of the Deluge witnesses of the Omnipotence of their Creator, transmitted the knowledge of him, and instilled the fear of him into all their descendants; the footsteps which we find in their Histories, will not let us doubt the truth of this.[52]

Conjectures of this kind were ultimately to rely upon historical, and even linguistic evidence. The possibility that China was a locus of ancient theology was considered in England mostly on evidence of the latter kind, and we shall be exploring these conjectures in some detail below. First, however, we shall give some attention to a major offshoot of ancient theology – comparative mythology.

COMPARATIVE RELIGION: MYTHOLOGY, EUHEMERISM, AND PAGANO-PAPISM

Questions about the authenticity of such documents as the *Hermetica* and the *Sibyls* had placed severe limitations on attempts to resurrect the Patristic and Renaissance doctrine of the ancient theology. Apart from the Cambridge circle with its apologia for Platonic thought and the French Jesuits with their reverence for Confucian ideals, the view fell considerably short of general acceptance. Another offshoot of the single-source theory which enjoyed considerably more vogue was comparative mythology. Like ancient theology, this approach stressed the derivative nature of all gentile mythologies, most often by reducing them to variants of Hebrew history. Like ancient theology, it had also been foreshadowed by the fathers and by Renaissance scholars. The sixteenth-century chronologer Joseph Scaliger had laid the foundations of this discipline in *De emendatione temporum* (1583).[53] Scaliger insisted that biblical chronology always be compared with, and interpreted by, profane histories:

> Wherefore, if someone most skilled in sacred history ... were able to refer none of these things to a certain epoch of Greek or Roman history, what assistance can he offer from careful study of this kind, either to himself or to those who are students of antiquities? For the end of all knowledge is to do with some purpose, and if you remove this from letters, all toil and effort spent on all studies is wasted.[54]

De emendatione was unique amongst chronologies of its time, in that it was a reconstruction of the past which was independent of moral and religious considerations. Scripture remained the most important focus, but other authorities for the first time were accorded an almost equal status.[55] While much of Scaliger's painstaking research proved useful to his fellow historians, few adopted his methods until the eighteenth century, when historical chronology was already in decline. At this time, Scaliger's approach was preserved in comparative mythology.

Perhaps the most popular eighteenth-century attempt to follow Scaliger's prescription was Samuel Shuckford's *Sacred and Profane History of the World Connected* (1728). This work contains most of the elements of comparative mythology, albeit in a rudimentary and unselfconscious form. Shuckford began with the now-familiar assertion of primitive monotheism: 'All the ancient Religions in the World were originally the same.'[56] Moreover, the ancient histories of the various authors were generally conformed to Mosaic history.[57] Three factors had contributed to the apparent proliferation of gods in antiquity – the corruption of the original religion by kings and rulers, the corruption of historical texts, and the linguistic habits of ancient peoples.[58] These together conspired to conceal the original unity of human religion.

The most interesting aspect of Shuckford's theory of religious evolution is his understanding of the parallel development of linguistic diversity and religious diversity. Admixture, travel, and climate are all identified by Shuckford as secondary causes of religious diversity, their primary influence being on language itself.[59] This linguistic diversity led in turn to an apparent religious diversity, which in time became actual. At first, names for the celestial deities were multiplied. The sun, for example, was variously designated Pil, Pal, Pel, Baal, Bal, Bel, Belo, Belus, Phel, Phil, Pul.[60] The uncritical antiquarian might easily be led to believe that each of these appellations referred to a different god, and thus be deceived into thinking that the various systems of pagan religion were more disparate and polytheistic than in fact they were. The key to a proper understanding of pagan religion was provided by etymological insights which enabled the careful researcher to penetrate superficial verbal differences and uncover a hidden religious unity. It was not only the names of heavenly bodies which were supposed to have proliferated. Shuckford points out that 'a Variety of Names are given to the Men of the first Ages, by writers of different nations'.[61] Only by tracing the mutations of names over time could the original identity of the actors in the old stories and myths be established. Given that many of these multi-named personages were later to have deity conferred upon them, the other vital key which would unlock the secrets of universal history was the theory of euhemerism. By assuming that the anthropomorphic gods of the ancient world had once been men, myths concerning the gods could be rendered into history. Says Shuckford: 'That *Mythology* came in upon this Alteration of their *Theology*, is obviously evident. for [sic] the mingling the [sic] History of these Men when Mortals, with what came to be ascribed to them when Gods, would naturally occasion it.'[62] Etymology and euhemerism could together show that despite appearances, pagan myths were all about the same thing, namely, important events in the first Ages of the world.

The more conservative of Shuckford's speculations involved equating the various pagan gods. The Egyptian 'Thyoth' was the same god as the Greek Hermes and the Roman Mercury.[63] His more imaginative constructions connected sacred history with pagan mythology. The Indian Bacchus was none other than Noah, whose ark had landed somewhere near India.[64] Noah was also the first king of China, known in their records as Fo-hi.[65] Noah's immediate offspring also figured in the myths of many cultures. His son Ham, for example, was known in pagan mythology as Chronus or Saturn.[66]

Many of Shuckford's points had already been made in the context of other discussions of man's early religious history, and a number of writers had similarly deployed euhemerism and to a lesser extent etymology. Sir Walter Raleigh informs us, on the authority of the fathers, that Cain, the son of Adam, 'was reputed for the first and ancient *Jupiter*', while Adam himself, 'for the first *Saturne*'.[67] The Cambridge Platonists similarly incorporated euhemerism into their accounts of religious development, to show how the vulgar, as distinct from those arcane custodians of the ancient theology, had perverted their original deposit of religion. Of the pagans, More informs us that '*Eminent* persons whom they could not but acknowledge as their great benefactors', came to be worshipped.[68] Cudworth made the explicit link to sacred history, and utilised the etymological method. The Egyptian equivalent of Jupiter, he notes, is 'Hammon' or 'Ammon', which was 'probably derived from Ham or Cham, the son of Noah, whose posterity reportedly settled in Egypt'. Thus too, the Greek Zeus was also named after Ham.[69]

Mainstream Christian apologists also relied on euhemerism, still claiming that the best in pagan religion was derived from the Judaeo-Christian tradition. Robert Jenkin declared, as if to a second-century audience, that 'it has been made evident by divers learned men, that the most ancient, and the very best of the Heathen Gods were but Men whom the Scriptures mention as worshippers of the True God, such as *Noah, Joseph, Moses*, etc.'[70] Matthew Hale identified Noah with Saturn, Japheth with Neptune, Ham with Jupiter, and Shem with Pluto.[71] Other stalwarts – Bishop Stillingfleet, Timothy Nourse, and Alexander Ross, to mention but three – also took up the theory with enthusiasm.[72]

At the other end of the theological spectrum, freethinkers favoured euhemeristic explanations second only to their beloved priestcraft theory. Herbert devoted a chapter of *The Antient Religion of the Gentiles* to 'the worship of heroes' in antiquity.[73] He also employed etymology to reduce the pagan pantheon to a manageable size.[74] Blount and Toland likewise made use of the theory.[75] Such were the attractions of comparative mythology and euhemerism that even the great Isaac Newton took time away from the laws of the physical universe to write a euhemerist history of religion.[76] Newton stated simply that the worship of one true God was observed 'by all nations while they lived together in Chaldea under the government of Noah and his sons & afterwards by the Chaldeans, Canaanites & Hebrews & til they began to worship to their dead kings'.[77]

If there were few novel elements in Shuckford's *Sacred and Profane History*, it is nonetheless true that his overall purpose was different from that of his predecessors. Shuckford wished to show that all of the historical and mythological writings of antiquity had the same subject – the first events of world history. In the second half of the eighteenth century this kind of project evolved into a self-conscious comparative mythology of the type most usually associated with Max Müller. Jacob Bryant's voluminous *Analysis of Antient Mythology* (vols. I, II, 1774, vol. III, 1776) is perhaps the first example of the genre. The true history of the first ages could be reconstructed, according to Bryant, by 'arranging and comparing the mythology of ancient times'. Moreover, the religious practices of the ancients could teach much about early history, 'the principal circumstances of which are continually observable in the rites and ceremonies of the first ages'.[78] 'All the rites and mysteries of the Gentiles', says Bryant, along with their 'antient hymns', are 'related to the history of the first ages, and to the same events which are recorded by Moses'.[79]

Of all the events of Mosaic history, that which provided the most conspicuous point of connection for all ancient myths and histories was the Flood. The Deluge was a natural focus for comparative historians because it appeared in a number of records of antiquity – Berosus, Polyhistor, Plato, and Strabo.[80] Bryant and his fellow mythologists thus tended to regard the Deluge as the most important feature of every Gentile history. It was the grand epoch of every ancient kingdom. From this it followed that if the genealogy of all of the princes of antiquity could be traced back across linguistic boundaries, it would be found that 'under whatever title he may come ... the first king in every country was Noah'.[81]

Bryant, like Shuckford, relied upon the indispensable tools of euhemerism and etymology.[82] Granted that the first king of every nation was Noah, and that ancient myths arose through the attribution of divine status to past heroes and kings, it followed that the gods of antiquity were actually Noah and his sons, disguised with other names, and dressed in the garb of divinity. Noah, according to Bryant, was 'one of the first among the sons of men to whom divine honours would be paid'.[83] Bryant fancifully asserts that Noah was variously styled Prometheus, Deucalion, Atlas, Theuth, Zuth, Xuthus, Inachus, Osiris, Helius, Zeus, Dios, Dionusos, Bacchus, Naus, and Nous.[84] Later, he tells us that Noah was also Thoth, Hermes and Menes, 'to which list a farther number of great extent may be added'.[85] Fortunately, Bryant does not furnish us with any more of Noah's divine alter-egos, beyond mentioning that he was also Saturn and Janus.

In the early decades of the seventeenth century, chronologists had tended to be conservative in the derivation of the names of heathen deities from the Jewish patriarchs. Bryant threw caution to the winds. When, for example, he encountered some difficulties relating pagan goddesses and the Oriental Buddha to Noah and his family, he reasoned along the following lines. The Indian Buto, or Budo, 'is the same name as Boutas of Egypt, Battus of Cyrene, and Boeotus of Greece'. These names, while apparently conferred upon the patriarch, actually refer to the Ark. This insight is established in the following derivation:

> One of the Amonian names for the Ark were [sic] Aren, and Arene: and Boeotus is said by Diodorus Siculus to have been the son of Neptune and Arne, which is a contraction of Arene, the ark. The chief city Boutus, in Egypt, where was the floating temple, signified properly the city of the float or Ark. The Boeotians, who, in the Dionusiaca, so particularly commemorated the Ark, were supposed to be descended from an imaginary personage Boeotus; and from him likewise their country was thought to have received its name. But Boeotus was merely a variation of Boutus, and Butus, the Ark; which in antient times was indifferently styled Theba, Argus, Aren, Butus, and Boeotus.[86]

In a similar vein, Bryant laboured to convince his readers that the Ark was also the origin of the heathen goddesses Melitta, Rhea, Cybele, Damater, Isis, and Athena.[87]

Bryant's speculations place him in a different category from Shuckford and his predecessors. No-one who has read Max Müller's *Introduction to the Science of Religion* or his *Comparative Mythology* can fail to be struck by the similarity between his etymological approach and that of Bryant.[88] Müller, of course, had many more materials at his disposal and was less committed to the centrality of the Deluge story. Yet for both Bryant and Müller, comparison had become a vital element of a scientific approach to texts and to history. As Müller was to express it: 'all higher knowledge is gained by comparison, and rests on comparison'. The fundamental character of scientific research was, according to Müller, comparative.[89] Bryant, despite his obvious preference for the sacred records of the Judaeo-Christian tradition, would have agreed. For Shuckford, on the other hand, and those who came before him, comparison was carried out for different reasons. Shuckford was still concerned to refute the claims of deism – that man could naturally attain, and in the first ages had naturally attained, the essential truths of religion. A comparison of sacred and profane history would, he believed, vindicate his position: that all of the religious knowledge of our remote ancestors had been revealed to a parent culture.[90] The bulk of the euhemerist-historians were even more overtly polemical. Much of the popularity of euhemerism as an explanation of pagan mythology derived from its inherent anti-Catholicism. The link between the worship of dead men and the Catholic veneration of the saints was an obvious one. 'Nor ought we to forget', says Toland, 'that this new Idolatry of the Christians is altogether grounded, as that of the antient Heathens, on the excessive veneration of dead Men and Women'.[91] The parallel between euhemerism and the Catholic cult of the saints was similarly exploited by Thomas Blount,

Theophilus Gale, Henry More, Henry Smith, Edward Stillingfleet, and many others.[92] Even Newton, on account of his euhemerist chronologies, was accused by French savant Nicolas Fréret of anti-Catholic bias.[93]

The incipient anti-Catholicism of euhemerism is but one example of a whole style of comparative religion which we have designated 'Pagano-papism'.[94] Luther, we recall, was the first to exploit other religions in anti-Catholic polemic. By comparing 'Papism', 'Mahometanism', and Judaism, he attempted to show that they were in essence the same, and that a number of parallels between their various beliefs and practices could be established. Numerous works in the seventeenth and eighteenth centuries adopted this as their theme.[95] Indeed, many so-called 'historical' investigations into the origin of idolatry were embarked upon with only one purpose in mind – to demonstrate that the idolatry of the heathens was no different in principle to that of the Catholics.[96] Of the polemical works of this type, the most thorough are perhaps Theophilus Gale's *The Court of the Gentiles* (1669–77), and the later piece by Conyers Middleton, *A Letter from Rome, shewing an Exact Conformity between Popery and Paganism* (1729). Gale's thesis was that pagan philosophy tended naturally to degenerate into idolatry, polytheism, and finally atheism.[97] Through the Greek fathers, this pagan philosophy had entered the Church, and had festered there unchecked until the Reformation.[98] Catholicism was thus the true heir of paganism. Specific examples of the vestiges of the old pagan ways included mystic and scholastic theology, canon law, the cult of the saints, hymns, fetes, plays, images, crosses, relics, the mass, the Catholic hierarchy, 'and many rites'.[99] Fifty years later the reading public had still not tired of hearing of these rather forced affinities between Rome and the heathen world. Middleton's *Letter from Rome* ran to a number of editions and was reprinted into the nineteenth century. Yet there is little in it which had not already been said. He traces the pagan origins of 'Incense, Holy Water, Lamps and Candles, Votive offerings, Images, Chapels on the way-sides and tops of Hills, Processions, Miracles', along with the cult of the saints, putative miracles, and the veneration of Mary.[100]

The papists were not the only ones to suffer by comparison. Parallels were also drawn between other religions and the deists and Socinians. John Toland, in particular, was singled out as an infidel. One 'Dr South' apparently dubbed him 'a certain *Mahometan Christian*',[101] while John Norris, in his critique of *Christianity not Mysterious*, thought him a Socinian who might as well be a Mahometan.[102] Jean Gailhard, who thought to dismiss both Toland and the Socinians with one protracted stroke of the pen, noted that the Jews were 'enemies to our Lord Jesus', who with Mahometans and Socinians join in blasphemy.[103] These criticisms show how any groups or individuals who questioned aspects of the mystery of the Trinity were liable to be regarded as 'Jewes' or 'Mahometans'. In his broad overview of Socinian beliefs, John Edwards maintained that Socinians had drunk deeply at the well of heterodoxy, their beliefs being a compound of virtually all of the trinitarian heresies which had ever been published. They were Ebionites, Sabellians, Samosatenians, Arians, Photinians, and Macedonians. But ultimately he identifies them not with the heretics, but with '*Jews, Pagans,* and *Mahometans*', all of whom deny the great mystery of the Trinity.[104]

The deists were by no means merely the victims of these sorts of comparisons. On the contrary, one of their chief objections to traditional Christianity was that it differed only superficially from heathenism. We have already considered their views of the role of the priests in all religions, but their comparisons went well beyond this. Toland pointed out that the Christian mysteries were virtually indistinguishable from those of the first century mystery religions, implying that Christian rites had a pagan origin.[105] The Christian appeal to Scripture rather than reason was compared to the 'Mahometans'' adherence to their 'Alcoran' or 'Poran'.[106] Finally, in their attempted suppression of free-thinking, the ecclesiastical authorities were little different from 'Popish' or 'Dominican inquisitors'.[107] Other odious comparisons abound in the writings of the free-thinkers, in keeping with the more critical deist view that all historical religions were so many different manifestations of superstition.[108]

The most strained comparisons of all attempted to establish connexions between the non-conforming Protestant sects and Papism. Strangely, many late seventeenth-century writers accused the Quakers of being Rome's fifth column. William Prynne believed the Quakers to be 'but the spawn of Romish frogs, Jesuites, and Franciscan Friars; sent from Rome to seduce the intoxicated giddy-headed English nation'.[109] John Brown, Francis Bugg, Charles Derby and many others pursued this unlikely thesis with vigour and determination.[110] Even more far-fetched was Sir Roger L'Estrange's claim that Presbyterianism was only superficially different from popery.[111]

Only a few isolated writers saw in the comparison of Christianity with other religions possibilities for the betterment of their own creed. Henry More, searching for a means of reconciling divine providence with the existence of so many barbarous nations, suggested that cultural differences were divinely ordained so that the natives of one country might learn by seeing their own faults expressed in different and exaggerated ways in those of other lands. Thus, says More, 'we become a mutual Theatre one to another, and are in a better capacity of censuring what is evil in our selves by reflecting upon others; the deformities we espie in others being nothing but a reprehensible Parable touching our selves'.[112] More's insight was later to find expression in the moral and didactic elements of the fantastic voyage literature. Swift's *Gulliver's Travels* and Montesquieu's *Lettres Persanes* are the better-known examples of the genre, but these are far more general in scope, and their fictional character distances them from specific studies of religion.

We can conclude that while much comparison of 'religions' took place in the seventeenth and eighteenth centuries, most of it was motivated not by any deep interest in the religious faith of other peoples, but by the desire to score points from theological adversaries. For this reason the so-called religions of the Orient were made in the image of their presumed western counterparts. Unfortunately, the paradigms of these new 'religions' were the undesirable religious forms of Christendom – be it papism, Calvinism, Socinianism, deism, Presbyterianism, or episcopacy. Only a few individuals saw in the comparison of religions possibilities for a systematic and objective study of religious phenomena. Herbert of Cherbury, Joseph Glanvill, and a few of the deists thought that some natural essence of religion might emerge from an examination of various religious forms, but these early ventures into comparative religion were severely hindered by a lack of accurate data, and by the researchers' predilection for *a priori* explanations. In any case, comparison was not thought to provide a sufficiently scientific basis for the study of religion. Natural history, it was thought, could place the study of religion on a similar footing to the natural sciences. Before we turn our attention to natural history, however, there was one further development in the history of religion which we should examine.

If the comparative aspect of Müller's science of religion began with seventeenth- and eighteenth-century chronologists and polemicists, the linguistic aspect began here as well – not only in the curious etymological speculations of such antiquarians as Bryant, but in more general theories of the origin and development of human language. Comparative linguistics, theories of a 'deep grammar', and the positivist critique of religious language are all present, albeit in a rudimentary form, in early speculations about the link between language and religion.

THE CONFUSION OF LANGUAGES AND LINGUISTIC THEORIES OF RELIGION

Whatever differences there might have been between them, sacred historians, comparative mythologists, and champions of the ancient theology all agreed that along with the Fall and the Deluge, the events which took place at Babel had had an irreversible effect upon the history of religion. Babel had led to dispersion – travel into different geographical areas which in one way or another had shaped religious beliefs and practices. Babel had, moreover, severed that link of communication between the earliest patriarchs and their descendants, effectively halting the transmission of ancient divine truths. Finally, because different names for God had arisen, Babel had led to an appearance of religious pluralism, which, it was generally agreed, led to a *de facto* pluralism.[113]

The possibility that the primitive language of mankind had been preserved somewhere on the globe excited many seventeenth-century imaginations. One hypothesis was that the speakers of the ancient language of mankind would have been able to preserve the religion, culture and science of the patriarchs. The French Jesuits, as we have seen, were inclined to the view that the inhabitants of China had maintained, more or less intact, the original language and religion of the world. While a fierce controversy raged on the continent between those unyielding institutions, the Sorbonne and the Société de Jésus, a related discussion was taking place in England about China. Here the approach was quite different, the primary focus being on the language and antiquity of China – questions which actually formed the prolegomena to the more ambitious claims of the Jesuit missionaries. China exercised a peculiar fascination over English minds in the seventeenth century, partly on account of its apparent 'deism', but also because of its unique mode of writing.[114] Interest in the latter aspect of Chinese culture began in England with a passing remark by Francis Bacon on the subject of Chinese characters. In *The Advancement of Learning* (1603), Bacon had noted that 'it is the use of China, and the kingdoms of the High Levant to write in characters real, which express neither letters nor words in gross, but things or notions'. As a result, he said, 'countries and provinces, which understand not one another's language, can nevertheless read one another's writings'.[115] 'Real Characters' (symbols which had a real, rather than an arbitrary link with the objects which they symbolised) were of interest to Bacon because they were a possible key to a universal language – a means of communication which would contribute considerably to the advancement of learning.

The discussions about the possibility of a universal language which were to become commonplace in the second half of the seventeenth century had two related aspects.[116] There were, for those of historical and speculative bent, questions about the language of Adam, the mode of its writing, the confusion of tongues at Babel, and the possibility that the primitive language had survived in some form to the present era. On the other side were those visionaries who thought more about the construction of an artificial universal language, and the power of good that such a language might exercise in the world.[117] The events which occurred at Babel were the key to both endeavours, for Babel was not just an event of momentous import in universal history, but had become a potent descriptive image of the contemporary religious situation. The shattering of the unity of a monolithic medieval Christendom had resulted in religious confusion of vast proportions, and while few English writers were inclined to liken the Reformation to Babel, many saw in the proliferation of Protestant sects a situation not unlike that which followed upon that momentous event on the plains of Shinar. 'Babel was never half so much confus'd', rued Samuel Butler.[118] On the positive side, more optimistic souls expressed the hope that the creation of a new universal language would overcome the set-back of Babel, and most importantly, bring about a reduction of religious conflicts. Indeed, it was the cherished ambition of many of the champions of a modern universal language to restore the kind of religious uniformity which they believed had characterised the antediluvian world with its single *Lingua Humana*.

In England such hopes were inspired by the activities of the Bohemian theologian and pedagogue, Johann Amos Comenius. Bacon's observations about real characters and a universal language, said Comenius, should not be idly dismissed as a fanciful dream. Rather they should act as a spur to research into a language based on real characters:

> If this is a good thing and seems to be advantageous, why should we not rather devote ourselves studiously to the discovery of a Real Language (which all men equally could understand, whether their business was to be done with the tongue or with the hand); to the discovery not only of a language but of thought and, what is more, of truth of things themselves at the same time?[119]

Bacon's interest in a universal language, as we might expect, was to do with the 'advancement of learning'. Comenius, for all his interest in education, saw it primarily as a means of healing religious breaches in the world. His vision was of a unified mankind sharing common expressions of those universal innate principles which comprise the 'roots of Human General Intelligence'.[120] The major obstacle to the achievement of this goal was 'the multitude, the variety, the confusion of languages'.[121] This confusion was particularly acute in religious disagreements, for wordy disputation was seen to cloud the common, innate core of all human religious experience. Comenius felt that when the 'terms and meanings' in such disputes were examined, differences would be found to exist 'not in fundamentals', but 'only in the manner of expressing them'.[122] Hence the need for a universal language. If such a language were propagated, says Comenius, 'all men will become as it were one race, one people, one household, one School of God'. There will be, he declares, 'universal Peace over the whole world, hatred and the causes of hatred will be done away, and all dissention between men'. 'For', he continues, 'there will be no ground for dissenting when all men have the same Truths clearly presented to their eyes'.[123]

There is little doubt that Comenius' work stimulated the well-known seventeenth-century interest in a universal language and a real character.[124] From the time of Comenius' visit in 1641, his *Via lucis* circulated in England in manuscript form until its publication in 1668, when it was dedicated to the Royal Society. Before this visit there were no publications on these topics, but quite a number thereafter.[125] Furthermore, two key writers on artificial languages – Samuel Hartlib and Bishop Wilkins – had close links with the Czech. The activities of Wilkins, one of the founders of the Royal Society, evidence the interest which that august body had in universal languages. In the same year as the appearance of Comenius' *Via Lucis*, Wilkins published his famous *Essay Towards a Real Character and a Philosophical Language* in which he outlined a scheme for an artificial universal language which, in the words of Robert Boyle, could 'make amends to mankind for what their pride lost to them at the tower of Babel'.[126] Seth Ward likewise averred that if the natural language of Adam was beyond recovery – and some of his contemporaries were to argue this very point – then a scheme such as Wilkins' was the next best thing: 'Such a language as this', he said, 'might not unjustly be termed a naturall Language, and would afford that which the *Cabalists* and *Rosycrucians* have vainly sought for in the Hebrew, and in the names of things assigned by Adam'.[127] The Bishop himself had high hopes for his invention. As well as facilitating communication in the sciences, it would, he said, 'very much conduce to the spreading of the knowledge of *Religion*', in much the same way that the gift of tongues had at Pentecost.[128] He went on to express the desire:

> That this design will likewise contribute much to the clearing of some of our Modern differences in *Religion*, by unmasking many wild errors, that shelter themselves under the disguise of affected phrases; which being Philosophically unfolded, and rendered according to the genuine and natural importance of Words, will appear to be inconsistencies and contradictions. And several of those pretended, mysterious, profound notions, expressed in great swelling words, whereby some men set up for reputation, being this way examined, will appear to be, either nonsense, or very flat and jejune.[129]

Another cleric, the Reverend Cave Beck, Rector of St Helen's, Ipswich, expressed similar hopes for his universal character, maintaining that it would be 'a singular means of propagating all sorts of Learning and true Religion in the world'.[130] Judging by the panegyrics which were printed along with the work, it too was well received. Ben Gifford likened Beck's achievement to the miracle of Pentecost, and spoke of 'reprieve' from 'Babel's curse'.[131] Other admirers spoke similarly of Beck's work as a reversal of Babel.[132] Yet another divine who saw in universal language a panacea for the religious ills of England was the Bishop of Kilmore, William Bedell.[133] Bedell was writing a work which dealt specifically with the link between religious disputation and ambiguous language, when the outbreak of the civil war prevented its completion.[134] According to Gilbert Burnet, Bedell's biographer, the Bishop cherished the hope that in the future controversies could be 'handled without the vain flourish of swelling words', and that this would consequently resolve many current difficulties and be 'useful to the Church'.[135]

The religious concord hoped for by Wilkins, Beck, and Bedell appears to be somewhat more restricted and parochial than the grand vision of Comenius. While they spoke grandly of Babel and Pentecost, it was probably the local squabbles between Protestants which they had in mind when they referred to the healing of religious breaches. They were formally committed to one creed of Christianity and when they spoke of religious discord, were disinclined (to use Locke's turn of phrase) to look beyond the smoke of their own chimneys. For the most part, only those who elevated an incorruptible innate religiosity over all of its particular expressions could disentangle themselves sufficiently from a restrictive loyalty to Protestantism to entertain the dream of a truly universal religion. Such men were the Platonists and free-thinkers. The latter, for their part, were more interested in utilising reason as a tool which could isolate religious fundamentals and bring about a religious peace and a common natural religion. Reason, for them, was the universal language.

One figure who, while not a Platonist, shared some of their commitments and subscribed to Comenius' vision of a universal religion and a universal language was the enigmatic figure John Webster.[136] Webster, whose writings betray an unlikely combination of influences ranging from Bacon to the German mystic Böhme, is of particular significance for us because he discusses the nature of the *Lingua Adamica*, and by implication suggests not the *construction* of an artificial universal language, but the *recovery* of the natural universal language. Unlike the deists, he saw little hope in ever giving expression to an innate, natural religion, except by means of an innate, natural language. Such a language was given by God to Adam:

> No truly, the mind receiveth but one single and simple image of every thing, which is expressed in all by the same motions of the spirits, and doubtlessly in every creature hath radically, and naturally the same sympathy in voice, and sound, but men not understanding these immediate sounds of the soul, and the true *Schematism* of the internal notions impressed, and delineated in the several sounds, have instituted and imposed others, that do not altogether concord, and agree to the innate notions, and so no care is taken for the recovery and restauration of the Catholique language in which lies hid all the rich treasury of natures admirable and excellent secrets.[137]

Webster makes it clear that Adam possessed these 'admirable and excellent secrets' of nature, for in his naming of objects, Adam correctly characterised their true nature: 'the name being exactly conformable, and configurate to the *Idæa* in his mind, the very prolation, and sound of the word' containing in it 'the vive expression of the thing'.[138] This meant that Adam had perfect knowledge of the 'internal natures, vertues, effects, operations, and qualities' of those objects for which he had names.[139] Thus, when this pure language of nature was 'so miserably lost and defaced' in the Fall, Adam's knowledge of the natural world and its workings was lost as well. Webster does imply, however, that some of this knowledge might have been preserved through the use of real characters. 'Was not the expressions of things by Emblems, and *Hieroglyphics* not only antient', he exclaims, 'but in and by them what great mysteries have been preserved and holden out to the world?'[140] Would not universal characters, such as those of the Chinese, 'have repaired the ruines of *Babell*, and have been almost a Catholick Cure for the confusion of tongues', he asks.[141]

Whether these hieroglyphics or the characters of the Chinese are, or derive from, the original real characters, Webster does not say. Two implications of his thoughts are clear, however. First is the possibility that the primitive language might well be recovered. Second, that the rediscovery of such a language might greatly contribute towards the knowledge of nature, for with the language of Adam would come the knowledge of Adam. This means that the goal of religious harmony should not be thought of as fundamentally different from that of establishing an Omni-Science and a means of communicating scientific knowledge universally.[142]

A universal language, then, would enable a clear and unambiguous expression of innate religiosity – 'those immediate sounds of the soul' – while at the same time unlocking the secrets of Nature's operations. For, in the words of Webster, what else is Nature but the '*Hieroglyphics* of his [God's] invisible power'. The language of nature was the Rosetta Stone which could make these hieroglyphics yield their secrets. As John Webb expressed it, recovery of the primitive language could unearth 'that GOLDEN-MINE of Learning, which from all ANTIQUITY hath lain concealed in the PRIMITIVE TONGUE'.[143] These sentiments better enable us to appreciate the considerable interest of the Royal Society in real characters – not that the Society was uninterested in promoting religious peace, on the contrary[144] – but there was also the optimistic belief that for the first time since Adam and the patriarchs, Nature's secrets were about to be divulged. The overcoming of Bacon's 'second curse' would also compensate for the losses of knowledge which accompanied the Fall. For this reason, the Royal Society hedged its bets regarding a universal language. While they were not unhappy with the achievements of Wilkins in crafting a language and a character, they also saw fit to commission Robert Hooke to investigate those ancient Chinese characters which some said were of the type first used by man. (Even Wilkins himself had admitted that 'no humane invention, but Divine creation can make any thing perfect on the sudden'.)[145] Thus the wheel turned full circle. The quest for a new universal language which would advance knowledge in all its forms led back to an enquiry into sacred history, and to the stories of Adam, Noah, and the tower of Babel, in hope of tracing the fortunes of the first language.

There were a number of conjectures concerning the possible fate of the language of Adam. First, it may not have survived even to the time of Babel, having degenerated because of the Fall or through natural processes.[146] Second, the language may have been preserved intact through the Deluge – perhaps because of the longevity of the first men, or because of the art of writing – but have been destroyed at Babel.[147] Third, the original language may have survived the confusion of tongues. This would be possible if not all peoples were present at Babel, or if there had been a form of writing before Babel which could still be deciphered afterwards. In either event, it was possible that the *Lingua Adamica* still existed in the world in some form – spoken or written. It was this third possibility which fired the imaginations of those dedicated to the rediscovery of the universal language.

Critics of the quest pointed out that those very mechanisms of corruption which were thought to have acted on natural religion would have changed the natural language beyond recognition. Admixture, travel and climate were cited as reasons why, even in the event of the survival of natural language beyond Babel, it was extremely unlikely that it should have lasted five thousand years to the present. The corruption of religion was closely linked with the corruption of language, and some went as far as to say that the latter was the cause of the former. John Milton noted that languages degenerate by 'the usually corrupt pronunciation of the lower classes' and by 'the habit of writing them falsely'. The philologist Richard Verstegan agreed.[148] Meric Casaubon spoke of the migrations of men, while Kircher referred to the mutual influence and mixture of languages.[149] Kircher also maintained with Brian Walton that climate would so effect the vocal cords as to make one language sound like another.[150]

But if one thing could ameliorate these agents of change and degeneration, it was a real character. If the language of Adam had been expressed in written form, its survival through the Babel era and successive periods of history was far more likely. The characters of China and Egypt, along with Hebrew letters, were favoured as original forms of the original language. While Hebrew was traditionally held to be the first form of writing, or at least of speech, Egyptian and Chinese symbols, on account of their much-vaunted antiquity and real nature, came into strong contention.[151] Sir Thomas Browne, for example, wrote that the Egyptians had managed to avoid much of the confusion which followed Babel because 'they invented a language of things, and spake unto each other by common notions in Nature'. This, he goes on to say, 'many conceive to have been the primitive way of writing and of greater antiquity than letters', concluding, 'this indeed might *Adam* well have spoken, who understanding the nature of things, had the advantage of natural expressions'.[152]

The possibility that the Egyptians had conversed and written in the language of Adam was made less attractive by the fact that their symbols remained intractably undecipherable. There was little point in having a real character if no-one could understand it. Chinese symbols, however, suffered from no such disadvantage. In 'Of Languages', Thomas Browne noted that because the confusion of languages fell only upon those present at Shinar, the primitive language of Noah might have been preserved 'in divers others'.[153] A few paragraphs later, he makes the pointed observation that the 'Chinoys, who live at the bounds of the earth', may possibly have a very ancient language, and by virtue of their 'common Character' have been able to record their history as far back as 'Poncuus, who is conceived our Noah'.[154] Browne, in other words, entertained the possibility that the Chinese, rather than the Egyptians, had possessed the most ancient form of writing.[155]

Browne's speculations show how sacred history was still very relevant to the quest for a universal language. While the gentlemen of the Royal Society were more inclined to invent such a language, or to examine existing languages on their present merits, Browne showed that the fortunes of Noah and his kin had an important bearing on the whole matter. Others had reached the same conclusion.[156] One of the more important points for consideration in this historical approach became the final resting place of the Ark. If it could be shown that Noah had disembarked in or near China, then it could be argued with some plausibility that the inhabitants of that land possessed the original language – provided, that is, that Noah had successfully preserved it. Raleigh had already proposed that the Ark had come to rest somewhere in the East.[157] Nathaniel Carpenter, Peter Heylyn, and later, Samuel Shuckford agreed.[158] Heylyn, however, still maintained that as the result of intercourse with other nations, the language of the district where Noah had settled would suffer change and undergo corruption.[159] This assertion was contested in 1669 by John Webb, in a remarkable work bearing the title *An Historical Essay, Endeavoring a Probability that the Language of the Empire of China is the Primitive Language.*[160]

Webb had no first-hand knowledge of China, or its languages, yet he was able through a reliance on the best authorities available (including the works of the Jesuits) to construct a most reliable account of Chinese language and culture.[161] It is Webb's thesis regarding the origin of the Chinese language, however, for which he is chiefly remembered. The language of 'our first Parents', he said, survived to the time of Babel without 'alteration either in the Form or Dialect and Pronunciation'.[162] Therefore, *'Noah* carried the *Primitive Language* into the Ark with him'.[163] As was evident from

Scripture and approved history, the Ark rested in the East, and from this it could be deduced that Noah and his offspring 'peopled the eastern parts of the world together with China'. Crucially, these settlers 'never came at *Babel*; and could not therefore be ingaged in that presumptuous work'.[164] Since 'the curse of *Confounded Languages* fell upon those only that were present upon the place at *Babel*', the Chinese had continued to use the primitive language.[165] Finally, such were the properties of Chinese characters, that these, along with the relative isolation of China and her limited cultural contact, ensured that the primitive language had survived there virtually intact up to the present day.[166]

To this point Webb's reasonings had the semblance of plausibility. But he was then to enter the fanciful world of comparative mythology. He first toyed with the notion that either Fotrius or Poncuus (Pan Ku) was the first monarch of China, and that perhaps one or other might be one of Noah's close descendants.[167] Webb, however, taking a cue from the fact that the Chinese themselves placed little faith in chronologies which went beyond the reign of Jaus, went on to propose on etymological grounds that Jaus or Yaus (Martinius, Kircher) was to be identified with Janus, who in turn was the same person as Noah.[168]

These historical speculations were further reinforced in two ways. First, Webb cited records to show that Chinese was a written language some 244 years before Babel.[169] This meant that the Chinese could preserve not only the language of Noah, but also his religion. A second strand of proof, therefore, came from an appeal to Chinese theology. Punctuating his work with frequent references to the Jesuits, Webb argued that the Chinese had practised a pure monotheism which had remained undefiled by idolatry for a considerable time. Confucius, like Christ, had preached the Golden Rule, and the Chinese ethic generally corresponded with the Judaeo-Christian. Even the Chinese dating of the creation accorded with the date suggested by biblical chronology. All of this, along with evidences of early Chinese expertise in mathematics, astronomy and astrology, was indicative of China's indebtedness to Noah.[170] In short, Webb's study of the language of China led him to a position virtually indistinguishable from that of the French Jesuits. In words which might have come directly from Le Comte or Couplet, he concluded that:

> the language of *China* affordeth us, the Acknowledgement of one only true God; Theology taught by *Noah*, Predictions of CHRIST in exotic Religions many Centuries of years before his Incarnation: devout Ejaculations, such as cannot (Oh the shame!) among Christians without difficulty be found.[171]

Thus Webb placed himself squarely in the tradition of the ancient theology, applying it, as had the Jesuits, to China.

Webb's thesis did not earn for him a large following, but the kinds of claims that he was making for Chinese characters were taken seriously enough to attract a number of refutations. Even before the appearance of the *Historical Essay*, Cave Beck, perhaps jealous of the ancient symbols which might compete with those of his own making, said that Egyptian letters were ambiguous and difficult to learn, while Chinese characters are difficult to draw – 'there being no proportion or method observed in their form'.[172] Wilkins noted simply that the Chinese language was in many respects 'very imperfect'.[173] Matthew Hale, in his *Primitive Origination of Mankind*, showed that he was at least familiar with Webb's thesis, for he dismissed it summarily as 'but a novel conceit'.[174] It fell to Robert Hooke, the first curator of the Royal Society, to make a reasoned examination of the claim that the language of Adam was related to the characters used by the present Chinese.[175] Hooke conceded that the Chinese seemed to possess the oldest form of writing, but judged 'the present *Chinese* Language to have no Affinity at all with the Character, the true Primitive or First Language, or Pronunciation of it, having been lost'.[176] William Wotton, author of *A Discourse Concerning the Confusion of Languages at Babel*, agreed, sarcastically observing that a language is hardly natural when 'eight or Ten of the best Years of a Man's life must be spent in learning to read'.[177]

Webb's chief significance for us lies not in his being representative of the views of his contemporaries, nor in the subsequent influence of his ideas, but in the fact that his theories illustrate the confluence of two important seventeenth-century tendencies: the first, a nostalgic quest for an ancient universal religion; the second, a forward-looking attempt to discover or invent a universal language. The first tendency we have seen in the Cambridge Platonists and the French Jesuits. With one or two exceptions, these groups represent the last appearances of this tendency in modern times. Michael Ramsay and Thomas Hyde were admittedly to make late sallies on behalf of the ancient theology, but their work exerted little influence, arousing only mild curiosity and well-placed criticism.[178]

The second tendency – the attempt to unearth or invent a universal language – led to a number of important projects which had a considerable bearing upon religious history. It should not be thought, therefore, that the two directions were unrelated or at cross purposes. It was merely that where one involved a preoccupation with the glories of the past, the other entertained the possibility that such glories might be recovered in the future. Indeed the eclipsing of ancient theology reflected the gradual resolution of the conflict between ancients and moderns in favour of the latter.

The 'linguistic' approach to religion begun in the seventeenth century was one which was to be of lasting influence, particularly in England where positivistic accounts of religious language have always attracted many supporters. The possibilities of a linguistic approach to religion were hinted at, again, by Francis Bacon, who anticipated so many intellectual developments of the seventeenth and eighteenth centuries. According to Bacon, chief among the 'idols and false notions which have taken possession of the human understanding' were the 'Idols of the Market-place'.[179] These idols, he said, 'crept into the understanding through the alliance of words and names', so that words now 'react on the understanding', rather than being controlled by it. This situation arose because words are 'commonly framed and applied according to the capacity of the vulgar', and thus, 'when an understanding of greater acuteness or a more diligent observation would alter those lines to suit the true divisions of nature, words stand in the way and resist the change'.[180] Thus, sophisticated thought is constrained by vulgar habit. Two kinds of linguistic mistake arose in this manner. There are found within language names of things which do not exist (like 'Prime Mover') and names of things which exist but which are 'confused and ill-defined'.[181] Hobbes was later to take up Bacon's point. He argued similarly that much false ontology arose from the introduction into languages of such words as 'est', 'is', and 'be'.[182] While Hobbes and Bacon declined to give their thoughts any application to theological language, the implications are clear. Ironically this application was left to such divines as Bishop Wilkins and the Reverend Mr Beck. As we saw earlier, both of these men cherished the ambitious hope that their artificial languages would render theological utterances immune from the pervasive idols of the marketplace.

Another seventeenth-century figure who could hardly be categorised as part of the theological establishment also made some interesting, if tantalisingly brief, remarks about language and religion. John Toland developed no comprehensive linguistic theory of the origins of religion, yet in some of his remarks we find the foundations of such a theory. He informs us in *Letters to Serena* that:

> Custom, (which is not unfitly call'd a second Nature) has imprest such a Stamp on the very Language of the Society, that what is deliver'd in these or those Words, tho never so contradictory or abstruse, passes ordinarily for current Truth.[183]

This view of language meshes neatly with Toland's contentions regarding 'mystery' and 'custom'. It was the burden of his *Christianity not Mysterious* that doctrines of the Christian faith only become dispute-engendering when no obvious meaning can be attached to the words used in their articulation. It is through custom and use that we have come to assume that such locutions have meaning. The insoluble disputes which these doctrines attract only serve to show their vacuous nature, and that they are not held to be true on any rational or reasonable grounds. The solution to these difficulties lay, for Toland, in historical analysis. Through the science of etymology the history of a term's meaning could be traced, and the gradual accumulation of those false or meaningless aspects, which exercise such a tyranny over those who use the words uncritically, could be detected. It is just such an analysis of 'mystery' that is set out in *Christianity not Mysterious*. The nearest Toland came to relating these thoughts to a theory of the origins of religion is in a marginal note in one of the works in his library. Here he notes that superstitions are 'almost as old as [names and] writing'.[184] It was Toland's belief that as soon as we name objects, we come to distort their nature, for we lack the advantages of the language of Adam.

These embryonic ideas of Toland we find in a more mature form in Max Müller's comprehensive linguistic theory of religion.[185] Briefly, Müller suggested that religion arose when figurative modes of speaking came to be thought of as expressing literal reality. Thus, the expression in primal language, 'the sun follows the dawn', led to the belief that the sun was an active agent.[186] Both Toland and Müller, in turn, anticipated the twentieth-century positivist critique of religious language,[187] in which the assumed analogy between religious propositions and empirical statements came under heavy attack. In the eighteenth century, however, linguistic theories had not sufficiently extricated themselves from biblical history to have achieved independent scientific status. Instead, linguistic theorising was channelled into another sphere – comparative linguistics, which in turn led to comparative mythology.

The seventeenth-century quest for a universal language was a failure. Certainly, Bishop Wilkins' unwieldy universal characters received the acclaim appropriate to such a valiant and scholarly achievement, but no-one saw fit to put his system to work. One loyal disciple, in an act of supreme irony, undertook the task of translating the work into Latin. By the time the following century was drawing to a close, Wilkins' *Real Character*, along with all those other undertakings of a similar kind, was regarded as little more than an historical curiosity. Yet the vision of universal communication, universal truths, and a universal religion, did not die, but rather found new expression in the age of Enlightenment. The medium which would make all these things possible was not a literal *lingua humana*, but the universal language of reason. In the sphere of religious history, reason was to be applied in a new way, to the old facts. Sacred history was to give way to *Histoire Raisonnée* – 'rational' or 'natural' history.

NATURAL HISTORY

'Nature', we have emphasised, was one of the controlling images of the seventeenth and eighteenth centuries. Of the various alternatives to waning ecclesiastical authority, the appeal to Nature and the natural was one of the most attractive. While the Cambridge Platonists might reaffirm the venerable traditions of Platonism and Neoplatonism, the burgeoning natural sciences pointed many others forward in quite a new direction. Herbert was perhaps unique in being able to hold both together, yet his explorations in natural history were definitive in a way that his covert Platonism was not. In the seventeenth and eighteenth centuries natural history was not only what we now think of as 'biology', but included attempts to set the study of human history on a similar footing to the natural sciences. Ultimately it failed to be either science or history, but natural histories of religion were an important foundation for subsequent attempts to devise a science of religion.

What, then, is natural history?[188] An important clue is provided by the Scottish writer Dugald Stewart, who, in the context of his discussion of Adam Smith's *Dissertation on the Origin of Languages* (1761), refers to a 'species of historical investigations' which he designates '*Theoretical* or *Conjectural History*, an expression which coincides pretty nearly in its meaning with that of *Natural History*, as employed by Mr. Hume, and with what some French writers have called *Histoire Raisonnée*'.[189] Stewart goes on to identify the characteristic features of this genre: 'In examining the history of mankind, as well as in examining the phenomena of the material world, when we cannot trace the process by which the event *has been* produced, it is often of importance to show how it *may have been* produced by natural causes.'[190] Stewart notes that in such histories, the ideal or natural development is of more significance than the actual development:

> In most cases, it is of more importance to ascertain the progress that is most simple, than the progress that is most agreeable to fact; for, paradoxical as the proposition may appear, it is certainly true, that the real progress is not always the most natural. It may have been determined by particular accidents, which are not likely again to occur, and which cannot be considered as forming any part of the general provision which nature has made for the improvement of the race.[191]

The distinction here is between 'natural', on the one hand, and 'factual' or 'accidental', on the other. The 'natural' or 'conjectural' history, therefore, is the ideal history of the institution – a theoretical account of its unimpeded development. This history is 'natural' because it attempts to penetrate the veil of historical accidents to uncover the true nature of the object of study.

The distinction here is between 'natural', on the one hand, and 'factual' or 'accidental', on the other. The 'natural' or 'conjectural' history, therefore, is the ideal history of the institution – a theoretical account of its unimpeded development. This history is 'natural' because it attempts to penetrate the veil of historical accidents to uncover the true nature of the object of study.

The distinction between the natural and the accidental can be traced to Aristotle, and it is worth considering how he originally set up the dichotomy, for here are to be found the roots of the notion that natural history is a science. Amongst the interminable definitions of *Metaphysics*, v, we find Aristotle distinguishing 'nature' (*physis*) from 'accident' (*symbebekos*). 'Nature' refers to the genesis of growing things, the immanent thing from which objects and institutions first begin to grow, the source from which the primary motion in every material object is induced.[192] Nature is thus to do with origins and growth, and indeed this concept links up with the Aristotelian *quadriga* of causes.[193] We can better understand the significance of this notion when we see how Aristotle applies it, as for example, in his efforts to determine the nature of the state. In *The Politics*, he says:

> In this subject as in others the best method of investigation is to study things in the process of development from the beginning . . .
>
> Hence every city-state exists by nature, inasmuch as the first partnerships so exist; for the city-state is the end of the other partnerships, and nature is an end, since that which each thing is when its growth is completed we speak of as being the nature of each thing . . .
>
> Thus also the city-state is prior in nature to the house-hold and to each of us individually.[194]

The nature of social institutions (in this instance, the state) is thus discovered by tracing the development of the institution from the beginning, at which stage its 'end', 'full development', or 'final cause' is already present. This procedure is a scientific one, because like the natural histories described by Stewart, it is one in which the influence of the accidental is omitted. For Aristotle, those things are accidental which occur neither necessarily nor usually.[195] Accidents have no definite cause, and cannot be the object of any of the sciences – practical, productive, or speculative.[196] As Plato had earlier observed, scientists concern themselves with proper ends, while only sophists attempt to make a study of the accidental.[197]

The most appropriate analogy to this Aristotelian approach to the history of social institutions is that of organic ontogeny. In the seed of a plant, for example, the fully-grown plant is, in a sense, already present. The science which elucidates the nature of the plant should properly give an account of its growth to maturity under ideal conditions. In this account, such accidents as the plant's being trampled by a careless foot, or being eaten by some beast, play no role.

The image of biological development as a model for the growth of social institutions, along with the related concepts of nature and science were a substantial part of the legacy of the Greek classical age to eighteenth-century historiography.[198] In retrospect, it was not a happy bequest. As R. J. Collingwood has pointed out, it was precisely this application of the classical view of nature to the sphere of history which prevented Enlightenment thinkers from developing a proper understanding of history.[199] Those very insights which were to place history on a scientific footing had quite the opposite effect, giving rise to a species of history which was neither scientific nor historical.

British historians, if they were the first to forsake the tried and trusted methods of sacred history in favour of the 'new' approach, were not the only ones to do so. As Stewart rightly pointed out, the natural history genre has obvious parallels in the *Histoires Raisonées* of the French. Here we find, as in the writings of the eighteenth-century Scots, fully developed examples of the genre of natural history. For our present topic nothing is more instructive than to observe Jean Jacques Rousseau's quite self-conscious approach to the historical task. Rousseau opens his *Discourse on the Origin of Inequality* (1755) with a restatement of the distinction between nature and convention. He then points out that the social philosophies of the past had committed the error of ascribing to the state of nature what in fact belonged to convention.[200] Rousseau attempted to negotiate this pitfall by making conjectures that were 'based solely on the nature of man, and the beings around him, concerning what might have become of the human race, *if it had been left to itself*'.[201] It is in the light of this goal that Rousseau's notorious statement about ignoring the facts is to be understood. 'Let us begin then', he says, 'by laying facts aside, as they do not affect the question'.[202] The social conventions which comprised 'the facts' were the very things which, according to Rousseau, obscured the true nature of man.[203] This is not to say that in these conjectural histories the facts played no role. Facts were adduced, but primarily to show how the normal course of development had been diverted. Rousseau's policy of laying facts aside is not an advocacy of wild speculation, but is instead an insistence that the historically-given state is not necessarily the naturally ordained one. The tension between the actual situation and conjectures as to what the ideal or natural state of affairs might have been led easily to more or less explicit programmes for the removal of those obstacles which had hindered the natural progress of mankind. Thus as in all forms of Enlightenment history, there is a didactic element in these historical accounts.[204]

By now it should be apparent that the deist histories of religion conform in most important respects to the pattern of natural history. Ignoring the story of Adam and Eve and their transgression, deist reconstructions of the earliest period of human history present the scenario of all mankind sharing the one, simple, monotheistic religion. In their natural state, men and women gave common expression to their inalienable religious instincts. Various accidents changed this agreeable situation – climate, admixture and travel, the problems of religious language, the limitations of the vulgar intellect, the pseudo-revelations of psychotic impostors, the excessive veneration of heroes and kings, and not least, the emergence of organised religion and the priestly hierarchy. As we can see, certain parallels exist between natural histories of religion and sacred histories. Both refer to a period of edenic bliss, a fall of some kind, continuing degeneration, and periodic attempts to regain original purity. But while these elements were common to both enterprises, natural history boasted a rational or scientific basis.

Herbert of Cherbury was the first to attempt a natural history of religion, a task which he undertook in *De Religione Gentilium* (1663).[205] For Herbert, the natural history of religion was essentially the history of natural religion. This is by no means a trite observation, for Hume's *Natural History of Religion*, for example, did not have natural religion as its subject. To make this claim then, is to say for Herbert, natural religion – the religion of the common notions – both constituted the essence of true religion, and was the pure and original form of religion. Herbert maintained that the first inhabitants of the earth came 'by degrees' to adore the supreme deity. This, he insisted, was the only form of religion at that time, for 'the Heathens hitherto had nothing to direct them, but common Notions imprinted in their Hearts'.[206] The major shortcoming of Herbert's thesis, as we have already seen, was that these *notitiae communes* did not appear to be, or ever to have been, universal: the known facts of history did not support the hypothesis. It was at this point, therefore, that the technique of 'laying facts aside' came into play. Herbert's conjectures about the early religious condition of mankind represent what should have been the case had natural instincts been given full rein. Moreover, had the human race been 'left to itself' indefinitely, the universal observation of the common notions would everywhere be in evidence. The present religious situation made it all too clear that our first parents had not been left to themselves. Instead, religious instincts had led to the development of social institutions – organised religion and the priesthood. These, in turn, had stifled those very affections and notions which gave them birth. As Herbert put it: 'afterwards, a certain sect of men sprang up, who persuaded them to entertain Rites and Ceremonies'.[207] In this manner the institution of a religious hierarchy brought about the fall of humanity. On the brighter side, none of these religious innovations, as far as Herbert was concerned, completely blotted out the heathens' common notions, for even in the most degraded forms of polytheism, 'symbolic' worship of the true God could be discerned. Herbert never tires of pointing out that the idolatrous heathen 'worshipped the *Supreme God* himself', for, 'almost all the Ancient Religion was Symbolical, and they do not worship this thing, in that, but one thing out of another'.[208] Hence the accidental never triumphed completely over the natural.

The natural historian of religion who is closest to Herbert, not only in years, but in overall intent, was Ralph Cudworth. In the ponderous *True Intellectual System*, Cudworth followed Herbert in upholding the thesis of primitive monotheism, similarly proposing that despite appearances to the contrary, heathen religion was actually monotheistic. Seemingly idolatrous pagans actually worshipped the supreme being in his earthly manifestations.[209] The pagans, according to Cudworth, always had access to a natural or philosophical theology, but on account of the difficulty in comprehending the deity, it was regarded as necessary that they be permitted to worship him 'in his works, by parts and piecemeal, according to the various manifestations of himself'.[210] The limitations of the vulgar intellect, rather than the deceits of the priests, here account for the diverting of natural religious development. The source of most errors was the quite valid theological insight that God is 'all in all', which unfortunately is 'easily liable to mistake and abuse'. Mistakes arising from this notion formed the 'chief ground and original of both seeming and real polytheism', for the heathen concluded that 'because God was in all things, and consequently all things God, that therefore God ought to be worshipped in all things, that is, in all the several parts of the world, and things of nature'.[211]

The deists who came after Herbert and Cudworth were less inclined to attribute deviations from natural religion to innocent theological mistakes. Moreover, they were more circumspect in arguing the thesis of primitive monotheism. Charles Blount, for example, concedes that there was a period of history when there was universal practice of a rational monotheism. 'The article of the one true God', he tells us, 'was common to both *Jews* and *Gentiles*, even before their Reception: the Universality of Religious Worship consisting in the practice of virtue and Goodness'.[212] The fall from this natural state was, in the most general sense, owing to human self-interest, which of course manifested itself in the practice of priestcraft.[213]

Blount's natural history, while essentially similar to Herbert's, had a slightly different emphasis. Herbert's *Antient Religion of the Gentiles* was a means of vindicating his five common notions, which could then be put forward as an alternative basis for those contemporary religious practices which had become so polarised because of their reliance upon revelatory and authoritative modes of truth. Herbert had taken particular care to safeguard his contention concerning the universality of monotheism by claiming that the supreme deity was worshipped in his earthly manifestations. While Blount in one place follows his mentor on this question,[214] he was far more equivocal about whether all religions had at their foundation some common notion or notions. He could admit the possibility that in antiquity there was a common religion, but to reach that religion now was a matter of selecting the best from all the religions, for all had been subject to corruption.[215] What current religions had in common was not any enduring 'essence', but merely a hypothetical common ancestry, some effete vestiges of which they still displayed. Blount was already moving towards the view that the positive religions were not based on some universal religious *a priori*, but in the final analysis rested upon another universal human characteristic – self-interest. The essence of religion lay here; the pure philosophical worship of God was practised, in Blount's own words, 'before Religion'.[216] In Blount, then, we see the beginnings of a natural history of religion which does not have as its focus natural religion, but rather some other more elemental affection such as self-interest or fear.

John Toland represents a further development of this tendency. He too spoke of a universal monotheism which eventually came to grief at the hands of the priests.[217] The first instances of idolatry were not initiated by the priests, however, but by the worship of dead heroes. Only after this did the priests seek to make a business out of polytheism and hero-worship.[218] Significantly, Toland regarded 'these false Notions of the Heathens about the Dead' to be 'the first, the most natural, the most universal' cause of heathenism.[219] What is remarkable about this development is that it attributes to heathenism a 'naturalness' which Herbert had reserved for natural religion. Toland claims for euhemerism that it was 'the first', the 'most natural' and the 'most universal' – the very criteria which Herbert claimed for his common notions. In Toland's view, the superstitious religions of the seventeenth-century world were no different from those of the remote past: 'THE present Heathens' who inhabit 'the greatest part of Africa, vast tracts of Asia, almost all America, and some few Corners of Europe, agree very much with the Antients in their Opinions.'[220] In asserting the antiquity and universality of heathenism, Toland did not mean to deprive true religion of its status as the primitive religion. Rather, natural religion and superstition together constituted humanity's natural religious condition, religion having had a bi-partite structure from the very earliest times. There was one religion for the philosophers, another for the plebeians. In this way Toland added historical reinforcement to the thesis of the twofold philosophy.

Toland was perfectly happy to speculate freely about primal religion, for so little was known of this period that virtually any theory could be put forward without fear of contradiction. The historical religions, however, could not easily be squeezed into the mould of conjectural history. If one wished to investigate the history of Judaism, Christianity, or Islam, there were widely accepted facts which could not be set aside. The histories of Herbert and Blount had avoided any direct mention of Christianity, expressing criticism by means of an implied comparison with the various forms of heathenism. Toland was the first of the deists to realise that the so-called revealed religions – the history of which was known in some detail – required separate historical treatment.

For all of the deists, and for many rationalistic divines as well, the fundamental theological question of the age of reason was how revealed religion was related to natural religion. Toland, like many of his contemporaries, came to the conclusion that revealed religion in its uncorrupted state was identical to natural religion – that original and rational form of human piety which any reasonable individual could arrive at. The difference between the two lay in the fact that revelation was a means of communication while reason provided the grounds of belief.[221] Reason, moreover, as for the Cambridge Platonists and John Locke, was a much-needed criterion of revelation, for, in Toland's words, 'we cannot otherwise discern [God's] *Revelations* but by their Conformity with our natural Notions of him, which is in so many words, to agree with our common Notions'.[222] This did not mean that reason was set up over and against revelation, but that it served to distinguish what was spurious from what was genuine. 'Reason', Toland insisted, in tones redolent of the Cambridge Platonists, 'is not less from God than *revelation*; 'tis the Candle, the Guide, the Judg he has lodg'd within every Man that cometh into this World'.[223]

When this view of the relation of reason and revelation is applied to the history of Christianity, the following syllogism results. Christianity as originally revealed was the same as natural religion. Contemporary Christianity is not the same as natural religion. Therefore contemporary Christianity is the result of a process of decay and admixture. This was one of the major themes of *Christianity not Mysterious*. In pursuing the thesis 'that there is nothing in the Gospel contrary to reason, nor above it', Toland argued that Jesus delivered a very simple message to the common people. The 'uncorrupted Doctrines of *Christianity*' consisted of 'the purest Morals' and 'reasonable Worship', and were not above the 'Reach or comprehension' of the common folk. The 'Gibberish of your *Divinity Schools*', Toland cannot resist adding, 'they [would] understand not'.[224] With the passing of time, Christianity had come to suffer the fate of the primitive natural religion, and through human proneness to superstition, and with the encouragement of the priests, had degenerated into its present condition. For while the disciples and followers 'kept to this simplicity for some considerable time', eventually Christianity had become 'miserably deform'd and almost ruined by those unintelligible and extravagant Terms, Notions, and Rites of *Pagan* or *Jewish* Original'.[225] It was Toland's firm belief that the inroads of paganism on Christianity had caused 'so divine an Institution' to 'degenerate into mere Paganism'.[226]

This thesis was reworked in some detail in the remarkable collection entitled *Nazarenus: or Jewish, Gentile and Mahometan Christianity*.[227] The anthology includes two essays – 'The History of the Ancient Gospel of Barnabas', and 'The Original Plan of Christianity' – both of which attempt to provide some 'hard' evidence for the embryonic historical thesis of Toland's first work. In 'The Original Plan of Christianity', Toland notes the existence of two groups within earliest Christianity – Gentile Christians and Jewish Christians or 'Nazarenes'. While the former group took the course described in *Christianity not Mysterious*, introducing pagan elements to Christianity, the Ebionites or 'Nazarenes', as Toland prefers to call them, observed the original precepts of Jesus, while at the same time preserving all that was of value in Judaism. But this situation did not last. In Toland's reckoning:

> the true Christianity of the Jews was overborn and destroyed by the more numerous Gentiles, who, not enduring the reasonableness and simplicity of the same, brought into it by degrees the peculiar expressions and mysteries of Heathenism, the abstruse doctrines and distinctions of the Philosophers, an insupportable pontifical Hierarchy, and even the altars, offrings, the sacred rites and ceremonies of their Priests, tho they would not so much as tolerate those of the Jews, and yet owning them to be divinely instituted.[228]

Details of the specific beliefs and rites of the Nazarenes remained somewhat sketchy. Toland believed these to be listed in a lost 'Gospel of the Hebrews'.[229] From the 'Apostolic Decree' in the *Acts of the Apostles*, however, Toland discovered that Jewish Christians were required to keep the Mosaic Law, while only the Noachite commandments were urged upon Gentile Christians.[230] The Mosaic Law he thought to have been a revealed form of that Moral Law, common to all mankind, which was otherwise attained through 'sound Reason, or the light of common sense'.[231] It was this Law, as we shall later see, that Toland considered to be the most perfect positive expression of the law of nature. The divine mission of Jesus was to restore this Mosaic Law to its original purity and to purge it of those elaborations and superstitions which had been introduced by the priests.[232] The Nazarenes had correctly discerned the mission of Jesus and had practised the legitimate form of Christianity – a form which Toland himself wished to re-establish. This religion was to be 'inward and spiritual, abstracted from all formal and outward performances', containing 'more objects of practice than belief' and in those objects of practice, nothing 'but what makes a man the better'.[233]

What makes Toland's thesis remarkable is not so much that Christianity is seen to be a recapitulation of the religion of nature,[234] for this becomes commonplace amongst the later deists. Toland goes much further, asserting that Judaism, in its ideal form, is exactly the same as true Christianity:

Thus therefore THE REPUBLIC OF MOSES might still have subsisted entire, such as it was, or rather ought to have been, in Judea, and yet the inhabitants be very good Christians too.[235]

Throughout *Nazarenus* and elsewhere Toland betrayed a considerable interest in the religion of the Jews. 'The religion that was true yesterday is not false today', he insisted, 'neither can it be false, if it was once true.'[236] In an appendix to *Nazarenus* he asks how the Jews could have preserved their national and religious identity to the present, while other ancient states had long since passed away.[237] He answers the question himself, proposing that the 'constitution of the Government', or 'a particular providence', or both, preserved the Jews.[238] The correlation of their positive law with the law of nature could, if they were resettled in Palestine, serve to make them 'more populous, rich, and powerful than any other nation in the world', Toland projected, suggesting that Christians give serious consideration to aiding the Jews to settle their own country.[239] In two other works as well – *Reasons for Naturalizing the Jews in Great Britain and Ireland* (1714) and *Origines Judaicae* (1709?) – Toland opposed the prevailing anti-semitism to give a positive evaluation of the Jewish people and religion.[240]

In view of Toland's assertion that members of the Jewish nation could be 'very good Christians', we should not be too surprised to find that he also regarded the 'Mahometans' to be 'a sort of Christians, and not the worst sort neither'.[241] In 1709, Toland had discovered in Amsterdam the manuscript of 'The Gospel of Barnabas' – a text which he clearly believed to be an authentic document from the apostolic age with a valid claim to canonicity.[242] It was from this document, he believed, that the Mahometans derived their doctrines. Islam was a religion much maligned, said Toland, there being many myths and fables about it 'to which the Musulmans are utter strangers'.[243] The truth was that Islamic doctrines were based not on the heterodox opinions of a Nestorian monk, as Medieval tradition would have it, but on 'the earliest documents of the Christian Religion'.[244] The document in question was, of course, the Gospel of Barnabas, which Toland declared was 'in a very great part the same book' as the 'Gospel of the Mahometans' (presumably the Qu'ran). The Mahometans, moreover, 'openly profess to believe the *Gospel*: tho they charge our copies with so much corruption and alteration'.[245] Toland's reasonings led him to the conclusion that the 'Mahometans', like the Jews, were really 'a sort or sect of Christians', and he even hinted that they were closer to the original plan of Christianity than was historical Christianity itself, the latter having suffered alteration through contact with paganism and being in addition based upon corrupted documents.[246] It is not hard to see how Toland got his reputation for being a 'Mahometan' Christian.

Toland's premature ecumènism won him few, if any supporters.[247] Even today, his achievements tend to be viewed through the eyes of his contemporary critics, and he is allocated but a minor role in the history of English religious thought.[248] Yet in his textual and historical researches he was far ahead of his detractors. It is true that his attempts to incorporate the three monotheistic religions under a united banner of Christianity foundered. So too, his pleas to see in other religions a means of criticising and improving one's own fell on deaf ears. One feature of his writings, however, was adopted by a number of subsequent thinkers.

Like Herbert, the Renaissance Platonists, and even Augustine, Toland had tried to extend the meaning of the term 'Christian' to include those outside the boundaries of the visible Church. Ideal Christianity, Toland had insisted, did not coincide with the Church of England, or any other form of positive Christianity, but was to be identified with a practice of natural religion which could take place under the guise of any number of religious traditions. This equating of genuine Christianity with natural religion became a platform of later deist thought. The classic statement of this thesis is Matthew Tindal's *Christianity as Old as the Creation: or the Gospel, a Republication of the Religion of Nature* (1730).

In contrast to Toland, whose contribution to English thought is seldom given due weight, Tindal is possibly the most overrated of the British freethinkers. Perhaps this is because surveyors of intellectual history can acquaint themselves with his major contribution to religious ideas simply by reading the title of his chief work. 'God at all times', Tindal informs those readers who persevere beyond the first page, 'has given Mankind sufficient Means of knowing whatever he requires of them'.[249] Whether the means be natural or revealed is of little account, for like Toland, Tindal insisted that '*Natural* and *Reveal'd* Religion differ in nothing, but the manner of their being conveyed to us'.[250] The logical outcome is that it is not inappropriate to designate natural religion 'Christianity', for the content of each should be the same: '*Christianity*, tho' the name be of a later Date, must be as old, as extensive, as humane Nature; and as the Law of our Creation, must have been Then implanted in us by God himself.'[251]

There follows upon this conclusion the barest bones of an historical thesis which shares the main features of other natural histories. Natural religion was the original religion. It was perverted by the priests. The natural religion which Jesus attempted to re-establish suffered the same fate. Tindal's project, if *passé*, nonetheless represents another stage in the erosion of the exclusive claims of Christianity.[252] If Toland had extended the boundaries of Christendom to include the Jews and 'Mahometans', Tindal had said that we might just as well include all forms of natural religion, even those which existed before the time of Christ. 'Christianity' was simply another term for 'True Religion', and 'True Religion' was for Tindal, as for his fellow free-thinkers, 'a constant Disposition of Mind to do all the Good we can, and thereby render ourselves acceptable to God in answering the End of his Creation'.[253]

A more original thinker than Tindal, and one possessed of considerably more historical sense, was the 'Christian deist', Thomas Morgan. Morgan's most important contribution to the history of religion lay in his rather tentative efforts to fit historical religions into the pattern of natural history. Like Toland, he attempted to show how both Christianity and Judaism were, in their original forms, valid expressions of natural religion which had been later corrupted by the introduction of a clerical hierarchy. He did not, however, share Toland's enthusiasm for Judaism. Moses and Aaron were together guilty of imposture, having introduced to the nation of Israel the priestly conventions of Egypt.[254] This 'inversion of Nature' led the people of Israel to perpetrate the most brutal follies in the name of their religion.[255]

Christianity had fared little better. The dual disasters which beset it were the survival of Jewish notions of atonement and sacrifice, and the sanctioning of the Christian religion by Rome. As Morgan saw it, Paul was the 'great freethinker of that age', who had defended and attempted to propagate Christ's pure religion of nature.[256] He had rejected both the Jewish Law and the 'Jewish' notion that Jesus' death was in some sense a propitiating sacrifice.[257] Unfortunately Paul was eventually forced to reach a compromise with Peter's Judaisers, and so a Catholic hierarchy arose which was little different in form to the old Jewish sacerdotal system.[258] Morgan thus took the opposite view to Toland who saw the Jews as the guardians of genuine religion in the face of Greek corruptions. The only 'true' Christians, according to Morgan, were those free-thinkers who were anathematised as gnostics.[259] The conversion of Constantine only made matters worse, for when the new religion was established by law, the people gave up only the appearance of paganism, remaining superstitious polytheists at heart:

> They had parted with, and discarded their old Gods, but they did not alter anything of the Form, or outward Appearance of Religion. They continued the same Sacrifices and public Festivals to their own Saints and Martyrs; they dedicated Churches and Temples to them; they prayed to and invoked them, and paid the same Sort of Worship to them that they had done to the heathen Idols before ... and within a hundred years Christians from Christians suffered more than ever Christians had suffered from Heathens.[260]

During the Reformation, history was to repeat itself, for while 'some of the grosser and more palpable absurdities of Popery' were dismissed, 'the outward Forms and Appearances of Religion were still the same'.[261]

In the histories of Blount, Toland, Tindal, and Morgan, almost impercep-

tibly the natural history of religion had become a natural history of superstition. Beneath the plethora of religious rites and creeds lay not natural
religion, but age-old patterns of superstition. In vain would the deists
project their own religious convictions onto the historical past, hoping that
they could find counterparts of themselves in every age, for it was becoming
increasingly apparent that superstition was more 'natural' than the religion
of nature itself. We encounter the first explicit recognition of the naturalness
of superstition in an essay by John Trenchard, simply entitled *The Natural
History of Superstition* (1709). The nub of Trenchard's thesis was that the
impostures of the heathen, of Muhammad, of papists and Protestants alike,
would never have succeeded 'unless something innate in our Constitution
made us easily to be susceptible of wrong Impressions, subject to panic
Fears, and prone to Superstition and Error'.[262] There is no mention here
of innate religious predispositions, but only a natural proneness to religious
error. Now, for the first time, this predisposition becomes the subject of
an historical enquiry. Trenchard went on to show that the theories of
religious pathology of Burton, Casaubon and More had a far wider
application than the original authors had thought. 'Nature, in many
circumstances', he says, 'seems to work by a sort of secret Magic, and by
ways unaccountable to us'.[263] It is nature which gives rise to those
'Phantasms and Images' which lead to superstition and fanaticism, yet this
is only possible when 'men have abandoned the natural Calm and Serenity
of their Minds'.[264]

More comprehensive than Trenchard's *Natural History* was David Hume's
The Natural History of Religion (1757?). This minor classic is at once the culmin-
ation of this genre, and its anti-type: to be Hegelian, its *Aufhebung*. The
title invites immediate comparison with Trenchard's pamphlet, and indeed
at the time of its publication it aroused much indignation simply by virtue
of the similarity of titles. It was apparent, even to the least perceptive reader,
that Hume's work was devoted to the same topic as Trenchard's, the difference being that Hume had been bold enough to imply that all religions
were merely socially acceptable superstitions. Hume's foray into natural
history is the terminus of the genre in that he refused to grant that there
is any 'hidden' essence of religion that can be discovered by historical investigation or through conjectures based on the assumption of some religious
a priori. In fact for Hume, there is no primary religious sentiment or predisposition.

The most radical aspect of Hume's theory of religious development is
his assertion that 'polytheism was the primary religion of man'.[265] This
cut across that cherished assumption of preceding natural historians, that
truth is older than error, and that the history of religion is the history of
an irreversible degeneration in religious beliefs and practices. Of equal

importance was Hume's implication that polytheism, was 'natural', for it was another axiom of natural history that what is natural is always original. Hume bases his claim on the dual premise that 'the mind rises gradually, from the inferior to the superior', and that once one becomes acquainted with the rational grounds of monotheism (Hume here means the argument from design), one can never regress into polytheism.[266] His conclusion:

> it must appear impossible, that theism could, from reasoning, have been the primary religion of the human race, and have afterwards, by its corruption, given rise to polytheism and to all the various superstitions of the heathen world. Reason, when obvious prevents these corruptions: When abstruse, it keeps the principles entirely from the knowledge of the vulgar, who are alone liable to corrupt any principle or opinion.[267]

If no religious instinct or conviction of the logical necessity of God's existence prompted the stirrings of human religion, how did religion begin? According to Hume, religion first arose through hopes and fears of the first humans, which were related to practical concerns. 'No passion', he says, 'can be supposed to work upon such barbarians, but the ordinary affections of human life'. It was not a religious instinct, but instincts far more fundamental which led to the discovery of the gods – 'the anxious concern for happiness, the dread of future misery, the terror of death, the thirst for revenge, the appetite for food and other necessaries'. These led early man to attempt to fathom the mainspring of future causes, and in this endeavour they found 'the first obscure traces of divinity'.[268] These obscure traces were then given shape by the human tendency to anthropomorphise:

> There is an universal tendency among mankind to conceive all beings like themselves, and to transfer to every object, those qualities, with which they are familiarly acquainted, and of which they are intimately conscious.[269]

The limited powers of these anthropomorphic deities meant that they were supposed to exist in vast numbers in order to account for the whole gamut of natural events.[270] Moreover, their proximity to the human prototype allowed for the speculation that they were 'nothing but a species of human creatures, perhaps raised from mankind'.[271] Hume thus admits euhemerism as part of the explanation of polytheism. In sum, Hume had a threefold explanation of the origin of polytheism, relying upon a fear theory, a projection theory and euhemerism.

Having set out an argument for the priority of polytheism, Hume proceeded to show how monotheism arose from polytheism. Again he denies that any reasoning processes were involved, insisting instead that men, attempting to ingratiate themselves with a particular deity thought to be more powerful than others, through the zeal of their praise eventually attributed complete sovereignty to this single deity. Henotheism was the stepping stone to monotheism. Even so, this monotheism could not be equated with genuine religion, for its tenets 'coincide, by chance, with the principles of reason and true philosophy'. Throughout history, most monotheists arrived at their beliefs 'not by reason, of which they are in a great measure incapable, but by the adulation and fears of the most vulgar superstition'.[272] Hume thus makes the claim that a religion may be true in content, and yet remain 'superstition' on account of the grounds by which it is held to be true.

The precarious nature of monotheistic belief is evidenced by the fact that monotheists invariably lapse back into polytheism. This did not contradict Hume's principle that the religion of the rational monotheist can never be corrupted into polytheism. For Hume, most monotheists were not of the rational variety. The whole history of religion was therefore a continual flux and reflux of polytheism and monotheism. The transcendence of the one God makes necessary the presence of intermediaries, who eventually encroach upon the worship of the supreme deity, and pave the way for the regression back into polytheism.[273] And so the cycle is completed.

The rest of Hume's *Natural History* is devoted to a comparison of the two 'types' of religion – polytheism and theism. It was Hume's sceptical judgement that while neither form of religion did much credit to the human race, polytheism at least allowed for diversity of religious expression.[274] Neither type, in Hume's view, provided an adequate conception of the deity, nor led to moral behaviour.[275] Religions were, in short, neither true nor useful.

Hume's *Natural History* sounded the death knell for natural histories of religion, not least because it distinguished the rational grounds of belief from the question of the historical origin of those beliefs. The rationalistic orientation of the deists, combined with their stress upon the potential rationality of every human being, led them to the view that the question of the reasonableness of religion could not be divorced from the investigation of its origins. At all times, in all places, individuals could arrive at the basic principles of natural religion through the simple exercise of reason – specifically by rehearsing the argument from design or the ontological argument. If there was any frailty in the rational faculty it was manifested not through an inability to arrive at the idea of God and love of neighbour, but through a subsequent susceptibility to the pious frauds of priests. For Hume, the frailty of reason was far more radical and pervasive. Reason played no role in the development of religion. It followed that the question of the reasonableness of religion was quite distinct from the question of its origins. Thus ended 'rational history' of religion.

With the demise of the first attempt at a genuine science of religion came a whole range of new possibilities for the study of religion. Hume distinguished himself from the free-thinkers who had preceded him by attacking religion on two fronts. While the *Dialogues* cut the ground from under natural religion, the essay 'Of Miracles' removed the external evidences which had shored up revealed religion; the *Natural History*, as we have seen, pushed the message home by providing empirical evidence of both the irrationality and moral bankruptcy of historical forms of religion, including 'revealed' religions. The discussion which had taken place, almost from the inception of the modern concept 'religion', of the relative merits of its natural and revealed forms, was to all intents and purposes at an end. From this time on, 'religion' became increasingly an outsider's term. Now the science of religion could no longer include the rational justification of certain religions, or types of religion. The apologetic 'impartial comparisons of the religions', which had been such an important part of religious literature of the English Enlightenment, now became data for, rather than the substance of, the science of religion. Rational discourse about religion had now to be distinguished from religious discourse itself. From its origins within theological polemic, the idea of religion had come of age in the secular world.

This secularisation of talk about religion was all the more significant because Hume had denied the 'naturalness' of religious sentiments. Not only had discourse about religion become non-religious, but it could also be reductive. Prior to Hume, even radical theories of religion were primarily theories which accounted for the corruption of (or, less pejoratively, the pluralism of expression of) pure and universal religious instincts. Now 'religion', even if acknowledged to be in some sense universal, could be explained in terms of non-religious instincts – for Hume, fear and the universal tendency to anthropomorphise. So it was that by the close of the eighteenth century, the 'reality' which the artificial construct 'religion' was supposed to represent, was itself seen as but an artifact.

EPILOGUE

I knew a real theologian once ... He knew the Brahmins, the Chaldeans, the Ignicoles, the Sabeans, the Syrians, the Egyptians, as well as he knew the Jews; he was familiar with the various readings of the Bible ... The more he grew truly learned, the more he distrusted everything he knew. As long as he lived, he was forbearing; and at his death, he confessed he had squandered his life uselessly.

Voltaire, 'Théologien', *Philosophical Dictionary*[1]

At the close of the seventeenth century it was John Toland who wished to clarify the meaning of concepts and terms by tracing their historical fortunes. For our own purposes we have followed his prescription for the terms 'religion' and 'the religions'. I hope to have shown that these two concepts appeared as an unintended consequence of a crisis within Western Christendom. They were not initially outsider's terms, as Cantwell Smith would have it, although certainly they have become that. Since the close of the eighteenth century, the two ideas have had a varied history. 'Religion' was taken up by Schleiermacher in the nineteenth century. He reacted against both the rationalists and Kant, asserting that the essence of religion was neither propositional nor moral, but to do with an inner feeling (*Gefühl*). This reaction swung the pendulum back to the medieval emphasis on piety, but at the same time helped to enshrine the centrality of 'religion' in accounts of what Christianity was supposed to be about. In our own century, however, there has been some disquiet within religious traditions themselves about the adequacy of the concept. Ironically, the strongest criticism has come from Protestant theologians. Karl Barth declared emphatically that Christianity was not to do with 'religion'. Barth believed that Christian theology took a wrong turn during the Enlightenment. A 'catastrophe' occurred, he says, 'in the movement of so-called rational orthodoxy at the beginning of the eighteenth century'. The result being that 'dogmatics now begin quite openly and unilaterally ... with the presupposition of the concept and the

description of a general and natural and neutral "religion"'.[2] Dietrich
Bonhoeffer, following Barth on this question, went as far as to suggest
the establishment of a 'religionless Christianity'.[3] In other traditions too
there is suspicion of the concept.[4]

The plural 'religions' has been even more contentious. In the nineteenth
century this idea was refined and its scope expanded. The three 'revealed
religions' – Christianity, Islam, Judaism – remain as the Western religions,
while the imprecise 'heathenism' became the so-called Eastern and primal
religions. 'Eastern religions' were born in the Western imagination in the
early 1800s – 'Boudhism' in 1821, 'Hindooism' in 1829, 'Taouism' in 1839,
and 'Confucianism' in 1862.[5] The discovery, or more correctly, the invention
of these religions by the West has been dealt with in some depth by Philip
Almond and Peter Marshall.[6]

Having considered the past of these crucial ideas it is worth considering
briefly what their future should be. It is not my intention to debunk these
notions merely by showing how they came to be constructed. Every system
of classification is artificial and to some extent arbitrary. Yet it seems to
me that the manner in which these concepts were created gives us some
insights into their inadequacies. The idea of religion leads to the view that
the religious life is primarily to do with subscribing to certain beliefs, carrying
out particular practices, and nothing more. In other words, because the
data which is available to the historian comprise only practices and beliefs,
it is taken for granted that these aspects make up the sum total of religious
commitment. It hardly needs to be said that this view is reductionistic. Admittedly, the description of these externals is all that the historian can hope
to do, but a mistake is made when it is assumed that religious persons
or communities so conceptualise these aspects of their own lives.

This problem carries over into 'the religions'. 'Religions' existed first
in the minds of Western thinkers who thought that the lives of other peoples
were governed by the kinds of concerns which were really only characteristic
of one episode of Western history. The 'world religions' were thus generated
largely through the projection of Christian disunity onto the world. It follows
that much of the perceived conflict between the so-called world religions
can be attributed to the grammar of the term 'religions', rather than to
substantive differences in matters of faith. It would be foolish to deny, of
course, that a belief in reincarnation is radically different to a belief in
resurrection of the body, or of immortality of the soul. But we must question
whether such differences are as significant as the concept of 'a religion',
propositionally conceived, makes them out to be.

The inertia of our linguistic habits makes it hard for us to relinquish
a grammar which seems to have served us well. Yet the time may now be
ripe for the adoption of new terms and new concepts. Cantwell Smith has

proposed that we guard against the distorting influence of our current conceptual framework by breaking 'religion' down into 'cumulative tradition' and 'faith'.[7] The former is to do with the externals of religion – those things to which every historian has access. The latter is the inner disposition of the individual which is largely unobservable, yet which underlies the visible structures of 'religion'. I must confess to having some reservations about Smith's notion of 'faith'. Briefly, if faith is not part of the objective, observable traditions, how can it be assumed to underly them all? Here we encounter the problem which plagued the champions of innate religiosity – the assertion of a religious *a priori* is neither falsifiable nor verifiable. We must take it on faith. Perhaps the best course of action is to proceed with our studies of the traditions armed with the knowledge that our concepts are at best inadequate, and at worst, misleading. In conclusion, I hope that this study has highlighted the need to revise some cherished assumptions about the constructs 'religion' and 'the religions' – assumptions held not only by those who carry out the academic study of religion, but also by those within religious traditions who have been dominated, to their detriment, by the idea of religion.

NOTES

INTRODUCTION

1. Wilfred Cantwell Smith, *The Meaning and End of Religion* (London: SPCK, 1978), pp. 48–50, and passim.
2. Louis Jordan's definitive *Comparative Religion: Its Genesis and Growth* (Edinburgh: T. and T. Clark, 1905), for example, devotes a mere three pages and a lengthy note (pp. 136–9, 505–8) to pre-nineteenth-century English contributions to comparative religion. Eric Sharpe's more recent *Comparative Religion: A History* (London: Duckworth, 1975), 2nd edn (1987), deals with 'deist' contributions to comparative religion in three pages as well (pp. 15–17). The only writers to give serious consideration to Enlightenment contributions to the science of religion have been Frank E. Manuel, *The Eighteenth Century Confronts the Gods* (Cambridge, Mass.: Harvard University Press, 1959), and David Pailin, *Attitudes to Other Religions: Comparative Religion in Seventeenth- and Eighteenth-Century Britain* (Manchester: Manchester University Press, 1984).
3. See, e.g., Manuel, *Eighteenth Century Confronts the Gods*; H. Pinard de la Boullaye, *L'Étude Comparée des Religions* (Paris, Gabriel Beauchesne, 1922), chs. 5, 6.
4. I am aware that a number of modern historians consider the spirit of Enlightenment to be essentially French. See, e.g., L. Crocker, *The Age of Enlightenment* (New York: Harper and Row, 1969); Peter Gay, *The Enlightenment: An Interpretation*, 1 (London: Weidenfeld and Nicolson, 1967). Curiously, this is not the view of the French *philosophes* themselves, and although we may suspect them of suffering from the fashionable *Anglomanie*, it is their judgements on the matter which I consider to be of prime importance. There is no doubt that Continental Europe looked to England as the source of Enlightenment. It is part of the burden of this book to vindicate this view. On the problems associated with some modern interpretations of 'the Enlightenment', see Roy Porter, 'The Enlightenment in England', in *The Enlightenment in National Context*, ed. Roy Porter and Mikuás Teich (Cambridge: Cambridge University Press, 1981), pp. 1–18; and J. G. A. Pocock, 'Post-Puritan England and the Problem of the Enlightenment', in *Culture and Politics From Puritanism to the Enlightenment*, ed. Perez Zagorin (Berkeley: University of California Press, 1980).
5. John Locke, *A Letter Concerning Toleration*, in *Treatise of Civil Government and A Letter Concerning Toleration*, ed. Charles L. Sherman (New York: Appleton-Century-Crofts, 1965), p. 191.
6. Henning Graf von Reventlow, *The Authority of the Bible and the Rise of the Modern World*, tr. John Bowden (Philadelphia: Fortress Press, 1984). Reventlow proposes that English deists had a much more significant role in the develop-

ment of biblical criticism than has previously been thought. See also Werner Kümmel, *The New Testament: The History of the Investigation of Its Problems*, tr. S. McLean Gilmore and Howard Kee (London: SCM, 1973), pp. 51–61.

1 ANTECEDENTS

1. See, e.g., Basil Willey, *The Eighteenth Century Background. Studies on the Idea of Nature in the Thought of the Period* (Ringwood: Penguin, 1967), p. 10.
2. Francis Bacon, *The Advancement of Learning* (1605), ed. Arthur Johnston, (Oxford: Clarendon, 1974), II.xxv.3 (p. 201).
3. On this understanding of 'nature', and its subsequent development, see Ernst Cassirer, *The Philosophy of the Enlightenment* (Princeton: Princeton University Press, 1951), pp. 40f.
4. Peter Gay refers to this aspect of the Enlightenment as the 'appeal to antiquity', *The Enlightenment*, I, xiii, and passim.
5. On the Reformation and the process of secularisation, see e.g., Peter Berger, *The Sacred Canopy* (New York: Anchor Books, 1969).
6. The *locus classicus* for this division is Romans 1.18–23.
7. See Smith, *Meaning and End of Religion*, p. 231, n. III.
8. Henricus Denzinger, *Enchiridion Symbolorum*, 33rd edn (Barcinone: Herder, 1965), 1622, 1650, 1670, 1785, 1806, 2145 (pp. 555, 562, 568, 588, 593, 688f.).
9. Commenting on Paul's assertion of evidence of God in nature, Calvin observes: 'When Paul says that that which may be known of God is manifested by the creation of the world, he does not mean such a manifestation as may be comprehended by the wit of man (Rom. i. 19); on the contrary, he shows that it has no further effect than to render us inexcusable. (Acts xvii. 27)' *Institutes of the Christian Religion*, tr. Henry Beveridge, 2 vols. (London: James Clark and Co., 1962), I.v (I, 62).
10. *Ibid.*, II. vi (I. 293).
11. 'Moreover, beyond the pale of the church no forgiveness of sins, no salvation, can be hoped for.' *Institutes*, IV.1.4; cf.; G. H. Williams, 'Erasmus and the Reformers on Non-Christian Religions and *Salus Extra Ecclesiam*', 361–3, in *Action and Conviction in Early Modern Europe*, ed. T. Rabb and J. Seigel (Princeton: Princeton University Press, 1969) pp. 319–70.
12. *Luther's Works* (Saint Louis: Concordia, 1955–75), hereafter *LW*, 19, 53.
13. Luther continues: 'So there is a vast difference between knowing that there is a God and knowing who or what God is. Nature knows the former – it is inscribed in everybody's heart; the latter is taught only by the Holy Spirit.' *LW* 19, 55. Cf. *Luther: Lectures on Romans*, ed. and tr. William Pauck (Philadelphia: Westminster, 1961), pp. 33, 41; *D. Martin Luthers Werke* (Weimar: Böhlaus, 1883–1948), hereafter *WA*, 30/1, 135; 56, 177.
14. *Ibid.*
15. 'nicht anders, denn was menschliche witze und vernunft wol leiden kan'. *WA* 30/2, 168.
16. *LW* 47, 175, 17. These false modes of faith, moreover, derived a unity not only from what they affirmed, but also from what they denied, and what they

denied, in Luther's view, was God's exclusive revelation in the person of Jesus Christ: 'Und durch deisen artickel [d.h. glaube an Jesus Christus] wird unser glaube gesondert von allen andern glauben auff erden, Denn die Jüden haben des nicht, Die Türken und Sarracener auch nicht, dazu kein Papist noch falscher Christ noch kein ander ungleubiger, sondern allein die rechten Christen.' *WA* 30/2, 186; cf. *LW* 12, 396f.; *WA* 37, 71f., *WA* 40/2, 451. Luther concludes that when a man does not have Christ in his heart 'da wird aus allem glauben ein glaube'. *WA* 37, 59. Jews, Turks and Papists, he goes on to declare, 'sind alle inn dem stück eins, das sie den glauben nicht haben und auff ander ding bawen.' *Ibid.*

17. *LW* 47, 177.

18. *LW* 46, 183f., *LW* 47, 175.

19. *LW* 46, 175, *WA* 21, 330, *WA* 53, 276f., 394f., *WA* 30/2, 168.

20. See Norman Daniel, *Islam and the West: The Making of an Image* (Edinburgh: Edinburgh University Press, 1960), esp. p. 252.

21. See, e.g., *LW* 47, 177; *LW* 46, 176, 183f. W. Holsten endorses this conclusion, stating that, for Luther, Catholicism is the 'gegenwärtige Gestalt nichtchristlicher Religion', *Christentum und nichtchristlicher Religion nach der Auffassung Luthers* (Gütersloh: Bertelsmann, 1932) p. 67.

22. David Pailin gives a valuable account of this vital aspect of the Enlightenment treatment of other traditions in the two chapters of his *Attitudes to other Religions* entitled 'The uses of "other religions" for instruction' and 'The uses of "other religions" in controversy' (pp. 105–36).

23. Said observes of the Orient: 'Thus the Orient acquired representatives, so to speak, and representations, each one more concrete, more internally congruent with some Western exigency, than the ones that preceded it. It is as if, having once settled on the Orient as a locale suitable for incarnating the infinite into a finite shape, Europe could not stop the practice; the Orient and the Oriental, Arab, Islamic, Indian, Chinese or whatever, became repetitious pseudoincarnations of some great original (Christ, Europe, the West) they were supposed to have been imitating.' *Orientalism* (London: Routledge and Kegan Paul, 1978) p. 62.

24. See Smith, *Meaning and End of Religion*, pp. 31–2.

25. *Ibid.*, p. 31.

26. Ernst Cassirer is one of the few writers who has appreciated the significance of this thinker as an influence on seventeenth-century English thought. See his *The Individual and the Cosmos in Renaissance Philosophy* (New York: Barnes and Noble, 1963), chs. 1, 2; *The Platonic Renaissance in England* (London: Nelson, 1953), pp. 11–24. An indirect avenue of Cusanus' influence which remains largely unexplored can be found in the writings of Giordano Bruno. Bruno himself subsequently became the hero of free-thinking fraternities at about the turn of the seventeenth century.

27. Max Müller, *Universal Religion* (Chicago, 1897) p. 21, qu. in Louis Jordan, *Comparative Religion*, p. 132.

28. Cassirer gives a useful summary of Cusanus' theological epistemology: 'Every spiritual being has its centre within itself. And its participation in the divine

consists precisely in this centring, in this indissoluble individuality. Individuality is not simply a *limitation*: rather it represents a particular *value* that may not be eliminated or extinguished. The One that is "beyond being" can only be grasped *through* this value. According to Cusanus, a *theodicy of religious forms and practices* is attainable only by means of this thought. For only by virtue of this thought do the multiplicity, the difference, and the heterogeneity of these forms cease to appear to be a contradiction of the unity and universality of religion and become instead a necessary expression of that universality itself.' *The Individual and the Cosmos*, pp. 28f.; also see Cassirer, *Das Erkenntnisproblem in der Philosophie und Wissenschaft der neueren Zeit*, 3 vols. (Berlin: B. Cassirer, 1906–20), I, 21f.

29. 'Cognoscitur igit inattingibilis veritatis unitas alteritate coniecturali.' *De conjecturis* i.2.fol. 76.; cf. i.13; in *Cusanus Texte*, ed. E. Hoffman, et al. (Heidelberg: Sitzungsberichte der Heidelberger Akademie der Wissenschaften, 1929–).

30. 'Oportet ut ostendatur non ex operibus, sed ex fide salvationem animae praesentari. Nam Abraham, pater fidei ominium credentium, sive Christianorum sive Arabum sive Iudaeorum, credidit Deo et reputatum est ei ad iustitiam: anima iusti haereditabit vitam aeternum. Quo admisso, non turbabunt varietates illae rituum. Nam ut signa sensibilia veritatis fidei sunt instituta et recepta. Signa autem mutationem capiunt, non signatum.' *De pace fidei*, ed. Raymundus Klibansky and Hildebrandus Bascour (Londinii: Instituti Warburgiani, 1956), XVI. fol. 121v. (pp. 51, l. 12 - 52, l. 2). Cf. 'Omnes qui umquam plures Deos coluerunt divinitatem esse praesupposuerunt. Illam enim in omnibus diis tanquam in participantibus eandem adorant. Sicut enim albedine non existente non sunt alba: ita divinitate non existente non sunt dii. Cultus igitur deorum confitetur divinitatem.' *Ibid.*, VI. fol. 116r. (p. 16).

31. 'Noli igitur amplius te occultare, Domine; sis propitius et ostende faciem tuam, et salvi erunt omnes populi ... Si sic facere dignaberis, cessabit gladius et odii livor, et quaeque mala; et congnoscent omnes quomodo non est nisi religio una in rituum varietate. Quod si forte haec differentia rituum tolli non poterit aut non expedit, ut diversitas sit devotionis adauctio, quando quaelibet regio suis cerimoniis quasi tibi regi gratioribus vigilantiorum operam impendet: saltem ut sicut tu unus es, una sit religio et unus latriae cultus.' *Ibid.*, I. fol. 114v. (p. 7, lines 4–15).

32. 'Cultusque diuinus ita fermè hominibus est naturalis, sicut equis hinnitus, canibusue latratus.' *Theologica Platonica*, bk. 14, ch. 9, *Opera*, 2 tom., (Basileæ: Ex officina Henrici petrina, 1576), I, 319–21, cf., Ficino, *De Christiana Religione*, ch. 1 (*Opera*, I, 2ff.). Also see Smith, *Meaning and End of Religion*, pp. 32–4, 221f.

33. 'Omnes hominum opiniones, affectus, mores, excepta religione, mutantur'. *Theologica Platonica*, 14.9 (*Opera*, I, 320).

34. 'Diuina prouidentia ... quamuis permittat uarijs locis atque temporibus, ritus adorationis uarios obseruari. Forsitan uero uarietas huiusmodi, ordinante Deo, decorem quendam parit in uniuerso mirabilem.' *Opera*, I, 4.

35. 'Christus est idea & exemplar uirtutum'. *Opera*, I, 4.

36. Ficino actually maintained that the religious orientation and the true philoso-

phical orientation are, in the end, the same – viz. orientation towards truth and Wisdom (God). Thus the best philosophers are also the best Christians.

37. 'Omnis religio boni habet nonnihil, modo ad deum ipsum creatorem omnium dirigatur Christiana sycera est.' *Ibid.*, I, 4.

38. It follows that other faiths will come under fire when their adherents pose some physical threat to the West. Luther's *Heerpredigt wider den Türken* (*WA* 30/2) is a conspicuous example of this principle.

39. Gay, *The Enlightenment*, I, passim.

40. *Ibid.*, I, 34.

41. 'But the theories of our modern men of enlightenment must be held to account for the mischief they cause. Now the effect of their compositions is this. When you and I produce our evidence of the existence of gods, and allege this very point – the deity or divinity of the sun, moon, planets and earth – the converts of these sages will reply that they are but earth and stones, incapable of minding human conduct, however plausibly we have coated them over with a varnish of sugared eloquence … this party [the sophists] asserts that gods have no real or natural, but only artificial being, in virtue of legal conventions, as they call them, and thus there are different gods for different places, conformably to the convention made by each group among themselves when they drew up their legislation.' Plato, *Laws*, X. 886 d, e; 889 e, in *The Collected Dialogues*, ed. Edith Hamilton and Huntington Cairns, Bollington Series LXXI (Princeton: Princeton University Press, 1982), pp. 1442, 1445.

42. Xenophanes of Colophon (fl. 540–500 BC) had earlier put forward a kind of projection theory, suggesting that humans tend to project their own qualities onto the Gods. 'The Ethiopians', he observed, 'make their Gods black and snub nosed; the Thracians say theirs have blue eyes and red hair.' *Die Fragmente der Vorsokratiker*, ed. H. Diels, 6th edn, 3 vols. (Dublin: Weidmann, 1966–7), frg. 16. In preceding fragments Xenophanes notes that 'if oxen and horses had hands, and could paint with their hands, and produce works of art as men do, horses would paint the forms of the gods as horses, and oxen like oxen, and make their bodies in the image of their several kinds' (frg. 15). Xenophanes' critique of the Olympian gods, however, is based more on theological grounds than naturalistic ones. He wished to commend the 'One god, the greatest among gods and men, neither in form like mortals, nor in thought … He sees all over, thinks all over, and hears all over. But without toil he sways all things by the thought of his mind' (frgs. 23, 24, 25).

43. 'and there are some who have supposed that we have arrived at the conception of Gods from those events in the world which are marvellous; which opinion seems to have been held by Democritus, who says – "For when men of old time beheld the disasters in the heavens, such as thunderings and lightnings, and thunderbolts and collisions between stars, and eclipses of sun and moon, they were affrighted, imagining the Gods to be the causes of these things."' Sextus Empiricus, *Against the Physicists*, 1.24, in *Sextus Empiricus*, tr. G. Bury, 3 vols., Loeb Classical Library (London: Heinemann, 1936), III, 13.

44. In fact this latter idea was older than Democritus, and harks back to the earlier Ionian scientists. Plutarch speaks of the influence of Anaxagoras on

Pericles: 'It appears that he [Pericles] was also lifted by him above superstition, that feeling which is produced by amazement at what happens in regions above us. It affects those who are ignorant of the causes of such things, and are crazed about divine intervention, and confounded through their inexperience in this domain; whereas the doctrines of natural philosophy remove such ignorance and inexperience, and substitute for timorous and inflamed superstition that unshaken reverence which is attended by good hope.' Plutarch, *Pericles*, VI.I, in *Plutarch's Lives*, tr. Bernadette Perrin, II vols., Loeb Classical Library (London: Heinemann, 1914–26), III, 15. Cf. Plato, *Laws*, VII. 821 d; *Epinomis*, 991.

45. Thomas Hobbes, *Leviathan*, ed. Michael Oakeshot (New York: Collier Books, 1962), ch. 12; Vico, *The New Science*, tr. T. G. Bergin and M. H. Frisch (Ithaca: Cornell University Press, 1948), section 337; Hume, *The Natural History of Religion*, ed. H. E. Root (Stanford: Stanford University Press, 1957), pp. 27f.

46. Sextus, *Against the Physicists*, I.19, 42 (Loeb edn, III, II, 23).

47. Eduard Zeller goes as far as to claim that Democritus was the first to set out upon this path which many subsequently followed: 'Democritus may so far be considered as the first who, in mediating between philosophy and popular religion, entered upon the course so often pursued in after times, viz., that of degrading the gods of polytheism into demons.' *A History of Greek Philosophy*, tr. S. F. Alleyne, 2 vols. (London: Longmans, 1881), II, 290.

48. See, e.g. Justin Martyr, *Apology*, I, 5,2; 9,1; 12, 5; 62,2; 64, 1; Clement of Alexandria, *Protreptikos*, 3, 42, 1; Theodoret, *The Cure of Hellenic Maladies*, 7, 3; Augustine, *City of God*, VII, 33 (p. 239).

49. Whether Critias himself held this view is not entirely clear. Almost certainly he was not the originator of this thesis. A. B. Drachmann proposed that Critias neither authored nor held this view. *Atheism in Pagan Antiquity* (London: Glynendal, 1922), p. 19. F. M. Cornford, on the other hand, holds that one may generally attribute to Greek dramatists the views of their characters. (*Greek Religious Thought from Homer to the Age of Alexander* (London: Dent, 1923), p. xiv.

50. Sextus, *Against the Physicists*, I.54 (Loeb edn, III, 31).

51. Plato, *Republic*, V.459c; cf. III.389b, 414b; *Laws*, VII.798b.

52. See e.g., Cicero, *On the Nature of the Gods*, II.71; III.3; Polybius, *Histories*, VI.56.

53. Sextus, *Against the Physicists*, I.18 (Loeb edn, III, II); cf. Cicero, *On the Nature of the Gods*, I.118.

54. Plato, *Protagoras*, 337, 341a; *Charmides*, 163d; *Euthydemus*, 277e; *Thaetetus* 151b. Apparently he also offered courses in 'terminology' for 50 drachma, which caused Socrates to complain that he could only afford the 1-drachma course. *Cratylus*, 384b. Actually 50 drachma was quite reasonable compared to the 100 minae which, according to Diogenes Laertius (IX. 52), Protagoras charged.

55. A. B. Drachmann has proposed something similar to this: 'Now he [Prodicus] found that Homer occasionally simply substituted the name of Hephaestus for fire, and that the other poets went even further on the same lines. Further-

more, while it was common knowledge to every Greek that certain natural objects, such as heavenly bodies and rivers, were regarded as divine and had names in common with their gods, this to Prodicus would be a specially attractive subject for speculation. It is plainly shown by his instances that it is linguistic observations of this kind which were the starting point of his theory concerning the origin of the conceptions of the gods.' *Atheism in Pagan Antiquity*, p. 43.

56. This tendency finds clear expression in Plato's *Cratylus*, in which the characters, in a somewhat tiresome manner, worry over the origins of various names. Consider, e.g., the following:

> I suspect that the sun, moon, earth, stars, and heaven, which are still the only gods of many barbarians, were the only gods known to the aboriginal Hellenes. Seeing that they were always moving and running, from their running nature they were called gods or runners (*theous, theontas*) . . .
>
> . . . other poets say truly that when a good man dies he has honour and a mighty portion among the dead, and becomes a daemon, which is a name given to him signifying wisdom. And I say too, that every wise man who happens to be a good man is more than human (*daimonion*) both in life and death, and is rightly called a demon . . .
>
> Poseidon is *posidesmos*, the chain of the feet. The original inventor of the name had been stopped by the watery element in his walks, and not allowed to go on, and therefore he called the ruler of this element Poseidon. (*Cratylus*, 396d, 398c, 402e (Hamilton and Cairns edn, pp. 435f, 439f.)

57. See, e.g., Herodotus, 'They call them gods (*theoi*) because of all things and the due assignment thereof were by them set in order (*thentes*)'. *Histories*, II.52, tr. A. D. Godley, 4 vols., Loeb Classical Library (London: Heinemann, 1920–5) I, 341.

58. Eduard Zeller, *Stoics, Epicureans and Sceptics*, tr. Oswald Reichel (London: Longmans, 1892), p. 468.

59. *Cratylus*, 398c (Hamilton and Cairns edn, p. 435).

60. The story is recounted in Diodorus Siculus, *History*, VI.I; Eusebius, *Evangelica Praeparatio*, II.2; Lactantius, *Divine Institutes*, I.14. Similar stories have also been attributed to Hecataeus of Miletus (fl. 500 BC) and Dionysius Scytobrachion (fl. 2nd century BC). See Diodorus Siculus, *History*, II.47; III.52–3; *Die Fragmente der griechischen Historiker*, ed. Felix Jacoby, 3 vols. (Leiden: Brill, 1954–64), I. 238f.; Polybius, *Histories*, XXXIV.2. Also see T. S. Brown, 'Euhemerus and the Historians', *Harvard Theological Review*, 39 (1946), 265. It should be noted that Brown seems to confuse Hecataeus of Miletus with Hecataeus of Abdera.

61. Sextus, *Against the Physicists*, I.17 (Loeb edn, III, 9–11).

62. Clement of Alexandria, *Cohortatio ad Gentes*, I.V. 55; Tertullian, *Ad Nationes*, II.13f.; Lactantius, *Divine Institutes*, I.XV.

2 RELIGION AND THE LIGHT OF NATURE

1. Calvin, *Institutes*, III. ii (I, 471).

2. There were many catechisms based on the Thirty-Nine Articles and the West-minster Confession. The following are representative: Anon., *The Summe of Christian Religion ... Serving for Instruction of the Simpler Sort* (London: Pr. by T. Creed for T. Man, 1607); Anon., *Short and Plain Catechism, Instructing the Learner of Christian Religion What he is to Believe, and What to Practise*, 4th edn (London: Pr. for Francis Tyton, 1668); Anon, *Short Questions and Answeares, contayning the Summe of Christian Religion* (London: Pr. by Iohn Dawson, 1641); Clement Ellis, *A Catechism wherein the Learner is at Once Taught to Rehearse, and Prove all the Main Points of the Christian Religion* (London: Pr. for Sam. Richards, 1674); T. Roberts, *The Catechisme in Meter, for the Easier Learnyng, and Better Remembryng of Prinples [sic] of Faithe* (London: Pr. by J. Kingston for R. Walley, 1583).

3. Thomas Rogers, *The Faith, Doctrin and Religion Professed in this Realme of England* (London: Pr. for William Hope, 1658) Preface.

4. *The Scotch Confession of Faith*, Art. XII, in Philip Schaff, *The Creeds of Christendom*, 4th edn 3 vols. (New York: Harper, 1919), III, 450f.

5. 'The Thirty-Nine Articles', Art. XVIII (Schaff, III, 499).

6. 'The Westminster Confession', I.I (Schaff, III, 600).

7. *The Confession of Faith, and the Larger and Shorter Catechisms together with The Summe of Saving Knowledge* (Edinburgh: Heirs of G. Anderson, 1652). David Dickson, author of the summary, later published it separately under the same title, *The Summe of Saving Knowledge* (Edinburgh: Pr. by George Swintoun, and Thomas Brown, 1671). Other works which stress the necessity of 'saving knowledge' are: John Brinsley (the Younger, 1600–65), *A Breviate of Saving Knowledge* (London: Pr. by G. M. for Iohn Burroughes, 1643), and *The Christian Cabala, or, Sure Tradition: Necessary to be Known and Believed, by All that Will be Saved* (London: Pr. for George Sawbridge, 1662); Samuel Cradock's two volumes, *Knowledge and Practise: Or a Plain Discourse of the Chief Things Necessary to be Known, Believ'd, and Practiced in Order to Salvation* (London: Pr. by J. Hayes, for John Rothwell, 1659), and *A Supplement to Knowledge and Practice, Wherein the Main Things Necessary to be Known and Believed in Order to Salvation are Fully Explained* (London: Pr. for Thomas Simmons, 1679). Note that in the twenty years between these two works, the salvific 'practices' have disappeared. Also John Davenport, *The Knovvledge of Christ Indispensibly Required of all Men that Would be Saved* (London: Pr. for L. Chapman, 1653); George Walker, *The Key of Saving Knowledge* (London: Pr. by Tho. Badger, 1641); Richard Younge, *A Short and Sure Way to Grace and Salvation: Being ... Three Fundamental Principles ... Which few do indeed know, and yet hee who knows them not, cannot bee saved* (London, 1658).

8. Because theological disputation in England at this time is often portrayed in terms of a struggle between Calvinism and Arminianism, it needs to be stressed that the doctrine of predestination is not the sum total of Calvinism, nor is it even the distinguishing feature of Calvinism. Augustine and many prominent schoolmen advocated election in this form, and Calvin's fellow reformers Luther and Zwingli were, if more circumspect, certainly no less committed to it than Calvin himself. See A. S. Martin, 'Election', *Encyclopaedia*

of Religion and Ethics, ed. James Hastings, 12 vols. (Edinburgh: T. & T. Clark, 1908–21), III, 146. Nonetheless, it is clear from the seventeenth- and eighteenth-century uses of the term, that for many, 'Calvinism' denoted that theological position which involved commitment to predestination. It is for this reason that Arminians were seen to be the great enemies of Calvinism, for Arminianism differs from Calvinism on this very point, namely the issue of election.

Some confusion also exists over the terms 'Puritan' and 'Presbyterian' which are often used synonymously and as equivalents for 'Calvinist'. The terms actually refer to discrete, if overlapping, groups. Certainly one could be a Puritan without being a Presbyterian, and the Calvinism of James I did nothing to stifle his anti-Puritan sentiments. For further clarification of these terms, see: Godfrey Davies, 'Arminian versus Puritan in England, *c.* 1620–1650', *Huntington Library Bulletin*, 5 (1934), 157–79; Nicholas R. N. Tyacke, 'Purita-nism, Arminianism, and Counter-Revolution', *Origins of the English Civil War*, ed. Conrad Russell (London: Macmillan, 1973).

9. 'Thirty-Nine Articles', Art. XVII (Schaff, III, 497).

10. See Schaff, I, 634–8.

11. Peter Baro, *In Ionam Prophetam Prælectiones 39* (Londini: Apud Joannem Dayum, 1579); *De fide, eiusque ortu, & Natura, explicato* (Londini: Apud R. Dayum, 1580). Cf. Schaff, III, 659.

12. 'The Lambeth Articles' (Schaff, III 523). The Queen took a dim view of the activities of the convocation (which had met without her sanction) and ordered the suppression of the articles and the prosecution of their authors. This action, however, was largely owing to royal pique and was not a systematic effort to hinder the progress of Calvinism. See Thomas Fuller, *Church History of Britain*, 6 pt (London: Pr. for J. Williams, 1655), V, 222.

13. 'Westminster Confession', III.iii (Schaff, III 609).

14. x.iv (Schaff, III 625).

15. Thus, A. A. Hodge comments on these articles: 'in the case of sane adult persons a knowledge of Christ and a voluntary acceptance of him is essential ... The heathen in mass, with no single definite and unquestionable exception on record, are evidently strangers to God, and going down to death in an unsaved condition. The possibility of being saved without a knowledge of Christ remains, after eighteen-hundred years, a possibility illustrated by no example.' *The Confession of Faith* (London: The Banner of Truth Trust, 1958), p. 176. Certainly this interpretation seems true to Calvin himself, who was sceptical of the possibility of salvation for any of the heathen: 'The more shameful, therefore, is the presumption of those who throw heaven open to the unbelieving and profane, in the absence of that grace which Scripture uniformly describes as the only door by which we enter into life ... Hence also Paul affirms, that all the Gentiles were "without God", and deprived of the hope of life'. *Institutes*, II.vi.1 (I, 293). Cf. Theophilus Gale, *The Court of the Gentiles*, 4 vols. (Oxford: Pr. by Will. Hall for Tho. Gilbert, 1669–77), pt II, preface; Robert South, *Twelve Sermons Preached Upon Several Occasions* (London: Pr. by J. H. for Thomas Bennet, 1692), p. 89. See also Williams, 'Erasmus and the Reformers on Non-Christian Religions and *Salus Extra*

Ecclesiam', pp. 361f.

16. 'Westminster Confession', XI.i,ii. (Schaff, III, 626).

17. Rosalie Colie writes: 'Arminianism had penetrated everywhere in England, except of course among the Presbyterians ... until in 1688 the technical triumph of Arminianism in England was complete.' *Light and Enlightenment* (Cambridge: Cambridge University Press, 1957), p. 21. The stages of the so-called 'rise of Arminianism' are by no means clear however. See e.g., Nicholas R. N. Tyacke, 'Puritanism, Arminianism and Counter-Revolution', pp. 119–43; Jonathan M. Atkins, 'Calvinist Bishops, Church Unity, and the Rise of Arminianism', *Albion*, 18 (1986), 411–27; Nicholas Tyacke and Peter White, 'Debate: The Rise of Arminianism Reconsidered', *Past and Present*, 115 (1987), 201–29.

18. 'Five Arminian Articles', I (Schaff, III, 545–9).

19. The terms 'natural religion' and 'revealed religion' did not gain currency until the latter half of the seventeenth century. Richard Baxter's *The Reasons of the Christian Religion* (Pr. by R. White for Fran. Titon, 1667), contains one of the earliest English uses of 'natural religion'. The work is divided into two parts, entitled respectively, 'Of Natural Religion or Godliness', and 'Of Christianity, and Supernatural Revelation'. Ralph Cudworth, at about the same time, begins to use the term 'revealed religion' in the 1678 edition of *The True Intellectual System of the Universe*. The dual expression is introduced in Timothy Nourse's *A Discourse of Natural and Reveal'd Religion in Several Essays* (London: Pr. for John Newton, 1691). From the last decade of the 1600s the terms become quite common. See, e.g., Thomas Beconsall, *The Grounds and Foundation of Natural Religion, Discover'd* (London: Pr. by W. O. for A. Roper, A. Bosvile, and G. West, 1698), Francis Gastrell, *The Certainty of the Christian Revelation ... in Opposition to ... Such as Pretend to Allow Natural Religion and Reject the Gospel* (London: Pr. for Thomas Bennet, 1699), Henry Hallywell, *A Defence of Revealed Religion* (London: Pr. for Walter Kettilby, 1694), Stephen Nye, *A Discourse Concerning Natural and Revealed Religion* (London: Pr. by T. W. for Jonathan Robinson, 1696), John Wilkins, *Of the Principles and Duties of Natural Religion* (London: Pr. by A. Maxwell, for T. Basset, H. Brome, R. Chiswell, 1675). Joseph Butler's eighteenth-century classic, *The Analogy of Religion, Natural and Revealed, to the Constitution and Course of Nature* (London: J., J. & P. Knapton, 1736), assured a permanent place for these terms in the theological lexicon. Also see Smith, *Meaning and End of Religion*, pp. 40–1, 231, n. 112. (Smith has these terms appearing a little later.)

20. Calvinist Thomas Halyburton provides the definitive statement of the orthodox position in *Natural Religion Insufficient; and Revealed Necessary to Man's Happiness in his Present State* (Edinburgh: Pr. by the Heirs and Successors of A. Anderson, 1714). Matthew Tindal is a spokesman for deism. See his *Christianity as Old as the Creation; or the Gospel, a Republication of the Religion of Nature* (London: 1730). Samuel Clarke's celebrated Boyle Lectures for the years 1704–5 expound the middle position. In particular, see 'The Evidences of Natural and Revealed Religion', in *A Discourse on the Being and Attributes of God*, 7th edn (London: Pr. by W. Botham, for James and John Knapton, 1728). Sir Leslie Stephen's *History of English Thought in the Eighteenth Century*, 3rd

edn, 2 vols. (New York: Peter Smith, 1949) still provides the best account of the controversy over the place of natural religion. For the significance of the debate in the assessment of the positive religions, see Pailin, *Attitudes to Other Religions*, pp. 23–44.

21. Nathaniel Crouch, *The Strange and Prodigious Religions, Customs, and Manners, of Sundry Nations* (London: Pr. for Henry Rhodes, 1683), pp. 27f. (The author given on the title page of this work is 'R. D.', but the Wing catalogue attributes it to Nathaniel Crouch.) Cf. Humphrey Prideaux: 'The grand and fundamental doctrine of the *Religion*, which *Jesus Christ* left his *Church*', 'the whole *Religion* which he taught them', 'the *Religion* which they taught', 'the *Religion* which they propagated'. These occur within the context of an attack on the natural religion of the 'Deists'. Humphrey Prideaux, *A Letter to the Deists* (1696), pp. 30f. and passim, in *The True Nature of Imposture Fully Display'd in the Life of Mahomet*, 2nd edn (London: William Rogers, 1697).

22. Rogers, *Faith, Doctrin and Religion*.

23. Younge, *A Short and Sure Way*, title page.

24. Nicholas Gibbon, *Theology Real, and Truly Scientifical* (London, 1687?).

25. William Ames, *The Svbstance of Christian Religion* (London: Pr. by T. Mabb for Thomas Davies, 1659); Hugh Binning, *The Common Principles of Christian Religion* (Glasgow: Pr. by Andrew Anderson, 1659); Edward Boughen, *The Principles of Religion* (Oxford: Pr. by Leonard Lichfield, 1646); Clement Ellis, *The Summe of Christianity* (London: Pr. for Will. Rogers, 1696); Edward Fisher, *Faith in Five Fundamental Principles* (London: Pr. for J. Wright, 1650); John Godolphin, *The Holy Arbor, contayning a Body of Divinity: or, The Summe and Substance of Christian Religion* (London: Pr. by John Field for Edmund Paxton, and William Roybould, 1651); Matthew Hale, *A Discourse of the Knowledge of God ... to which are added A Brief Abstract of the Christian Religion* (London: Pr. by B. W. for William Shrowsbery, 1688); Henry Isaacson, *The Summe and Substance of Christian Religion* (London: 1646); Edward Leigh, *A Systeme or Body of Divinity ... Wherein the Fundamentals and Main Grounds of Religion are Opened Up* (London: Pr. by A. M. for William Lees, 1654); Herbert Palmer, *An Endeavovr of Making the Principles of the Christian Religion... Plaine and Easie*, 3rd edn (London: Pr. for Thomas Vnderhill, 1644); Matthew Scriver, *A Course of Divinity: Or, An Introduction to the Knowledge of the True Catholic Religion* (London: Pr. by Tho. Roycroft for Robert Clavil, 1674); Richard Steele, *A Scheme and Abstract of the Christian Religion* (London: Pr. for Samuel Sprint, 1684); John Tickell, *The Sum and Substance of Religion* (Exeter, 1665?); James Ussher, *A Body of Divinitie, or the Summe and Substance of Christian Religion, Catechistically Propounded* (London: Pr. by M. F. for Tho. Downes and Geo: Badger, 1645); T. W., *The Key of Knowledge Opening the Principles of Religion* (London: Pr. for Tho. Parkhurst, 1682); William Wake, *The Principles of the Christian Religion Explained* (London: Pr. for Richard Sare, 1699); William Whitaker, *A Short Sum of Christianity* (London: Pr. for J. E., 1651) etc.

26. (My emphasis) Harris quotes with approval the words of James in rather loose translation: 'Pure religion [*threskeia*] – is this, to visit the Fatherlesse and

widowes in their affliction, and to keep himselfe unspotted from the World', *True Religion in the Old Way of Piety and Charity* (London: Pr. by John Bartlet, 1645).

27. Richard Allestree, *The Causes of the Decay of Christian Piety, Or, An Impartial Survey of the Ruins of Christian Religion, undermin'd by Christian Practice* (London, 1667). Allestree was Regius Professor of Divinity at Oxford, and possibly authored *The Whole Duty of Man* (Oxford, 1684). Richard Baxter, a man of obvious piety and moderation, distinguishes 'falsely pretended knowledge' from 'true saving knowledge and love', denying that mere cognisance of religious doctrines was sufficient. *A Treatise of Knowledge and Love Compared* (London: Pr. for Tho. Parkhurst, 1689).

28. See, e.g., Anon., *An Impartial Account of the Doctrines of the Church of Rome* (London: Pr. by H. L., 1679); John Bradley, *An Impartial View of the Truth of Christianity* (London: Pr. by W. Downing for Michael Johnson, 1699); Gilbert Burnet, *An Impartial Survey and Comparison of the Protestant Religion* (1685); John Cockburn, *An Enquiry into the Nature, Necessity and Evidence of Christian Faith* (London: Pr. for William Keblewhite, 1697–9); Robert Grove, *The Protestant and Popish Way of Interpreting Scripture, Impartially Compared* (London: Pr. for Walter Kettilby, 1689); Henry Hammond, *Of the Reasonableness of the Christian Religion* (London: Pr. by J. R. for R. Royston, 1650); Robert Jenkin, *The Reasonableness and Certainty of the Christian Religion*, 2nd edn (London: Pr. for P. B. and R. Wellington, 1700); John Locke, *The Reasonableness of Christianity* (London: Pr. for Awnsham and John Churchill, 1695); James Lowde, *The Reasonableness of the Christian Religion* (London: Pr. for Walter Kettilby, 1684); John Owen, *A Brief and Impartial Account of the Nature of the Protestant Religion* (London: Pr. by J. A., 1682); Francis Roberts, *Believers Evidences* (London: Pr. by T. R. and E. M. for George Calvert, 1649); Edward Stillingfleet, *A Rational Account of the Grounds of Protestant Religion* (London: Pr. by Rob. White for Henry Mortlock, 1665); Abraham Woodhead, *A Rational Account of the Doctrine of Roman Catholics* (London: Pr. 1673). So pervasive was the spirit of rationalism that even non-propositional, devotional aspects of Christianity were 'rationalised'. Thus we find two anonymous works dealing with prayer and 'daily religion': *A Rational Discourse concerning Prayer* (London, 1669), and *A Rational Method of Daily Religion* (London, 1697).

29. Richard Younge, *The Cause and Cure of Ignorance, Error, Enmity, Atheisme, Prophanesse etc.* (London: Pr. by R. I., for N. Brook, 1648).

30. John Edwards, *Some Thoughts Concerning the Several Causes and Occasions of Atheism* (London: Pr. for J. Robinson, 1695).

31. Jean Le Clerc, *A Treatise of the Causes of Incredulity* (London: Pr. for Awnsham and John Churchill, 1697).

32. John Flavell, *Planelogia. A Succinct and Seasonable Discourse of the Occasions, Causes, Nature, Rise, Growth, and Remedies of Mental Errors* (London: Pr. by R. Roberts, for T. Cockerill, 1691), pp. 2f., 9.

33. John Muirhead, *The Platonic Tradition in Anglo-Saxon Philosophy* (Cambridge: Cambridge University Press, 1931) p. 28.

34. Jonathan Swift, *Gulliver's Travels* (Ringwood: Penguin, 1985), IV. 5 (p. 292).

35. Introductions to the group may be found in the following: Ernst Cassirer, *The Platonic Renaissance in England*; John Muirhead, *The Platonic Tradition in Anglo-Saxon Philosophy*; W. C. de Pauley, *The Candle of the Lord: Studies in the Cambridge Platonists* (London: SPCK, 1937); Frederick Powicke, *The Cambridge Platonists: A Study* (Hildesheim: George Olms Verlag, 1970); John Tulloch, *Rational Theology and Christian Philosophy in England in the Seventeenth Century*, 2nd edn, 2 vols. (Edinburgh: Blackwood, 1874), II.

36. 'Those things upon which all men agree must necessarily be true', Cicero, *De Natura Deorum*, I.17.

37. On the relation of Descartes to the Cambridge Platonists see J. E. Saveson, 'Differing Reactions to Descartes among the Cambridge Platonists', *Journal of the History of Ideas*, 21 (1960), 560–7; also Saveson's 'Descartes' Influence on John Smith', *Journal of the History of Ideas*, 20 (1959), 258–63; and Danton B. Sailor, 'Cudworth and Descartes', *Journal of the History of Ideas*, 23 (1962), 133–40.

38. See Calvin, *Institutes*, I.iii.1.

39. Joseph Glanvill, *Two Choice and Vseful Treatises* (London: Pr. for James Collins and Sam Lowndes, 1682), p. 157. The issue of the goodness of a predestining Deity caused wide-ranging debate in the latter half of the seventeenth century. See, e.g. Henry Hallywell, *Deus Justificatus: Or, the Divine Goodness* (London: Pr. by E. Cotes for Walter Kettilby, 1668), esp. pp. 91, 255 (The British Museum Catalogue attributes this work to Laurence Womock, Bishop of St David's); Samuel Parker, *An Account of the Nature and Extent of the Divine Dominion and Goodnesse* (Oxford: Pr. by W. Hall for R. Davis, 1666); E[dward] W[arren], *No Præexistence* (London: Pr. by T. R. for Samuel Thomson, 1667), p. 8. Also Samuel Hoard, *God's Love Unto Mankind* (London: Pr. for John Clark, 1656); William Twisse, *The Riches of God's Love unto the Vessels of Mercy Consistent with his Absolute Hatred or Reprobation* (Oxford: Pr. by L. L. and H. H. for Tho. Robinson, 1653).

40. Richard Hooker, *Of the Lawes of Ecclesiastical Politie* (1593–7) I.ii.5–6, in *Works*, ed. W. Speed Hill, Folger Library edn (Cambridge, Mass.: Harvard University Press, 1977), pp. 71f.

41. George Rust, 'A Discourse of Truth', in Glanvill, *Two Treatises*, p. 177. I am aware that there has been considerable discussion about the positive relationship between Calvinist theology and the new science. The classic statement of the 'Protestantism/Puritanism science hypothesis' (derived from Weber's and Tawney's linking of capitalism and protestant ideology) is Robert Merton's 'Science, Technology and Society in Seventeenth-Century England', *Osiris*, 4 (1938), 414–38. For a discussion of this thesis, see papers by S. F. Mason, H. F. Kearney, Christopher Hill, Theodore Rabb, and Barbara Shapiro in Charles Webster (ed.), *The Intellectual Revolution of the Seventeenth Century* (London: Routledge and Kegan Paul, 1974). Also, see, more recently, Margaret Jacob, *The Radical Enlightenment: Pantheists, Freemasons and Republicans* (London: George Allen and Unwin, 1981), ch. 1. On this particular issue, however, I believe we have a clear instance in which the principles of the new science counted against Calvinism, and to the extent that puritanism was Calvinist,

against puritanism.

42. As is the case with all such designations, this one is somewhat contentious. Some have suggested that Henry More is a more obvious candidate. See, e.g., C. A. Staudenbauer, 'Platonism, Theosophy and Immaterialism: Recent Views of the Cambridge Platonists', *Journal of the History of Ideas*, 35 (1974), 157–69. The problem is compounded by the fact that Whichcote did not publish during his life-time, and consequently his influence is difficult to trace. Be that as it may, if the viewpoint outlined here was not influential, it was at least typical.

43. A detailed account of Whichcote's understanding of the relation of reason and revelation is given in J. D. Roberts Senr., *From Puritanism to Platonism in Seventeenth-Century England* (The Hague: Marinus Nijhoff, 1968), ch. 6.

44. Benjamin Whichcote, *The Works of the Learned Benjamin Whichcote, D.D.* (Aberdeen, Pr. by J. Chalmers for Alexander Thomson, 1751), III, 20. Whichcote was subsequently to modify this view, suggesting that knowledge of God's (moral) nature is natural, while knowledge of his will is revealed. But in any case, he seems to regard the former as being the core of religion. Morality, the chief part of religion, may be communicated to us either by reason, or by revelation.

45. This view of the relation between reason and revelation was to become prevalent amongst both the Cambridge Platonists and the deists. For example, Matthew Tindal, one of the deist writers of the next century, declared that '*Natural* religion ... differs not from *reveal'd* but in the manner of its being communicated.' *Christianity as Old as the Creation* (London, 1730), p. 3.

46. *Ibid.*, 20, 28.

47. Some discussion of the meaning of 'reason' in this context is given by Jackson I. Cope, *Joseph Glanville, Anglican Apologist* (St Louis: Washington University Studies, 1956), pp. 70–2.

48. *Meno*, 100.b,c.

49. Richard Baxter, *The State of Souls Moderately Examined*, Baxter MSS. Treatises, iv, ff. 227–55; Qu. in Vivian de Sola Pinto (the Elder), *Peter Sterry, Platonist and Puritan, 1613–1672* (Cambridge: Cambridge University Press, 1934).

50. *Works*, III, 163; cf. *Moral and Religious Aphorisms* (London: Mathews & Morrot, 1930), no. 76.

51. John Locke, *An Essay Concerning Human Understanding*, ed. A. C. Fraser (New York: Dover, 1959), II, IV.xviii.10 (p. 425).

52. Thus, John Toland: 'For as 'tis by *Reason* we arrive at the Certainty of God's own Existence, so we cannot otherwise discern his *Revelations* but by their Conformity with our natural Notices of him, which is in so many words, to agree with our common Notions.' *Christianity not Mysterious* (London, 1696), p. 30; Thomas Chubb: 'Reason is the judge of the meaning and sense of divine revelation. Reason ought to be the judge of *every part* of that revelation.' *The Comparative Excellence and Obligation of Moral and Positive Duties* (London: Pr. for J. Roberts, 1730), p. 26, cf. p. 15; Thomas Morgan: 'The moral Truth, Reason, or Fitness ... is the only Mark or Criterion of any Doctrine as coming from God, or as making any Part of true Religion.' *The Moral Philosopher*

(London: Pr. for the Author, 1737), [vol. 1] pp. viii, cf. pp. 429f. For Anthony Collins, subjecting all to the bar of reason was the essence of 'free-thinking'. *A Discourse of Free-Thinking* (London, 1713).

53. *Works*, IV, 147.

54. *Works*, III, 20f, 31.

55. 3 vols., ed. John Harrison (London: Thomas Tegg, 1845). The numbering of the sections of the original work is rather erratic. When referring to this work I have given the original section numbers which are followed by the volume and page numbers of the Harrison edition. Cudworth's *Treatise concerning Eternal and Immutable Morality* is appended to the third volume of this edition.

56. *Ibid.*, I. IV.xxxvi (II, 312f.). Cudworth's view was of course not entirely novel. A number of the early Fathers (in particular Lactantius, Clement of Alexandria and Eusebius) had made similar claims. A more complete discussion of this tradition of 'Ancient Theology' will be given in the fifth chapter.

57. *Ibid.*, (II, 313). So too, Henry More: 'Wherefore it is very plain that *Pythagoras* had his *Philosophy* from *Moses.*' *Conjectura Cabbalistica*, p. 101, cf. 102f., in *A Collection of Several Philosophical Writings of D. Henry More*, 2nd edn (London: Pr. by J. Flesher for W. Morden, 1662); and Nathaniel Culverwel: 'the whole generality of the Heathen went a gleaning in the Jewish Fields', *An Elegant and Learned Discourse of the Light of Nature* (London: Pr. by T. R. and E. M. for John Rothwell, 1652), p. 67.

58. *Ibid*, I. IV.xxxiii (II, 480).

59. Henry More, *An Antidote Against Atheisme* (London: Pr. by Roger Daniel, 1653), bk I, ch. 10 (p. 29).

60. Anthony Ashley Cooper, Third Earl of Shaftesbury, *Characteristics of Men, Manners, Opinions, Times*, ed. John M. Robertson (Indianapolis: Bobbs- Merril, 1964), Treatise I, sec. VI (p. 35).

61. See, e.g., Drachmann, *Atheism in Pagan Antiquity*, passim.

62. David Hume, *An Enquiry Concerning Human Understanding*, 17, in *Enquiries Concerning Human Understanding and Concerning the Principles of Morals*, ed. L. A. Selby-Bigge, 3rd edn (Oxford: Clarendon Press, 1975), p. 22. Cf. Locke, *An Essay Concerning Human Understanding*, bk I, (Frazer edn, pp. 37–118). Locke's criticisms were directed explicitly at Herbert of Cherbury and implicitly at Descartes, who had spoken of certain ideas which were 'née & produite auec moy', *Meditations*, iii.58, in *Oeuvres de Descartes*, ed. Charles Adam and Paul Tannery, 12 vols. and suppl. (Paris: Léopold Cerf, 1897–1913), IX, 41.

63. The Cambridge Platonists generally do not rely on the term 'innate' at all, preferring such terms as 'instinct', 'natural', 'connate' and 'prolepsis'.

64. Joseph Glanvill, 'The Agreement of Reason and Religion', p. 17, in *Essays on Several Important Subjects in Philosophy and Religion* (London: Pr. by J. D. for John Baker, 1676).

65. *Ibid.*, p. 4.

66. *Ibid.*, pp. 4, 5.

67. *Ibid.*, p. 5.

68. *Ibid.*, p. 17. Calvinist thinkers, on the other hand, while they admitted some natural knowledge of God, insisted that this knowledge was invariably stifled or corrupted. *Institutes*, I.iv (pp. 46–9).

69. *Ibid.*, p. 6.

70. *Antidote Against Atheisme*, bk I, ch. 10 (pp. 31f.). Here More deliberately rejected the comparison of empirical knowledge (the earth revolves around the sun) and knowledge of God. In empirical knowledge the senses can deceive reason, as when it was universally accepted that the sun moved around the earth. Knowledge of God, however, is more like *a priori* geometrical knowledge.

71. *True Intellectual System*, I.IV.xxxvi (II, 486).

72. 'Notes Directed Against a Certain Programme' (1647), in *The Philosophical Works of Descartes*, ed. and tr. Elizabeth S. Haldane and G. R. T. Ross, 2 vols. (Cambridge: Cambridge University Press, 1911–12), I, 442.

73. Smith, 'The Immortality of the Soul', *Select Discourses* (London: Pr. by J. Flesher for W. Morden, 1660), p. 80. Cf. Cudworth, 'knowledge is an inward and active energy of the mind itself, and the displaying of its own innate vigour from within ... and the intelligible forms by which things are understood or known, are not stamps or impressions passively printed upon the soul from without, but ideas vitally potended or actively exerted from within itself'. *Eternal and Immutable Morality*, IV.i, in *True Intellectual System*, III, 578; and More, 'There is an active and *actuall Knowledge* in a man, of which these outward Objects are rather the reminders than the first begetters or implanters.' *Antidote Against Atheisme*, p. 19.

74. Smith, 'The Difference of the true Prophetic Spirit from all Enthusiastical Imposture', *Ibid.*, p. 190.

75. Smith, 'Of Atheism', *Ibid.*, p. 49; cf. 'An Account of Men's Mistakes about Religion', *Ibid.*, p. 351.

76. More, *An Explanation of the Grand Mystery of Godliness* (London: Pr. by James Flesher for W. Morden, 1660), III.i.2 (p. 57).

77. More, *Antidote Against Idolatry*, p. 14. Cf. More, *Enthusiasmus Triumphatus*, p. 1, in *A Collection*.

78. Cudworth, *Eternal and Immutable Morality*, in *True Intellectual System*, III, 566.

79. Nathaniel Culverwel, *Light of Nature*, p. 91.

80. Cf. Locke, *Essay Concerning Human Understanding*, I.ii.20 (I, 85f.).

81. Culverwel, *Light of Nature*, p. 91.

82. Richard Cumberland, *A Treatise of the Laws of Nature* (London: Pr. by Richard Phillips, 1727), p. 14.

83. Culverwel, *Light of Nature*, p. 52.

84. Cumberland, *Laws of Nature*, p. 14.

85. IV.xi, section 2; see *The Oxford English Dictionary*, 2nd edn, sv. 'Religion', 4.a.

86. References from the 5th(?) edn (London: Pr. for Samuel Mearne, John Martyn and Henry Herringman, 1674). Brerewood served as a reference for such varied writers as Robert Burton, Henry More, and John Wesley. This work was followed in mid-century by Alexander Ross's equally influential *Pansebeia: or A View of all the Religions in the World* (1st edn, 1653) citations from 3rd

edn (London: Pr. for John Saywell, 1658). The next great encyclopaedic work on 'the religions' in this century was William Turner's ambitious, *The History of all Religions in the World, from Creation down to this Present Time* (London: Pr. for John Dunton, 1695). Also see Smith, *Meaning and End of Religion*, pp. 41–4.

87. Ross admittedly structured *Pansebeia* around the religions 'of Asia', 'of Africa and America', and 'of Europe', but nonetheless still subscribed to the fourfold distinction. Turner augmented the four types by dividing 'paganism' into 'ancient heathen', 'modern heathen', and 'diabolical'.

88. Thus Richard Baxter, 'Four sorts of Religions I find only considerable upon earth: The meer Naturalists, called commonly Heathens and Idolaters: the Jews: the Mahometans: and the Christians. The Heathens by their Oracles, Augures and Aruspices, confess the necessity of some supernatural light; and the very Religion of all the rest consisteth in it.' *Reasons of the Christian Religion*, p. 198.

89. Peter Sterry, *The Appearence of God to Man in the Gospel* (London, 1710), p. 20.

90. *Ibid.*, pp. 102f.

91. *Ibid.*, pp. 102f.

92. Ralph Cudworth, *True Intellectual System*, I.iv.xiii (I, 365). Cf. Henry More, *Grand Mystery of Godliness*, III.i.7 (p. 59).

93. *Ibid.*, v.i (III, 71). Cf. *Eternal and Immutable Morality*, IV.i.5, in *True Intellectual System*, III, 581.

94. *Light of Nature*, p. 78.

95. *Ibid.*, pp. 78ff. Cf.: 'The World is full of looking-glasses: for God hath communicated several resemblances of himself to the creature, as the face sheds that image or species upon the glass whereby it self is represented.' 'Spiritual Opticks', p. 15, in *Ibid.*

96. *Ibid.*, p. 79.

97. *Ibid.*, p. 83.

98. *Ibid.*, p. 85.

99. *Ibid.*, p. 86.

100. Whichcote, *Works*, III, 214.

101. Peter Sterry, *A Discourse of the Freedom of the Will* (London: Pr. for John Starkey, 1675), p. 124. Cf. *The Appearence*, p. 151.

102. Joseph Glanvill, 'Against Confidence in Philosophy and Matters of Speculation', p. 24, in *Essays*.

103. Joseph Glanvill, *The Vanity of Dogmatizing* (London: Pr. by E. C. for Henry Eversden, 1661), p. 128.

104. *Ibid.*

105. *Ibid.*, p. 228. Babel was a very common image for the religious pluralism of the times.

106. Glanvill, *Discourses, Sermons and Remains*, p. 78.

107. More, *Conjectura Cabbalistica*, p. 28.

108. More, *Grand Mystery of Godliness*, II.x.4 (p. 50).

109. *Ibid.*, II.x.4,5 (p. 50). Cf. John Smith, 'An Account of Mens Mistakes about

Religion', *Select Discourses*, p. 375.
110. More, *Grand Mystery of Godliness*, x.iv.4 (p. 501).
111. Whichcote, *Works*, III, 21.
112. *Ibid.*, 20.
113. *Ibid.*, I. 22; cf. *Aphorisms*, no. 153.
114. *Works*, II, 20.
115. *Ibid.*, I, 33.
116. *Aphorisms*, no. 114.
117. *Works*, III, 30.
118. *Ibid.*
119. *Ibid.*, 31.
120. *Ibid.*, 32f.
121. *Ibid.*, 36.
122. *Ibid.*, 36.
123. *Ibid.*, 214. Sterry insisted in similar terms that moral rectitude is the measure of the truth of belief: '*Spiritual knowledge is not a* notional, verbal, *and* talking: *but a* real living, *and* practical *thing.*' Thus, he continues, 'Holiness *is the* Character *and* seal *of the Spirit of Truth*'. Sterry, cited in J. White's preface to *The Rise, Race and Royalty of the Kingdom of God in the Soul of Man* (London: Pr. for Thomas Cockman, 1683).
124. *Ibid.*, 214.
125. While it is evident that, in principle, Whichcote is tolerant of all shades of Christianity, in fact 'Popery' attracts strong criticism, again, on moral grounds. See, 'The Malignity of Popery', *Works*, I, 160–2.
126. More, *Grand Mystery of Godliness*, x.v (pp. 502–4). More elsewhere deferred to the Thirty-Nine Articles on this question, and actually upheld the notion of God's 'absolute decree'. Presumably he adopted the so-called 'Arminian interpretation' of the Articles. See *Antidote Against Idolatry*, p. 430.
127. *Ibid.*, pp. 490f.
128. More, *Antidote Against Idolatry*, p. 112.
129. The extent of Culverwel's Calvinism has been debated. John Tulloch claims that in *The Discourse of the Light of Nature*, little remained of Culverwel's Calvinism. *Rational Theology and Christian Philosophy in England in the 17th Century*, II, 424. Frederick Powicke disputes this, maintaining that there is 'the persistence and triumph in Culverwel of that harsh Calvinism against which Whichcote and his friends protested'. *The Cambridge Platonists: A Study*, p. 134. The truth of the matter almost certainly lies with Powicke. Culverwel's other writings are uncompromising in their presentation of the doctrine of predestination. See, e.g., 'The White Stone', passim, and 'The Act of Oblivion', p. 44, both in *The Light of Nature*. Even in *The Light of Nature* itself we find such sentiments as 'The lamp of the Moralist may waste it self in doing good to other, and yet at length may go out in a snuff, and be cast into utter darknesse' (p. 204). Tulloch is correct to this extent, that within the confines of a predestinarian understanding of salvation, Culverwel took as charitable a view as was possible.
130. Culverwel, *Light of Nature*, p. 84.

131. *Ibid.*, p. 16.
132. *Ibid.*, p. 17.
133. *Ibid.*, p. 16.
134. *Ibid.*, p. 208; cf.: 'Many Heathens have liv'd more accurately and exactly than some Christians in their unregenerate condition, and yet one out of all possibility of salvation, and the others efficaciously called. He may do with his own what he will, and he hath mercy on whom he will have mercy.' 'The Act of Oblivion', p. 44, in *Ibid.*
135. *Ibid.*, pp. 208f.; cf. 'The Act of Oblivion', p. 44, in *Ibid.* Culverwel in an earlier passage remarks that the moral excellence of these noble pagans sprang not from nature but grace: 'That *Socrates* was any better then *Aristophanes*, was not nature, but a kinde of common gift and grace of the Spirit of God, for there are the same seminal principles in all.' *Ibid.*, p. 205. This would seem to counter Culverwel's claim that insisting upon the salvation of noble pagans is a form of Pelagianism.
136. *Ibid.*, pp. 209f.
137. 'Yet God has reveal'd his minde expressely, and 'tis the constant voice of the Gospel it self, that there are but few of these precious souls that be sav'd.' 'The Worth of Souls', in *Ibid.*, p. 207.
138. 'The Act of Oblivion', p. 40, in *Ibid.*
139. *Ibid.*, p. 41.
140. *Ibid.*, p. 204.
141. *Ibid.*, p. 204. There was some precedent for this scheme of graded punishments. See, e.g., Augustine, *Enchiridion*, 110.
142. 'The Act of Oblivion', p. 45.
143. Peter Sterry, *The Rise, Race and Royalty of the Kingdom of God in the Soul of Man*, p. 8.
144. *Ibid.*, p. 5.
145. Sterry, *The Appearence of God to Man in the Gospel* (London: 1710), 126f., and *Discourse of the Freedom of the Will* (London, Pr. for John Starkey, 1675), Preface (my transliteration).
146. Sterry, *Freedom of the Will*, p. 127. Sterry's understanding of redemption and anthropology and his application of these to the question of the status of non-Christian religions shows some remarkable affinities with the more recent views of Karl Barth. For Barth too, the truth about nature of humanity is to be found in Jesus Christ. *Church Dogmatics* (Edinburgh: T. and T. Clark, 1936–69), III/2, 43, 132f., cf., *Christ and Adam* (London: Oliver and Boyd, 1956), p. 42 and passim. This implies that salvation includes all men, with some simply being unaware of their salvation. See Barth, *The Humanity of God* (London: Collins, 1961), *Church Dogmatics* IV/3, 874.
147. 'Our Blessed Saviour, in dying, by dying, in that very moment, by that very act, dissolves, and defaceth at once the whole frame of Nature, and of the first Creation. He blotteth out every natural image.' 'The State of a Saints Soul and Body in Death', in *The Rise, Race and Royalty*, p. 47.
148. Sterry, *The Rise, Race and Royalty*, pp. 40f. This is very much in accord with Ficino's view that true philosophy and true religion are one and the same

thing. Ficino, *Laus Philosophiae moralis, Opera*, I, 668.

149. Sterry, *The Appearence of God to Man*, pp. 102, 201f.
150. Sterry, *The Rise, Race and Royalty*, p. 507.
151. Sterry's conception of hell is outlined in a manuscript essay entitled 'That the state of wicked men after this life is mixed of evil & good things'. The manuscript is in the possession of Mrs E. Poolman of Melbourne, Australia. Reference to it is made by Vivian de Sola Pinto, *Peter Sterry, Platonist and Puritan*, (Cambridge: Cambridge University Press, 1934), pp. 103f. For a comprehensive over-view of the changing attitudes towards hell during this period, see D. P. Walker, *The Decline of Hell* (London: Routledge and Kegan Paul, 1964).
152. 'Arminianism', like the derogatory terms 'atheist', 'deist', 'socinian', 'unitarian', was often applied quite indiscriminately as a general term of theological abuse. William Narne, e.g., seems to apply it to universalists, speaking of 'that erroneous, detestable, and damnable doctrine of the Arminians, dreaming of vniuersall grace as they call it', *Christs Starre* (London, Pr. by J. L. for P. Stephens and C. Meredith, 1625), p. 281. The reason for this confusion is doubtless because Arminius affirmed that Christ died for *all*, not merely, as for Calvinists, the elect. Traditional Arminianism, however, requires that in this life a conscious appropriation of that saving grace be made.

Universalism was not the sole preserve of the Cambridge Platonists. Richard Baxter had no great affection for the Cambridge School, whose thought he regarded as 'a mixture of *Platonisme*, Origenisme & Arianisme' (Baxter MSS, Treatises, iv, fols. 227–55.) Yet he set forth a version of universalism little different in outcome from that proposed by Rust, though devoid of reference to the pre-existence of souls: 'As those that know not God nor his Creation, are yet Gods Subjects as Creator, and he their Lord: So those that know not Christ nor his redemption, are yet his Redeemed, and his Subjects as Redeemed, and he their Lord Redeemer as to his Right and Law, and their obligation.' (Richard Baxter, *Universal Redemption of Mankind* (London: Pr. for John Salisbury, 1694), prop. XXIV, p. 37). All nations of the world, says Baxter, have some kind of religion, and thus may cherish some hope of obtaining mercy for their sins. They remain under the covenant made with Adam which requires (according to Baxter) only their taking God to be their sole redeemer, loving him and expecting mercy from him, repenting of sin, and following the law. (*Ibid.*, props. XXIX, XXX, pp. 38f.) Baxter insists that any mercies given to the heathen are purchased with the blood of Christ, and also insists on the reality of hell and everlasting torment. (props. XLV, LV, pp. 44, 47).

Isaac Barrow was another prominent divine with no direct connexion to the Cambridge school who defended the thesis of apokatastasis. *Theological Works*, 9 vols., ed. Alexander Napier (Cambridge: Cambridge University Press, 1859), IV, 270–3. Other advocates of universalism at this time include: Richard Coppin, *Divine Teachings*, 2nd edn (London: Pr. by William Larner and Richard Moon, 1653); Paul Hobson, *A Treatise containing Three Things* (London, 1653); Samuel Richardson, *A Discourse of the Torments of Hell* (London, 1660);

Gerrard Winstanley, *The Mysterie of God, Concerning the Whole Creation* ([London], 1648). One of Sterry's young contemporaries at Cambridge – Jeremiah White – also published, much later, an influential work on universalism, *The Restoration of All Things* (London, 1712). An equal number of works were devoted to refuting this heresy. See, e.g., Jean Pierre Camus, *A Draught of Eternity*, tr. Miles Car (Doway: By the Widowe of Marke Wyon, 1632); Richard Clerke, *Sermons* (London: Pr. by T. Cotes for Thomas Alchorn, 1637), pp. 22, 550; Samuel Gott, *An Essay of the True Happiness of Man* (London, 1650), p. 280; Peter Hausted, *Ten Sermons* (London: Pr. for J. Clark, 1636), pp. 137ff.; John Wall, *Christian Reconcilement* (Oxford, 1658), p. 9. Obadiah Howe, in *The Vniversalist Examined and Convicted* (London: Pr. for John Rothwell, 1648) provides a useful guide to the variety of views of salvation current in the seventeenth century. He sets out eight soteriologies, including universalist options, and then gives his assessment of them. Also see C. A. Patrides, 'The Salvation of Satan', *Journal of the History of Ideas*, 28 (1967), 468–78.

153. Frederick Seebohm, *The Oxford Reformers* (London: Dent, 1914), p. 437.

154. John Donne, *Sermons*, III, 115–16, qu. in Patrides, 'Salvation of Satan', p. 475.

155. There remains some doubt about its authorship, however. See the discussion in Walker, *The Decline of Hell*, pp. 124ff.

156. George Rust, *A Letter of Resolution Concerning Origen and the Chief of his Opinions* (London, 1661), pp. 31f.

157. Plato, *Euthyphro*, 10.d. Cf. Cudworth, *Eternal and Immutable Morality*, bk II, in *True Intellectual System*, III, 525–40.

158. Rust, *Letter of Resolution*, p. 29.

159. *Ibid.*, p. 31.

160. Glanvill, *Lux Orientalis, Or An Enquiry into … the Præexistence of Souls*, in *Two Choice and Vseful Treatises*; More, *Divine Dialogues* I, 503; Franciscus van Helmont, *Seder Olam* (London: Pr. for Sarah Howkins, 1694) and *Two Hundred Queries Moderately Propounded Concerning the Doctrine of the Revolution of Humane Souls* (London: Pr. for Rob. Kettlewell, 1684); N. N., *A Letter to a Gentleman Touching the Treatise … concerning the Revolution of Humane Souls* (London: Pr. for A. Churchill, 1690); C. P., *A Dissertation concerning the Pre-existency of Souls* (London: Pr. for J. Wickins and Rob. Kettlewell, 1684). Of these, van Helmont and 'N. N.' put forward the possibility of reincarnation. Thus 'N. N.': 'all Men, of all ages, and in all Places of the World, that have lived and died without ever hearing of THAT VERY GOSPEL of the Kingdom … shall live again in the world in some Age and Place where they shall hear it'. (p. 16)

Critiques of the doctrine of Pre-existence may be found in Isaac Barrow, *Animæ Humanæ Corporibus non Præexistunt*, in *The Works*, IV (London: Pr. by M. Flesher for Brabazon Aylmer, 1687); John Dunton, *The Visions of the Soul before it comes into the Body* (London: Pr. for John Dunton, 1692); Samuel Parker, *A Free and Impartial Censure of the Platonick Philosophy with an Account of the Origenian Hypothesis Concerning the Preexistence of Souls* (Oxford: Pr. by W. Hall for R. Davis, 1666), Edward Warren, *No Præexistence*. One Bulstrode Whitelocke also wrote on transmigration, but mostly with a view to distancing Pythagoras from the 'barbarous' doctrine of modern pagans. See *An Essay of Transmigration, in Defence of Pythagoras* (London: Pr. by E. H. for Tho. Basset, 1692).

161. Rust, *Letter of Resolution*, p. 31.

162. There are five dialogues all told, spread across two volumes. The first three are found in *Divine Dialogues* (which I refer to as Vol. 1), the last two in *The Last Two Dialogues* (London: Pr. by J. Flesher, 1668). There is some confusion because the 'second' volume actually appeared earlier in 1668 than the first.

163. More, *Divine Dialogues*, 1, 361.

164. *Ibid.*, 1, 362.

165. *Ibid.*, 1, 363.

166. *Ibid.*, 1, 401.

167. *Ibid.*, 1, 402–13, 426. More's source on the religions of the New World is Josephus Acosta, *Historia natural y moral de las Indias* (1590), which appeared in English translation in 1604.

168. *Ibid.*, 1, 411. It is not clear whether 'superlapsarianism' is equivalent to the modern '*supra*lapsarianism' – that most severe form of the Calvinist doctrine – or not. From the context it could apply equally well to either infra- or supra-lapsarianism.

169. *Ibid.*

170. *Ibid.*, 1, 365.

171. *Ibid.*, 1, 419f.

172. *Ibid.*, 1, 420.

173. *Ibid.*, 1, 461ff.

174. *Ibid.*

175. *Ibid.*, 1, 503

176. *Ibid.*, 1, 462.

177. More, *Antidote Against Idolatry*, p. 107, cf. pp. 40, 46, 53.

178. *Ibid.*, p. 112.

179. *Ibid.*, p. 430.

180. *Divine Dialogues*, 1, 491.

181. *Grand Mystery of Godliness* pp. 502–4.

182. Thomas Burnet, *The Sacred Theory of the Earth* (London: Centaur, 1965), p. 89. This version is a reprint of the 2nd edn of 1691. Pagination differs.

183. See John Brooke, 'Science and the Fortunes of Natural Theology: Some Historical Perspectives', *Zygon* 24 (1989), 3–22; James Force, *William Whiston* (Cambridge: Cambridge University Press, 1985), pp. 34–9.

3 RELIGIOUS INSTINCT AND PRIESTLY CORRUPTIONS

1. The most comprehensive work on Herbert is Mario M. Rossi's *La Vita, le opere, i tempi di Edoardo Herbert di Chirbury*, 3 vols. (Florence: 1947). To date this work has not been translated into English. For English readers, Ronald Bedford's *The Defence of Truth: Herbert of Cherbury and the Seventeenth Century* (Manchester: Manchester University Press, 1979) gives an introduction to Her-

bert's life and thought.

2. Thomas Halyburton, *Natural Religion Insufficient* (Edinburgh: Pr. by the heirs and successors of A. Anderson, 1714); Bedford, *Defence of Truth*, p. 21.

3. *The Life of Edward, First Lord Herbert of Cherbury*, ed. J. M. Shuttleworth, (London: Oxford University Press, 1976).

4. Thomas Halyburton, *Natural Religion Insufficient*, p. 219.

5. (London: T. Tegg and Son, 1837), p. 3. The first two letters of the work are devoted to Herbert.

6. Blount, says Leslie, 'set himself at the head of the deists' and it is he 'after whom they all copy'. *A Short and Easy Method with the Deists* (1697), in *Works*, 7 vols. (Oxford: Oxford University Press, 1832), I. 7.

7. See, e.g., discussions in G. Gawlick, 'Deismus', *Historisches Wörterbuch der Philosophie*, II, ed. J. Ritter (Basel: Schwabe & Co., 1972), 44–8; also see Gawlick's discussion in 'Hume and the Deists: a reconsideration', *David Hume: Bicentenary Papers*, ed. G. P. Morice (Edinburgh: Edinburgh University Press, 1977), p. 133; S. G. Hefelbower, 'Deism Historically Defined', *American Journal of Theology*, 24 (1920), 217–23; Gordon Rupp, *Religion in England, 1688–1791* (Oxford: Clarendon Press, 1986), pp. 257–61; Robert Sullivan, *John Toland and the Deist Controversy* (Cambridge, Mass.: Harvard University Press, 1982), pp. 205–34; C. W. Welsh, 'Note on the Meaning of "Deism"', *Anglican Theological Review*, 38 (1956), 160–5; A. R. Winnett, 'Were the Deists "Deists"?', *Church Quarterly Review*, 161 (1960), 70–7. For an eighteenth-century definition, see Samuel Clarke, *A Discourse Concerning the Being and Attributes of God*, pp. 157–74.

8. I am here assuming that deism was largely an English phenomenon. Louis Bredvold has warned of the pitfalls of this view, and certainly the use of the term pre-dates the writings of most of those regarded as representative of the movement. Bredvold believes that this indicates that many of the tenets of deism were subscribed to quite early in the seventeenth century on the continent, but owing to the harsh measures against heterodoxy which were then in place, there was no visible movement nor was there a canon of writings. See his 'Deism Before Lord Herbert', *Papers of the Michigan Academy of Science, Arts and Letters*, 4 (1924) 431–42, esp. pp. 431f; Cf. also F. E. Manuel, *The Changing of the Gods* (London: University Press of New England, 1983), p. 27. With regard to this, my point is simply that in Britain in the late seventeenth and early eighteenth centuries we have an overt, flourishing movement, with public leading figures, and a body of controversial literature.

9. Sir Sidney Lee thus observes that 'Herbert's true affinity is with the Cambridge Platonists'. *Dictionary of National Biography*, Leslie Stephen and Sidney Lee, eds., (London: Oxford University Press, 1917–), IX, 631a. Cf. also Bedford, *The Defence of Truth*, p. 258.

10. In the period from Renaissance to Enlightenment we often encounter difficulty distinguishing the various influences from classical antiquity. Such was the eclecticism of Renaissance thinkers that elements of Aristotelianism, Stoicism, and Neoplatonism are melded into a cohesive whole. See, e.g., Rossi's comments, *La Vita*, I, 293–5.

11. Herbert, *De Religione Laici*, ed. and tr. Harold R. Hutcheson, (New Haven: Yale University Press, 1944), p. 87.

12. Matthew Tindal, *Christianity as Old as the Creation*, p. 242. Cf. Thomas Morgan: 'The Distinction of Fundamentals and Non-Fundamentals had prov'd to be of great and excellent Use till of late; but since these Fundamentals themselves came to be disputed, and many of them thrown off by Scripture Authority, the Matter of historical Faith was very much perplex'd.' *The Moral Philosopher* I, 407, cf. p. 419.

13. Edward Herbert, *De Veritate*, tr. Meyrick H. Carré, (Bristol: J. W. Arrowsmith, 1937), p. 303. In this connexion also, we should note that the Reformation made possible a degree of religious toleration which would have been quite anomalous in medieval Christendom. On the face of it, admittedly, the ideology of the reformers had nothing to do with religious liberty. Certainly heretics fared no better under Lutheran or Calvinist authorities than they would have done under Rome. Indeed, the Reformation created more heretics – everyone was a heretic of one kind or another. At a deeper level, however, the Reformation established the social and political conditions requisite for religious toleration. See J. B. Bury, *A History of Freedom of Thought*, 2nd edn (London: Oxford University Press, 1952). In any case, matters of ideology were not completely irrelevant here, for there was considerably less justification for the persecution of heretics if one held seriously to the Reformation doctrine of election. Whereas the Catholic Church might be able to mount a reasonable argument to the effect that torture and death in the temporal realm was justified in the light of its eternal benefits – the untidy death of non-conformists might serve as a spur to genuine piety in those tempted to stray from the confines of orthodox belief – the logic of Calvinism was such that the burning of heretics made not one iota of difference to who was going to be saved and who was to suffer eternal damnation, such considerations having been determined before the world began.

There was also, for medieval Catholicism, a warrant for persecution on the grounds that it reinforced civil order. This principle maintained its inertia despite the Reformation, but after such events as the Thirty-Years War and the revolution in England, lost considerable momentum. The civil unrest occasioned by lack of toleration thus counted decisively against the practice of persecution, and accounts in large part for the degree of religious liberty enjoyed by Englishmen during the period of the Restoration.

14. Nicholas of Cusa had already realised that religious practices constituted a far greater barrier to religious dialogue than religious belief. *De pace fidei*, 15 (pp. 47–50).

15. London editions of the Latin appeared in 1633, 1645, and 1656. Most of Herbert's works were first published abroad, and many were not translated for some time. *De Veritate*, e.g., appeared in French in 1639, but to my knowledge an English translation was not made until 1937.

16. See Herbert's autobiography, *The Life of Edward, First Lord Herbert of Cherbury*, p. 120. Herbert here relates that he was persuaded to publish *De Veritate* when he received a sign from heaven. This episode is most intriguing because

it shows that Herbert did not deny the possibility of revelation, although he does seem generally to distrust second-hand reports of revelation.

17. For accounts of Herbert's epistemology see, R. D. Bedford, *The Defence of Truth*, chs. 2–4; W. R. Sorley, 'The Philosophy of Herbert of Cherbury', *Mind*, 3, NS (1894), 491–508 (dated, but still useful). Also see introductions to Herbert's works, *De Religione Laici*, ed. and tr. Harold R. Hutcheson; *De Veritate*, tr. Meyrick H. Carré.

18. Immanuel Kant, *Critique of Pure Reason*, ed. and tr. Norman Kemp Smith, 2nd edn (London: Macmillan, 1929), preface.

19. This omission forms the basis of Trendelenburg's criticism of Kant's epistemology as applied to space and time.

20. Herbert, *De Veritate*, Eng. edn, p. 115.

21. *Ibid.*, p. 44.

22. *Ibid.*, p. 150.

23. Cf. *Ibid.*, ch. xiii.

24. Despite this there are no grounds for Locke's complaint (*Essay*, I.iii.16) that Herbert regards the Natural Instinct as the home only to the five common notions pertaining to religion. It is clear that Herbert regarded, *inter alia*, certain ethical maxims as Common Notions, such as 'Do as thou wouldst be done unto' (to use Locke's own suggestion). See *De Veritate*, Eng. edn, p. 312. Richard Baxter, incidentally, raised a similar objection against Herbert, in his 'Animadversions on the Treatise *De Veritate*', in *More Reasons for the Christian Religion and No Reason Against It* (London: Pr. for Nevil Simmons, 1672) p. 118.

25. *De Veritate*, Eng. edn, p. 154, cf. p. 148. Herbert, admittedly, did muddy the waters somewhat with his notion of universal consent, but with a liberal definition of insanity, this problem need not be insurmountable: those who did not profess the common notions were in some way mentally deficient or deviant.

26. F. D. E. Schleiermacher, *On Religion: Speeches to its Cultured Despisers*, tr. from the 3rd edn by John Oman (New York: Harper Torchbooks, 1958), p. 71.

27. Rudolf Otto, *The Idea of the Holy*, tr. John Harvey (Oxford: Oxford University Press, 1950) p. 8.

28. Herbert, *De Veritate*, Eng. edn, p. 289.

29. *Ibid.* This was to become a common argument of the deists. See, e.g., Toland, *Christianity not Mysterious*, pp. 31, 141f.; Anthony Collins, *A Discourse of Free-thinking*, pp. 41f.

30. Herbert, *De Veritate*, Eng. edn, p. 291.

31. In fact Herbert was relying on a traditional Catholic test of orthodoxy. Vincent of Lérins, around the year 434, had established the view that genuine tradition consisted of that which had been believed 'everywhere, always, by all' – *quod ubique, quod semper, quod ab omnibus creditum est. Commonitorum*, 2, 3, in M. de la Bigne, *Magna Bibliotheca Veterum Patrum*, 15 tom. (Coliniae Agrippinae, 1618–22). Herbert applied the same criteria, but widened their scope to include not just the positive institution of the Catholic Church, but the 'true catholic church' from which no one was excluded.

32. Herbert, *De Veritate*, Eng. edn, p. 294.

33. *Ibid.*, p. 295.

34. Herbert is less restrained in later parts of the work, referring to 'our most popular windbags', who 'weave their spells from the pulpit'. This clearly implies that the divines of Herbert's day were as guilty of imposture as those from antiquity.

35. Herbert, *De Veritate*, Eng. edn, p. 295.

36. *Ibid.*, p. 297.

37. *Ibid.*, p. 298.

38. *Ibid.*, p. 299.

39. *Ibid.*, p. 300.

40. See, e.g., Anselm, *Cur Deus Homo*, chs. 21–3; Aquinas, *Summa Theologica*, iii, Q. 1, Art. II, 3.

41. Herbert, *De Veritate*, Eng. edn, p. 301.

42. *Ibid.*, p. 302.

43. *Ibid.* Herbert does not appear, however, to believe in eternal damnation. See *A Dialogue between a Tutor and his Pupil* (London: Pr. for W. Bathoe, 1768), p. 26.

44. *Ibid.*, p. 30.

45. Locke deals specifically with Herbert's theories in *Essay*, I.iii.

46. 'though we possess certain *a priori* internal faculties they cannot function apart from the external faculties', *De Veritate*, p. 209. Also see Hutcheson's comment in his introduction to *De Religione Laici*, p. 37.

47. Herbert, *De Veritate*, Latin edn, p. 175. In the *Elenchus Verborum*, 'Natura' is defined as 'providentia divina universalis'. See W. R. Sorley, 'The Philosophy of Herbert of Cherbury', p. 501, n. 5. Also cf. Grotius: 'that natural Law of which we have spoken ... though it proceed from principles internal to man, yet it may deservedly be ascribed to God, because it was his will that such principles should be in us.' *Of the Law of Warre and Peace* (London: Pr. by T. Warren for William Lee, 1755), preface. (The first edition of *De Jure Belli et Pacis* appeared in 1625, one year after *De Veritate*.

48. Sorley argues for the former identification, 'The Philosophy of Herbert of Cherbury', p. 501.

49. John Ogilvie, *An Inquiry into Causes of the Infidelity and Scepticism of the Times* (London, 1783), pp. 56, 179.

50. Locke, *Essay*, I.iii.8 (pp. 95–8). From the middle of the seventeenth century until well into the eighteenth, there was considerable debate about whether there actually existed 'nations of atheists'. Locke, we should note, did not actually identify those who came later to be known as Theravadins. In fact, out of his five examples of nations of atheists, only the Chinese 'literati' deserved the title. It was Locke's sources (numbering about six) which were chiefly at fault here. Many proponents of universal theism were thus correct to question those sources. See, e.g., Charles Gildon, 'To Dr. R. B— of a God', in Charles Blount, *Miscellaneous Works* (London, 1695), p. 180; Shaftesbury, *Characteristics* I, Treatise 3, pt 3, sec. ii (pp. 222f.).

51. Herbert, *De Veritate*, Eng. edn, p. 301.

52. Locke echoes this complaint: 'but concerning innate Principles, I desire these Men to say, whether they can, or cannot, by Education and Custom, be blurr'd and blotted out: If they cannot, we must find them in all Mankind alike, and they must be clear in everybody; and if they may suffer variation from adventitious Notions, we must then find them clearest and most perspicuous, nearest the Fountain, in Children and illiterate People, who have received least impression from foreign Opinions. Let them take which side they please, they will certainly find it inconsistent with visible matter of fact, and daily observation.' *Essay*, I.ii.20 (pp. 85f.).

53. Grotius, *Of the Law of Warre and Peace*, Preface.

54. Schleiermacher, *The Christian Faith*, sections 6,7.

55. Herbert actually regards these as criteria of truth. *A Dialogue*, p. 10.

56. Herbert, *The Antient Religion of the Gentiles*, tr. William Lewis (London: Pr. for John Nutt, 1705), p. 3; cf. pp. 12f., 41, 271; *De Veritate*, Eng. edn, pp. 294f.; *A Dialogue*, pp. 27, 33.

57. 'Great is Diana of the Ephesians: or, The Original of Idolatry, together with the Politick Institution of the Gentile Sacrifices' (London: 1695), p. 3; in Charles Blount, *Miscellaneous Works*.

58. *Ibid.*, pp. 6, 14.

59. *Ibid.*, pp. 7, 9.

60. Blount, *The Oracles of Reason* (London, 1693) p. 125. It is difficult to know whether Blount himself was committed to a belief in rewards and punishments in the afterlife. It appears as an article of belief in Blount's version of the five common notions – 'A Summary Account of the Deists Religion', *Oracles of Reason*, pp. 88–96. This seems to suggest, the connexion with imposture notwithstanding, that Blount held such a view.

61. Blount, 'The Original of Idolatry', pp. 8, 27, 29.

62. Blount, 'A Summary Account of the Deists Religion', *Oracles of Reason*, p. 92.

63. Blount, 'The Original of Idolatry', preface (Fol. F 4.v).

64. *Ibid.*, preface (Fols. F 5.r–F 6.v).

65. Blount, *The Oracles of Reason*, p. 123.

66. John Toland, *Letters to Serena* (London: Pr. for Bernard Lintot, 1704), Letter III.

67. *Ibid.*, p. 71.

68. *Ibid.*, pp. 72, III.

69. *Ibid.*, pp. 76–81.

70. *Ibid.*, pp. 87f.

71. *Ibid.*, pp. 104f.

72. *Ibid.*, p. 130.

73. Thomas Morgan, *The Moral Philosopher*, I, 94.

74. Morgan, *The Moral Philosopher*, 2nd edn, 3 vols. (London, 1738–40), III, 94. The first edition of this work was a single volume. Accordingly, when reference is made to vol. I, the first edition is referred to. All references from vols II and III come from the second edition.

75. *Ibid.*, III, 95f.

76. *Ibid.*, III, 93.
77. *Ibid.*
78. *Ibid.*, III, III. Cf. Prideaux, *A Discourse for the Vindicating of Christianity from the Charge of Imposture, offered by Way of a Letter to the ... Deists*, 2nd edn (London: Pr. by J. H. for W. Rogers, 1697), p. 7.
79. *Ibid.*, III, 99.
80. Collins, *A Discourse of Free-Thinking*, p. 46.
81. Tindal, *Christianity as Old as the Creation*, p. 93.
82. Richard Bentley, *Remarks upon a Late Discourse of Free-Thinking* (London: Pr. for John Morphew, 1713) p. 12.
83. See R. N. Stromberg, 'History in the Eighteenth Century', *Journal of the History of Ideas*, 12 (1951), 295–304 (esp. p. 302).
84. Bentley, *Remarks Upon a Late Discourse*, p. 47.
85. See, e.g., Anon., *Hieragnosticon: or Coray's Doom, being an Answer to two Letters of Enquiry* (London: Pr. for Tho. Milbourne for Dorman Newmann, 1672); Anon., *Mrs Abigail: or, an Account of a Female Skirmish between the Wife of a Country Squire, and the Wife of a Doctor in Divinity* (London: H. Baldwin, 1702); Anon., *An Occasional Paper wherein the Honour of the English Clergy ... is vindicated from a Late Pamphlett called Mrs. Abigail* (London: Pr. for J. Nutt, 1703); Anon., *Priest-craft Exposed, Shewing the Wicked Politics and Practices of the Pretended Clergy* (London, 1691); William Bayley, *A Word of Reproof from the Lord to the Priests of England* (London, 1659); William Prynne, *The Antipathie of the English Lordly Prelacie* (London: Pr. by Authority for Michael Sparke Senior, 1641), and *Nevvs from Ipswich* (n.p.: Repr. for T. Bates, 1641); William Tomlinson, *A VVord of Reproof to the Priests or Ministers* (London: Pr. for Giles Calvert, 1656); Ralf Wallis, *Room for the Cobler of Gloucester and his Wife, with Several Cartloads of Abominable Irregular, Pitiful Stinking Priests* (London, 1668).
86. *The Spectator*, no. 21 (Sat. March 24, 1711), no. 609 (Wed. October 20, 1714).
87. John Eachard, *The Grounds and Occasions of the Contempt of the Clergy and Religion* (London: Pr. by W. Goodbid for N. Brooke, 1670), p. 3.
88. T. B. Macaulay, *History of England*, 3 vols. (London: Dent, n.d.), I. 253. (The volumes of this edition do not correspond with those of the original.)
89. See C. H. Mayo, 'The Social Status of the Clergy in the Seventeenth and Eighteenth Centuries', *English Historical Review*, 37 (1922), 258–66.
90. See, e.g., John Bramhall, *An Answer to a Letter of Enquiry into the Grounds and Occasions of the Contempt of the Clergy* (London: Pr. for Nath. Ranew and J. Robinson, 1671); Lancelot Addison, *A Modest Plea for the Clergy* (London: Pr. for William Crook, 1677).
91. Edmund Hickeringill, *Priestcraft, its Character and Consequences*, Pt I, 3rd edn (London, 1708), p. 2.
92. Hickeringill, *The Black Non-Conformist Discover'd in More Naked Truth* (London, 1682), Introduction.
93. Hickeringill, *Priestcraft*, Pt II, p. 22.
94. The religious types of Max Weber are already present in the deists' philosophy of religion. They quite explicitly oppose 'prophet' and 'priest'. The priest

is the distorter of natural religion, the prophet the one who attempts to re-establish it. For Weber's types of religious leader see Max Weber, *The Sociology of Religion*, tr. Ephraim Fischoff (Boston: Beacon, 1964), pp. 46–79; also Joachim Wach, *Sociology of Religion* (Chicago, University of Chicago Press, 1962), pp. 346–51, 360–8.

95. Jonathan Swift, *Mr C—ns's Discourse of Free-Thinking put into Plain English, by way of Abstract, for the Use of the Poor* (1713), in *The Prose Works of Jonathan Swift, D. D.*, ed. Temple Scott, 12 vols. (London: George Bell and Sons, 1909), III, 171.

96. William Warburton, *The Divine Legation of Moses*, I, xxiii.

97. Swift thus ridicules the notion that 'the Trinity was an invention of the statesmen and politicians'. *Mr C—ns's Discourse of Free-Thinking*, p. 187.

98. Collins, *Discourse of Free-Thinking*, p. 43.

99. Swift, *Mr C—ns's Discourse of Free-Thinking*, p. 182. 'Reason', Swift observed elsewhere, serves only 'to aggravate our *natural* corruptions' and helps us 'acquire new ones which Nature had not given us.' *Gulliver's Travels*, IV. 7 (p. 306).

100. *Ibid.*, p. 172.

101. Swift in *The Examiner*, no. 29 (Feb. 22, 1710).

102. See, e.g., what Swift has to say in *The Examiner*, nos. 19, 22, 25, 29, 39 (1710–11). From the remarks here it is evident that Swift regards Toland, Tindal, and Collins as all of a kind in their advocacy of free-thinking and in their denigration of the clergy. Also see Margaret Jacob, *The Newtonians and the English Revolution, 1689–1720* (Hassocks: Harvester Press, 1976), pp. 201–50, for an account of the link between Whig politics and radical religion.

103. Bentley, *Remarks Upon a late Discourse*. p. 47.

104. See, e.g., Hilkiah Bedford, *A Defence of the Church of England from Priestcraft* (London: Pr. for R. Wilkin, 1711); Samuel Chandler, *Reflections on the conduct of the Modern Deists* (London: Pr. for John Chandler, 1727); Thomas Cockman, *Freethinking Rightly Stated* (London: Pr. for George Strahan, 1713); Anon., *An Answer to the Discourse of Free-thinking ... by a Gentleman of Cambridge* (London: Pr. by J. Morphew and A. Dodd, 1713).

105. *The Spectator*, no. 186, (Wednesday Oct. 3, 1711).

106. Bentley, *Remarks Upon a Late Discourse*, p. 12.

107. In fact Eachard notes the vast difference between the London clergy and their rural counterparts, but nonetheless tends to over-generalise.

108. Macaulay, *History of England*, I, 257.

109. The Whig Addison, for example, rued the fact that the country clergy did not simply repeat the printed sermons of their more distinguished city colleagues. *The Spectator*, 106, July 2, 1711.

110. Toland, *Letters to Serena*, Letter I.

111. *Ibid.*, p. 3.

112. *Ibid.*, pp. 6, 7.

113. *Ibid.*, p. 9.

114. John Milton, *The Doctrine and Discipline of Divorce* (rev. edn, 1644), in *Prose Writings*, ed. K. M. Burton (London: Dent, 1965), p. 248.

115. Glanvill, *The Vanity of Dogmatizing*, pp. 126f.
116. Sir Thomas Pope Blount, *Essays on Several Subjects* (London: Pr. for Richard Bentley, 1697), pp. 105f. The Blount brothers seem to have possessed a lively talent for plagiarism. Charles, in his *De Religione Laici*, had simply reproduced enormous chunks of Herbert of Cherbury's piece of the same name. Thomas, in the passage cited above, borrows from Glanvill's *Vanity of Dogmatizing* in which we find this observation: 'The *half-moon* or *Cross*, are indifferent to its reception; and we may with equal facility write on this *rasa Tabula* Turk or Christian.' (p. 128). Thomas Blount was clearly influenced by Glanvill, and his last essay – 'The Variety of Opinions' – reiterates Glanvill's thesis that pluralism arises from uncertainty.
117. Tindal, *Christianity as Old as the Creation*, pp. 167f.
118. This reliance on other theories can in part be attributed to the realisation that neither in the primal religions of the Pacific and the Americas, nor in the religions of antiquity, were there historical founder-figures who could be accused of imposture. This in turn illustrates a dissatisfaction with the view that Islam was the paradigmatic non-Christian religion, and that other religions were more like heresies with corresponding heresiarchs.
119. Swift, *Gulliver's Travels*, ii.6 (p. 172).
120. Interestingly, Lancelot Addison, in his dispute with John Eachard, maintained that the clergy had always played a part in all religions from the beginning. In this sense, they were 'natural': 'there was never any Religion that had not *Separate Persons* to whom was committed the *Power* and *Care* of *prescribing*, *directing*, and administering the rites thereof, and whom by an easie figure we may call their Clergy.' *A Modest Plea for the Clergy*, p. 6. The participation of the Clergy in religion was for Addison as fundamental an idea as any of Herbert's common notions. 'The antiquity of the Clergy', he insists, 'is to be placed among those verities which are manifest and known of themselves', and which are a matter of 'universal acknowledgement'. And further: 'ever since the Creation, a Deity, Religion, and Priesthood, do as much mutually infer each other, as the most *natural relations*'. *Ibid.*, p. 12. Addison also broaches the issue of the educational role of the clergy in his *Primitive Institution* (1674). Here he demonstrates that the 'imprinting' of 'younger minds' by the Clergy was both ancient and universal, and thus was as natural a part of the process of religious development as the acquisition of common notions. *The Primitive Institution, or A Seasonable Discourse of Catechizing* (London: Pr. by J. C. for William Crook, 1674). Addison's neglected arguments show clearly that the logical conclusion of the tendency to see the priesthood as a universal feature of all religions is that priests are as natural a part of religion as any common notions.
121. Tyndale, *The Practyse of Prelates* (London: Anthony Scoloker & William Seres, 1548); also, *Expositions and Notes on Sundry Portions of the Holy Scriptures*, ed. H. Walter, (London: Parker Society, 1849), 237–344. Cf. William Clebsch, *England's Earliest Protestants* (New Haven: Yale University Press, 1964), pp. 159ff.
122. William Turner, *The Huntying and Fyndyng out of the Romish Foxe* (Basel:

R. Potts, 1534), p. 28.

123. John Milton, *An Apology against a pamphlet call'd A Modest Confutation of the Animadversions of the Remonstrant against Smectymnuus* (1642), in *Prose Writings*, pp. 108f.

124. Stephen Marshal, Edmund Calamy, Thomas Young, Matthew Newcomen, and William Spurstow, whose initials form the pseudonym 'Smectymnuus'.

125. See, e.g., *Areopagitica* (1644), in *Ibid.*, pp. 172–7, and passim. On John Milton's 'deist' tendencies, see Joseph Frank, 'John Milton's Movement Toward Deism', *Journal of British Studies*, 1 (1961), 38–51.

126. Anon., *A Defence of True Protestants Abused for the Service of Popery* (London: Pr. for N. P., 1680). Cf. Anon., *The Bishops Manifest* (London: Pr. for W. R., 1641); Hugh Edmonds, *Presbytery Popish, not Episcopacy* (London: Pr. for Philemon Stephens, 1661).

127. Locke, *A Letter concerning Toleration*, p. 191.

128. John Toland, *Pantheisticon: or, the Form of Celebrating of the Socratic Society* (London: Pr. by Sam. Paterson, 1751), p. 57.

129. Diodorus Siculus, *History*, 1.27.6; Plutarch, *Isis and Osiris*, 354; Cicero, *On the Nature of the Gods*, II.71, III.3; Lucretius, *On the Nature of Things*, IV.14f.; Clement of Alexandria, *Stromateis*, V.iv.664; Origen, *Contra Celsum*, I.12; Lactantius, *Divine Institutes*, II.3.2; Augustine, *City of God*, IV.30–1. See also *Diogenes Laertius*, 9.22.

130. The 'multitude', according to Origen, is incapable of receiving the deep spiritual truths of the Scriptures; these are evident only to the 'lovers of wisdom'. *On First Principles*, tr. G. W. Butterworth, (Gloucester, Mass.: Peter Smith, 1973), I.preface.3, IV.ii.6–8 (pp. 2, 278–85); 'The simple minded masses', he says in *Contra Celsum* IV.9, 'cannot comprehend the complex theology of the wisdom of god ... and must be content with the *ipse dixit* of Jesus rather than anything beyond this'. *Contra Celsum*, tr. Henry Chadwick (Cambridge: Cambridge University Press, 1953), (p. 190), cf. 1.7, (pp. 10f). The apostles and fathers, says Basil, 'guarded the awful dignity of the mysteries in secrecy and silence, for what is bruited abroad at random among the common folk is no mystery at all'. *On the Spirit*, XXVII.66, 'Nicene and Post-nicene Fathers', VIII (Grand Rapids: Erdmans, 1955), 40–2.

There is, arguably, a New Testament basis for this view. 'Give not that which is holy unto the dogs,' says Jesus, 'neither cast your pearls before the swine'. (Matthew 7.6) So too Paul, 'we speak wisdom among the perfect; yet a wisdom not of this world'. (1 Corinthians 2.6) Such passages formed the basis of Toland's argument that the twofold philosophy had been a part of Christianity since its inception. See *Clidophorus, or, Of the Exoteric and Esoteric Philosophy*, in Toland, *Tetradymus* (London: Pr. by J. Brotherton & W. Meadows, 1720), pp. 78f.

131. Blount specifically links double truth to the twofold philosophy, arguing on the authority of Averroës that 'there is properly neither Truth nor Falsehood' in fables which are propagated by rulers for reasons of political expediency. *Oracles of Reason*, p. 125. Stuart MacClintock has pointed out that the doctrine of the double truth, as commonly understood, can hardly be attributed to

Averroës, who spoke rather of different modes of apprehending the truth. Neither, he argues, can this view be found in any of the medieval school men. See 'Averroës' and 'Averroism' in *The Encyclopedia of Philosophy*, ed. Paul Edwards (New York: Macmillan, 1972), I, 220–6; cf. Martin Pine, 'Pomponazzi and the Problem of "Double Truth"', *Journal of the History of Ideas* 29 (1968), 163–76. These more recent writings challenge some of the conclusions of Renan's *Averroès et L'Averroïsme*.

132. Francis Bacon, *Novum Organum*, I.lxv, in *The English Philosophers from Bacon to Mill*, ed. E. Burtt, Modern Library Series (New York: Random House, 1967), (pp. 44f.); *The Advancement of Learning*, II. xxv (pp. 200–12). Also see Basil Willey, *The Seventeenth Century Background: Studies in the Thought of the Age in Relation to Poetry and Religion* (London: Chatto and Windus, 1953), pp. 27–30.

133. Blount, *The Oracles of Reason*, pp. 202f.

134. Herbert, *A Dialogue*, p. 47.

135. Toland, *Letters to Serena*, pp. 89, 114f.

136. Both appeared in 1720, the Latin *Pantheisticon* in Holland under the title 'Cosmopoli', listing one 'Junius Edganesius' as its author.

137. Toland, *Clidophorus*, p. 89, in Toland, *Tetradymus*.

138. Some of the more important responses include Thomas Beverly, *Christianity the Great Mystery* (Dondon [sic]: Pr. for W. Marshall and J. Marshall, 1696); Peter Browne, *A Letter in Answer to a Book Entitled Christianity not Mysterious* (Dublin: Pr. by John Ray for John North, 1697); Jean Gailhard, *Blasphemous Socinian Heresie Disproved and Confuted* (London: Pr. for R. Wellington and J. Hartley, 1697); John Norris, *An Account of Reason and Faith: in Relation to the Mysteries of Christianity* (London: Pr. for S. Manship, 1697); Edward Synge, *A Gentleman's Religion*, 7th edn (London: T. Trye, 1752). Other critiques are listed in *A Collection of Several Pieces of Mr John Toland* (London: Pr. for J. Peele, 1726), pp. xvf.

139. Toland, *Christianity not Mysterious*, p. iv.

140. *The Guardian*, 3, (March 14, 1713).

141. Thomas Woolston, *Six Discourses on the Miracles of our Saviour* (London: Pr. for the author, 1727–9).

142. Peter Annet, *A Collection of the tracts of a Certain Free Enquirer noted by his sufferings for his opinions* (London, c. 1750).

143. The accusation was made by Peter Brown, in *A Letter*, p. 199. Also see Toland, *A Collection of Several Pieces of Mr John Toland*, p. xx; *Apology for Mr Toland*, pp. 6f.

144. Toland, *Pantheisticon*, p. 108.

145. *Ibid.*, p. 99.

146. *Pantheisticon* has been variously interpreted. See, e.g., F. H. Heinemann, 'John Toland and the Age of Reason', *Archiv für Philosophie*, 4 (1950), 35–66; Ernst Campbell Mosner, 'John Toland', *Encyclopedia of Philosophy*, 8, 142.

147. *Pantheisticon*, pp. 108–10; 57f.

148. Seigneur de La Noue, *Discours Politiques et Militaires* (Basel: 1587), pp. 6, 34.

149. Cited in F. Strowski, *Histoire du sentiment religieux en France au XVII siècle. Pascal et son Temps* (Paris: Plon-Nourrit, 1907), I, 138f.

150. Voltaire, *Pièces détachées*, II, 94, qu. in Louis Brevold, 'Deism before Lord Herbert', *Papers of the Michigan Academy of Science, Arts and Letters*, 4 (1924), 431–42, (p. 442).

151. See, e.g., Bredvold, 'Deism before Lord Herbert'; Robert Niklaus, *A Literary History of France: The Eighteenth Century* (New York: Barnes and Noble, 1970), pp. 123–33; I. O. Wade, *The Clandestine Organization and the Diffusion of Philosophical Ideas in France, 1700–1750* (New York: Octagon, 1967).

152. Qu. in Douglas Bush, *English Literature in the Earlier Seventeenth Century*, 2nd edn (Oxford: Clarendon, 1962) p. 339.

153. Horneck's introduction to Bénédict Pictet, *An Antidote against a Careless Indifferency in Matters of Religion*, 2nd edn (London: Pr. for Henry Rhodes and John Harris, 1698).

154. Jean Gailhard, *The Blasphemous Socinian Heresie disproved and Confuted*, Epistle Dedicatory.

155. 'When a sett of Men find themselves agree in any Particular, tho' never so trivial, they establish themselves into a kind of Fraternity, and meet once or twice a Week, upon the Account of such a Fantastick Resemblance.' Addison in *The Spectator*, no. 9, March 10, 1711. 'Christian deist' Thomas Morgan confessed that the foundations of his *Moral Philosopher* were laid by 'a Society, or Club of Gentlemen' who met specifically 'to enter impartially into the Consideration of the Grounds and Principles of Religion in general.' *The Moral Philosopher*, I, pp. viif.

156. See Margaret Jacob, *The Radical Enlightenment*, p. 37; also see her *Newtonians and the English Revolution*, pp. 222–7. Cf. Rupp, *Religion in England*, p. 260. It is possible that Toland was the translator of the 1713 English edition of *Spaccio*. See Giordano Bruno, *The Expulsion of the Triumphant Beast*, ed. and tr. Arthur D. Imerti (New Brunswick: Rutgers University Press, 1964), p. 281, n. 4. The works of Bruno had become so coveted by some elements of London society that *Spaccio* fetched the 'extravagant Price' of thirty pounds at auction in 1712. Budgell, noting this event in *The Spectator* (no. 389, May 27, 1712) labelled Bruno 'a professed Atheist, with a design to deprecate religion', and charitably remarked that 'a solemn judicial death' was 'too great an honour' for such as he.

157. Jacob, *The Radical Enlightenment*, ch. 5; cf. *The Newtonians*, pp. 222–7.

158. *Ibid.*, p. 153.

159. Jacob presents us with an extract of a record of the meeting of the Knights – a document which was found among Toland's unpublished manuscripts and deposited in the British Library (ADD 4295, fols 18–19). Yet Toland was not a signatory to the document, which might have been expected were he a major figure in the movement. In this work generally, I think, Jacob places too great a burden of speculation on the evidence which she has accumulated. Yet *The Radical Enlightenment* is an important book which makes a timely and valuable contribution to our knowledge of Toland's circle.

160. Toland, *Pantheisticon*, p. 108. Cf. *Clidophorus*, pp. 95f.

161. *Ibid.*, pp. 94f.

162. On the influence of Bruno on Toland in particular and Deism generally, see Jacob, *The Newtonians*, 226–34, 245–7, *The Radical Enlightenment*, 35–9; J. F. Nourrisson, *Philosophies de la Nature. Bacon, Boyle, Toland, Buffon* (Paris: Perrin, 1887), pp. 85ff. Spinoza's pantheism was not acceptable to Toland, as his 'Confutation of Spinosa' shows. *Letters to Serena*, Letter IV, pp. 131–62. It is also worth noting that Toland seems to have coined the term 'pantheism', and thus has the liberty of giving to it what meaning he will. See F. H. Heinemann, 'Prolegomena to a Toland Bibliography', *Notes and Queries*, 185 (1943), pp. 182–6 (p. 182).

163. As Toland himself implies, *Pantheisticon*, p. 107.

164. *Ibid.*, p. 73.

165. *Ibid.*, pp. 85f.

166. The lesser free-thinkers were Erasmus, Father Paul, Joseph Scaliger, Cartesius, Gassendus, Grotius, Hooker, Chillingworth, Lord Falkland, Lord Herbert, Selden, Hales, More, William, and Locke. *Discourse of Freethinking*, p. 177. Toland, we might add, had a similar list of individuals from antiquity who were 'Votaries of Truth'. He included Socrates, Plato, Xenophon, Cato, Cicero, Parmenides, Confucius, and quite a few others. *Pantheisticon*, p. 64.

167. Admittedly, there was a tendency in the Greek fathers to attribute virtual apostolic status to such figures as Socrates and Plato, but they stopped short of equating the beliefs of these men with the essential teachings of Jesus. See, e.g., Justin Martyr, *Apology*, I.46; II.13. In any case, the truth which was granted to these pagan writers was most often attributed to plagiarism, rather than reason or direct revelation.

168. See, e.g., Augustine, *City of God*, IV, 30–2; Lactantius, *Divine Institutes*, II.3.iii.

169. Origen, *On First Principles*, I.preface.3–8.

170. Origen, *Contra Celsum*, III.44–6, 52, 59.

171. Schleiermacher, *On Religion*, pp. 1, 14, 18.

172. Toland, *Clidophorus*, p. 95. Toland attributes this saying to Shaftesbury.

173. David Hume, *Enquiry Concerning Human Understanding*, VII.i.65 (p. 83).

174. Toland, *Letters to Serena*, p. 129. Cf., 'Superstition is always the same in Vigour, though sometimes different in Rigour', *Pantheisticon*, p. 98.

175. Royal Society, Gregory MS. 247. See also Crauford Gregory, 'Notice concerning an Autograph Manuscript by Sir Isaac Newton', *Transactions of the Royal Society of Edinburgh*, 12 (1834), 64–76.

176. For a more complete account of the contents of the Scholia, see J. E. McGuire and P. M. Rattansi, 'Newton and the "Pipes of Pan"', *Notes and Records of the Royal Society of London*, 21 (1966), 108–43.

177. Gregory MS. 247, fols 11–12. Qu. in *Ibid.*, p. 117.

178. For the background of this conflict see R. F. Jones, *Ancients and Moderns: A Study of the Background of the Battle of the Books* (Gloucester, Mass.: Peter Smith, 1961).

179. Toland, *Christianity not Mysterious*, p. v.

180. Plato's political writings exhibit a similar tension between utopianism and primitivism. See in particular Karl Popper's interpretation of Plato, *The Open*

Society and its Enemies, 5th edn, 2 vols. (London: Routledge and Kegan Paul, 1966) I, 39–49.

181. This is not to say that these other theories found no application at all. Euhemerism was commonly used by the deists to account for the cult of the saints, which was consequently argued to have pagan origins. See, e.g., Toland, *Letters to Serena*, p. 123. The projection theory was also given applications, Toland, *Ibid.*, p. 72.

182. For all this, veiled, and at times not so veiled, biblical criticism was a feature of many of the deists' writings. See, e.g., Herbert of Cherbury, *De Veritate*, Eng. edn, p. 316; Toland, *Christianity not Mysterious*, pp. 31f., 49, 109; *Amyntor*, pp. 14f., 42f.; Collins, *A Discourse of Free-Thinking*, pp. 85–93, *A Discourse of the Grounds and Reasons*, passim. Also see Henning Graf von Reventlow, *The Authority of the Bible*, passim.

183. *True Intellectual System*, I.IV.xvii (I, 531–6); cf. I.IV.xxxvi (II, 300f.).

184. William Warburton, *The Divine Legation of Moses*, I, 317f.

185. Thomas Burnet, *Of the State of the Dead and Those that are to Rise*, tr. M. Earberry, 2nd edn, 2 vols, (London: E. Curll, 1728), II, 97. Earberry was quite undeterred by Burnet's admonition in the original Latin text: 'Therefore if any shall translate what has been said by learned Men upon this Subject into the vulgar Language, they can have no good Scope or View thereby.' Earbery made two comments in the notes. First he observed that Burnet's position sounded very much like priestcraft. He then pointed out that there was really no more universal language than Latin (p. 97).

186. Qu. in Warburton, *Divine Legation of Moses*, I, 314f.

187. *The Spectator*, no. 186 (Wed. Oct. 3, 1771).

188. Lancelot Addison, not to be confused with the above-mentioned Joseph Addison, argued along similar lines that even if it is admitted that religion is 'a meer Engine of Government', it is nonetheless in the best interests of government to continue to instil in people 'a belief and fear of the *Invisible Powers*, and this dismal apprehension of a future State'. *A Modest Plea for the Clergy*, p. 146.

189. But this, too, was changing. The rise of the middle classes in the seventeenth century threatened the old class structure from which the twofold philosophy derived a measure of support. The growth of literacy reduced the more obvious gap between the vulgar and the learned. It was the role of *The Spectator*, for example, to bring 'Philosophy out of Closets and Libraries, Schools and Colleges, to dwell in Clubs and Assemblies, at Tea-tables, and in Coffee-houses.' Addison, in *The Spectator* no. 16, Monday March 12, 1711.

4 SACRED HISTORY AND RELIGIOUS DIVERSITY

1. Henry Smith, *God's Arrow Against Atheists* (London: Pr. for John Wright and G. Sawbridge, 1656), pp. 31f. (The first edition of this work appeared in 1593.) The same attitude is found in the fathers, from Tertullian to Augustine. Thus Tertullian, 'Extreme antiquity gives books authority. For Moses was the first prophet ... He is discovered to have lived about three hundred years before

your most ancient [Gentile] man.' *Apology*, XIX, ed. and tr. T. R. Glover, Loeb edn (London: Heinemann, 1931). And Eusebius: 'The race of Hebrews is not new but is honoured among all men for its antiquity and is well known to all. Now, stories and documents belonging to it concern ancient men, few and scarce in number, yet remarkable for piety and righteousness and all other virtues.' *Ecclesiastical History*, I.4, ed. and tr. K. Lake, Loeb edn (London: Heinemann, 1926).

2. Thomas Hearne, *Ductor Historicus* (London: Pr. for Tim. Childe, 1698), pp. II, 127; cf. pp. 145f.

3. Timothy Nourse, *A Discourse of Natural and Reveal'd Religion* (London: Pr. for John Newton, 1691), pp. 178–84.

4. David Collyer, *The Sacred Interpreter* (London: Pr. for Thomas Astley, 1732) p. 146.

5. See, e.g., Matthew Hale, *The Primitive Origination of Mankind* (London: Pr. by W. Goodbid for W. Shrowsbery, 1677), preface, p. 136; Peter Heylyn, *Microcosmus: or A Little Description of the Great World*, 2nd edn (Oxford: Pr. by Iohn Lichfield and William Tvrner, 1625), p. 19; Simon Patrick, *A Commentary on the First Book of Moses, called Genesis* (London: Pr. for Ri. Chiswell, 1695), preface; Sir Walter Raleigh, *The Historie of the World in Five Bookes* (London: Pr. for R. Best, Jo. Place and Sam. Cartwright, 1652), I.8.ii (p. III); Edward Stillingfleet, *Origines Sacrae* (London: Pr. for Henry Mortlock, 1675), pp. 14–73, and passim; William Warburton, *The Divine Legation of Moses*, II, 302.

6. Thus, Robert Jenkin: 'And here we must have recourse to the History of the Bible; since it is acknowledged by all learned men to be so much the ancientest Book, which can give us an Account of Religion, in the World.' He goes on to note that even if the Bible's divine authority is not taken into account, it is at the very least 'an Historical relation of Things past'. *The Reasonableness and Certainty of the Christian Religion*, 2nd edn (London: Pr. for P. B. and R. Wellington, 1700), pp. 58f. Henry More, *Grand Mystery of Godliness*, II.i.2 (p. 157); cf. *Antidote Against Idolatry*, p. 14.

7. Henry More, *Grand Mystery of Godliness*, II.i.2 (p. 157); cf. *Antidote Against Idolatry*, p. 14.

8. The 'Stratonician presumption', first formulated by Strato, lies at the heart of the British empiricist tradition. Antony Flew defines it as the belief that 'all qualities observed in things are qualities belonging by natural right to those things themselves'. *God and Philosophy* (New York: Dell, 1966), 3.20. In suggesting that such naturalism was the basis of all idolatry, More was in part attempting to counter an increasing tendency towards materialistic and naturalistic explanations.

9. Robert South, 'Man was Created in the Image of God', in *Twelve Sermons*, p. 89; cf. Gale, *The Court of the Gentiles*, pt II, preface.

10. Thomas Browne, *Pseudodoxia Epidemica* (London: Pr. for the assigns of Henry Dod, 1669), pp. 1, 5.

11. *Ibid.*, pp. 37, 40.

12. More, *Grand Mystery of Godliness*, III.ix.2 (p. 76); cf. *Antidote Against Idolatry*, p. 124. If it were the case that angels had established the pagan religions,

then it was clear that the people had corrupted the original institutions. More makes no comment on how such religions would have differed from Judaism, neither did he address the issue of their validity.

13. Robert Burton, *The Anatomy of Melancholy*, 8th edn (London: Pr. for Peter Parker, 1676) p. 389, cf. p. 187. Also see Thomas Bromhall, *An History of Apparitions, Oracles, Prophecies, and Predictions ... and the Cunning Delusions of the Devil*, tr. from the French (London: Pr. by John Streater, 1658); Robert Jenkin, *The Reasonableness and Certainty of the Christian Religion*, bk 1, pp. 400f.; Charles Leslie, *The History of Sin and Heresie Attempted* (London: Pr. for H. Hindmarsh, 1698) pp. 51–3; Walter Raleigh, *Historie of the World*, 1.6.ix (pp. 82f.), 1.11.vii (pp. 178f.); Alexander Ross, *Pansebeia*, p. 74; Henry Smith, *God's Arrow against Atheists*, p. 21.

14. Margaret Hodgen's *Early Anthropology in the 16th and 17th Centuries* (Philadelphia: University of Pennsylvania Press, 1964) outlines the main features of early theories of human diversity. The application of these theories to the problem of religious diversity which follows owes much to the fifth chapter of this excellent work.

15. Warburton, *The Divine Legation of Moses*, 11, 14f.; cf. Van Dale, *The History of the Oracles and the Cheats of the Pagan Priests*, pp. 1–3, in Mrs Behn, *Histories, Novels and Translations*, 4th edn (London: Pr. by W. O. for S. B., 1700).

16. Burton, *Anatomy of Melancholy*, p. 389.

17. Raleigh, *Historie of the World*, 1.11.VII (pp. 178f.).

18. Origen, *On First Principles*, 11.1.i (p. 77).

19. Etienne Gilson, *History of Christian Philosophy in the Middle Ages* (New York: Random House, 1955), p. 573, n. 39.

20. See, e.g., More, *Divine Dialogues*, pp. 503f.; Rust, *A Letter of Resolution*, pp. 28–31.

21. Victor Harris traces the fortunes of this theory in the seventeenth century in *All Coherence Gone* (London: Frank Cass, 1966).

22. See Donald Cameron Allen, 'The Degeneration of Man and Renaissance Pessimism', *Studies in Philology*, 35 (1938), 202–27; Clarence Glacken, *Traces on the Rhodian Shore: Nature and Culture in Western Thought from Ancient Times to the End of the Eighteenth Century* (Berkeley: University of California Press, 1973), pp. 162f., 379–92; Hodgen, *Early Anthropology*, pp. 254–94; George Williamson, 'Mutability, Decay, and Seventeenth-Century Melancholy', *Journal of English Literary History*, 2 (1935), 121–51.

23. Even in the middle of the seventeenth century there were reasonable men who wished to deny, almost *a priori*, the accuracy of those astronomical observations which pointed to changes in the heavens. See, e.g., Meric Casaubon, *A Treatise of Vse and Cvstom* (London: Pr. by Iohn Legatt, 1638), pp. 71ff. Also see Williamson, 'Mutability, Decay and Melancholy', pp. 122–6.

24. For computations of the proportion of Christians in the world, see Edward Brerewood, *Enquiries Touching the Diversity of Languages and Religions, through the Chief parts of the World* (London: Pr. for Samuel Mearne, John Martin and Henry Herringman, 1674), (1st edn 1614); Burton, *Anatomy of Melancholy*, p. 386; Brerewood's estimate is also cited by Henry More, *Grand Mystery*

of Godliness, x.i.5 (p. 491).

25. The latin motto appears in *Phisiologiae Stoicorum* by the Flemish Neo-stoic, Justus Lipsius, *Opera Omnia* (Antverpiae, 1637).

26. *Faerie Queene* v, pro. 1. Also see Spenser's *Mutabilitie* cantos, and Edwin Greenlaw, 'Spenser and Lucretius', *Studies in Philology*, 17 (1920), 439–64; W. P. Cumming, 'The Influence of Ovid's *Metamorphoses* on Spenser's "Mutability" Cantos', *Studies in Philology*, 28 (1931), 241–56.

27. John Dove, *A Confutation of Atheism* (London: Pr. by E. Able for H. Rockett, 1605), p. 92. Cf. also John Donne's Holy Sonnets, I and v.

28. Genesis 3.17, cf. Romans 8.18–23.

29. Burnet, *Sacred Theory*, I.12 (p. 126).

30. William Whiston, 'Of the Mosaick History of the Creation', p. 91, in *A New Theory of the Earth* (London: Pr. by R. Roberts for Benj. Tooke, 1696); cf. *New Theory*, pp. 168–74. Cf. also John Woodward (1665–1736), fellow of the Royal Society and professor of physics at Gresham College, who maintained that the Deluge had altered the earth for the worse so that its condition would correspond with that of fallen humanity. *An Essay Towards a Natural History of the Earth* (London: Pr. for Ric. Wilkin, 1695), pp. 83, 90, 92.

    Relying upon the same premise, some theologians had taken the opposite tack, attempting to prove the Fall by an appeal to the evidences of a decaying universe. See, e.g., Godfrey Goodman, *The Fall of Man, or the Corruption of Nature Proved by Natural Reason* (London: F. Kyngston, 1616).

31. Thomas Pope Blount, *Essays on Several Subjects* (London: Pr. for Richard Bentley, 1697), p. 139. (1st edn 1692).

32. Casaubon, *Vse and Cvstom*, p. 80.

33. George Hakewill, *Apologie or Declaration of the Power and Providence of God in the Government of the World, Consisting in an Examination and Censure of the Common Errour touching Nature's Perpetual and Universal Decay* (Oxford: J. Lichfield and W. Turner, 1627). One John Jonston 'of Poland' also wrote a work refuting the thesis that 'the world universally and perpetually doth grow to be worse', *An History of the Constancy of Nature* (London: Pr. for John Streater, 1657). Hakewill and Jonston were belatedly and somewhat ambiguously supported by Hale, *Primitive Origination*, pp. 169–74. Bodin, we should mention, also denied degeneration as an explanation of diversity. 'They are mistaken', he said, 'who think that the race of men always deteriorates.' *Methodus ad facilem historiarum cognitionem* (Parisiis: Apud M. Iuuenam, 1566), p. 302. As we shall see, Bodin attributed diversity to climate.

34. See Richard Jones, *The Battle of the Books*.

35. Josephus, *Jewish Antiquities*, tr. H. Thackeray *et al.*, 9 vols., Loeb edn (London: Heinemann, 1961–9), I.66 (IV.31).

36. Philo, *De Posteritate Caini*, 42 (Loeb edn II, 351).

37. More, *Grand Mystery of Godliness*, Contents, III.i.2 (p. 57), cf. II.12.5 (p. 54). More almost certainly invested the birth of Cain with some deeper symbolic significance.

38. Leslie, *A Supplement upon occasion of a History of Religion*, in *Works*, II, 643.

39. Dionisius Petavius, *The History of the World: or, an Account of Time* (London:

Pr. by J. Streater, 1659), p. 3.

40. *Ibid.*, p. 4. The puzzling scriptural reference to the 'sons of God' (Gen. 6.1) has been variously interpreted. Josephus seems to have begun a tradition that the 'sons of God' were angels, and in this he is supported by the Alexandrinus manuscript of the Septuagint. He is later contradicted by rabbinical interpretations which from about the second century onwards suggest that the 'sons of God' were actually members of aristocratic families. See Josephus, *Jewish Antiquities*, 1.73. Josephus seems to have influenced the views of Lactantius and Eusebius. On the other side, Augustine declared that the 'sons of God' were merely men (*City of God*, XV.23). This, in all probability, was the favoured reading in the seventeenth century. See, e.g., Walter Raleigh, *Historie of the World*, 1.5.vii (p. 69); Collyer, *Sacred Interpreter*, p. 146. It is important for our purposes that the 'sons of God' were considered to be men, for as we shall see below, it was the admixture of pure and defiled religious 'types' which was thought to play an important part in the formation of heathen religions.

41. The Biblical injunctions against the 'mixing of kinds' are well known. Genesis reports that the various species were created 'each after his kind', implying set limits to species variation. The Pentateuch's prohibition of the mixing of kinds makes this ban on the crossing of specific boundaries more explicit. Bestiality was punishable by death (Exodus 22.19, Leviticus 20.15), cross-breeding was forbidden, animals of different kinds were not to be yoked together, seeds of different kinds could not be sown in the same field, and even the wearing of clothes made of different materials was proscribed (Leviticus 19.19, Deuteronomy 22.9–11). Also see Hayden White, 'The Forms of Wildness: Archaeology of an Idea', pp. 9, 14–17, in *The Wild Man Within*, ed. Edward Dudley and Maximillian Novak (Pittsburgh: Pittsburgh University Press, 1972), pp. 3–38. This biblical view was influential until at least early modern times. The Renaissance environmentalist Jean Bodin, e.g., reinforced his climatic theory of human diversity with a theory of admixture. 'The fusion of peoples', he maintained, 'changes the customs and nature of men not a little' *Method for the Easy Comprehension of History*, tr. Beatrice Reynolds (New York: Columbia University Press, 1945), p. 145.

42. Raleigh, *Historie of the World*, 1.2.v, (p. 61). Philo had expressed a similar opinion. The land of Nod, he says, 'is the country called "Tossing"'. Cain and his spiritual progeny were thus creatures of 'wavering and unsettled impulses ... subject to tossing and tumult.' *De Posteritate Caini*, 22 (Loeb edn, II, 341). Cf. John Flavel, *Discourse of the Occasions of Mental Errors*, pp. 2f.

43. *Ibid.*, 1.5.vii (p. 69). Aspects of this 'latter' Fall were prefigured in the original one. Augustine, e.g., observed that 'this calamity, as well as the first, was occasioned by woman'. *City of God*, XV.22 (p. 510).

44. For an account of the story of Noah and its place in explanations of the dispersion of the human race, see Don Cameron Allen, *The Legend of Noah: Renaissance Rationalism in Art, Science and Letters* (Urbana: University of Illinois Press, 1949) esp. ch. 6.

45. Patrick, *A Commentary*, p. 226.

46. Genesis 9, 10. The cursing of Ham's son on account of Ham's 'looking upon Noah's nakedness' has caused exegetes not a few problems throughout history. Not only does it seem unfair, but the nature of Ham's 'crime' is puzzling. Petrus Comestor observed, with penetrating insight, that the story showed (at the very least) that underwear had not been invented in Noah's time. *Historical Scholastica*, in *Patrologiae cursus completus*, Series Latina, ed. J. P. Migne, 217 vols. (Paris, 1844–1905), CXCVIII, 187. More illuminating interpretations of the passage and its significance are given in Allen, *Legend of Noah*, pp. 73f.

47. Genesis 10.6; Diodorus Siculus, *History*, 1.28, 82; Herodotus, *Histories*, II.7; Juvenal, XV; Lucian, *De Syria Dea*, I.2.

48. Augustine, *City of God*, XVI.2.

49. Gregory of Tours, *History of the Franks* I.5, ed. and tr. Lewis Thorpe (Ringwood: Penguin, 1974), p. 71.

50. Joannes Boemus, *The Fardle of Façions*, tr. W. Waterman (London: Pr. by Jhon Kingstone and Henry Sutton, 1555), Fol. B.iiii.v– B.iiii.r. Also see Hayden White, 'The Forms of Wildness: Archaeology of an Idea', pp. 15f., in *The Wild Man Within*, pp. 3–38.

51. *Ibid.*, B v.v.

52. Raleigh, *Historie of the World*, 1.6.ii-iii (p. 72). Raleigh relies here on both Genesis and Herodotus (*Histories*, II.7) as sources. The re-occurence of the 'effects of the former poyson' in Noah's line had long been recognised as a difficulty, for it seems to make the Deluge rather pointless. Joannes Gerhardus, e.g., thought that perhaps God should have destroyed Noah and his family as well, for while they betrayed no outward sign of it, they too possessed the seeds of wickedness and went on to father nations of idolaters, *Commentarius super Genesin* (Leipzig, 1693), pp. 194f.

53. John Dryden, *Works* (Edinburgh, 1884), X, 12. Qu. in Hodgen, *Early Anthropology*, p. 262.

54. Joseph Glanvill, *Scepsis Scientifica*, ed. John Owen (London: Kegan Paul and Co., 1885), p. 211.

55. See, e.g., Casaubon, *Vse and Custom*, p. 1.

56. William Strachey, *The Historie of Travell into Virginia Britania* (1612) (London: Hakluyt Society, 1953) pp. 54f. Qu. in Hodgen, *Early Anthropology*, p. 262.

57. *Ibid.*

58. See, e.g., Josephus, *Jewish Antiquities*, 1.122–50; Epiphanius, *Adversus Haereses*, in *Patrologia cursus completus*, Series Graeca, ed. J. P. Migne, 162 vols. (Paris, 1857–66), XLI. 160f.

59. There was considerable discussion in the mid 1600s in England as to whether the American Indians might be part of one of the lost tribes of Israel. See, e.g., Thomas Thorowgood, *Iewes in America, or Probabilities that the Americans are of that Race* (London: Pr. by W. H. for Tho. Slater, 1650); Menasseh ben Israel, *The Hope of Israel* (London: Pr. by R. I. for Hannah Allen, 1650); Hamon l'Estrange, *Americans no Jewes, or Improbabilities that the Americans are of that Race* (London: Pr. by W. W. for Henry Seile, 1652). These specula-

tions were intimately linked to millennial hopes. See Richard Popkin, 'Jewish Messianism and Christian Millenarianism', in *Culture and Politics from Puritanism to the Enlightenment*, ed. Perez Zagorin (Berkeley: University of California Press, 1980), pp. 67–90.

60. See, e.g., Edmund Dickinson, *Diatriba de Noae in Italia adventu*, appended to *Delphi Phoenicizantes* (Oxoniae: Excudebat H: Hall, impensis Ric. Davis, 1655); Jean Lemaire de Belges, *Les illustrations de Gaule et singularitatez de Troye*, in *Oeuvres* (Brussels: Académie Impériale et Royale, 1882); Richard Lynche, *An Historical Treatise of the Travels of Noah into Europe* (London: A. Islip, 1601); Gulielmus Postellus, *Cosmographicae disciplinae compendium* (Basel: per Ioannem Oporinum, 1561); Alphonso Tostado, *Commentaria in Genesim*, in *Opera omnia*, 23 tom. (Venice, 1728).

61. George Harry, *The Genealogy of the High and Mighty Monarch James ... King of Brittayne ... with his lineall descent from Noah* (London: Pr. by S. Stafford for T. Salisbury, 1604).

62. Robert Sheringham, *De Anglorum gentis origine disceptatio* (Cantabrigiae: Excudebat Joann. Hayes, impensis Edvardi Story, 1670); Edmund Campion, *A Historie of Ireland* (1571), in *The Historie of Ireland*, ed. Sir James Ware (Dublin: Pr. by the Societie of Stationers, 1663)). Historians of other nations took up similar projects. On behalf of the Germans, for example, Wolfgang Lazius proved the Hebrew origins of the Teutonic peoples, *De gentium aliquot migrationibus ... libri X* (Francofurti: Apud A. Wecheli Heredes, 1600).

63. On 'typological' interpretation see Erich Auerbach, *Mimesis* (Princeton: Princeton University Press, 1968), pp. 48ff., 73ff., 194ff., 555; Hans Frei, *The Eclipse of Biblical Narrative* (New Haven: Yale University Press, 1974), ch. 1.

64. Raleigh, *Historie of the World*, 1.5.ii, (p. 61). Raleigh cites Cyril as his source for this view. The writer of *The Originall of Idolatries* (London: Pr. by G. Purslowe and M. Flesher for N. Butter, 1624), a work wrongly attributed to Isaac Casaubon, likewise maintained that the Jews 'are at this day vagabonds' (p. 77). Heylyn notes that in the first century the Jews suffered many massacres before their final dispersion. These, he charitably observes, 'were not more cruelly inflicted on them by their enemies, then justly deserued by themselves: they wishing (though, I suppose, not desiring) that the innocent bloud of our Sauiour should be on them and their children'. Their just fate was that they were 'generally banished [sic] their natiue country and neuer permitted to inhabit it, otherwise then as strangers. After this desolation, the *Iewes* were dispersed all ouer the world.' *Microcosmvs*, pp. 580f. Burton informs us that the modern Jews are 'a company of vagabonds' who are 'scattered over all parts', *Anatomy of Melancholy*, p. 388. James Howell, in the Epistle Dedicatory of Josippon, *The VVonderful, and Most Deplorable History of the Latter Times of the Jews* (London: Pr. for John Stafford, 1652), describes the Jews as 'straglers', and 'Runnagates and Landlopers' who were 'dispersed and Squandered here and there upon the surface of the earth'. Even Warburton, who was comparatively sympathetic towards the Jews, spoke of their state as representing 'the irremissible infamy of an unsettled vagabond condition'. *Divine Legation of Moses*, III, xvii.

The legend of the 'Wandering Jew' (variously named Ahasuerus, Joseph Cartaphilus, Giovanni Buttadeo) is also part of this tradition. The story is that Ahasuerus was condemned to spend his endless life wandering as a punishment for mocking Jesus when on his way to the cross.

65. Theophilus Gale, 'Of Philosophy' (1670), preface, part II of *The Court of the Gentiles* (London: Pr. by A. Maxwell and R. Roberts, for T. Cockeril, 1669–77). Gale was championing a view made famous by Tertullian, who maintained against the early Greek apologists that 'philosophy is the parent of heresy', *De Praescriptione Haereticorum*, 7. It is also worth noting that Robert Jenkin maintained the minority view that mixing did not lead to corruption, but allowed the Gentiles to come into contact with the true religion. *Reasonableness and Certainty*, pp. 76f.

66. Boemus, *Fardle of Façions*, Fols. P. v. r., P. vi. r. Boemus also noted that Mohammad's land of birth was inhabited by many races – Turks, Greeks, Armenians, Saracens, Jacobites, Nestorians, Jews, and Christians. (P. v. v.).

67. Henry Smith's expression, in *God's Arrow Against Atheists* (London: Pr. for John Wright and George Sawbridge, 1656), p. 44.

68. Humphrey Prideaux, *The True Nature of Imposture Fully Display'd in the Life of Mahomet*, 2nd edn (London: William Rogers, 1697), p. 47. See also Heylyn, *Microcosmvs* p. 613; Richard Simon, *The Critical History of the Religions* (London: Pr. by J. Hepinstall for Henry Fairthorn and John Kersley, 1685), p. 148.

69. Robert Burton, *Anatomy of Melancholy*, pp. 404f.

70. Henri Boulainvilliers, *The Life of Mahomet*, tr. from the French (London: Pr. for W. Hinchliffe, 1731), p. 139.

71. Louis Le Roy, *Of the Interchangeable Course, or Variety of Things in the Whole World*, tr. R. Ashley (London: C. Yetsweirt, 1594), Fol. 14 v.

72. *Ibid.*, 13r. Heylyn similarly describes the Arabs as 'a vagabond and theeuish people', *Microcosmvs*, p. 609.

73. The construction of new religions from elements of old ones forms part of Anthony Collins' theory of the origin of the religions. See *Discourse of the Grounds and Reasons*, p. 21. Also see Warburton's response, *Divine Legation of Moses*, II, 380f.

74. A comprehensive account of this history may be found in Glacken, *Traces on the Rhodian Shore*.

75. George Sarton, *A History of Science*, 2 vols. (Cambridge, Mass.: Harvard University Press, 1959), I, 338, 343, 368.

76. Hippocrates, *Airs, Waters, Places*, tr. W. H. S. Jones, 4 vols., Loeb edn (London: Heinemann, 1939), xxiv (I, 133–5); Glacken, *Traces on the Rhodian Shore*, pp. 86f. Cf. Plato, *Timaeus*, 82.a, b; Aristotle, *Politics*, VII.vii; Herodotus, *Histories*, 1.105.

77. See, e.g., Glacken, *Traces on the Rhodian Shore*, pp. 265–71, 434–47; Marian Tooley, 'Bodin and the Medieval Theory of Climate', *Speculum*, 28 (1953), 64–83.

78. Bodin, *Method*, p. 110.

79. Bodin, *Republique*, v, i. This work was translated into English by Richard Knowles and appeared in 1606 as *The Six Books of a Commonweale* (London:

Imprinted A. Islip, impensis G. Bishop, 1606). Page references come from this edition. See pp. 548, 550, 561.

80. *Ibid.*

81. *Ibid.*, pp. 550, 561.

82. Bodin's influence can be found in the works of such diverse thinkers as Bolton, Burton, Carpenter, Meric Casaubon, Hakewill, William Harrison, Heylyn, Hobbes, Holinshed, Milton, Nash, Sidney, Spenser, and Wheare. Thus, e.g., Burton: 'The Clime changeth not so much customs, manners, wits ... as constitutions of their bodies, and temperature it self. In all particular Provinces we see it confirmed by experience, as the Air is, so are the inhabitants, dull, heavy, witty, subtle, neat, cleanly, clownish, sick and sound.' Burton, *Anatomy of Melancholy*, p. 164. And Casaubon: 'it is not possible ... that men that live under different clymates should all live after one fashion'. *Vse and Cvstom*, p. 80. Also see Z. S. Fink, 'Milton and the Theory of Climatic Influence', *Modern Language Quarterly*, 2 (1941), 67–80; Leonard F. Dean, 'Bodin's *Methodus* in England before 1625', *Studies in Philology*, 39 (1942), 160–6.

83. Louis Le Roy, *Of the Interchangeable Course, or Variety of Things*, fols. 10r–16r, quotation from 11r.

84. Giovanni Botero, *Relations of the Most Famous Kingdomes and Common-weales thorough the World* (London: Pr. by Iohn Havilland, 1630).

85. Cf. Heylyn, *Microcosmvs*, p. 16.

86. *Ibid.*, p. 9; cf. *Cosmographie in Foure Bookes* (London: Pr. for Henry Seile, 1652), p. 18.

87. Nathaniel Carpenter, *Geographie Delineated*, 2nd edn (Oxford: Pr. by Iohn Lichfield for Henry Cripps, 1635), Bk. II, p. 221.

88. *Ibid.*, p. 250.

89. *Ibid.*, p. 276. Similar attitudes to climate and colonisation prevailed during the French Enlightenment – the Abbé Corneille de Pauw: 'Since it is principally to the climate of the New World that we have attributed causes vitiating the essential qualities of men and the degeneration of human nature, we are doubtless justified in asking if any derangement has been observed in the faculties of the Creoles, that is, of Europeans born in America of parents native to our continent ... All animals taken from the Old World to the New have undergone, without any exception, a notable deterioration, either in their form or in their instinct. This would lead us immediately to presume that men also have experienced some effects caused by the air, the land, the water, and the food'. Corneille de Pauw, *Recherches philosophiques sur les Américains, ou Mémoires intéressants pour servir à l'Histoire de l'Espèce humaine* (London: 1774), II, 107–22, in *Was America a Mistake?* ed. H. S. Commager and E. Giordanetti (New York: Harper, 1967), p. 100.

90. *Ibid.*, p. 278.

91. See, e.g., George C. Taylor, *Milton's Use of Du Bartas* (Cambridge, Mass.: Harvard University Press, 1934); Heylyn, *Cosmographie*, p. 20, n.

92. Du Bartas, *Les Colonies*, lines 623f. Heylyn noncommitally quotes du Bartas on the same point (*Cosmographie*, p. 18, n.).

O see how full of wonders strange is Nature,
Sith in each *Climate*, not along in stature,
Strength, colour, hair; but that men differ do
Both in their humours, and their manners too.

93. Wotton, *A Discourse Concerning the Confusion of Languages at Babel* (London: Pr. for S. Austin and W. Bowyer, 1730), p. 50. Josephus, incidentally, also saw Babel merely as bringing about the dispersion which God had originally intended. *Jewish Antiquities*, I. 110–13.

94. George Walker, *The History of the Creation* (London: Pr. for John Bartlett, 1641), p. 100.

95. On the principle of plenitude, see Arthur O. Lovejoy, *The Great Chain of Being* (Cambridge, Mass.: Harvard University Press, 1936), passim.

96. Casaubon, *Vse and Cvstome*, pp. 80–2.

97. Burnet, *Sacred Theory*, Bk. II, ch. I, (p. 137). This view of the antediluvian cosmos was subsequently adopted by Samuel Shuckford, *The Sacred and Profane History of the World Connected*, 3rd edn (London: Pr. for J. and R. Tonson, 1743), I, 33. Henry More, incidentally, maintained precisely the opposite, arguing that the tilt of the earth on its axis was an indication of divine providence, for 'an orderly *vicissitude* of things is most pleasant unto us.' *Antidote Against Atheisme*, Bk. II, ch. ii, 1–4 (pp. 40–2). So too, his Cambridge colleague Cudworth, *True Intellectual System*, v.v.3 (III, 464f.). This serves to illustrate the point that the Platonists generally viewed variety in a more kindly light.

98. Whiston, *New Theory*, p. 181.

99. *Ibid.*, p. 292.

100. Prideaux, *The True Nature of Imposture*, p. 25.

101. *Ibid.*

102. See, e.g., Anon. *The History of Mahomet, the Great Impostor* (Falkirk: T. Johnston, 1821), p. 17; Bernard de Mandeville, *An Enquiry into the Origin of Honour* (London, 1732), p. 29; *Pantologia* (London: G. Kearsley et al., 1813), 7, 143. Edward Stillingfleet, *A Letter to a Deist* (London: Pr. by W. G., 1677), p. 44.

103. William Paley, *The Works* (Edinburgh: Peter Brown and Thomas Nelson, 1831), p. 408.

104. Herbert, *A Dialogue*, p. 19.

105. *Ibid.*, p. 41.

106. Shaftesbury, *Characteristics*, II, Misc. ii, ch. 1 (p. 184; cf. pp. 188, 215).

107. David Collyer, *The Sacred Interpreter*, I, 116f.

108. Charles Montesquieu, *De L'Esprit des Loix* (Paris: Société Les Belle Lettres, 1950–61), XIV.5; Glacken, *Traces on the Rhodian Shore*, pp. 565–81.

109. *Ibid.*, XIV.5, 7.

110. *Ibid.*, XVI.2.

111. Thomas Blount, 'The Variety of Opinions', *Essays*, pp. 213–23.

112. *Ibid.*, p. 226.

113. *Ibid.*, p. 240.

114. Glacken, *Traces on the Rhodian Shore*, p. 445.

115. Almost certainly a pseudonym, possibly of George Sale.

116. Abdulla Mahumed Omar, *A Defence of Mahomet: A Paradox*, in *Miscellanea Aurea: or, the Golden Medley* (London: A. Bettesworth and J. Pemberton, 1720), p. 170. Here Omar also takes up the issue of the 'naturalness' of the mores of Christianity and Islam, for it had often been argued that Christian monogamy was more natural given the even proportions of the sexes. For a discussion of arguments of this kind, see Alfred A. Owen, 'Polygamy and Deism', *The Journal of English and Germanic Philology*, 48 (1949), 343–60.

117. *Paradise Lost*, IX.41–5.

118. Montesquieu, e.g., defended his speculations about climatic determination of religion in *De l'Esprit des Loix* by use of this stratagem. See his 'Défence de l'Esprit des Lois', *Oeuvres Complètes de Montesquieu*, ed. Edouard Laboulaye (Paris: Garnier Frères, 1875–9), VI.

119. Matthew Hale, for example, observes: 'Animals, even of the same Original, Extraction and *Species*, be diversified by accustomable residence in one Climate from what they are in another.' *Primitive Origination*, p. 201. John Bulwer, in the introduction to his *A View of the People of the Whole World* (London: Pr. by William Hunt, 1654), applies this view of variation to humans, claiming that certain human customs will bring about inherited changes. See also L. J. Jordanova, *Lamarck* (Oxford: Oxford University Press, 1984), p. 2.

120. 'Original sin standeth not in the following of Adam (as the Pelagians do vainly talk); but it is the fault and corruption of the Nature of every man, that naturally is engendered of the offspring of Adam.' 'Thirty-Nine Articles', IX (Schaff, III, 492f). Cf. 'They [Adam and Eve] being the root of all mankind, the guilt of this sin was imputed, and the same death in sin and corrupted nature conveyed to all their posterity descending from them by ordinary generation.' 'Westminster Confession', VI.iii (Schaff, III, 615).

121. More, *Antidote Against Idolatry*, p. 14 (my emphasis).

122. More, *Enthusiasmus Triumphatus*, p. 4.

123. Burton, *Anatomy of Melancholy*, p. 383.

124. *Ibid.*, p. 386.

125. *Ibid.*

126. *Ibid.*

127. *Ibid.*, pp. 387, 389.

128. Meric Casaubon, *A Treatise Concerning Enthusiasme, As it is an Effect of Nature: but is mistaken by Many for either Divine Inspiration, or Diabolical Possession* (London: Pr. by R. D., 1655), p. 17.

129. *Ibid.*, p. 16.

130. *Ibid.*, p. 4.

131. Also see Cudworth, *True and Intellectual System*, IV.xvii (I, 513); John Smith, *Select Discourses*, pp. 41, 190. Burton, the Cambridge Platonists, and even some of the deists regarded atheism and enthusiasm as two sides of the same coin. See Thomas Morgan, *The Moral Philosopher*, I, 219; Burton, *Anatomy of Melancholy*, p. 386.

132. More, *Enthusiasmus Triumphatus*, p. 1.

133. *Ibid.*, pp. 5–8.

134. *Ibid.*, p. 8.

135. *Ibid.*, pp. 10f.

136. *Ibid.*, p. 12.

137. *Ibid.*, pp. 15–29. Muhammad was often portrayed as the enthusiastic–impostor *par excellence*. This was due at least in part to his supposed 'epilepsy'. On epilepsy and its connexion with religious imposture see Oswei Temkin, *The Falling Sickness*, 2nd edn (Baltimore: Johns Hopkins, 1971), pp. 148–61. More's last reference – 'Chymists' – is probably to Paracelsus.

138. *Ibid.*, p. 48.

139. *Ibid.*, p. 47. This parallels More's theological position on the operation of divine grace. While it may seem that the elect is predetermined, human choice nonetheless plays an important role. See *Grand Mystery of Godliness*, x.v (pp. 501–4).

140. Burton, *Anatomy of Melancholy*, p. 410.

141. *Ibid.*

142. Henry More, in another context, advocated toleration: 'It is manifest therefore, *That Liberty of religion is the common and natural right of all nations and Persons*', *Grand Mystery of Godliness*, x.x.9 (p. 521).

143. *Ibid.*, p. 412. Only 'some of them', because presumably there would be some practical difficulties associated with housing all of the superstitious idolaters, Ethnicks, Mahometans, Jews, Hereticks, Enthusiasts, Divinators, Prophets, Sectaries, Schismaticks, Monks, Heremites, Epicures, Libertines, Atheists, Hypocrites, and Infidels.

144. More, *Enthusiasmus Triumphatus*, pp. 3f. More followed Aristotle here. The Philosopher believed that during sleep or in certain emotional or diseased states, man is guided by imagination, not reason. See, e.g., Aristotle, *On the Soul*, III.3.429a.5ff.; *On Dreams*, I.459a.21. Cf. Avicenna, *De Anima*, 4.2.

145. *Ibid.*, p. 4.

146. *Ibid.*, p. 5. Compare this with Thomas Browne, according to whom the *second* cause of error, after the more general first cause of the Fall is the 'erroneous disposition' or 'vulgar capacities' of the people. *Pseudodoxia Epidemica*, p. 8. Browne goes on to note that such religious forms as Islam, Paganism, and brute worship result directly from this vulgar malady.

147. Shaftesbury, *Characteristics*, I, Tr. I, sec. vi (p. 35). Cf. II, Tr. 6, misc. 2, ch. I (p. 179).

148. John Trenchard, *The Natural History of Superstition*, in John Trenchard and Thomas Gordon, *A Collection of Tracts*, I (London: Pr. for F. Cogan, 1751) p. 380.

149. *Ibid.*

150. Hume, *Natural History of Religion*, p. 75.

151. *Ibid.*, p. 76.

152. d'Holbach's *Contagion sacrée* is discussed in some detail in Manuel, *Eighteenth Century Confronts the Gods*, ch. 6. The Baron relied quite heavily upon the English deists: his library contained works by Trenchard, Woolston, Collins, Toland, and of course, Hume.

153. Augustine, *City of God*, XVI.9. (p.532).

154. Something similar had happened when the Ptolemaic theory of the solar system

had been defended on biblical grounds by the ecclesiastical authorities. Moreover, just as the heliocentric view removed the earth from the centre of the universe, so the New World destroyed the old symmetry which placed Christendom in the centre of the known world.

155. Abbé Corneille de Pauw, *Recherches philosophiques*, I, I, in *Was America a Mistake?*, ed. Commager and Giordanetti, p. 76. His fellow cleric and compatriot Roubaud agreed, stating that the discovery of America had 'changed the face of the universe'. Pierre-Joseph Roubaud, *Histoire générale de l'Asie, de l'Afrique, et de l'Amérique*, 5 vols. (Paris, 1775), v. 186, in *ibid.*, p. 160.

156. Strachey, *The Historie of Travell*, p. 55.

157. Heylyn, *Cosmography*, pp. 98–100.

158. Petavius, *The History of the World*, pp. 130f.; Patrick, *A Commentary*, pp. 217f.

159. Hale, *Primitive Origination*, pp. 189–94.

160. Burnet, *Sacred Theory*, II.viii (pp. 194ff.).

161. Corneille de Pauw, *Recherches philosophiques*, I.32f., in *Was America a Mistake?*, ed. Commager and Giordanetti, p. 90.

162. As some commentators realised. See Simon Patrick, *A Commentary*, p. 217.

163. 'their ordinary vent for them' said the Bishop, 'is a certaine high hill in the North of *America*', though it sometimes happened 'that they mistake their aim, and fall upon Christendom, Asia and Affricke.' *The Man in the Moon*, tr. E. M. (London: Pr. by J. Norton for J. Kirton and T. Warren, 1638), p. 105.

164. More, *Divine Dialogues*, I, 503f.; Rust, *Letter of Resolution*, p. 31.

165. Heylyn, *Cosmographie*, p. 18. Cf. Hale, *Primitive Origination*, p. 182. Heylyn, of course, was satisfied that his environmental theories adequately accounted for this diversity.

166. Paracelsus, *Philosophiæ Sagacis* (Frankfurt, 1605), lib. i, c. II, tom. x, p. 110; Bruno, *Expulsion of the Triumphant Beast*, pp. 250, 307, n. 52, *Jordani Bruni Nolani Opera Latine Conscripta*, ed. F. Fiorentino, V. Imbriani and G. M. Tallarigo, I. pt 2, p. 282. C. Vanini, *De admirandis naturæ reginæ Deæq. mortalium arcanis* (Paris, 1616), lib. iv, dial. xxxvii. Also see Richard Popkin, *Isaac La Peyrère (1596–1676)* (Leiden: Brill, 1987), pp. 26–41; Thomas Bendyshe, 'The History of Anthropology', *Memoirs of the Anthropological Society of London*, I (1863–4), 335–60.

167. R. H. Popkin, 'Pre-Adamism in 19th Century American Thought: "Speculative Biology" and Racism', *Philosophia*, 8 (1978), 206. Popkin's comprehensive *Isaac La Peyrère* spells out in detail the far-reaching consequences of the preadamite controversy. Cf. A. Klempt, *Die Säkularisierung der universalhistorischen Auffassung: zum Wandel des Geschichtsdenkens im 16. und 17. Jahrhundert* (Göttingen: Musterschmidt Verlag, 1960), pp. 89–96; David Livingstone, 'Preadamites: The History of an Idea from Heresy to Orthodoxy', *Scottish Journal of Theology*, 40 (1987), 41–66.

168. Admittedly, there did exist polygenetic theories within the Judaeo-Christian tradition. Origen seems to have at least considered the idea, and according to some of the rabbinic writings God created man in two distinct formations. See Livingstone, 'Preadamites', p. 42; Bendyshe, 'History of Anthropology',

pp. 345f.

169. Pierre Poivre, a pre-Adamite, suggested that the Americans neither inherited original sin, nor required salvation. He also relates the observation of a Spanish priest that since God had not given grapes to the Americans it was clear that he did not wish them to celebrate the mass, and thus did not wish them to be Christians. See *Was America a Mistake?*, ed. Commager and Giordanetti, p. 30.

170. Goodwin, *The Man in the Moon*, Epistle to the Reader.

171. The work appeared in England under the title 'The Theory or System of Several New Inhabited Worlds', in Mrs. Behn, *Histories, Novels and Translations*. See pp. 43, 46f., 87.

172. See, e.g., Joseph Addison, *The Spectator*, no. 519 (October 25th, 1712); Pierre Borel, *A New Treatise Proving a Multiplicity of Worlds* (London: Pr. by John Streater, 1658); Thomas Burnet, *Sacred Theory*, II.II. (p. 220); Robert Burton, *Anatomy of Melancholy*, p. 161.; Ralf Cudworth, *True Intellectual System*, V.I. (II, 601); William Derham, *Astro-Theology* (London: Pr. by W. Innes, 1715), pp. xxxviii-xlii; Joseph Glanvill, 'The Usefulness of Real Philosophy to Religion', p. 37, in *Essays*; Matthew Hale, *Primitive Origination*, p. 7; Henry More, *Divine Dialogues*, I, 525, 533; *Democritus Platonissans*, p. 51. Cusanus, Bruno, and Campanella had made similar speculations in preceding centuries.

173. John Wilkins, *A Discovery of the New World, or a Discourse Tending to Prove that there may be another Habitable World in the Moon*, 5th edn (London: Pr. for J. Gellibrand, 1684), p. 125. Tommaso Campanella, in his *Apologia pro Galileo* suggested that extra-terrestrials, if they existed, 'did not originate from Adam and are not infected by his sin'. Qu. in Popkin, *Isaac La Peyrère*, p. 39.

174. There was, e.g., growing acceptance of the Copernican model of the solar system. The Church had claimed scriptural warrant for the geocentric view, and to the discredit of both Church and Scripture, the heliocentric theory had triumphed. This was also, in part, a triumph for Classical/Renaissance solar symbolism. It is interesting that Richard Popkin regards this development as of less significance than Pre-Adamism for the decline of the biblical view of humanity (Popkin, 'Pre-Adamism', p. 206). I have argued that in fact these events cannot be separated. Pre-Adamism was simply a reaction to the exclusive claims of the Christian history of redemption – the first Adam and the second Adam stand or fall, (no pun intended) together. The heliocentric theory led to a similar challenge, albeit indirectly. In this way, the discoveries of the New World and those of the 'new astronomy' combined to yield this new picture of the nature and destiny of the human race.

175. While it has generally been assumed that historical biblical criticism was born in nineteenth-century Germany, Henning Reventlow has correctly stressed the importance of earlier English contributions to the historical–critical method (Reventlow, *The Authority of the Bible*). It is no accident that the initiators of this tradition were the same individuals who began writing alternative histories of the origin of religion – the British deists. On the continent as well, the radical ideas of Spinoza and La Peyrère had forced reshaping of

traditional methods of biblical study. See Popkin, *Isaac La Peyrère*, pp. 43–59. Largely in reaction to these critics do we find the development of a small but significant critical tradition within the religious establishment. In the seventeenth century, Richard Simon's *Critical Histories* of the Old and New Testaments appeared. In the century which followed, Johann Michaelis produced his *Introduction to the Divine Scriptures of the New Covenant* (1750) and Johann Semler published the influential (though virtually incomprehensible) *Treatise on the Free Investigation of the Canon* (1771–5).

176. By the middle of the seventeenth century two distinct traditions of biblical chronology had developed. Chronologists generally could be placed into one of two broad and opposing groups: the English (e.g. Ussher, Marsham, Stillingfleet), who tended to be classical and Protestant in their approach, and the French (e.g. Petavius, Bousset, Chevreau), who were rather more medieval and Catholic. On the significance of this distinction see James Johnson, 'Chronological Writing: Its Concepts and Development', *History and Theory*, 2 (1962), 124–45, esp. p. 137.

177. Frei, *The Eclipse of Biblical Narrative*, p. 130.

5 FROM SACRED HISTORY TO NATURAL HISTORY

1. *City of God*, XVI.1 (p. 521).
2. Richard Simon, *Histoire critique du Viex Testament* (Suivant la Copie, imprimée a Paris, 1680), p. 229; 'en un mot tout ce que nous avons de Chronologie de la Bible n'est pas point suffisant pour nous donner une connoissance exacte du nombre des Siècles qui se sont passez depuis la creation du monde'.
3. Such truths included, e.g., the pre-existence and immortality of the soul, and the triune nature of the Godhead. See Henry More, *Conjectura Cabbalistica*, pp. 1–3, 45; Andrew Michael Ramsay, *The Philosophical Principles of Natural and Revealed Religion* (Glasgow, F. P., 1748–9) II, 215; Isaac Newton, *Opera quae exstant omnia*, ed. S. Horsely (London: J. Nichols, 1779–85) V, 299.
4. Robert Fludd, *Mosaicall Philosophy: Grounded upon the Essential Truth or Eternal Sapience* (London: Pr. for H. Moseley, 1659), p. 17.
5. *Ibid.*, p. 40.
6. *Ibid.*, pp. 18–24. Fludd was by no means alone in this view. Theophilus Gale suggested that pagan mathematics and physics had been plagiarised from Moses, Job and Solomon. *Court of the Gentiles*, Pt III, 32–4. Henry More proposed that Abraham was the father of mathematics, and Moses, of 'Atomical philosophy'. *Conjectura Cabbalistica*, pp. 43, 102. Simon Patrick had Moses the father of history. *A Commentary*, preface. Cf. also Josephus, *Jewish Antiquities*, I.166–8. The single-source theory was not unanimously accepted, however. See, e.g., Warburton, *Divine Legation*, I, 375f., II, 23.
7. The most comprehensive account of 'ancient theology' is found in D. P. Walker's *The Ancient Theology* (Ithaca: Cornell University Press, 1972). Also see his 'Orpheus the Theologian and Renaissance Platonists', *Journal of the Warburg and Courtauld Institutes*, 16 (1953), 100–20; 'The *prisca theologia* in France', *Journal of the Warburg and Courtauld Institutes*, 17 (1954), 204–59; and

F. A. Yates, *Giordano Bruno and the Hermetic Tradition* (Chicago: Chicago University Press, 1964); J. Dagens, 'Hermetism et Cabale en France, de Lefèvre d'Etaples à Boussuet', *Revue de littérature comparée*, 35 (Paris, 1961), 5–16; Charles B. Schmidt, 'Perennial Philosophy: from Agostino Steuco to Leibniz', *Journal of the History of Ideas*, 27 (1966), 505–32.

8. Matthew Hale, *Primitive Origination*, p. 168.

9. Walker, *The Ancient Theology*, p. 20.

10. There are even two English translations of Hermes from this period – *The Divine Pymander* (London: Pr. by Robert White, for Tho. Brewster and Greg. Moule, 1650), and *Hermes Trismegistus his Divine Pymander* (London: Pr. by J. S. for Thomas Brewster, 1657). John Harvey also translated some of the Hermetic material in the preceding century in his *An Astrological Addition ... Whereunto is Adjoyned his Translation of Hermes Trismegistus* (London: R. Watkins, 1583). Ficino, as mentioned earlier, postponed his Latin translation of Plato to give the West its first Latin version of Hermes.

11. *An Essay on Man*, IV: 35–8.

12. Henry More, *Conjectura Cabbalistica*, p. 1. cf. p. 99. More, it is important to note, was never a Cabbalist in the true sense. See Allison Coudert, 'A Cambridge Platonist's Kabbalist Nightmare', *Journal of the History of Ideas*, 36 (1975), 633–52. For an account of 'Christian Cabbala' in England, see Francis Yates, *The Occult Philosophy in the Elizabethan Age* (London: Routledge and Kegan Paul, 1979).

13. *Ibid.*, pp. 43, 102.

14. *Ibid.*, Epistle Dedicatory.

15. *Ibid.*, p. 99.

16. *Ibid.*, Epistle Dedicatory, p. 101.

17. *Ibid.* Cf. Justin Martyr, *Apology*, 1.46, II.13; Clement of Alexandria, *Stromateis*, 1.5.28. 1–3.

18. *Ibid.*, pp. 54f.

19. *Ibid.*, p. 28.

20. More, *Grand Mystery of Godliness*, II.xi.4 (pp. 50f.); cf. Glanvill, *Some Discourses, Sermons and Remains* (London: Pr. for Henry Mortlock and James Collins, 1681), pp. 67, 77f; Smith, *Select Discourses*, p. 357; and Fludd, *Mosaicall Philosophy*, p. 9.

21. More, *Conjectura Cabbalistica*, p. 49 (my italics).

22. *Ibid.*, p. 50, cf. pp. 61f.

23. Sextus Empiricus, *Against the Physicists*, 1.18; Cicero, *On the Nature of the Gods*, 1.119. More also relies upon Plato's derivation of the name 'god', from the Greek *theous, theontas*. Plato, *Cratylus*, 397d.

24. More, *Antidote Against Idolatry*, pp. 14, 40, 46, 53, 111.

25. *Ibid.*, p. 112.

26. Glanvill, *Discourses, Sermons and Remains*, pp. 77f.

27. Cudworth, *True Intellectual System*, I.IV.xviii (I, 518–72).

28. *Ibid.* Cudworth's source here is probably Herodotus, who informs us that '*Amun* is the Egyptian name for Zeus' (*Histories* II. 43 (p. 146)).

29. *Ibid.*, I.IV.xviii (I, 531f.).

30. *True Intellectual System*, I.IV.xxxiii (II, 480).

31. *Ibid.*, I.IV.xvii (I., 510); I.IV.xxxvi (II, 312f). The trinitarian formulations of the Persians are regarded by Cudworth as superior to others (I.IV.xvi (I, 482)). This view was shared by John Selden, *Joannis Seldeni I. C. de dis Syris syntagmata* (London: G. Stansbeius, 1617), p. 31. Robert Jenkin also noted that the Brachmins believed in a trinity of divine nature. *Reasonableness and Certainty*, p. 130.

32. *Ibid.*, I.IV.xxxvi (II, 313).

33. Isaac Casaubon, *De rebus sacris et ecclesiasticis exercitationes XVI* (Londini: Ioan Billium, 1614) p. 87. On Casaubon's redating of the *Hermetica* and *Sibylline Oracles*, see F. Yates, *Bruno and the Hermetic Tradition*, pp. 398–402.

34. Robert Fludd, *Utriusque cosmi, majoris scilicet et minoris, metaphysica atque technica historia*, 2 vols. (Francofurti: Oppenheimii, 1617), I, IIf., II, 72, and passim; *Mosaicall Philosophy*, passim; Athenasius Kircher, *Oedipus Ægyptiacus* (Romæ: V. Mascardi, 1652–4), I, 103, II, 506.

35. Cudworth actually distances himself from what he calls Fludd's 'fanaticism', *True Intellectual System*, I.IV.xvii (I, 513).

36. Ralph Cudworth, *True Intellectual System*, I.IV.xviii (I, 540–55). Matthew Hale later noted that Moses was more ancient than any other writer with the exception of Hermes Trismegistus, but that no writings of the latter had survived, *Primitive Origination*, p. 137.

37. More, *The Immortality of the Soul*, p. 113.

38. Jenkin, *Reasonableness and Certainty*, p. 58.

39. *Ibid.*, pp. 64f.

40. *Ibid.*, p. 98.

41. *Ibid.*, pp. 76, 117, 425.

42. *Ibid.*, pp. 129–38.

43. Culverwel, *Light of Nature*, p. 67. Cf. e.g., Jacob Bryant, *A New System, or, An Analysis of Antient Mythology*, 3rd edn, 6 vols. (London: Pr. for J. Walker et al., 1807), I, 216; Cudworth, *True Intellectual System*, I.IV.xxxvi (II, 313); Gale, *Court of the Gentiles*, pt. II, passim; Charles Leslie, *Short and Easy Method*, in *Works* (London: Oxford University Press, 1832) I, 47; John Marsham, *Chronicus canon Aegyptiacus Graecus et disquisitiones* (London: Excudebat Tho. Roycroft, prostant apud Guliel. Wells and Rob. Scott, 1672), p. 149; More, *Conjectura Cabbalistica*, pp. 101f.

44. Pierre-Daniel Huet, *Demonstratio Evangelica* (Parisiis: Apud Stephanum Michallet, 1679), pp. 68–165. On Huet, see A. Dupront, *Pierre-Daniel Huet et l'Exégèse comparatiste au XVIIe siècle* (Paris, 1930); Arnold H. Rowbotham, 'The Jesuit Figurists and Eighteenth-Century Religious Thought', *Journal of the History of Ideas*, 17 (1956), 471–85; Walker, *The Ancient Theology*, pp. 214–20.

45. On ancient theology in France see: Virgile Pinot, *La Chine et la Formation de l'Esprit Philosophique en France (1640–1740)* (Genève: Slatkine Reprints, 1971); Rowbotham, 'The Jesuit Figurists'; Walker, *The Ancient Theology*, pp. 194–230.

46. i La Chine a conservé pendant plus de 2000 ans avant la naissance de Jésus-Christ la connaisance du vrai Dieu.

ii Elle a eu l'honneur de lui sacrifier dans le plus ancien temple de l'univers.

iii Elle l'a honoré d'une manière qui peut servir d'exemple même aux chrétiens.

iv Elle a pratiqué une morale aussi pure que la religion.

v Elle a eu la foi, l'humilité, le culte intérieur et extérieur, le Sacerdoce, les Sacrifices, la Sainteté, les miracles, l'esprit de Dieu et la plus pure charité, qui est le caractère et la perfection de la véritable religion.

vi De toutes les nations du monde, la Chine a été la plus constamment favorisée des grâces de Dieu.

Qu. in Pinot, *La Chine et la Formation de l'Esprit Philosophique*, p. 98.

47. 2 vols. (Paris: J. Anisson, 1696).

48. (London: Pr. for Benjamin Tooke, 1699). Other editions appeared in 1697, and later in 1737 and 1739.

49. Phillipe Couplet, *Confucius Sinarum Philosophus, sive Scientia Sinensis Latine exposita* (Parisiis, Danielem Horthemels, 1687).

50. *Ibid.*, p. lxix.

51. *Ibid.*, p. lxxvii. This was true, of course, of the Chinese of antiquity, who preserved true religion from its institution after the Deluge for some two thousand years. After this, they slid into superstition. Cf. Le Comte, *Memoirs and Observations*, p. 311.

52. Le Comte, *Memoirs and Observations*, p. 310; cf. Couplet, *Confucius*, lxxiif. Jean Baptiste Du Halde, *The General History of China*, 4 vols., tr. R. Brookes (London, 1736), II, 1–2, III, 5–16.

53. On Scaliger's contribution to historical method in the seventeenth century, see Anthony T. Grafton, 'Joseph Scaliger and Historical Chronology: The Rise and Fall of a Discipline', *History and Theory*, 14 (1975), 156–85.

54. 'Quod si aliquis sacrae historiae peritissimus ... nihil tamen ex illis ad certam epocham historiae Graecae, aut Romanae referre possit: quodnam adiumentum is ex eiusmodi diligentia adferre potest aut sibi, aut studiosis rerum antiquarum? Nam omnis cognitionis finis ad usum aliquem spectat, quem si ex medio literarum sustuleris, ingratis est omnis labor et opera, quaecumque in omne studium impenditur.' Joseph Scaliger, *Opus de emendatione temporum*, 3rd edn (Geneva, 1629), 2.

55. 'non mirum est, si alia a nobis pronuncient, quibus alia est historia sacra, alia etiam, ut ipsi loquuntur, profana ... Neque curamus, quid somniant profanarum literarum contemptores. Nulla veritas profana est. In ore profani hominis omnis veritas sacra est.' ('It is not surprising if they, to whom sacred history is one thing, and profane history, as they call it, another, declare different things from us ... Nor are we concerned about the fantasies of those who despise profane letters. No truth is profane. In the mouth of a profane man all truth is sacred.') *De emendatione*, 398.

56. Samuel Shuckford, *The Sacred and Profane History of the World Connected*, 3rd edn, I, (Pr. for J. and R. Tonson, 1743), p. 313. Shuckford specifically states that the Persian, Chaldean, Arabian, Canaanite and Egyptian religions were originally little different from the religion of Abraham. *Ibid.*, 305–11.

57. 'these ancient Writers, before their writings were corrupted, left Accounts very agreeable to that of *Moses*'. *Ibid.*, xxv.

58. *Ibid.*, 353, xxxiv, xxxv.

59. The mutability of language, says Shuckford, is due to: '(1) The Difference in Climates. (2) An intercourse or Commerce with the different nations; or (3) The unsettled Temper and Disposition of Mankind.' *Ibid.*, p. 125.

60. *Ibid.*, 330–53.

61. *Ibid.*, xxxv, cf. vol. II, 3rd edn (London: Pr. for J. and R. Tonson, 1743), 49, 299f.

62. Shuckford, *The Creation and Fall of Man, A Supplemental Discourse to the Preface of the First Volume of The Sacred and Profane History of the World Connected* (London: Pr. for J. and R. Tonson and S. Draper, 1753), p. xx. Some writers refer to this work as *Sacred and Profane History Connected*, vol. IV.

63. Shuckford, *Sacred and Profane History Connected*, I, 330.

64. *Ibid.*, II, 50f.

65. *Ibid.*, I, 29, 102f., 236, 244; II, 60.

66. *Ibid.*, II, 300.

67. Raleigh, *Historie of the World*, I.vi.4 (p. 73). Cf. Augustine, *City of God*, VII.26, Cicero, *On the Nature of the Gods*, I.118; II.62.

68. More, *Grand Mystery of Godliness*, p. 73. More actually used all theories – fall, devil, utility theory, euhemerism, pathology, and imposture.

69. Cudworth, *True Intellectual System*, I.IV.xviii (I. 572).

70. Jenkin, *Reasonableness and Certainty*, p. 391.

71. Hale, *Primitive Origination*, pp. 133f., 166f.

72. See e.g., Edward Stillingfleet, *Origines Sacrae*, p. 579; Timothy Nourse, *A Discourse of Natural and Reveal'd Religion*, pp. 4f.; Alexander Ross, *Pansebeia*, pp. 60, 74. Also see Simon Patrick, *A Commentary*, p. 169; Humphrey Prideaux, *A Discourse*, p. 149.

73. Herbert, *Antient Religion*, pp. 161–83.

74. *Ibid.*, pp. 26–32, and passim.

75. Blount, *The Original of Idolatry*, p. 8; Toland, *Letters to Serena*, pp. 72f. Toland also relied upon a number of other theories. Conspicuously absent from the free-thinkers' accounts of religion, however, are any indications that the great men of the past were the biblical patriarchs.

76. See in particular, Frank Manuel, *Isaac Newton: Historian* (Cambridge, Mass.: Harvard University Press, 1963), ch. 7 (pp. 103–22) and *The Religion of Isaac Newton* (Oxford: Clarendon Press, 1974).

77. Isaac Newton, New College MSS, II, fol. 160. Qu. in Manuel, *Isaac Newton: Historian*, p. 112.

78. Bryant, *Antient Mythology*, III, 114.

79. *Ibid.*, I, xl.

80. Berosus, *Babyloniaca*; Alexander Polyhistor, *Historicus*, both in *Fragmenta Historicorum Graecorum*, ed. Karl Ludwig Müller, 5 vols. (Parisiis: Excudebat Firmin Didot Fratres, 1848–74), II, 495–510, III, 206–14; Plato, *Laws*, III.677; Strabo, *Geography*, XIII.1. *The Epic of Gilgamesh* was not known at this time.

81. Bryant, *Antient Mythology*, I, xxxix. Vico and Boulanger had already made

the Deluge the single most important historical event in the shaping of early religion. See Manuel, *The Eighteenth Century Confronts the Gods*, pp. 155, 213. Shuckford also had suggested that Noah, if not the first king of every country, was certainly the first king of China.

82. Admittedly, Bryant seems in places to be hesitant about accepting the theory of euhemerism. Elsewhere, however, he thoroughly endorses it. Cf. eg., *Antient Mythology*, I, 323, 382, II, 174, III, 6.

83. *Ibid.*, III, 6.

84. *Ibid.*, 7–9.

85. *Ibid.*, III, 75.

86. Bryant, *Antient Mythology*, III, 171.

87. *Ibid.*, p. 341.

88. See Müller's *Comparative Mythology*, passim, in *Chips from a German Workshop*, II (London: Longmans, Green, and Co., 1868).

89. Müller, *Introduction to the Science of Religion* (London: Longmans, Green, and Co., 1909), p. 9.

90. Shuckford, *Sacred and Profane History*, I, 354, 365f.

91. Toland, *Letters to Serena*, p. 123.

92. Blount, *Essays*, pp. 4, 8; Gale, *Court of the Gentiles*, pt III, pp. 187, 204; More, *Antidote Against Idolatry*, p. 53; Smith, *God's Arrow*, pp. 74–9; Stillingfleet, *A Discourse Concerning the Idolatry Practised in the Church of Rome*, 2nd edn (London: Pr. by Robert White for Henry Mortlock, 1672), pt III.

93. See Manuel, *The Eighteenth Century Confronts the Gods*, p. 108.

94. The term 'pagano-papism', as far as I can ascertain, first appears in the title of Joshua Stopford's *Pagano-papismvs, or an Exact Parallel between Rome–Pagan and Rome–Christian in Their Doctrines and Ceremonies* (London: Pr. by A. Maxwell for R. Clavel, 1675). It is similar in meaning to Henry More's 'Pagano-christianism'.

95. See e.g., Anon., *The Anatomy of Popery* (London: Pr. by Tho. Passenger, 1673); Samuel Johnson, *Julian the Apostate* (London: Pr. for Langly Curtis, 1682); Joseph Mede, *The Apostacy of Latter Times, or The Gentiles Theology of Daemons Revived in the Latter Times*, in *Works*, 4th edn (London: Pr. by Roger Norton for Richard Royston, 1677); Joshua Stopford, *Pagano-papismvs*; Simon Patrick, Bk. 7 in Grotius, *The Truth of the Christian Religion*, tr. Simon Patrick (London: Pr. for Richard Royston, 1680).

96. See Anon., *The Originall of Idolatries*; Henry More, *Antidote Against Idolatry*; Edward Stillingfleet, *A Discourse concerning the Idolatry practised in the Church of Rome*; Thomas Tenison, *Of Idolatry* (London: Pr. for Francis Tyton, 1678); Daniel Whitby, *A Discourse concerning the Idolatry of the Church of Rome* (London: Pr. by Tho. Basset and Ja. Magnes, 1674). Cf. Thomas Godden's response to Stillingfleet, *Catholics no Idolaters* (Paris: Pr. for Rene Guignard, 1677).

97. Gale, *Court of the Gentiles*, pt. III, 32–4.

98. *Ibid.*, 131–4.

99. *Ibid.*, 149–225.

100. Conyers Middleton, *A Letter from Rome, shewing an Exact Conformity between Popery and Paganism*, 5th edn (London: Pr. for the Editor, 1812).

101. Toland, *A Collection of Several Pieces of Mr. John Toland*, p. xxvi. Robert South, D.D., is in all probability the doctor referred to. In view of the substance of Toland's *Nazarenus*, South's label was not too far wide of the mark.

102. Norris, *An Account of Reason and Faith*, p. 329.

103. Gailhard, *The Blasphemous Socinian Heresie Disproved*, Epistle Dedicatory.

104. John Edwards, *The Socinian Creed: Or, a brief Account of the Professed Tenets and Doctrines of the Foreign and English Socinians* (London: Pr. for J. Royston and J. Wyat, 1697), p. 221.

105. Toland, *Christianity not Mysterious*, pp. 68f.

106. *Ibid.*, pp. 31, 100.

107. Toland, *Apology for Mr. Toland* (London, 1697), pp. 26, 47.

108. See e.g., Chubb, *Moral and Positive Duties*, pp. 31, 81f; Collins, *Discourse of Free-thinking*, pp. 41f., 52f., 103.

109. William Prynne, *The Quakers Unmasked* (London: Pr. for Edward Thomas, 1664), title page.

110. John Brown, *Theses Theologicae, Quakerism the Pathway to Paganisme* (Edinburgh: Pr. by John Cairns, 1678); Francis Bugg, *Battering Rams against the New Rome* (London: Pr. for Joh. Gwillim, 1690–1); Charles Derby, *Truth Triumphant: in a Dialogue between a Papist and a Quaker: whereupon it is made Manifest, that Quaking is the Offspring of Popery* (London: Pr. for A. D., 1669). Also John Alexander (of Leith), *Jesuitico-Quakerism Examined* (London: Pr. for Dorman Newman, 1680); George Hickes, *The Spirit of Popery Speaking out of the Mouths of Phanatical-Protestants* (London: Pr. by R. Hills, 1680); William Russell, *Quakerism is Paganism* (London: Pr. for Francis Smith, 1674).

111. Roger L'Estrange, *The Growth of Knavery and Popery under the Mask of Presbytery* (London: Pr. for Henry Brome, 1678). Cf. Hugh Edmonds, *Presbytery Popish, not Episcopacy* (London: Pr. for Philemon Stephens, 1661); David Owen, *Pvritano-Iesvitismvs, The Puritan tvrned Jesuite* (London: Pr. for William Sheares, 1643).

112. More, *Divine Dialogues*, I, 364f.

113. Thus John Selden: 'Quemadmodum autem ab unnumero *idolorum, columnarum, & symbolorum* numero, sic a *Nominum* in sacris adhibitorum *multitudine*, ingens indigitamentis fiebat accessio. & quæ primum nomina tantummodo, numina deinde diuersa æstimabantur sic *Luna* quæ & *Isis*, & *Lucina*, & *Diana*, & *Triuia*, & *Hecate* dicebatur, tot demum, atq; innumeras alias peperit Deas. nomen enim vnumquodq; numen singulare devenit. *De Dis Syris Syntagmata II*, Prolegomena, pp. 52f.

114. Ch'ien Chung-Shu, 'China in the English Literature of the Seventeenth Century', *Quarterly Bulletin of Chinese Bibliography*, 1 (1940), 351–84; Walter W. Davis, 'China, the Confucian Ideal, and the European Age of Enlightenment', *Journal of the History of Ideas*, 64 (1983), 523–48.

115. Bacon, *The Advancement of Learning*, Bk. 2, XVI.2 (p. 131).

116. On the seventeenth-century English pre-occupation with universal languages, see Sidonie Clauss, 'John Wilkins' Essay Towards a Real Character', *Journal of the History of Ideas*, 43 (1982), 531–53; Jonathan Cohen, 'On the Project of a Universal Character', *Mind*, 63 (1954), 49–63; Clark Emery, 'John Wilkins'

Universal Language', *Isis*, 38 (1947–8), 174–85; Russell Fraser, *The Language of Adam* (New York: Columbia University Press, 1977); Otto Funke, *Zum Weltsprachenproblem in England im 17. Jahrhundert, Anglistishe Forschungen*, Heft 69, (Heidelberg, C. Winter, 1929); R. F. Jones, 'Science and Language in England of the Mid-Seventeenth Century', *The Journal of English and Germanic Philology*, 31 (1932), 315–31; James Knowlson, *Universal Language Schemes in England and France, 1600–1800* (Toronto: University of Toronto Press, 1975).

117. Here again we see the historical ambivalence of the age. The pendulum eventually was to swing towards the future and to the idea of progress. In the linguistic sphere this meant the triumph of conventional signs over natural ones. See Michel Foucault, *The Order of Things* (London: Tavistock, 1974), pp. 61f.

118. Qu. in Arno Borst, *Der Turmbau von Babel*, 6 vols. (Stuttgart: Anton Hiersemann, 1957–63), III/1, 1333.

119. *The Way of Light of Comenius*, tr. E. T. Campagnac, (London: 1938), p. 187.

120. *Ibid.*, p. 7, cf. pp. 203f.

121. *Ibid.*, p. 8.

122. *Ibid.*, p. 198.

123. *Ibid.*, pp. 198, 202. In this dream of universal religion, Comenius was strongly influenced by Rosicrucian J. V. Andreae and mystic Jakob Böhme. Both men 'believed in a mystical harmony of nations and hoped to form a universal Christian brotherhood of wise men devoted to the pursuit of knowledge that would unite mankind', Benjamin DeMott, 'Comenius and the Real Character in England', *PMLA*, 70 (1955), 1068–81 (p. 1070, n. 10). DeMott points out in the same place that Böhme spoke of a perfect 'language of Nature' (*Natursprache*) which had originally been given to man. Cf. Johann Valentin Andreae, *Christianopolis*, tr. F. E. Held (New York: Oxford University Press, 1916), p. 11; Jakob Böhme, *Sämmtliche Werke*, ed. K. W. Scheibler (Leipzig, 1831–46) IV, 83ff. On the Rosicrucian influence on Comenius, see Francis Yates, *The Rosicrucian Enlightenment* (London: Routledge and Kegan Paul, 1972), 156–70.

124. See particularly DeMott, 'Comenius and the Real Character in England'.

125. The more important ones being: Cave Beck, *The Universal Character* (London: Pr. by Tho. Maxey for William Weekley, 1657); George Dalgarno, *Ars Signorum, vulgo character universalis et lingua philosophica* (Londini: Excudebat J. Hayes, 1661); Francis Lodowyck, *A Common Writing* (London: Pr. for the author, 1647) and *The Ground-work, or Foundation Laid ... For the Framing of a New Perfect Language* (London, 1652); Sir Thomas Urquhart, *Logopandecteision, or an Introduction to the Universal Language* (London: Pr. by Giles Calvert and Richard Tomlins, 1653); John Wilkins, *An Essay towards a Real Character and a Philosophical Language* (London: Pr. for Sa. Gellibrand and John Martin, 1668). Also of significance is Isaac Newton's manuscript 'Of an Universall Language', now published in Ralf Elliott, 'Isaac Newton's "Of an Universall Language"', *Modern Language Review*, 52 (1957), 1–18.

126. Robert Boyle in a letter to Samuel Hartlib, dated 19th March, 1646, qu. in Clark Emery, 'John Wilkins' Universal Language', p. 175.

127. Seth Ward, *Vindiciae Academiarum* (Oxford: Pr. by Leonard Lichfield for Tho-

mas Robinson, 1654), pp. 20f. Despite Ward's disavowal of the Rosicrucian project, many of his contemporaries (including Wilkins) strongly sympathised with Rosicrucians' ideals, and were influenced by the Renaissance magico-scientific tradition as exemplified by John Dee and Robert Fludd. See Yates, *The Rosicrucian Enlightenment*, pp. 183–8; cf. her translation of the *Confessio Fraternitatis*, appended to this work, p. 257.

128. Wilkins, *Essay Toward a Real Character*, Epistle Dedicatory.

129. *Ibid.*

130. Beck, *Universal Character*, preface.

131. *Ibid.*

132. See the poems of Nath. Smart and Jos. White printed at the beginning of *Universal Character*. Bacon himself had noted that in cultivating the 'art of Grammar', man had sought to overcome the 'second general curse', which was the confusion of tongues at Babel, *Advancement of Learning*, bk. 2, XVI.4 (p. 132).

133. On Bedell's contribution to this discussion see DeMott, 'Comenius and the Real Character', pp. 1074f.

134. Gilbert Burnet maintained that the 'rebellion' curtailed Bedell's labours, *The Life of William Bedell, D.D.* (London: Pr. for John Southby, 1685). In fact Bedell died in 1642 – the year the war began – and this also may have slowed his literary output.

135. *Ibid.*, pp. 78f., 137.

136. Webster (1610–82) should not be confused with his namesake, playwright John Webster (1580–1625). While he was not obviously a Platonist, and in fact sometimes drew their ire, he was, like Comenius, drawn to the mysticism of Jakob Böhme. This, in part, helps explain his preoccupation with a universal language.

137. John Webster, *Academiarum Examen* (London: Pr. for Giles Calvert, 1654) p. 32.

138. *Ibid.*, p. 30.

139. This was a common view at the time. See e.g., Thomas Browne, *Pseudodoxia Epidemica*, p. 300; Kircher, *Oedipus Ægyptiacus*, II, 42–57; George Walker, *The History of the Creation*, pp. 192f.; John Webb, *An Historical Essay, Endeavoring a Probability that the Language of the Empire of China is the Primitive Language* (London: Pr. for Nath. Brook, 1669), p. 147. There were some exponents of a universal character, however, who disputed the existence of such a natural language with these almost magical properties. See Seth Ward, *Vindicae Academiarum*, p. 22.

140. One of the differences between hieroglyphics and alphabetical characters was that hieroglyphics, apart from their supposed real character, could be used to conceal deep truths from the vulgar. Thus Webb informs us that whereas the literal meaning of alphabetical letters is patent even to the vulgar, of 'signative' characters – those which 'involved mystically the whole conception of some certain matter' – 'the vulgar came to know nothing, but what vulgarly befitted them for to know.' *Historical Essay*, p. 151. Also see the discussion in Warburton, *Divine Legation of Moses*, II, 96, III, 70–83.

141. *Ibid.*, pp. 24f.

142. Comenius, e.g., looked forward to a time when there would be a science of 'all the things under Heaven which it is granted for us to know, to say, or to do'. *The Way of Light*, p. 7. Wilkins also spoke of a 'Universal Philosophy' which consisted of 'such things and notions, as are to be known, and to which names are to be assigned'. *Real Character*, p. 297. Again we should recall that many scientists of the seventeenth century saw 'progress' as being the recovery of ancient truths, hence the curious picture of Newton scanning the writings of the sages of antiquity for confirmation of his 'discoveries'. Leibniz, too, modestly considered his binary arithmetic a 'rediscovery' of the Fu Hsi's mathematical inventions which were originally set out in the *I Ching*. See Donald Lach, 'Leibniz and China', *Journal of the History of Ideas*, 6 (1945), 436–55. What this means is that the belief in a *prisca theologia* was often accompanied by a similar belief in a *prisca sapientia*. For this reason we can say that the quest for a universal language was both progressive and nostalgic at the same time.

143. John Webb, *Historical Essay*, Epistle Dedicatory.

144. Admittedly Robert Hooke had written that the 'business and design' of the Society did not include 'meddling with Divinity, Metaphysics, Moralls, Politicks, Grammar, Rhetoric, or Logick'. Qu. in C. R. Weld, *A History of the Royal Society*, 2 vols. (London: J. W. Parker, 1848) i, 146. This meant only that one of the ways which the Royal Society could promote religious harmony was to avoid the rarefied air of theological disputation.

145. Qu. in Webb, *Historical Essay*, p. 187.

146. Browne, e.g., doubted that a single tongue was spoken between the time of creation and Babel because of the natural corruption of language, *Of Languages*, p. 70. Phylastrius was of like mind; see Torneillus, *Annales Sacri et Profani* (Coloniae Agrippinae, 1622), p. 127.

147. This was widely accepted because it is the most literal reading of the Babel story in Genesis ii. See e.g., Heylyn, *Cosmographie*, p. 18.

148. Milton, *Logica*; Richard Verstegan, *Restitution of Decayed Intelligences in Antiquity* (London: Pr. for Sam. Mearne et al., 1673), pp. 212–21, both cited in D. C. Allen, 'Theories of Language in Milton's Age', pp. 6, 11. Cf. Edward Brerewood, *Enquiries Touching the Diversity of Languages*, p. 51.

149. Meric Casaubon, *De Quatuor Linguis Commentationis* (London: Typis J. Flesher, sumptibus Ric. Mynne, 1650), p. 15; Kircher, *Turris Babel* (Amsterdam, 1679), p. 130; cited in Allen, 'Theories of Language in Milton's Age', p. 11. Cf. Wilkins, *Real Character*, p. 6; Edward Brerewood, *Enquiries Touching the Diversity of Languages*, p. 51.

150. Kircher, *Turris Babel*, pp. 130f.; Brian Walton, *In Biblia Polyglotta Prolegomena* (Cambridge, 1827), i, 36–55, cited in Allen, 'Theories of Language in Milton's Age', pp. 11f. Cf. Shuckford, *Sacred and Profane History Connected*, i, 124f.

151. On the primacy of Hebrew, Browne non-committally presented the common view: 'that children committed unto the school of Nature, without institution, would naturally speak the primitive language of the world, was the opinion of the antient heathens, and continued since by Christians: who will have

it to be the Hebrew tongue.' *Pseudodoxia Epidemica*, p. 309. Herodotus was one of those ancients. He reported that children, left to their own devices, would speak Phrygian (*Histories*, II.1). Gulielmus Postellus was the first to attempt to prove that Hebrew was the primitive language on etymological grounds, *De Originibus seu Hebraicae Linguae & Gentis Antiquitate, deque Variarum Linguarum* (Parisiis, 1538), Fols. A iii r–A iv r. J. H. Heidegger listed a number of subsequent attempts to do the same thing, including those of Avenarius, Cruciger, Guichartus, Lamphaus, Scaliger, Casaubonus, Grotius, Salmasius, Heinsius, Martinius, Vossius, Bochartus, Daviesius, and Lyscandrus. [*R'SY 'BWT*] *sive de Historia sacra Patriarchum*, 2 tom. (Amstelodami, 1667–71), I, 462–3. Brief discussions of the originality of Hebrew are also found in Simon Patrick, *A Commentary*, pp. 218f., Richard Simon, *A Critical History of the Old Testament* (London: Pr. by Jacob Tonson, 1682), I.xiv (pp. 97–101), and John Selden, *De Synedriis ... Veterum Ebraeorum*, prolegomenon, cap. III; Cf. H. Pinard de la Boullaye, *L'Etude Comparée des Religions* (Paris: Gabriel Beauchesne, 1922) section 90 (pp. 158–63).

Other languages also vied for the honour of having been the first. Some scholars followed Herodotus in favouring Phrygian. Others, like Nicholas Serarius, thought Samarian, *Prolegomena Biblicae* (Moguntiaci, 1612) pp. 7–16. Matthew Hale thought either Hebrew or 'Samaritan', *Primitive Origination*, p. 162. Most interesting of all perhaps were the claims of those whose patriotism outran their scholastic ability. Johannes Becanus, e.g., proposed that the language in which Adam conversed was not Hebrew, but Low German, *Origines Antwerpianiae* (Antverpiae: Christophori Plantini, 1569), p. 534. If we discount over-zealous nationalism and anti-semitism, however, one factor that in the seventeenth century seemed to count decisively against the primacy of Hebrew was the fact that it was alphabetical and therefore lacked the real character, which according to tradition, the primitive language had. Accordingly, John Webb declared: 'In vain do we search for the PRIMITIVE Language to remaining with those Nations whose Languages consist in Alphabets.' *An Historical Essay*, p. 150. Hebrew was one such language.

152. Browne, *Pseudodoxia Epidemica*, p. 300.

153. Thomas Browne, *Of Languages, and Particularly of the Saxon Tongue* (1683?), in *Works*, ed. Geoffrey Keynes (London: Faber and Faber, 1928), III, 71.

154. *Ibid.*, 72. Cf. Shuckford, *Sacred and Profane History Connected*, I, 122, 236, 244.

155. The Jesuit Athenasius Kircher resolved the difficulty of deciding between Egypt and China by stating that both the religion and the form of writing of China were borrowed from the Egyptians, *Of the Various Voyages and Travels Undertaken into China*, appended to Peter de Goyer and Jacob de Keyzer, *An Embassy from the East India Company of the United Provinces to the Grand Tartar Cham Emperour of China* (London: Pr. by John Macock, 1669), pp. 75f. Cf. his *Oedipus Ægyptiacus*, pt. II.

156. John Webb, e.g., expresses his preference for an historical approach, slighting the contribution of 'vulgar Traditions', and 'licentious Etymologies of Words', while extolling the virtues of 'sacred truth' and 'Scripture'.

157. Raleigh, *Historie of the World*, I.vii.10 (p. 96).

158. Carpenter, *Geographie Delineated*, p. 213; Heylyn, *Cosmographie*, p. 18; Shuckford, *Sacred and Profane History Connected*, II, 51. Also see discussion in Simon Patrick, *A Commentary*, pp. 145–7.

159. Heylyn, *Cosmographie*, p. 18.

160. On Webb, see William W. Appleton, *A Cycle of Cathay* (New York: Columbia University Press, 1951), ch. 2; Ch'ien Chung-Shu, 'China in the English Literature of the Seventeenth Century'; Ch'en Shou-yi, 'John Webb: A Forgotten Page in the Early History of Sinology in Europe', *Chinese Social and Political Science Review*, 19 (1935–6), 295–330.

161. On Webb's sources, see Ch'en Shou-yi, 'John Webb', pp. 302–5.

162. Webb, *Historical Essays*, p. 16.

163. *Ibid.*, p. 17.

164. *Ibid.*, p. 35. Some orthodox exegetes admitted this possibility. See, e.g., Simon Patrick, *A Commentary*, p. 227.

165. *Ibid.*, p. 36.

166. *Ibid.*, pp. 38–44, 143–5.

167. Webb, *Historical Essay*, pp. 51, 58. Relying upon similar considerations, Thomas Browne and Samuel Shuckford, as we saw earlier, proposed that Poncuus (or Fo-hi) was actually the same person as Noah.

168. *Ibid.*, p. 60. Webb maintained that Father Martini Martinii (*Sinicae historiae decas prima* (1658) I, 3) held a similar view. See *Ibid.*

169. *Ibid.*, p. 154. So too Shuckford, *Sacred and Profane History*, I, 236.

170. *Ibid.*, pp. 86–117.

171. *Ibid.*, p. 206.

172. Beck, *Universal Character*, Preface.

173. Wilkins, *Real Character*, p. 10.

174. Hale, *Primitive Origination*, p. 163.

175. R. Hooke, 'Some Observations, and Conjectures concerning Chinese Characters', *Philosophical Transactions of the Royal Society*, XVI (1686), 63–78.

176. *Ibid.*, pp. 65, 73.

177. William Wotton, *Reflections of Ancient and Modern Learning* (London: Pr. by J. Leake for Peter Buch, 1694) p. 154.

178. A Platonic mystic, Ramsay revered Cudworth's *True Intellectual System*, and like many of the English Platonists adhered to 'Origenism', or the belief in universal salvation. These influences combine with those of the French Jesuits in Ramsay's *Travels of Cyrus*, 2 vols. (London: T. Woodward and J. Peele, 1727) and *The Philosophical Principles of Natural and Revealed Religion*, 2 vols. (Glascow: F. P., 1748–9). Ramsay accepted virtually all of the premises of the ancient theology which were accepted by Cudworth and More, and to these were added the Jesuit view: 'In these last and dangerous times... perhaps Providence has opened a communication to China, that so we might find vestiges of our sacred religion in a nation which had no communication with the ancient Jews, and whose original books, yea, the principal commentaries upon them having been wrote long before the coming of our Saviour, cannot be suspected of imposture.' *Philosophical Principles*, II, 185. Ramsay did not mean by this that the Chinese had received a unique revelation of their own,

but merely that the communication of divine revelation was closer to the time of the Flood than the Exodus: 'Tis a common notion that all the footsteps of natural and reveal'd religion which we see in the heathen Poets and Philosophers, are originally owing to their having read the books of Moses; but 'tis impossible to answer the objections which are made against this opinion. The Jews and their books were too long concealed in a corner of the earth, to be reasonably thought the primitive light of the Gentiles. We must go further back, even to the deluge.' *Discourse on the Theology and Mythology of the Ancients*, in *ibid.*, p. 93. Ramsay's affinities with Webb and the French Jesuits are obvious.

The Englishman Thomas Hyde is also worth mentioning as a late proponent of ancient theology. In one of the few eighteenth-century works on Zoroastrianism, *Historia Religionis Veterum Persarum* (Oxonii, e theatro Sheldoniano, 1700), Hyde maintained that despite its apparent idolatry and dualism, there was a cortex of true religion in Zoroastrianism. Zoroaster, though a false prophet, had learnt much from the Jews, had included aspects of their prophecies in his writings, and had even foretold the coming of Christ. On Hyde, see P. J. Marshall and Glyndwr Williams, *The Great Map of Mankind* (Melbourne: Dent and Sons, 1982) pp. 102f.

In fact there was no 'major' religion for which the claim was not advanced that it had been originally true and might even be presently relatively uncorrupt. Boulainvilliers, whose positive assessment of Muhammad was published in English translation in 1731, declared: 'tis highly probable that the *Arabians* had long preserved, or rather had never lost the notion of a supreme God, the Creator of the Universe', *Life of Mahomet*, p. 137. Some of Boulainvilliers' compatriots made the same claim for the Hindus. In the anonymous work *The Travels of Several Learned Missionaries of the Society of Jesus* (London: Pr. for R. Gosling, 1714), we find Abraham being named as the founder of Hinduism (p. 12). Claims of this kind about Indian religions were indeed quite rare. Because the connexion between Indian and European language groups remained obscure, the etymological conjectures which were a vital link in tracing the development of religion were absent. See La Boullaye, *L'Etude Comparée des Religions*, section 90 (pp. 162f.).

179. Bacon, *Novum Organum*, 1. xxxviii, lix (pp. 34, 40).
180. *Ibid.*, 1, lix.
181. *Ibid.*, 1, lx.
182. Hobbes, *Leviathan*, pt. 4, ch. 46, (pp. 482–6).
183. Toland, *Letters to Serena*, p. 13.
184. See Stephen Daniel's timely work on Toland – *John Toland: His Methods, Manner, and Mind* (Kingston: McGill-Queen's University Press, 1984) p. 118. The words 'names and' in the quotation are enclosed in square brackets because they were later crossed out.
185. It is not insignificant that Müller spoke highly of Wilkins' *Real Character*. See his *Lectures on the Science of Language*, 9th edn (London: Longmans, Green and Co., 1877), II, 50–65.
186. *Ibid*, I, 12f.
187. As indeed they themselves had been anticipated by various writers in antiquity.

The famous sophist, Prodicus of Ceos had put forward a thesis that such poetic conventions as substituting the name of Haphaestus for fire led to the belief that fire itself was divine. A. B. Drachmann concludes that 'linguistic observations of this kind... were the starting point of his [Prodicus'] theory concerning the origin of the conceptions of the gods'. *Atheism in Antiquity*, p. 19, cf. Sextus Empiricus, *Against the Physicists*, 1.24. Cotta, in Cicero's *On the Nature of the Gods* also notes that 'the beings which are called gods are really natural forces and are not personal deities at all'. He continues, like a good logical positivist, that 'it is the task of philosophers to dispel such errors'. *On the Nature of the Gods*, III.63 (p. 219), cf. III.40 (p. 209). According to Cicero, Zeno likewise believed that the gods Jupiter, Juno and Vesta were 'merely names given symbolically to mute and inanimate forces', 1.36 (p. 85).

188. For the account of natural history which follows I have drawn upon the following: Gladys Bryson, *Man and Society: The Scottish Inquiry of the Eighteenth Century* (Princeton: Princeton University Press, 1945); Ernst Cassirer, *The Philosophy of the Enlightenment*, esp. chs. 2 and 4; R. G. Collingwood, *The Idea of History* (Oxford: Oxford University Press, 1946) III. sections 8–10, v section 1; Robert Nisbet, *Social Change and History: Aspects of the Western Theory of Development* (London: Oxford University Press, 1969); F. J. Teggart, *Theory of History* (New Haven: Yale University Press, 1925).

189. *Collected Works of Dugald Stewart*, ed. William Hamilton, 11 vols. (Edinburgh: T. Constable, 1854–60), X, 34.

190. *Ibid.*

191. *Ibid.*, p. 37.

192. Aristotle, *Metaphysics*, v.iv.1–3. For a concise discussion of Aristotle's view of nature and its relation to history, see Nisbet, *Social Change*, pp. 24f.

193. *Ibid.*, 1.iii.1–2.

194. Aristotle, *Politics*, 1.i.3, 8, 11 (Loeb edn pp. 5–11).

195. Aristotle, *Metaphysics*, v.xxx.1.

196. *Ibid.*, v.xxx.2–3; vi.ii.1; xi.viii.1.

197. Plato, *Sophist*, 254.a.; cf., Aristotle, *Metaphysics*, xi.viii.3.

198. At times this debt is quite explicitly acknowledged. The frontpiece of Rousseau's *Discourse on Inequality*, e.g., bears this quotation from Aristotle's *Politics*: 'We should consider what is natural not in things which are depraved but in those which are rightly ordered according to nature' (1.ii). The same statement is paraphrased by Grotius in *Of the Law of Warre and Peace*. 1.v.

199. Collingwood, *The Idea of History*, pp. 208, 228.

200. Jean Jacques Rousseau, *The Social Contract and Discourses*, tr. G. D. H. Cole (London: Dent, 1968), p. 160.

201. *Ibid.*, p. 162 (my emphasis).

202. *Ibid.*, p. 161.

203. There were also the 'facts' of sacred history which Rousseau wanted leave to ignore.

204. Thus John Trenchard, in his *Natural History of Superstition*: 'for til we know from what Source or Principle we are so apt to be deceived by others, and by ourselves, we can never be capable of true Knowledge, much less of true

Religion', in Trenchard and Gordon, *A Collection of Tracts*, I, 380. The didactic element is even more explicit in Malthus' *Essay on the Principle of Population* (London, 1803), which though it comes much later conforms almost exactly to the scheme of natural history: 'In an inquiry concerning the improvement of society, the mode of conducting the subject which naturally presents itself, is (1) To investigate the causes that have hitherto impeded the progress of mankind towards happiness; and (2) To examine the possibility of total or partial removal of these causes in the future.' (p. 1).

There is a remarkable similarity both of form and intent between natural histories and the 'fantastic voyage' literature of this period. The fantastic voyage literature was mostly a French phenomenon, but Swift's *Gulliver's Travels*, was a popular English example of the genre. On the French works of this kind, see Atkinson's two-volume *Extraordinary Voyage in French Literature*.

205. Published originally in Amsterdam, this work was translated into English by William Lewis, and appeared in London in 1705 bearing the title *The Antient Religion of the Gentiles*.

206. Herbert, *Antient Religion*, pp. 11f.

207. *Ibid.*

208. *Ibid.*, p. 31; cf., pp. 23, 32, 49, 87, 160, 296, 326, 374.

209. Cudworth, *True Intellectual System*, I.IV.xii (I, 365). Cf. More, *Grand Mystery of Godliness*, III.i.7 (p. 59).

210. *Ibid.*, I.IV.xxxiv (II, 304).

211. *Ibid.*, I.IV.xvii (I, 515f.).

212. 'Concerning the Original of the Jews', in *Oracles of Reason*, p. 135. Elsewhere, Blount appears to prevaricate on this issue. In a translation of *The Life of Apollonius* – a work in which his voluminous sceptical notes so aroused the ire of the censor that few copies have survived – Blount informs us that mankind had at no time entertained common views about religious matters. *The First Two Books of Philostratus, concerning the life of Apollonius Tyraneus* (London: Pr. for Nathaniel Thompson, 1680), p. 32.

213. Blount, *Life of Apollonius*, preface, p. 5, n. 1. Blount replaced the more theological concept 'sin' with that of 'self-love', which he regarded as lying at the basis of most human ills.

214. Blount, 'A Summary Account of the Deists Religion', *Oracles of Reason*, p. 92.

215. Blount, 'The Original of Idolatry', preface.

216. *Ibid.*, p. 3.

217. Toland, 'The Origin of Idolatry, and Reasons of Heathenism', *Letters to Serena*, Letter III.

218. *Ibid.*, p. 88.

219. *Ibid.*

220. *Ibid.*, p. 124, cf. p. 129; *Pantheisticon*, p. 98.

221. Toland, *Christianity not Mysterious*, pp. 14f., 30, 38, 146.

222. *Ibid.*, p. 30, cf. p. 133.

223. *Ibid.*, p. 146.

224. *Christianity not Mysterious*, pp. 147, 158.

225. *Ibid.*, p. 148.

226. *Ibid.*, p. 168. (This is the most general application of the thesis of pagano-papism.)

227. (London: J. Roberts, J. Brown, and J. Brotherton, 1718).

228. *Ibid.*, p. 77.

229. *Ibid.*, pp. 78f.

230. *Ibid.*, pp. 42f., 62.

231. *Ibid.*, pp. 64ff.

232. *Ibid.*, pp. 69f.

233. *Ibid.*, pp. v, xiv.

234. 'one main design of Christianity was to improve and perfect the knowledge of the Law of nature, as well as to facilitate and inforce the observation of the same.' *Ibid.*, p. 67.

235. *Ibid.*, p. 44.

236. *Ibid.*, p. 65.

237. 'Two Problems, historical, political and theological, concerning the Jewish Nation and Religion', pp. 3f.

238. *Ibid.*, p. 5.

239. *Ibid.*, p. 8.

240. Toland, *Reasons for Naturalizing the Jews in Great Britain and Ireland* (London: J. Roberts, 1714); *Origines Judaicae* in *Adeisidaemon, sive Titus Livius a Superstitione Vindicatus* (The Hague, 1709). See also M. Weiner, 'John Toland and Judaism', *Hebrew Union College Annual*, 16 (1941), 215–42. The possibility of readmitting the Jews to England (they had been expelled in 1290, and were not legally readmitted until the nineteenth century) was actively discussed in seventeenth-century England, particularly during the rule of Cromwell, when millennarian expectations were rife. The high point of the discussion was the year 1656, when Menasseh ben Israel was in England to plead the Jewish cause. The extent of the debate in the year 1656 alone can be seen from the following: Joseph Copley, *The Case of the Jews is Altered* (London, 1656); John Dury, *A Case of Conscience, whether it be lawful to admit Jews* (London: Pr. for Richard Wodenothe, 1656); Rhys Evans, *Light for the Jews* (London, 1656); Margaret Fell, *For Menasseh ben Israel, The call of the Jewes* (London: Pr. for Giles Calvert, 1656); William Hughes, *Anglo-Jvdævs* (London: Pr. by T. N. for Thomas Heath, 1656); Henry Jessey, *A Narrative of the Late Proceed's at Whitehall, concerning the Jews* (London: Pr. for L. Chapman, 1656); D. L., *Israel's Condition and Cause Pleaded* (London: Pr. by P. W. for William Larnar and Jonathan Bull, 1656); Menasseh ben Israel, *Vindiciae Judaeorum* (London, 1656); R. R., *The Restoration of the Jewes* (London: Pr. by A. Maxwell, 1665); William Tomlinson, *A Bosome Opened to the Jewes* (London: Pr. for Giles Calvert, 1656). Also see Popkin, 'Messianism and Millennarianism', in *Culture and Politics*, ed. Zagorin.

241. Toland, *Nazarenus*, p. iii.

242. *Ibid.*, p. ii. The extant Gospel of Barnabas, M. R. James informs us, 'is in Italian, a forgery of the late fifteenth or sixteenth century, by a renegade from

Christianity to Islam'. *The Apocryphal New Testament* (Oxford: Clarendon Press, 1972) p. 23. The text of the Gospel has been translated and edited by L. and L. Ragg, *The Gospel of Barnabas* (Oxford: Clarendon, 1907). This gospel still plays an important role in many forms of Islam, in particular in Muslims' dialogue with Christians. Toland was perhaps justified in assuming an earlier date for this work, for a 'Gospel of Barnabas' is listed in the Gelasian Decree 'Of Books to be received and not to be received' which dates from before the sixth century. This gospel has been lost. There are, however, indications that some parts of the extant gospel date from the early Christian period. See William Axon, 'The Mohammedan Gospel of Barnabas', *Journal of Theological Studies*, 3 (1902), 441–51; Per Beskow, *Strange Tales about Jesus* (Philadelphia: Fortress Press, 1983), ch. 3; Lonsdale Ragg, 'The Gospel of Barnabas', *Journal of Theological Studies*, 6 (1909), 423–33.

243. *Ibid.*, p. 4. Toland's source for Islam was Reland's 'The Compendious Mahometan Theology' published in *Four Treatises Concerning the Doctrine, Discipline and Worship of the Mahometans* (London: Pr. for J. Darby, 1712), which, as Toland rightly put it, 'exploded many myths'. *Nazarenus*, pp. 4, 10.

244. *Ibid.*, p. 5.

245. *Ibid.*, pp. 11f.

246. *Ibid.*, p. 4.

247. To my knowledge, the only European writer within fifty years of Toland to give such a positive evaluation of Islam was Henri Boulainvilliers, in his *Life of Mahomet* (London: Pr. for W. Hinchliffe, 1731). Even this work was restrained compared to Toland's.

248. This is due in part, I believe, to Leslie Stephen's influential *English Thought in the Eighteenth Century* which is marred only by his peculiar prejudice against the deists, Toland included. In the last decade a number of writers (Stephen Daniel, Margaret Jacob, Robert Sullivan, e.g.) have recognised Toland's importance.

249. Tindal, *Christianity as Old as the Creation*, p. 1.

250. *Ibid.*, p. 3.

251. *Ibid.*, p. 4.

252. If we can judge by the response which it excited amongst Tindal's contemporaries, then it was certainly not a tired thesis for them. Of the many rejoinders elicited, the following are representative: John Balguy, *A Second Letter to a Deist* (London: J. Pemberton, 1731); Simon Browne, *A Defence of the Religion of Nature, and the Christian Revelation* (London: Pr. for R. Ford, 1732); Thomas Burnet, *The Argument Set Forth in a Late Book* (London: A. Bettesworth, 1731); Thomas Cockman, *Salvation by Jesus Christ Alone Asserted and Vindicated*, 4th edn (London: S. Austen, 1733); John Conybeare, *A Defence of Reveal'd Religion* (London: Pr. for S. Wilmot, 1732); William Law, *The Case of Reason, or Natural Religion, Fully Stated* (London: W. Innys, 1731); Conyers Middleton, *A Letter to Dr Waterland* (London: Pr. for J. Peele, 1731); Henry Stebbing, *A Defence of Dr. Clarke's Evidences of Natural and Revealed Religion* (London: Pr. for J. Pemberton, 1731) and *A Discourse concerning the Use and Advantages of the Gospel Revelation* (London: J. Pemberton, 1730); George Turnbull, *Christianity*

Neither False nor Useless, tho' not as Old as the Creation (London: R. Willcock, 1732); Daniel Waterland, *Scripture Vindicated* (London: Pr. for W. Innes, 1730–1).

253. Tindal, *Christianity as Old as the Creation*, p. 92.

254. Morgan, *The Moral Philosopher*, III, 93.

255. *Ibid.*, 114f.

256. *Ibid.*, I, 71.

257. *Ibid.*, 210.

258. *Ibid.*, 379f.

259. *Ibid.*, III, 109.

260. *Ibid.*, 108f.

261. *Ibid.*, p. 109.

262. Trenchard, *Natural History of Superstition*, p. 380.

263. *Ibid.*, p. 380.

264. *Ibid.*, p. 384.

265. Hume, *Natural History of Religion*, p. 23.

266. *Ibid.*, pp. 24f.

267. *Ibid.*, p. 26.

268. *Ibid.*, p. 26.

269. *Ibid.*, p. 29. Hume's projection theory had been anticipated not only by Xenophanes (*Fragments*, 15f.), but also Fontenelle. See Bernard de Fontenelle, *De l'origene des fables*, ed. J. B. Carré (Paris: F. Alcan, 1932), pp. 17, 32. Also, Manuel, *Eighteenth Century Confronts the Gods*, pp. 44f.

270. *Ibid.*, p. 31.

271. *Ibid.*, p. 30.

272. *Ibid.*, p. 43.

273. *Ibid.*, pp. 43, 47.

274. *Ibid.*, p. 49.

275. *Ibid.*, pp. 66, 70.

EPILOGUE

1. Qu. in Pailin, *Attitudes to Other Religions*, p. 40.

2. Barth, *Church Dogmatics*, I/2, 288.

3. Dietrich Bonhoeffer, *Letters and Papers from Prison* (New York: Macmillan, 1962), pp. 161–9, 194–200, 226.

4. Smith, *Meaning and End of Religion*, pp. 125–8.

5. *Ibid.*, p. 61.

6. Philip C. Almond, *The British Discovery of Buddhism* (Cambridge: Cambridge University Press, 1988); P. J. Marshall (ed.), *The British Discovery of Hinduism in the Eighteenth Century* (Cambridge: Cambridge University Press, 1970).

7. Smith, *Meaning and End of Religion*, chs. 6, 7.

REFERENCES

A NOTE ON SOURCES

Since the 1950s University Microfilms International has been placing onto microfilm all works listed in Donald Wing's *Short Title Catalogue* (1641–1700) and Pollard and Redgrave's *Short Title Catalogue* (1475–1640). This undertaking is almost finished and its completion will mean that virtually all works published in England between 1475 and 1700 will be available on microfilm. The Central Library of the University of Queensland has the complete collection to date and most of my research was carried out there. Material published after 1700 was gathered from a variety of sources the most important of which were the Australian National Library, and the Sterling and Beinecke libraries at Yale University. Also at Yale is a useful collection entitled 'British Tracts', which includes many of the deists' writings. I am grateful to the staffs of these libraries and would like to thank in particular the reference librarians and inter-library loan staff at the University of Queensland.

PRIMARY SOURCES

Acosta, Joseph de, *Historia Natural y Moral de las Indias* (Sevilla: J. de Leon, 1590).
 The Naturall and Morall Historie of the East and West Indies, tr. E. G[rimstone] (London: Pr. by V. Sims for E. Blount and W. Aspley, 1604).
Addison, Lancelot, *A Modest Plea for the Clergy* (London: Pr. for William Crook, 1677).
 The Primitive Institution, or, A Seasonable Discourse of Catechizing (London: Pr. by J. C. for William Crook, 1674).
Alexander, John (of Leith), *Jesuitico–Quakerism Examined* (London: Pr. for Dorman Newman, 1680).
Allestree, Richard, *The Causes of the Decay of Christian Piety* (London, 1667).
Ames, William, *The Svbstance of Christian Religion* (London: Pr. by T. Mabb for Thomas Davies, 1659).
Andreae, Johann Valentin, *Christianopolis*, tr. F. E. Held (New York: Oxford University Press, 1916).
 Fraternitatis Roseae Crucis Fama e Scanzia Redux (Frankfort, 1618).
Annet, Peter, *A Collection of the Tracts of a Certain Free Enquirer Noted by his Sufferings for his Opinions* (London, c. 1750).
Anonymous, *The Anatomy of Popery* (London: Pr. by Tho. Passenger, 1673).

An Answer to the Discourse of Free-Thinking . . . by a Gentleman of Cambridge (London: Pr. by J. Morphew and A. Dodd, 1713).

The Bishops Manifest (London: Pr. for W. R., 1641).

A Defence of True Protestants Abused for the Service of Popery (London: Pr. for N. P., 1680).

Four Treatises Concerning the Doctrine, Discipline and Worship of the Mahometans (London: Pr. for J. Darby, 1712).

Hieragnosticon: or, Coray's Doom, being an Answer to two Letters of Enquiry (London: Pr. by Tho. Milbourne for Dorman Newmann, 1672).

The History of Mahomet, the Great Imposter (Falkirk: T. Johnston, 1821).

An Impartial Account of the Doctrines of the Church of Rome (London: Pr. by H. L., 1679).

Miscellanea Aurea: or, The Golden Medley (London: A. Bettesworth and J. Pemberton, 1720).

Mrs. Abigail: or, an Account of a Female Skirmish between the Wife of a Country Squire, and the Wife of a Doctor in Divinity (London: H. Baldwin, 1702).

An Occasional Paper wherein the Honour of the English Clergy . . . is vindicated from a Late Pamphlet called Mrs. Abigail (London: Pr. for J. Nutt, 1703).

The Originall of Idolatries: or, the Birth of Heresies, tr. from Fr. by A. Darcie, (Pr. [by G. Purslowe and M. Flesher] for N. Butter, 1624). (Wrongly attr. to Isaac Casaubon.)

Priestcraft Exposed (London, 1691).

A Rational Discourse Concerning Prayer (London, 1669).

A Rational Method of Daily Religion (London, 1697).

Short and Plain Catechism, Instructing a Learner of Christian Religion What he is to Believe, and What to Practise, 4th edn (London: Pr. for Francis Tyton, 1668).

Short Questions and Answeares, Contayning the Summe of Christian Religion (London: Pr. by Iohn Dawson, 1641).

The Summe of Christian Religion . . . Serving for Instruction of the Simpler Sort (London: Pr. by T. Creed for T. Man, 1607).

The Travels of Several Learned Missionaries of the Society of Jesus (London: Pr. for R. Gosling, 1714).

Aristotle, *Politics*, tr. H. Rackham, Loeb Classical Library (London: Heinemann, 1932).

Atkinson, Benjamin, *Christianity not Older than the First Gospel Promise* (London: R. Ford, 1730).

Augustine, *The City of God*, tr. Marcus Dodds, Modern Library Series (New York: Random House, 1950).

Bacon, Francis, *The Advancement of Learning*, ed. Arthur Johnston (Oxford: Clarendon, 1974).

Balguy, John, *A Second Letter to a Deist* (London: J. Pemberton, 1731).

Banier, Abbé Antoine, *The Mythology of the Ancients, Explain'd from History*, 4 vols. (London: Pr. by A. Millar, 1738–40).

Baro, Peter, *De fide, eiusque ortu, & Natura, explicato* (Londini: Apud R. Dayum, 1580).

In Ionam Prophetam Præelectiones 39 (Londini: Apud Joannem Dayum, 1579).

Barrow, Isaac, *Theological Works*, ed. Alexander Napier, 9 vols. (Cambridge: Cambridge University Press, 1859).

The Works, 4 vols. (London: Pr. by M. Flesher for Brabazon Aylmer, 1683–7).

The Works, 3 vols. (London: Pr. by Brabazon Aylmer, 1700).

Basil the Great, *On the Spirit*, Nicene and Post-Nicene Fathers, VIII (Grand Rapids: Eerdmans, 1955).

Baxter, Richard, *More Reasons for the Christian Religion and No Reason Against It* (London: Pr. by N. Simmons, 1672).

The Reasons of the Christian Religion (Pr. by R. White for Fran. Titon, 1667).

A Treatise of Knowledge and Love Compared (London: Pr. for Tho. Parkhurst, 1689).

The Universal Redemption of Mankind (London: Pr. for John Salisbury, 1694).

Bayley, William, *A Word of Reproof from the Lord to the Priests of England* (London, 1659).

Becanus, Johannes, *Origines Antwerpianiae, sive Cimmeriorum Becceselana novem libres complexa* (Antverpiae: Christophori Plantini, 1569).

Beck, Cave, *Universal Character* (London: Pr. by Tho. Maxey for William Weekley, 1657).

Beconsall, Thomas, *The Grounds and Foundation of Natural Religion, Discover'd* (London: Pr. by W. O. for A. Roper, A. Bosvile, and G. West, 1698).

Bedford, Hilkiah, *A Defence of the Church of England from Priestcraft* (London: Pr. by R. Wilkin, 1711).

Behn, Mrs. (ed.), *Histories, Novels and Translations* (London: Pr. by W. O. for S. B., 1700).

Bentley, Richard, *The Folly and Unreasonableness of Atheism*, 4th edn (London: Pr. by J. H. for H. Mortlock, 1699).

Remarks Upon a Late Discourse of Freethinking, 5th edn (London: Pr. for J. Morphew and P. Crownfield, 1716).

Beverly, Thomas, *Christianity the Great Mystery. In Answer to a late Treatise, Christianity not Mysterious* (Dondon [sic]: Pr. for W. Marshall and J. Marshall, 1696).

Biddle, John C., *The Apostolic and True Opinion Concerning the Holy Trinity, Revived and Asserted* (London, 1653).

Binning, Hugh, *The Common Principles of Christian Religion* (Glasgow: Pr. by Andrew Anderson, 1659).

Bishop, George, *A Looking Glass for the Times* (London: Pr. in the Year 1668).

Blount, Charles (tr.), *The First Two Books of Philostratus, concerning the Life of Apollonius Tyraneus* (London: Pr. for Nathaniel Thompson, 1680).

Miscellaneous Works (London, 1695).

The Oracles of Reason (London, 1693).

Blount, Sir Thomas Pope, *Essays on Several Subjects* (London: Pr. for Richard Bentley, 1697).

Bodin, Jean, *Methodus ad facilem historiarum cognitionem* (Parisiis: Apud M. Iuuenem, 1566).

Method for the Easy Comprehension of History, tr. Beatrice Reynolds (New York: Columbia University Press, 1945).

The Six Books of a Commonweale, tr. Richard Knowles (London: Imprinted A. Islip, impensis G. Bishop, 1606).

Boemus, Joannes, *The Fardle of Façions*, tr. W. Waterman (London: Pr. by Jhon Kingstone and Henry Sutton, 1555).

Böhme, Jakob, *Sämmtliche Werke*, ed. K. W. Scheibler, 6 vols. (Leipzig: 1831–46).

Borel, Pierre, *A New Treatise, Proving a Multiplicity of Worlds* (London: Pr. by John Streater, 1658).

Botero, Giovanni, *Relations of the Most Famous Kingdomes and Common-weales thorough the World* (London: Pr. by Iohn Haviland, 1630).

Boughen, Edward, *The Principles of Religion* (Oxford: Pr. by Leonard Lichfield, 1646).

Boulainvilliers, Henri, Count of, *The Life of Mahomet*, tr. from the Fr. (London: Pr. for W. Hinchliffe, 1731).

Bradley, John, *An Impartial View of the Truth of Christianity* (London: Pr. by W. Downing for Michael Johnson, 1699).

Bramhall, John, *An Answer to a Letter of Enquiry into the Grounds and Occasions of the Contempt of the Clergy* (London: Pr. for Nath. Ranew, and J. Robinson, 1671).

Brerewood, Edward, *Enquiries Touching the Diversity of Languages and Religions, through the Chief Parts of the World* (London: Pr. for Samuel Mearne, John Martyn and Henry Herringman, 1674).

Brinsley, John (the Younger, 1600–65), *A Breviate of Saving Knowledge* (London: Pr. by G. M. for Iohn Burroughes, 1643).

  The Christian Cabala, or, Sure Tradition: Necessary to be Known and Believed, by All that Will be Saved (London: Pr. for George Sawbridge, 1662).

Bromhall, Thomas, *An History of Apparitions, Oracles, Prophecies and Predictions*, tr. from Fr. (London: Pr. by John Streater, 1658).

Brown, John, *Thesis Theologicae, Quakerism the Pathway to Paganisme* (Edinburgh: Pr. for John Cairns, 1678).

Browne, Peter, *A Letter in Answer to a Book Entitled Christianity not Mysterious* (Dublin: Pr. by John Ray for John North, 1697).

Browne, Simon, *A Defence of the Religion of Nature, and the Christian Revelation* (London: Pr. for R. Ford, 1732).

Browne, Sir Thomas, *The Workes of Sir Thomas Browne*, ed. Geoffrey Keynes, 4 vols. (London: Faber and Faber, 1928–37).

  Pseudodoxia Epidemica, 5th edn (London: Pr. for the assigns of Henry Dod, 1669).

  Religio Medici (London: Pr. for Andrew Crooke, 1642).

Bruno, Giordano, *The Expulsion of the Triumphant Beast*, tr. and ed. Arthur Imerti (New Brunswick: Rutgers University Press, 1964).

  Jordani Bruni Nolani Opera Latine Conscripta, ed. F. Fiorentino, V. Imbriani and G. M. Tallarigo (Naples, 1879–91).

  Spaccio de la Bestia Trionfante (Paris [London], 1584).

Bryant, Jacob, *A New System, or, An Analysis of Antient Mythology*, 3rd edn, 6 vols. (London: Pr. for J. Walker et al., 1807).

Bugg, Francis, *Battering Rams Against the New Rome* (London: Pr. for Joh. Gwillim, 1690–1).

Bulwer, John, *A View of the People of the Whole World* (London: Pr. by William Hunt, 1654).

Burnet, Gilbert, *An Impartial Survey and Comparison of the Protestant Religion* (London: Pr. for Richard Chiswell, 1685).

The Life of William Bedell, D. D. Bishop of Kilmore (London: Pr. for John Southby, 1685).

Burnet, Thomas, *The Argument Set Forth in a Late Book, Entitled, Christianity as Old as the Creation* (London: A. Bettesworth, 1731).

The Sacred Theory of the Earth (London: Centaur, 1965) Repr. of 2nd edn of 1691, pagination different.

Of the State of the Dead and Those that are to Rise, tr. M. Earberry, 2nd. edn, 2 vols. (London: E. Curll, 1728).

Burton, Robert, *The Anatomy of Melancholy*, 8th edn (London: Pr. for Peter Parker, 1676).

Butler, Joseph, *The Analogy of Religion, Natural and Revealed, to the Constitution and Course of Nature* (London: J., J. & P. Knapton, 1736).

Calvin, John, *Institutes of the Christian Religion*, tr. Henry Beveridge, 2 vols. (London: James Clarke and Co., 1962).

Camus, Jean Pierre, *A Draught of Eternity*, tr. Miles Car (Doway: By the Widowe of Marke Wyon, 1632).

Carpenter, Nathaniel, *Geography Delineated Forth in Two Bookes*, 2nd edn (Oxford: Pr. by Iohn Lichfield for Henry Cripps, 1635).

Casaubon, Meric, *De Quattuor Linguis Commentationis* (London: Typis J. Flesher, sumptibus Ric. Mynne, 1650).

A Treatise Concerning Enthusiasme, as it is an Effect of Nature: but is Mistaken by Many for either Divine Inspiration, or Diabolical Possession (London: Pr. by R. D., 1655).

A Treatise of Vse and Cvstom (London: Pr. by I[ohn]. L[egatt]., 1638).

Casaubon, Isaac, De rebus sacris et ecclesiasticis exercitationes XVI (Londini: Ioan Billium, 1614).

Chandler, Samuel, *Reflections on the Conduct of Modern Deists* (London: Pr. for John Chandler, 1727).

Charron, P., *Of Wisdom*, tr. Samuel Lennard (London: Pr. for Luke Fawn, 1651).

Chubb, Thomas, *The Comparative Excellence and Obligation of Moral and Positive Duties* (London: Pr. for J. Roberts, 1730).

Cicero, *On the Nature of the Gods*, tr. Horace C. P. McGregor, (Ringwood: Penguin, 1972).

Clarke, Samuel, *A Discourse Concerning the Being and Attributes of God*, 7th edn (London: Pr. by W. Botham for James and John Knapton, 1728).

Clerke, Richard, *Sermons* (London: Pr. by T. Cotes for Thomas Alchorn, 1637).

Cockburn, John, *An Enquiry into the Nature, Necessity, and Evidence of Christian Faith, in Several Essays* (London: Pr. for William Keblewhite, 1697–9).

Cockman, Thomas, *Freethinking Rightly Stated* (London: Pr. for George Strahan, 1713).

Collins, Anthony, *A Discourse of Free-Thinking* (London, 1713).

A Discourse of the Grounds and Reasons of the Christian Religion (London, 1724).

Priestcraft in Perfection (London: B. Bragg, 1710).

Collyer, David, *The Sacred Interpreter*, 2nd edn, 2 vols. (London: Pr. for

T. Astley, 1732).

Comenius, Johann Amos, *The Way of Light of Comenius*, tr. E. T. Campagnac (London: Hodder and Stoughton, 1938).

Conybeare, John, *A Defence of Reveal'd Religion* (London: Pr. for S. Wilmot, 1732).

The Confession of Faith, and the Larger and Shorter Catechisms together with The Summe of Saving Knowledge (Edinburgh: Heirs of G. Anderson, 1652).

Coppin, Richard, *Divine Teachings: in Three Parts*, 2nd edn (London: Pr. by William Larner and Richard Moon, 1653).

Couplet, Philippe, et al., *Confucius Sinarum Philosophus, sive Scientia Latine exposita* (Parisiis: Danielem Horthemels, 1687).

Cradock, Samuel, *Knowledge and Practise: or A Plain Discourse of the Chief Things Necessary to be Known, Believ'd, and Practiced in Order to Salvation* (London: Pr. by J. Hayes, for John Rothwell, 1659).

A Supplement to Knowledge and Practise (London: Pr. for Thomas Simmons, 1679).

Crouch, Nathaniel, *The Strange and Prodigious Religions, Customs, and Manners, of Sundry Nations* (London: Pr. for Henry Rhodes, 1683).

Cudworth, Ralph, *The True Intellectual System of the Universe* and *A Treatise Concerning Eternal and Immutable Mortality*, ed. John Harrison, 3 vols. (London: Thomas Tegg, 1845).

Culverwel, Nathaniel, *An Elegant and Learned Discourse of the Light of Nature* (London: Pr. by T. R. and E. M. for John Rothwell, 1652).

Cumberland, Richard, *A Treatise of the Laws of Nature*, tr. from Lat. by John Maxwell (London: Pr. by R. Phillips, 1727).

Cusanus, Nicholas, *Cusanus Texte*, ed. E. Hoffman et al. (Heidelberg: Sitzungsberichte der Heidelberger Akademie der Wissenschaften, 1929–).

De Pace Fidei, ed. Raymondus Klibansky and Hilderbrandus Bascour (Londinii: In Aedibus Instituti Warburgiani, 1956).

Of Learned Ignorance, tr. G. Heron (London: Routledge, 1954).

Dalgarno, George, *Ars Signorum, vulgo character universalis et lingua philosophica* (Londini: Excudebat J. Hayes, 1661).

Davenport, John, *The Knowledge of Christ Indispensibly Required of all Men that Would be Saved* (London: Pr. for L. Chapman, 1653).

Denzinger, Henricus, *Enchiridion Symbolorum*, 33rd edn (Barcinone: Herder, 1965).

Derby, Charles Stanley, 8th Earl of, *Truth Triumphant* (London: Pr. by A. D., 1669).

Derham, William, *Astro-Theology, or, a Demonstration of the Being and Attributes of God from a Survey of the Heavens* (London: Pr. by W. Innes, 1715).

Descartes, René, *Discourse on Method and the Meditations*, tr. F. E. Sutcliffe (Ringwood: Penguin, 1968).

Oeuvres de Descartes, ed. Charles Adam and Paul Tannery, 12 vols. and supp. (Paris: Léopold Cerf, 1897–1913).

The Philosophical Works of Descartes, ed. and tr. Elisabeth S. Haldane and G. R. T. Ross, 2 vols. (Cambridge: Cambridge University Press, 1911–12).

Dickenson, Edmund, *Delphi Phoenicizantes* (Oxoniae: Excudebat H. Hall, impensis Ric. Davis, 1655).

Dickson, David, *The Summe of Saving Knowledge* (Edinburgh: Pr. by George Swintoun, and Thomas Brown, 1671).

Diels, H. (ed.), *Die Fragmente der Vorsokratiker*, 6th edn, 3 vols. (Dublin: Weidmann, 1966–7).

Dove, John, *A Confutation of Atheism* (London: Pr. by E. Able for H. Rockett, 1605).

Du Halde, Jean Baptiste, *The General History of China*, tr. R. Brookes, 4 vols. (London: Pr. by R. Brookes, 1736).

Dunton, John, *The Visions of the Soul before it comes into the Body* (London: Pr. for John Dunton, 1692).

Eachard, John, *The Grounds and Occasions of the Contempt of the Clergy and Religion* (London: Pr. by W. Goodbid for N. Brooke, 1670).

Edmonds, Hugh, *Presbytery Popish, not Episcopacy* (London: Pr. for Philemon Stephens, 1661).

Edwards, John, *Some Thoughts Concerning the Several Causes and Occasions of Atheism* (London: Pr. for J. Robinson, 1695).

   The Socinian Creed: Or, a Brief Account of the Professed Tenets and Doctrines of the Foreign and English Socinians (London: Pr. for J. Royston and J. Wyat, 1697).

Edwards, Thomas, *Gangræna: or A Catalogue and Discovery of many of the Errors*, 2nd edn (London: Pr. for Ralph Smith, 1646).

Ellis, Clement, *A Catechism Wherein the Learner is at Once Taught to Rehearse, and Prove all the Main Points of the Christian Religion* (London: Pr. for Sam. Richards, 1674).

   The Summe of Christianity (London: Pr. for Will. Rogers, 1696).

Erberry, William, *The Babe of Glory* (London: Pr. by J. C. for Giles Calvet [sic], 1653).

Ficino, Marsilio, *Opera*, 2 tom. (Basileæ: Ex officina Henrici Petrina, 1576).

Firmicus Maternus, Julius, *De Errore Profanarum Religionum* (Argentine: 1562).

Fisher, Edward, *Faith in Five Fundamental Principles* (London: Pr. for J. Wright, 1650).

Flavell, John, *Planelogia, A Succinct and Seasonable Discourse of the Occasions, Causes, Nature, Rise, Growth and Remedies of Mental Errors* (London: Pr. by R. Roberts for T. Cockerill, 1691).

Fludd, Robert, *Mosaicall Philosophy* (London: Pr. for Humphrey Moseley, 1659).

   Utriusque cosmi, majoris scilicet et minoris, metaphysica atque technica historia, 2 vols. (Francofurti: Openhemii, 1617–1619).

Fontenelle, Bernard de, *De l'origene des fables* (1724), ed. J. R. Carré (Paris: F. Alcan, 1932).

Gailhard, Jean, *Blasphemous Socinian Heresie Disproved and Confuted ... with Animadversions on a Book call'd Christianity not Mysterious* (London: Pr. for R. Wellington and J. Hartley, 1697).

Gale, Theophilus, *The Court of the Gentiles*, 4 vols. (Oxford: Pr. by Will. Hall for Tho. Gilbert, 1669–77).

Gastrell, Francis, *The Certainty of the Christian Revelation* (London: Pr. for Thomas Bennet, 1699).

Gerhardus, Joannes, *Commentarius super Genesin* (Leipzig: 1693).

Gibbon, Nicholas, *Theology Real, and Truly Scientifical* (London, 1687?).

Glanvill, Joseph, *Essays on Several Important Subjects in Philosophy and Religion* (London: Pr. by J. D. for John Baker, 1676).

Scepsis Scientifica, or Confest Ignorance the way of Science; in an Essay of the Vanity of Dogmatizing ... with a Reply to the Exceptions of the Learned Thomas Albius, ed. John Owen (London: Kegan Paul and Co., 1885).

Some Discourses, Sermons and Remains (London: Pr. for Henry Mortlock and James Collins, 1681).

Two Choice and Vseful Treatises (London: Pr. for James Collins and Sam Lowndes, 1682).

The Vanity of Dogmatizing (London: Pr. by E. C. for Henry Eversden, 1661).

Godden, Thomas, *Catholics no Idolaters* (Paris: Pr. for Rene Guignard, 1677).

Godolphin, John, *The Holy Arbor, Contayning a Body of Divinity; or, The Summe and Substance of Christian Religion* (London: Pr. by John Field for Edmund Paxton, and William Roybould, 1651).

Goodman, Godfrey, *The Fall of Man, or the Corruption of Nature Proved by Natural Reason* (London: F. Kyngston, 1616).

Goodwin, Francis, *The Man in the Moon, or a Discourse of a Voyage Thither by D. Gonsales*, tr. E. M[abon]. (London: Pr. by J. Norton for J. Kirton and T. Warren, 1638).

Goodwin, John, *Apolutrosis Apolutroeas, or Redemption Redeemed* (London: Pr. by John Macock, for Lodowick Lloyd and Henry Cripps, 1651).

Gott, Samuel, *An Essay of the True Happiness of Man* (London, 1650).

Goyer, Peter de, and Keyzer, Jacob de, *An Embassy from the East India Company of the United Provinces to the Grand Tartar Cham Emperour of China* (London: Pr. by John Macock, 1669).

Gregory of Tours, *The History of the Franks*, ed. and tr. Lewis Thorpe (Ringwood: Penguin, 1974).

Grotius, Hugo, *Of the Law of Warre and Peace* (London: Pr. by T. Warren for William Lee, 1755).

The Truth of the Christian Religion, in six books, tr. into English with the addition of a seventh book by Simon Patrick (London: Pr. for Richard Royston, 1680).

Grove, Robert, *The Protestant and Popish Way of Interpreting Scripture, Impartially Compared* (London: Pr. for Walter Kettilby, 1689).

A Short Defence of the Church Clergy of England (London: Pr. by J. Macock for Walter Kettilby, 1681).

Hakewill, George, *An Apologie ... Consisting in an Examination and Censure of the Common Errour touching Natures perpetuall and Universal Decay* (Oxford: J. Lichfield and W. Turner, 1627).

Hale, Matthew, *A Discourse of the Knowledge of God, and of Ourselves ... To Which are Added A Brief Abstract of the Christian Religion* (London: Pr. by B. W. for William Shrowsbury, 1688).

The Primitive Origination of Mankind Considered and Examined According to the Light of Nature (London: Pr. for W. Shrowsbury, 1677).

Hall, Joseph, *A Letter ... concerning Some Slanderous Reports Lately Raised against the Bishops* (London: Pr. in the year 1641).

Hallywell, Henry, *A Defence of Revealed Religion* (London: Pr. for Walter Kettilby, 1694).

Deus Justificatus: Or, the Divine Goodness (London: Pr. by E. Cotes for Walter

Kettilby, 1668).

Halyburton, Thomas, *Natural Religion Insufficient* (Edinburgh: Pr. by the Heirs and Successors of A. Anderson, 1714).

Hammond, Henry, *Of the Reasonableness of the Christian Religion* (London: Pr. by J. G. for R. Royston, 1650).

Harris, John, *The Atheistical Objections Against the Being of a God* (London: Pr. by J. I. for Richard Wilkin, 1698).

Harris, Robert, *True Religion in the Old Way of Piety and Charity* (London: Pr. for John Bartlet, 1645).

Harry, George Owen, *The Genealogy of the High and Mighty Monarch James ... King of Brittayne ... with his lineall descent from Noah* (London: Pr. by S. Stafford for T. Salisbury, 1604).

Harvey, John, *An Astrological Addition ... Whereunto is Adjoyned his Translation of Hermes Trismegistus* (London: R. Watkins, 1583).

Hausted, Peter, *Ten Sermons* (London: Pr. for J. Clark, 1636).

Hearne, Thomas, *Ductor Historicus, or A Short System of Universal History*, partly tr. from the Fr. of M. de Vallemont, but chiefly composed by W. J. M. H. (London: Pr. for Tim. Childe, 1698).

Heidegger, Johann Heinrich, [*R'SY 'BWT*] *Sive de Historia Sacra Patriarchum Exercitationes Selectæ*, 2 tom. (Amstelodami, 1668).

Helmont, Franciscus Mercurius van, *Seder Olam* (London: Pr. for Sarah Howkins, 1694).

Two Hundred Queries Moderately Propounded concerning the Doctrine of the Revolution of Humane Souls (London: Pr. for Rob Kettlewell, 1684).

Herbert of Cherbury, Edward, 1st Lord, *The Antient Religion of the Gentiles*, tr. from Lat. by William Lewis (London: Pr. for John Nutt, 1705).

A Dialogue between a Tutor and his Pupil (London: Pr. for W. Bathoe, 1768).

The Life of Edward, First Lord Herbert of Cherbury, ed. J. M. Shuttleworth (London: Oxford University Press, 1976).

De Religione Gentilium Errorumque apud Eos Causis (Amsterdam, 1663).

De Religione Laici, ed. and tr. Harold H. Hutchéson (New Haven: Yale University Press, 1944).

De Veritate (Paris, 1624).

De Veritate, tr. Meyrick H. Carré (Bristol: J. W. Arrowsmith, 1937).

Hermes Trismegistus, *The Divine Pymander* (London: Pr. by Robert White, for Tho. Brewster and Greg. Moule, 1650).

Hermes Trismegistus his Divine Pymander (London: Pr. by J. S. for Thomas Brewster, 1657).

Herodotus, *Histories*, tr. A. D. Godley, 4 vols., Loeb Classical Library (London: Heinemann, 1920–5).

Heylyn, Peter, *Cosmographie in Foure Bookes* (London: Pr. for Henry Seile, 1652).

Microcosmvs; or A Little Description of the Great World, 2nd edn (Oxford: Pr. by Iohn Lichfield and William Tvrner, 1625).

Hickeringill, Edmund, *The Black Non-Conformist Discover'd in More Naked Truth* (London, 1682).

Priestcraft, its Character and Consequences, 3rd edn (London, 1708).

Hickes, George, *The Spirit of Popery Speaking out of the Mouths of Phanatical-Protestants* (London: Pr. by R. Hills, 1680).

Hippocrates, tr. W. H. S. Jones and E. T. Withington, 4 vols., Loeb Classical Library (London: Heinemann, 1939).

Hoard, Samuel, *God's Love unto Mankind, Manifested by Disproving his Absolute Decree for their Damnation* (London: Pr. for John Clark, 1656).

Hobbes, Thomas, *Leviathan*, ed. Michael Oakeshot (New York: Collier Books, 1962).

Hobson, Paul, *A Treatise containing Three Things* (London: Pr. by M. S. for Tho. Brewster, 1653).

Hooke, Robert, 'Some Observations and Conjectures concerning Chinese Characters', *Philosophical Transactions of the Royal Society*, 16 (1686), 63–78.

Hooker, Richard, *Works*, ed. W. Speed Hill, Folger Library edn (Cambridge, Mass.: Harvard University Press, 1977).

Howard, Sir Robert, *The History of Religion* (London: Pr. in the year 1694).

Howe, Obadiah, *The Vniversalist Examined and Convicted* (London: Pr. for John Rothwell, 1648).

Huet, Pierre Daniel, *Demonstratio Evangelica* (Parisiis: Apud Stephanum Michallet, 1679).

Hume, David, *Dialogues Concerning Natural Religion*, ed. Norman Kemp Smith (Indianapolis, Bobbs-Merrill, 1985).

Enquiries Concerning Human Understanding and Concerning the Principles of Morals, repr. from 1777 edn, ed. L. A. Selby-Bigge, 3rd edn rev. by P. H. Nidditch (Oxford: Clarendon Press, 1975).

The Natural History of Religion, ed. H. E. Root (Stanford: Stanford University Press, 1957).

Hyde, Thomas, *Historia Religionis Veterum Persarum* (Oxonii: e theatro Sheldoniano, 1700).

Isaacson, Henry, *The Summe and Substance of Christian Religion* (London, 1646).

Jacoby, Felix (ed.) *Die Fragmente der griechischen Historiker*, 3 vols. (Leiden: Brill, 1954–64).

Jenkin, Robert, *The Reasonableness and Certainty of the Christian Religion*, 2nd edn (London: Pr. for P. B. and R. Wellington, 1700).

Johnson, Samuel, *Julian the Apostate* (London: Pr. for Langly Curtis, 1682).

Jonston, John, *An History of the Constancy of Nature* (London: Pr. for John Streater, 1657).

Josephus, tr. H. Thackeray, et al., 9 vols., Loeb Classical Library (London: Heinemann, 1961–69).

Josippon, *The VVonderful, and Most Deplorable History of the Latter Times of the Jews* (London: Pr. for John Stafford, 1652).

Kant, Immanuel, *Critique of Pure Reason*, ed. and tr. Norman Kemp Smith, 2nd edn (London: Macmillan, 1929).

Kircher, Athenasius, *Turris Babel* (Amsterdam, 1679).

Oedipus Ægyptiacus, 3 tom. (Rome: V. Mascardi, 1652–4).

La Bigne, M. de, *Magna Bibliotheca Veterum Patrum*, 15 tom. (Coloniae Agrippinae, 1618–22).

La Loubère, Simon de, *A New Historical Relation of the Kingdom of Siam* (London:

Pr. by F. L. for Tho. Horne et al., 1693).

La Noue, Seigneur de, *Discours Politiques et Militaires du Seigneur de la Noue* (Basel, 1587).

La Peyrère, Isaac de, *Men Before Adam* (London, 1656).

Law, William, *The Case of Reason, or Natural Religion, Fully Stated* (London: W. Innys, 1731).

Lazius, Wolfgang, *De gentium aliquot migrationibus ... Libri X* (Francofurti: Apud A. Wecheli Heredes, 1600).

Le Clerc, Jean, *A Treatise of the Causes of Incredulity. Wherein are Examin'd the General Motives and Occasions which Dispose Unbelievers to Reject the Christian Religion* (London: Pr. for Awnsham and John Churchill, 1697).

Le Comte, Louis, *Memoirs and Observations ... Made in a Late Journey through the Empire of China*, tr. from Fr. (London, 1697).

Noveaux Mémoirs sur l'état présent de la Chine, 2 vols. (Paris: J. Anisson, 1696).

Leigh, Edward, *A Systeme or Body of Divinity ... Wherein the Fundamentals and Main Grounds of Religion are Opened Up* (London: Pr. by A. M. for William Lee, 1654).

Leland, John, *A View of the Principal Deistical Writers* (London: T. Tegg & Son, 1837).

Lemaire de Belges, Jean, *Oeuvres* (Brussels: J. Stecher, 1882).

Le Roy, Louis, *Of the Interchangeable Course, or Variety of Things in the Whole World*, tr. R[obert]. A[shely] (London: Pr. by C. Yetsweirt, 1594).

Leslie, Charles, *The History of Sin and Heresie Attempted* (London: Pr. for H. Hindmarsh, 1698).

Works, 7 vols. (Oxford: Oxford University Press, 1832).

L'Estrange, Hamon, *Americans no Jewes* (London: Pr. by W. W. for Henry Seile, 1652).

L'Estrange, Roger, *The Growth of Knavery and Popery under the Mask of Presbytery* (London: Pr. for Henry Brome, 1678).

Lipsius, Julius, *Opera Omnia* (Antverpiae, 1637).

Locke, John, *An Essay Concerning Human Understanding*, ed. A. C. Fraser, 2 vols. (New York: Dover, 1959).

The Reasonableness of Christianity (London: Pr. for Awnsham and John Churchill, 1695).

Treatise Concerning Civil Government and A Letter Concerning Toleration, ed. Charles L. Sherman, (New York: Appleton-Century-Crofts, 1965).

Lodowyck, Francis, *A Common Writing* (London, 1647).

The Ground-work, or Foundation Laid ... For the Framing of a New Perfect Language (London, 1652).

Lowde, James, *The Reasonableness of the Christian Religion* (London: Pr. for Walter Kettilby, 1684).

Luther, Martin, *Lectures on Romans*, ed. and tr. William Pauck (Philadelphia: Westminster, 1961).

D. Martin Luthers Werke (Weimar: Böhlaus, 1883–1948).

Luther's Works (St Louis, Concordia, 1955–75).

Lynche, Richard, *An Historical Treatise of the Travels of Noah into Europe*, Done into English out of Berosus (London: A. Islip, 1601).

Macaulay, Thomas Babington, *The History of England from the Accession of James II*, 3 vols. (London: Dent, n.d.).

Malthus, Thomas, *An Essay on the Principle of Population*, 2nd edn (London, J. Johnson, 1803).

Mandeville, Bernard de, *An Enquiry into the Origin of Honour and the Usefulness of Christianity in War*, 2nd edn (London, 1732).

Marsham, John, *Chronicus canon Aegyptiacus Graecus et disquisitiones* (London: Excudebat Tho. Roycroft, prostant apud Guliel. Wells & Rob. Scott, 1672).

Mede, Joseph, *Works*, 4th edn (London: Pr. by Roger Norton for Richard Royston, 1677).

Menasseh Ben Israel, *The Hope of Israel* (London: Pr. by R. I. for Hannah Allen, 1650).

Middleton, Conyers, *A Letter From Rome, Shewing an Exact Conformity between Popery and Paganism*, 5th edn (London: Pr. for the Editor, 1812).

A Letter to Dr Waterland (London: Pr. for J. Peele, 1731).

Miscellaneous Works (London: R. Manby, 1752).

Migne, Jacques Paul (ed.), *Patrologiae cursus completus*, Series Graeca, 162 vols. (Paris, 1857–66).

(ed.), *Patrologiae cursus completus*, Series Latina, 217 vols. (Paris, 1844–1905).

Milton, John, *Prose Writings*, ed. K. M. Burton (London: Dent, 1965).

Montesquieu, Charles, *De l'Esprit des Loix*, 4 vols. (Paris: Société Les Belles Lettres, 1950–61).

Oeuvres Complètes de Montesquieu, ed. Edouard Laboulaye (Paris: Garnier Frères, 1875–9).

More, Henry, *An Antidote Against Atheisme* (London: Pr. by Roger Daniel, 1653).

A Collection of Several Philosophical Writings of D. Henry More, 2nd edn (London: Pr. by J. Flesher for W. Morden, 1662).

Democritus Platonissans; or An Essay upon the Infinity of Worlds out of Platonic Principles (Cambridge: Pr. by Roger Daniel, 1646).

Divine Dialogues, 2 vols. (London: Pr. by James Flesher, 1668).

Enthusiasmus Triumphatus, or, A Brief Discourse of the Nature, Causes, Kinds, and Cure of Enthusiasm (London: Pr. by James Flesher for William Morden, 1662).

An Explanation of the Grand Mystery of Godliness (London: Pr. by James Flesher for W. Morden, 1660).

An Exposition of the Seven Epistles to the Seven Churches; together with a Brief Discourse of Idolatry, with Application to the Church of Rome (London: Pr. by James Flesher, 1669).

The Last Two Dialogues (London: Pr. by J. Flesher, 1668).

The Philosophical Writings of Henry More, ed. Flora Isobel Mackinnon (New York: Oxford University Press, 1929).

Morgan, Thomas, *The Moral Philosopher* (London: Pr. for the Author, 1737).

The Moral Philosopher, 2nd. edn, 3 vols. (London: Pr. for the Author, 1738–40).

Müller, Karl Ludvig (ed.), *Fragmenta Historicorum Graecorum*, 5 vols. (Parisiis: Excudebat Firmin Didot Fratres, 1848–74).

N., N., *A Letter to a Gentleman Touching the Treatise ... concerning the Revolution of Humane Souls* (London: Pr. for A. Churchill, 1690).

Narne, William, *Christ's Starre* (London: Pr. by J. L. for P. Stephens and C. Meredith, 1625).

Newton, Isaac, *Opera quae exstant omnia*, ed. S. Horsely, 5 vols. (London: J. Nichols, 1779–85).

Norris, John, *An Account of Reason and Faith: in Relation to the Mysteries of Christianity* (London: Pr. for S. Manship, 1697).

Nourrisson, J. F., *Philosophies de la Nature, Bacon, Boyle, Toland, Buffon* (Paris: Perrin, 1887).

Nourse, Timothy, *A Discourse of Natural and Reveal'd Religion in Several Essays* (London: Pr. for John Newton, 1691).

Nye, Stephen, *A Discourse Concerning Natural and Revealed Religion* (London: Pr. by T. W. for Jonathan Robinson, 1696).

Ogilvie, John, *An Inquiry into the Causes of the Infidelity and Scepticism of the Times* (London, 1783).

Origen, *Contra Celsum*, tr. Henry Chadwick (Cambridge: Cambridge University Press, 1953).

On First Principles, tr. G. W. Butterworth (Gloucester, Mass.: Peter Smith, 1973).

Owen, David, *Pvritano-Iesvitismvs, the Puritan tvrn'd Jesuite* (London: Pr. for William Sheares, 1643).

Owen, John, *A Brief and Impartial Account of the Nature of the Protestant Religion* (London: Pr. by J. A., 1682).

P., C., *A Dissertation Concerning the Pre-existency of Souls* (London: Pr. for J. Wickins and Rob. Kettlewell, 1684).

Pagitt, Ephraim, *Christianography: The Description of the Multitude and Sundry Sorts of Christians, in the World, not Subject to the Pope* (London: Pr. for Robert Clavell, 1674).

Heresiography, or A Description of the Hereticks and Sectarians of these Latter Times, 3rd edn (London: Pr. for W. L., 1647).

Paley, William, *The Works*, (Edinburgh: Peter Brown and Thomas Nelson, 1831).

Palmer, Herbert, *An Endeavovr of Making the Principles of the Christian Religion ... Plaine and Easie*, 3rd edn (London: Pr. for Thomas Vnderhill, 1644).

Pantalogia (London: G. Kearsley et al., 1813).

Paracelsus, *Philosophiæ Sagacis* (Frankfurt, 1605).

Parker, Samuel, *An Account of the Nature and Extent of the Divine Dominion and Goodnesse* (Oxford: Pr. by W. Hall for R. Davis, 1666).

A Free and Impartial Censure of the Platonick Philosophy with an Account of the Origenian Hypothesis Concerning the Preexistence of Souls (Oxford: Pr. by W. Hall for R. Davis, 1666).

Patrick, Simon, *A Commentary upon the First Book of Moses, Called Genesis* (London: Pr. for Ri. Chiswell, 1695).

Petavius, Dionisius, *The History of the World, or, An Account of Time* (London: Pr. by J. Streater, 1659).

Philo, tr. F. H. Colson, G. H. Whittaker, et al., 10 vols. and supps., Loeb Classical Library (London: Heinemann, 1971–9).

Pictet, Bénédict, *An Antidote against a Careless Indifferency in Matters of Religion*, 2nd edn, intro. by Anthony Horneck (London: Pr. for Henry Rhodes and John Harris, 1698).

Pine, Martin, 'Pomponazzi and the Problem of "Double Truth"', *Journal of the History of Ideas*, 29 (1968), 163–76.

Plato, *The Collected Dialogues*, ed. Edith Hamilton and Huntington Cairns, Bollington Series LXXI (Princeton: Princeton University Press, 1982).

Plutarch, *Plutarch's Lives*, tr. Bernadette Perrin, 11 vols., Loeb Classical Library (London: Heinemann, 1914–26).

Pocock, Edward, *Specimen Hist. Arabum* (Oxonii, 1650).

Postellus, Gulielmus, *Cosmographic disciplinae compendium* (Basileae: Per Ioannem Oporinum, 1561).

De Originibus seu de Hebraicae Linguae & Gentis Antiquitate, deque Variarum Linguarum (Paris: 1538).

Prideaux, Humphrey, *The True Nature of Imposture Fully Display'd in the Life of Mahomet*, 2nd edn (London: William Rogers, 1697).

Prynne, William, *The Antipathie of the English Lordly Prelacie* (London: Pr. by Authority for Michael Sparke Senior, 1641).

Nevvs from Ipsvvich (n.p.: Repr. for T. Bates, 1641).

The Quakers Unmasked, and Clearly Detected to be but the Spawn of Romish Frogs, 2nd edn (London: Pr. for Edward Thomas, 1664).

Raleigh, Walter, *The Historie of the World in Five Bookes* (London: Pr. for R. Best, Jo. Place, and Sam. Cartwright, 1652).

Ramsay, Andrew Michael, *The Philosophical Principles of Natural and Revealed Religion*, 2 vols. (Glasgow: F. P., 1748–9).

The Travels of Cyrus, 2 vols. (London: T. Woodward and J. Peele, 1727).

Richardson, Samuel, *A Discourse of the Torments of Hell* (London, 1653).

Roberts, Francis, *Believers Evidences* (London: Pr. by T. R. and E. M. for George Calvert, 1649).

Roberts, T., *The Catachisme in Meter, for the Easier Learnyng, and Better Remembryng of Prinples [sic] of Faithe* (London: Pr. by J. Kingston for R. Walley, 1583).

Rogers, Thomas, *The Faith, Doctrin and Religion Professed in this Realme of England* (London: Pr. for William Hope, 1658).

Rogers, Timothy (of Essex), *Saving Belief* (London: Pr. by G. M. for Edward Brewster, 1644).

Ross, Alexander, *Pansebeia: or A View of all the Religions in the World*, 3rd edn (London: Pr. for John Saywell, 1658).

Rousseau, Jean Jacques, *The Social Contract and Discourses*, tr. G. D. H. Cole (London: Dent, 1968).

Russell, William, *Quakerism is Paganism* (London: Pr. for Francis Smith, 1674).

Rust, George, *A Discourse of the Use of Reason in Matters of Religion*, tr. by H. Hallywell (London: Pr. by Hen. Hills jun. for Walter Kettilby, 1683).

(attr.) *A Letter of Resolution Concerning Origen and the Chief of his Opinions* (London, 1661).

Scaliger, Joseph, *Opus de emendatione temporum*, 3rd edn (Geneva, 1629).

Schedius, Elias, *E. Schedii de Diis Germanie, sive veteri Germanorum, Gallorum, Brittanorum, Vandalorum religione, syngrammata quator* (Amsterdami: Apud L.

Alzcuririum, 1648).

Schleiermacher, F. D. E., *The Christian Faith*, ed. H. R. Mackintosh and J. S. Stewart (Edinburgh: T. & T. Clarke, 1976).

On Religion: Speeches to its Cultured Despisers, tr. from the 3rd edn by John Oman (New York: Harper Torchbooks, 1958).

Scriver, Matthew, *A Course of Divinity: Or, An Introduction to the Knowledge of the True Catholic Religion* (London: Pr. by Tho. Roycroft for Robert Clavil, 1674).

Selden, John, *Joannis Seldeni I.C. de dis Syris syntagmata II* (London: G. Stansbeius, 1617).

De Synedriis et Praefecturis Juridicis Veterum Ebraeorum (Amstelaedami, 1679).

Serarius, Nicholas, *Prolegomena Biblicae* (Moguntiaci, 1612).

Sextus Empiricus, tr. R. G. Bury, 3 vols., Loeb Classical Library (London: Heinemann, 1936).

Shaftesbury, Anthony Ashley Cooper, 3rd Earl of, *Characteristics of Men, Manners, Opinions, Times*, ed. J. M. Robertson (Indianapolis: Bobbs-Merrill, 1964).

Sheringham, Robert, *De Anglorum gentis origine disceptatio* (Cantabrigiae: Excudebat Joann. Hayes, impensis Edvardi Story, 1670).

Shuckford, Samuel, *The Sacred and Profane History of the World Connected*, vols. 1 and 2, 3rd edn (London: Pr. for J. and R. Tonson, 1743).

The Sacred and Profane History of the World Connected, vol. 3, 2nd edn (London: Pr. for H. Knaplock and J. and R. Tonson, 1740).

The Creation and Fall of Man, A Supplemental discourse to the Preface of Sacred and Profane History (London: Pr. for J. and R. Tonson and S. Draper, 1753).

Simon, Richard, *The Critical History of the Old Testament* (London: Pr. by Jacob Tonson, 1682).

A Critical History of the Religions and Customs of the Eastern Nations (London: Pr. by J. Hepinstall for Henry Fairthorn and John Kersley, 1685).

Histoire critique du Vieux Testament (Suivant la Copie, imprimée a Paris, 1680).

Sleidanus, Johannes, *The Key of History*, 4th edn (London: Pr. for William Shears, 1661).

Smith, Henry, *God's Arrow Against Atheists* (London: Pr. for John Wright and George Sawbridge, 1656).

Smith, John, *Select Discourses* (London: Pr. by J. Flesher for W. Morden, 1660).

South, Robert, *Twelve Sermons Preached Upon Several Occasions* (London: Pr. by J. H. for Thomas Bennet, 1692).

Spencer, John, *De legibus Hebraeorum ritualibus et earum rationibus* (London: Richardi Chiswell, 1685).

Stebbing, Henry, *A Defence of Dr. Clarke's Evidences of Natural and Revealed Religion* (London: Pr. for J. Pemberton, 1731).

A Discourse Concerning the Use and Advantages of the Gospel Revelation (London: J. Pemberton, 1730).

Steele, Richard, *A Scheme and Abstract of the Christian Religion* (London: Pr. for Samuel Sprint, 1684).

Stephens, William, *An Account of the Growth of Deism in England* (London: Pr. for the Author, 1696).

Sterry, Peter, *The Appearance of God to Man in the Gospel* (London, 1710).

Discourse of the Freedom of the Will (London: Pr. for J. Starkey, 1675).

The Rise, Race and Royalty of the Kingdom of God in the Soul of Man (London: Pr. for Thomas Cockerill, 1683).

Stewart, Dugald, *Collected Works of Dugald Stewart*, ed. William Hamilton, 11 vols. (Edinburgh: T. Constable, 1854–60).

Stillingfleet, Edward, *A Discourse concerning the Idolatry Practised in the Church of Rome*, 2nd edn (London: Pr. by Robert White for Henry Mortlock, 1672).

A Letter to a Deist (London: Pr. by W. G., 1677).

Origines Sacrae; or A Rational Account of the Grounds of the Christian Faith, 4th edn (London: Pr. by R. W. for Henry Mortlock, 1675).

A Rational Account of the Grounds of the Protestant Religion (London: Pr. by Rob. White for Henry Mortlock, 1665).

Stopford, Joshua, *Pagano-papismvs, or An Exact Parallel between Rome–Pagan and Rome–Christian in their Doctrines and Ceremonies* (London: Pr. by A Maxwell for R. Clavel, 1675).

Strachey, William, *Historie of Travell into Virginia Britania* (London: Hakluyt Society, 1953).

Swift, Jonathan, *Gulliver's Travels*, ed. John Chalker, (Ringwood: Penguin, 1985).

Mr C—ns's Discourse of Free-Thinking put into Plain English, by way of Abstract, for the Use of the Poor (London: Pr. for John Morphew, 1713).

The Prose Works of Jonathan Swift, D. D., ed. Temple Scott, 12 vols. (London: George Bell and Sons, 1909).

Synge, Edward, *A Gentleman's Religion*, 7th edn (London: T. Trye, 1752).

Taylor, Jeremy, *Ductor Dubitantium: or The Rule of Conscience in all her General Measures*, 2nd edn (London: Pr. by Roger Norton for Richard Roysten, 1671).

Temple, William, *An Essay upon the Ancient and Modern Learning*, ed. J. E. Spingarn, (Oxford: Clarendon, 1909).

Tenison, Thomas, *Of Idolatry* (London: Pr. for Francis Tyton, 1678).

Thorowgood, Thomas, *Iewes in America, or Probabilities that the Americans are of that Race* (London: Pr. by W. H. for Tho. Slater, 1650).

Tickell, John, *The Sum and Substance of Religion* (Exeter, 1665?).

Tindal, Matthew, *Christianity as Old as the Creation* (London, 1730).

Toland, John, *Adeisidaemon, sive titus Livius a Superstitione Vindicatus* (The Hague, 1709).

Amyntor, or A Defence of Milton's Life (London, 1699).

An Appeal to Honest People Against Wicked Priests (London: Pr. for Mrs Smith, 1710).

Apology for Mr Toland (London, 1697).

Christianity not Mysterious (London, 1696).

A Collection of Several Pieces of Mr John Toland, 2 vols. (London: J. Peele, 1726).

Letters to Serena (London: Pr. by B. Lintot, 1704).

Nazarenus, or, Jewish, Gentile and Mahometan Christianity (London: J. Brown, J. Roberts, & J. Brotherton, 1718).

Pantheisticon: or, The Form of Celebrating of the Socratic Society (London: Pr. by Sam. Paterson, 1751).

Reasons for Naturalizing the Jews in Great Britain and Ireland (London:

J. Roberts, 1714).

Tetradymus (London: Pr. by J. Brotherton & W. Meadows, 1720).

Vindicus Liberius: or, Mr Toland's Defence of Himself (London: 1702).

Tomlinson, William, *A VVord of Reproof to the Priests or Ministers* (London: Pr. for Giles Calvert, 1656).

Tostado, Alphonso, *Opera Omnia*, 23 tom. (Venetiis, 1596).

Tostado, Alphonso, *Opera Omnia*, 27 tom. (Venice, 1728).

Torneillus, Augustinus, *Annales Sacri et Profani* (Coloniae Agrippinae, 1622).

Trenchard, John, and Gordon, Thomas, *A Collection of Tracts*, 2 vols. (London: Pr. for F. Cogan, 1751).

Tuckney, Anthony, *None but Christ* (London: Pr. for J. Rothwell and S. Gellibrand, 1654).

Turnbull, George, *Christianity Neither False nor Useless, tho' not as Old as the Creation* (London: R. Willcock, 1732).

Turner, William (d. 1568), *The Huntyng and Fyndyng out of the Romish* Foxe (Basel: R. Potts, 1534).

Turner, William (1653–1701), *The History of all Religions in the World, from Creation down to this Present Time* (London: Pr. for John Dunton, 1695).

Twisse, William, *The Riches of God's Love unto the Vessels of Mercy Consistent with his Absolute Hatred or Reprobation* (Oxford: Pr. by L. L. & H. H. for Tho. Robinson, 1653).

Tyndale, William, *Expositions and Notes on Sundry Portions of the Holy Scriptures*, ed. H. Walter (London: Parker Society, 1849).

The Practyse of Prelates (London: Anthony Scoloker & Willyam Seres, 1548).

Urquhart, Thomas, *Logopandecteision, or An Introduction to the Universal Language* (London: Pr. by Giles Calvert and Richard Tomlins, 1653).

Ussher, James, *A Body of Divinitie, or the Summe and Substance of Christian Religion, Catechistically Propounded* (London: Pr. by M. F. for Tho. Downes and Geo. Badger, 1645).

Vanini, C., *De admirandis naturæ reginæ deæq. mortalium arcanis* (Paris, 1616).

Verstegan, Richard, *A Restitution of Decayed Intelligences in Antiquity* (London: Pr. for Sam. Mearne et al., 1673).

Vico, Giambattista, *The New Science of Giambattista Vico*, tr. from 3rd edn by T. G. Bergin and M. H. Frisch (Ithaca: Cornell University Press, 1948).

Voltaire, François Marie Arouet de, *Pièces Détachées* (Paris: P. Didot L'ainé, 1820).

Vossius, Gerhardus Joannes, *De Theologica Gentili, et physiologia Christiana sive de origine ac progressu idolatriæ* (Amsterdam, 1641).

W., T., *The Key of Knowledge Opening the Principles of Religion* (London: Pr. for Tho. Parkhurst, 1682).

Wake, William, *The Principles of the Christian Religion Explained* (London: Pr. for Richard Sare, 1699).

Walker, George, *The History of Creation* (London: Pr. for John Bartlett, 1641).

The Key of Saving Knowledge (London: Pr. by Tho. Bader, 1641).

Wall, John, *Christian Reconcilement* (Oxford, 1658).

Wallis, Ralf, *Room for the Cobler of Gloucester and his Wife, with Several Cartloads of Abominable Irregular, Pitiful Stinking Priests* (London: Pr. for the

Author, 1668).

Walton, Brian, *In Biblia Polyglotta Prolegomena*, 2 vols. (Cambridge: 1827).

Wanley, Nathaniel, *The Wonders of the Little World; or, A General History of Man* (London: Pr. for T. Basset et al., 1673).

Warburton, William, *The Divine Legation of Moses Demonstrated*, 2nd edn, 4 vols. (London: Pr. for Fletcher Gyles, 1738–65).

Ward, Seth, *Vindiciae Academiarum* (Oxford: Pr. by Leonard Lichfield for Thomas Robinson, 1654).

Ware, Sir James (ed.), *The Historie of Ireland* (Dublin: Pr. by the Societie of Stationers, 1663).

Warren, Edward, *No Praeexistence* (London: Pr. by T. R. for Samuel Thomson, 1667).

Waterland, Daniel, *Scripture Vindicated* (London: Pr. for W. Innys, 1730–1).

Webb, John, *An Historical Essay, Endeavoring a Probability that the Language of the Empire of China is the Primitive Language* (London: Pr. for Nath. Brook, 1669).

Webster, John, *Academiarum Examen* (London: Pr. for Giles Calvert, 1654).

Whichcote, Benjamin, *Moral and Religious Aphorisms* (London: Mathews and Marrot, 1930).

   Select Sermons of Dr. Whichcot (London: Pr. for Awnsham and John Churchill, 1698).

   The Works of the Learned Benjamin Whichcote, 4 vols. (Aberdeen: Pr. by J. Chalmers for Alexander Thomson, 1751).

Whiston, William, *A New Theory of the Earth* (London: Pr. by R. Roberts for Benj. Took, 1696).

Whitaker, William, *A Short Sum of Christianity* (London: Pr. for J. E., 1651).

Whitby, Daniel, *A Discourse concerning the Idolatry of the Church of Rome* (London: Pr. by Tho. Basset, and Ja. Magnes, 1674).

White, Jeremiah, *The Restoration of all Things* (London, 1712).

Whitelocke, Bulstrode, *An Essay of Transmigration, in Defence of Pythagoras* (London: Pr. by E. H. for Tho. Basset, 1692).

Wilkins, John, *A Discovery of the New World, or a Discourse Tending to Prove that there may be another Habitable World in the Moon*, 5th edn (London: Pr. for J. Gellibrand, 1684).

   An Essay towards a Real Character and a Philosophical Language (London: Pr. for Sa. Gellibrand & John Martin, 1668).

   Of the Principles and Duties of Natural Religion (London: Pr. by A. Maxwell for T. Basset, H. Brome, R. Chiswell, 1675).

Winstanley, Gerrard, *The Mysterie of God, Concerning the Whole Creation* ([London], 1648).

Woodhead, Abraham, *A Rational Account of the Doctrine of Roman Catholics* (London, 1673).

Woodward, John, *An Essay Towards a Natural History of the Earth ... with an Account of the Deluge; and of the effects that it had upon the Earth* (London: pr. by Richard Wilkin, 1695).

Woolston, Thomas, *Six Discourses on the Miracles of our Saviour* (London: Pr. for the Author, 1727–9).

Wotton, William, *A Discourse Concerning the Confusion of Languages at Babel* (London: Pr. for S. Austin & W. Bowyer, 1730).

Reflections of Ancient and Modern Learning (London: Pr. by J. Leake for Peter Buch, 1694).

Younge, Richard, *A Short and Sure Way to Grace and Salvation; Being a ... Tract, upon Three Fundamental Principles of Christian Religion, which few do indeed know, and yet hee who knows them not, cannot bee saved* (London, 1658).

The Cause and Cure of Ignorance, Error, Enmity, Atheisme, Prophanesse etc.; or, A Most Hopeful and Speedy Way to Salvation (London: Pr. by R. I. for N. Brook, 1648).

SECONDARY SOURCES

Allen, Donald Cameron, 'The Degeneration of Man and Renaissance Pessimism', *Studies in Philology*, 35 (1938), 202–27.

The Legend of Noah: Renaissance Rationalism in Art, Science and Letters (Urbana: University of Illinois Press, 1949).

'Some Theories of the Growth and Origin of Language in Milton's Age', *Philological Quarterly*, 28 (1949), 5–16.

Almond, Philip C., *The British Discovery of Buddhism* (Cambridge: Cambridge University Press, 1988).

Appleton, William W., *A Cycle of Cathay* (New York: Columbia University Press, 1951).

Atkins, Jonathan M., 'Calvinist Bishops, Church Unity, and the Rise of Arminianism', *Albion*, 18 (1986), 411–27.

Atkinson, Geoffrey, *The Extraordinary Voyage in French Literature before 1700* (New York: Burt Franklin, 1960).

The Extraordinary Voyage in French Literature from 1700 to 1720 (New York: Burt Franklin, 1960).

Auerbach, Erich, *Mimesis* (Princeton: Princeton University Press, 1968).

Axon, William, 'On the Mohammedan Gospel of Barnabas', *Journal of Theological Studies*, 3 (1902), 441–51.

Barth, Karl, *Christ and Adam* (London: Oliver and Boyd, 1956).

Church Dogmatics, 4 vols. (Edinburgh: T. & T. Clarke, 1936–69).

The Humanity of God (London: Collins, 1961).

Bedford, Ronald, *The Defence of Truth: Herbert of Cherbury and the Seventeenth Century* (Manchester: Manchester University Press, 1979).

Bendyshe, Thomas, 'The History of Anthropology', *Memoirs of the Anthropological Society of London*, 1 (1863–4), 355–60.

Berger, Peter, *The Sacred Canopy* (New York: Anchor Books, 1969).

Beskow, Per, *Strange Tales about Jesus* (Philadelphia: Fortress Press, 1983).

Bonhoeffer, Dietrich, *Letters and Papers from Prison* (New York: Macmillan, 1962).

Borst, Arno, *Der Turmbau von Babel; Geschichte der Meinungen über Ursprung und Vielfalt der Sprachen und Völker*, 6 vols. (Stuttgart: Anton Hiersemann, 1957–63).

Bredvold, Louis, 'Deism Before Lord Herbert', *Papers of the Michigan Academy of Science, Arts, and Letters*, 4 (1924), 431–42.

Brooke, John, 'Science and the Fortunes of Natural Theology: Some Historical Perspectives', *Zygon*, 24 (1989), 1–22.

Brown, T. S., 'Euhemerus and the Historians', *Harvard Theological Review*, 39 (1946), 259–74.

Bryson, Gladys, *Man and Society: The Scottish Inquiry of the Eighteenth Century* (Princeton: Princeton University Press, 1945).

Burtt, Edwin (ed.), *The English Philosophers from Bacon to Mill*, Modern Library Series (New York: Random House, 1967).

Bury, J. B., *The Idea of Progress* (London: Macmillan, 1920).

A History of Freedom of Thought, 2nd edn (London: Oxford University Press, 1952).

Bush, Douglas, *English Literature in the Earlier Seventeenth Century*, 2nd edn (Oxford: Clarendon, 1962).

Cassirer, Ernst, *Das Erkenntnisproblem in der Philosophie und Wissenschaft der neueren Zeit*, 3 vols. (Berlin: B. Cassirer, 1906–20).

The Individual and the Cosmos in Renaissance Philosophy, tr. Mario Domandi (New York: Barnes and Noble, 1963).

The Philosophy of the Enlightenment (Princeton: Princeton University Press, 1951).

The Platonic Renaissance in England, tr. James P. Pettigrove (London: Nelson, 1953).

Chung-Shu, Ch'ien, 'China in the English Literature of the Seventeenth Century', *Quarterly Bulletin of Chinese Bibliography*, 1 (1940), 351–84.

Clauss, Sidonie, 'John Wilkins' Essay Towards a Real Character', *Journal of the History of Ideas*, 43 (1982), 531–53.

Clebsch, William A., *England's Earliest Protestants* (New Haven: Yale University Press, 1964).

Cohen, J., 'On the Project of a Universal Character', *Mind*, 63 (1954), 49–63.

Colie, Rosalie Littel, *Light and Enlightenment: A Study of the Cambridge Platonists and Dutch Arminians* (Cambridge: Cambridge University Press, 1957).

Collingwood, R. J., *The Idea of History* (Oxford: Oxford University Press, 1946).

Commager, H. S., and Giordanetti, E. (eds.), *Was America a Mistake?* (New York: Harper, 1967).

Cope, Jackson I., '"The Cupri-Cosmits": Glanville on Latitudinarian Anti-Enthusiasm', *Huntington Library Quarterly*, 17 (1954), 269–86.

Joseph Glanville, Anglican Apologist (St Louis: Washington University Studies, 1956).

Cornford, F. M., *Greek Religious Thought from Homer to the Age of Alexander* (London: Dent, 1923).

Coudert, Allison, 'A Cambridge Platonist's Kabbalist Nightmare', *Journal of the History of Ideas*, 36 (1975), 633–52.

Crocker, L., *The Age of Enlightenment* (New York: Harper and Row, 1969).

Cumming, W. P., 'The Influence of Ovid's *Metamorphoses* on Spenser's "Mutability" Cantos', *Studies in Philology*, 28 (1931), 241–56.

Dagens, J., 'Hermetism et Cabale en France, de Lefèvre d'Etaples à Bossuet', *Revue de littérature comparée*, 35 (1961), 5–16.

Daniel, Norman, *Islam and the West: The Making of an Image* (Edinburgh: Edinburgh University Press, 1960).

Daniel, Stephen H., *John Toland, His Methods, Manners and Mind* (Kingston,

Montreal, McGill-Queens University Press, 1984).

Davies, Godfrey, 'Arminian versus Puritan in England, c. 1620–50', *Huntington Library Bulletin*, 5 (1934), 157–79.

Davis, Walter W., 'China, the Confucian Ideal, and the European Age of Enlightenment', *Journal of the History of Ideas*, 64 (1983), 523–48.

Dean, Leonard F., 'Bodin's *Methodus* in England', *Studies in Philology*, 39 (1942), 160–6.

DeMott, Benjamin, 'Comenius and the Real Character in England', *PMLA*, 70 (1955), 1068–81.

Drachmann, A. B., *Atheism in Pagan Antiquity* (London: Glynendal, 1922).

Dudley, Edward, and Novak, Maximillian E. (eds.), *The Wild Man Within: An Image in Western Thought from Renaissance to Romanticism* (Pittsburgh, Pa.: University of Pittsburgh Press, 1972).

Dupront, Alphonse, *Pierre-Daniel Huet et l'Exégèse comparatiste au XVIIe Siècle* (Paris, 1930).

Edwards, Paul (ed.), *The Encyclopedia of Philosophy*, 8 vols. (New York: Macmillan, 1972).

Elliot, Ralph W. V., 'Isaac Newton's "Of an Universall Language"', *Modern Language Review*, 52 (1957), 1–18.

Emery, Clark, 'John Wilkins' Universal Language', *Isis*, 38 (1947–8), 174–85.

Fink, Z. S., 'Milton and the Theory of Climatic Influence', *Modern Language Quarterly*, 2 (1941), 67–80.

Flew, Antony, *God and Philosophy* (New York: Dell, 1966).

Force, James, *William Whiston* (Cambridge: Cambridge University Press, 1985).

Fordice, C. J., and Knox, T. M., 'Jesus College Library', *Proceedings and Papers of the Oxford Bibliographic Society*, 5 (1936–7), 54–115.

Foucault, Michel, *The Order of Things* (London: Tavistock, 1974).

Frank, Joseph, 'John Milton's Move Toward Deism', *Journal of British Studies*, 1 (1961), 38–51.

Fraser, Russell, *The Language of Adam* (New York: Columbia University Press, 1977).

Frei, Hans, *The Eclipse of Biblical Narrative* (New Haven: Yale University Press, 1974).

Freudenthal, J., 'Beiträge zur Geschichte der englischen Philosophie', *Archiv für Geschichte der Philosophie*, 4 (1892), 450–77, 578–603.

Fuller, Thomas, *Church History of Britain*, 6 pt, (London: Pr. for J. Williams, 1655).

Funke, Otto, *Zum Weltsprachenproblem in England im 17, Jahrhundert, Anglistiche Forschungen*, Heft 69 (Heidelberg: C. Winter, 1929).

Gay, Peter, *The Enlightenment: An Interpretation*, 2 vols. (London: Weidenfeld and Nicolson, 1967).

Gilson, Etienne, *The History of Christian Philosophy in the Middle Ages* (New York: Random House, 1955).

Glacken, Clarence J., *Traces on the Rhodian Shore: Nature and Culture in Western Thought from Ancient Times to the End of the Eighteenth Century* (Berkeley: University of California Press, 1973).

Grafton, Anthony T., 'Joseph Scaliger and Historical Chronology: The Rise and Fall of a Discipline', *History and Theory*, 14 (1975), 156–85.

Greenlaw, Edwin, 'Spenser and Lucretius', *Studies in Philology*, 17 (1920), 439–64.

Gregory, Crauford, 'Notice concerning an Autograph Manuscript by Sir Isaac Newton', *Transactions of the Royal Society of Edinburgh*, 12 (1834), 64–76.

Harris, Victor, *All Coherence Gone* (London: Frank Cass, 1966).

Hastings, James (ed.), *Encyclopaedia of Religion and Ethics*, 12 vols. (Edinburgh: T. & T. Clark, 1908–21).

Hefelbower, S. G., 'Deism Historically Defined', *American Journal of Theology*, 24 (1920), 217–23.

The Relation of John Locke to English Deism (Chicago: University of Chicago Press, 1918).

Heimann, P. M., 'Voluntarism and Immanence: Conceptions of Nature in 18th Century Thought', *Journal of the History of Ideas*, 39 (1978), 271–83.

Heinemann, F. H., 'John Toland and the Age of Enlightenment', *Review of English Studies*, 20 (1944), 125–46.

'John Toland and the Age of Reason', *Archiv für Philosophie*, 4 (1950), 35–66.

'Prolegomena to a Toland Bibliography', *Notes and Queries*, 185 (1943), 182–6.

Hick, John, *God and the Universe of Faiths* (London: Fount, 1977).

(ed.), *Truth and Dialogue in the World Religions: Conflicting Truth Claims* (London: Sheldon Press, 1974).

Hodge, A. A., *The Confession of Faith* (London: Banner of Truth Trust, 1958).

Hodgen, Margaret, *Early Anthropology in the 16th and 17th Centuries* (Philadelphia: University of Pennsylvania Press, 1964).

Holsten, W., *Christentum und nichtchristlichen Religion nach der Auffassung Luthers* (Güttersloh: Bertelsmann, 1932).

Hutcheson, Harold R., 'Lord Herbert and the Deists', *Journal of Philosophy*, 43 (1946), 219–21.

Jacob, Margaret C., *The Newtonians and the English Revolution, 1689–1720* (Hassocks, Harvester Press, 1976).

The Radical Enlightenment: Pantheists, Freemasons and Republicans (London: George Allen and Unwin, 1981).

James, M. R., *The Apocryphal New Testament* (Oxford: Clarendon, 1972).

Johnson, James, 'Chronological Writing: Its Concepts and Development', *History and Theory*, 2 (1962), 124–45.

Jones, Richard Foster, *Ancients and Moderns: A Study of the Background of the Battle of the Books*, 2nd edn (Gloucester, Mass.: Peter Smith, 1961).

'Science and Language in England of the Mid-Seventeenth Century', *Journal of English and Germanic Philology*, 31 (1932), 315–31.

Jordan, Louis, *Comparative Religion: its Genesis and Growth* (Edinburgh: T. and T. Clark, 1905).

Jordanova, L. J., *Lamarck* (Oxford: Oxford University Press, 1984).

Klempt, A., *Die Säkularisierung der universalhistorischen Auffassung: zum Wandel des Geschichtsdenken im 16, und 17 Jahrhundert* (Göttingen: Musterschmidt Verlag, 1960).

Knowlson, James, *Universal Language Schemes in England and France, 1600–1800* (Toronto: University of Toronto Press, 1975).

Kümmel, Werner, *The New Testament: The History of the Investigation of Its Problems,* tr. S. McLean Gilmore and Howard Kee (London: SCM Press Ltd., 1973).

La Boullaye, H. Pinard de, *L'Etude Compareé des Religions* (Paris: Gabriel Beauchesne, 1922).

Lach, Donald F., 'Leibniz and China', *Journal of the History of Ideas*, 6 (1945), 436–55.

Lechler, Gotthard V., *Geschichte des Englischen Deismus* (Stuttgart: J. G. Cotta, 1841).

Livingstone, David N., 'Preadamites: The History of an Idea from Heresy to Orthodoxy', *Scottish Journal of Theology*, 40 (1987), 41–66.

Lovejoy, Arthur O., *The Great Chain of Being* (Cambridge, Mass.: Harvard University Press, 1936).

Manuel, Frank E., *The Changing of the Gods* (London: University Press of New England, 1983).

   The Eighteenth Century Confronts the Gods (Cambridge, Mass.: Harvard University Press, 1959).

   Isaac Newton, Historian (Cambridge, Mass.: Harvard University Press, 1963).

   The Religion of Isaac Newton (Oxford: Clarendon Press, 1974).

Marshall, P. J. (ed.), *The British Discovery of Hinduism in the Eighteenth Century* (Cambridge: Cambridge University Press, 1970).

Marshall, P. J., and Williams, Glyndwr, *The Great Map of Mankind* (Melbourne, J. M. Dent and Sons, 1982).

Massa, Daniel, 'Giordano Bruno's Ideas in Seventeenth-Century England', *Journal of the History of Ideas*, 38 (1977), 227–42.

Mayo, C. H., 'The Social Status of the Clergy in the Seventeenth and Eighteenth Centuries', *English Historical Review*, 37 (1922), 258–66.

McGuire, J. E., and Rattansi, P. M., 'Newton and the "Pipes of Pan"', *Notes and Records of the Royal Society of London*, 21 (1966), 108–43.

Merton, Robert, 'Science, Technology and Society in Seventeenth-Century England', *Osiris*, 4 (1938), 414–38.

Morice, G. P. (ed.), *David Hume: Bicentenary Papers* (Edinburgh: Edinburgh University Press, 1977).

Muirhead, John H., *The Platonic Tradition in Anglo-Saxon Philosophy* (Cambridge: Cambridge University Press, 1931).

Müller, F. Max, *Chips from a German Workshop*, 4 vols. (London: Longmans, Green, and Co., 1867–75).

   Introduction to the Science of Religion (London: Longmans, Green, and Co., 1909).

   Lectures on the Science of Language, 9th edn, 2 vols. (London: Longmans, Green, and Co., 1877).

Niklaus, Robert, *A Literary History of France: The Eighteenth Century* (New York: Barnes and Noble, 1970).

Nisbet, Robert A., *Social Change and History: Aspects of the Western Theory of Development* (London: Oxford University Press, 1969).

Otto, Rudolf, *The Idea of the Holy*, tr. John W. Harvey, 2nd edn (London: Oxford University Press, 1950).

Owen, Alfred A., 'Polygamy and Deism', *The Journal of English and Germanic Philology*, 48 (1949), 343–60.

Pailin, David A., *Attitudes to Other Religions: Comparative Religion in Seventeenth- and Eighteenth-Century Britain* (Manchester: Manchester University Press, 1984).

Patrides, C. A., '"The Beast with many Heads": Renaissance views on the Multitude', *Shakespeare Quarterly*, 16 (1965), 241–6.

(ed.), *The Cambridge Platonists* (London; Edward Arnold, 1969).

'The Salvation of Satan', *Journal of the History of Ideas*, 28 (1967), 468–78.

Pauley, W. C. de, *The Candle of the Lord: Studies on the Cambridge Platonists* (London: SPCK, 1937).

Pinot, Virgile, *La Chine et la Formation de l'Esprit Philosophique en France, 1640–1740* (Genève: Slatkine Reprints, 1971).

Pinto, Vivian de Sola (the Elder), *Peter Sterry, Platonist and Puritan, 1613–1672* (Cambridge: Cambridge University Press, 1934).

Pollard, A. W., and Redgrave, G. R., *A Short Title Catalogue of Books Printed in England, Scotland and Ireland and of English Books Printed Abroad, 1475–1640*, 2nd edn, 2 vols. (London: The Bibliographic Society, 1986).

Popkin, R. H., *Isaac La Peyrère: His Life, Work, and Influence* (Leiden: E. J. Brill, 1987).

'Pre-Adamism in 19th Century American Thought', *Philosophia*, 8 (1978), 205–39.

Popper, Karl, *The Open Society and its Enemies*, 5th edn, 2 vols. (London: Routledge and Kegan Paul, 1966).

Porter, Roy, and Teich, Mikuás (eds.), *The Enlightenment in National Context* (Cambridge: Cambridge University Press, 1981).

Powicke, Frederick, *The Cambridge Platonists: A Study* (Hildesheim: George Olms Verlag, 1970).

Rabb, T., and Seigel, J. (eds.), *Action and Conviction in Early Modern Europe* (Princeton: Princeton University Press, 1969).

Ragg, Lonsdale (ed. and tr.), *The Gospel of Barnabas* (Oxford: Clarendon, 1907).

'The Mohammedan Gospel of Barnabas', *Journal of Theological Studies*, 6 (1909), 423–33.

Renan, Ernest, *Averoès et l'Averoisme* (Paris: Calman-Levy, 1903).

Reventlow, Henning Graf von, *The Authority of the Bible and the Rise of the Modern World*, tr. John Bowden (Philadelphia: Fortress Press, 1985).

Ritter, J. (ed.), *Historisches Wörterbuch der Philosophie* (Basel: Schwabe & Co., 1971–).

Roberts, James D. Senr., *From Puritanism to Platonism in Seventeenth-Century England* (The Hague: Martinus Nijhoff, 1968).

Rossi, Mario M., *La Vita, le opere, i tempi di Edoardo Herbert di Chirbury*, 3 vols. (Florence: G. C. Sansoni, 1947).

Rowbotham, Arnold H., 'The Jesuit Figurists and Eighteenth-Century Religious Thought', *Journal of the History of Ideas*, 17 (1956), 471–85.

Rupp, Gordon, *Religion in England* (Oxford: Clarendon Press, 1986).

Russell, C. (ed.), *The Origins of the English Civil War* (London: Macmillan, 1973).

Said, Edward W., *Orientalism* (London, Routledge and Kegan Paul, 1978).

Sailor, Danton B., 'Cudworth and Descartes', *Journal of the History of Ideas*, 23 (1962), 133–40.

Sarton, George, *A History of Science*, 2 vols. (Cambridge, Mass.: Harvard University Press, 1959).

Saveson, J. E., 'Descartes' Influence on John Smith', *Journal of the History of Ideas*, 20 (1959), 258–63.

'Differing Reactions to Descartes among the Cambridge Platonists', *Journal of the History of Ideas*, 21 (1960), 560–7.

Schaff, Philip, *The Creeds of Christendom*, 4th edn, 3 vols. (New York: Harper, 1919).

Schmidt, Charles B., 'Perennial Philosophy: from Agostino Steuco to Leibniz', *Journal of the History of Ideas*, 27 (1966), 505–32.

Seebohm, Frederick, *The Oxford Reformers* (London: Dent, 1914).

Sharpe, Eric, *Comparative Religion: A History* (London: Duckworth, 1975).

Shou-yi, Ch'en, 'John Webb, a Forgotten Page in the Early History of Sinology in Europe', *Chinese Social and Political Science Review*, 19 (1935), 295–330.

Smith, Wilfred Cantwell, *The Meaning and End of Religion* (London: SPCK, 1978).

Sorley, W. R., 'The Philosophy of Herbert of Cherbury', *Mind*, 3 (1894), 491–508.

Staudenbaur, C. A., 'Platonism, Theosophy and Immaterialism: Recent Views of the Cambridge Platonists', *Journal of the History of Ideas*, 35 (1974), 157–69.

Stein, Arnold, 'Donne's Obscurity and the Elizabethan Tradition', *Journal of English Literary History*, 13 (1946), 98–118.

Stephen, Leslie, *History of English Thought in the Eighteenth Century*, 3rd edn, 2 vols. (New York: Peter Smith, 1949).

Stephen, Leslie and Lee, Sydney (eds.), *Dictionary of National Biography*, 21 vols. and supp. (London: Oxford University Press, 1917–).

Stromberg, R. N., 'History in the Eighteenth Century', *Journal of the History of Ideas*, 12 (1951) 295–304.

Strowski, F., *Historie du sentiment Religieux en France au XVIIe Siècle, Pascal et son Temps* (Paris: Plon-Nourrit, 1907).

Sullivan, Robert E., *John Toland and the Deist Controversy* (Cambridge, Mass.: Harvard University Press, 1982).

Taylor, George C., *Milton's Use of Du Bartas* (Cambridge, Mass.: Harvard University Press, 1934).

Teggart, F. J., *The Ideas of Progress* (Berkeley: University of California Press, 1929).

Theory of History (New Haven: Yale University Press, 1925).

Temkin, Oswei, *The Falling Sickness* (Baltimore: Johns Hopkins University Press, 1971).

Tooley, Marian J., 'Bodin and the Medieval Theory of Climate', *Speculum*, 28 (1953), 64–83.

Tulloch, John, *Rational Theology and Christian Philosophy in England in the Seventeenth Century*, 2nd edn 2 vols. (Edinburgh: Blackwood, 1874).

Tyacke, Nicholas, and White, Peter, 'Debate: The Rise of Arminianism Reconsidered', *Past and Present*, 115 (1987), 201–29.

Wach, Joachim, *The Sociology of Religion* (Chicago: University of Chicago Press, 1962).

Wade, I. O., *The Clandestine Organization and the Diffusion of Philosophical Ideas in France from 1700–1750* (New York: Octagon, 1967).

Walker, Daniel Pickering, *The Ancient Theology: Studies in Christian Platonism from 15th–18th Century* (Ithaca: Cornell University Press, 1972).

The Decline of Hell (London: Routledge and Kegan Paul, 1964).

'Orpheus the Theologian and Renaissance Platonists', *Journal of the Warburg and Courtauld Institutes*, 16 (1953), 100–20.

'The *prisca theologia* in France', *Journal of the Warburg and Courtauld Institutes*, 17 (1954), 204–59.

Weber, Max, *The Sociology of Religion*, tr. Ephraim Fischoff (Boston: Beacon Press, 1964).

Webster, Charles (ed.), *The Intellectual Revolution of the Seventeenth Century* (London: Routledge and Kegan Paul, 1974).

Weiner, M., 'John Toland and Judaism', *Hebrew Union College Annual*, 16 (1941), 215–42.

Weld, Charles Richard, *A History of the Royal Society*, 2 vols. (London: J. W. Parker, 1848).

Welsh, Clement W., 'A Note on the Meaning of "Deism"', *Anglican Theological Review*, 38 (1956), 160–5.

Willey, Basil, *The Eighteenth Century Background: Studies on the Idea of Nature in the Thought of the Period* (Ringwood: Penguin, 1967).

The Seventeenth Century Background: Studies in the Thought of the Age in Relation to Poetry and Religion (London: Chatto and Windus, 1953).

Williamson, George, 'Mutability, Decay, and Seventeenth-Century Melancholy', *Journal of English Literary History*, 2 (1935), 121–50.

Wing, Donald, *A Short-Title Catalogue of Books Printed in England, Scotland, Ireland, Wales, and British America and of English Books Printed in Other Countries, 1641–1700*, 2nd edn, 3 vols. (New York: Modern Language Association of America, 1972–).

Winnett, A. R., 'Were the Deists "Deists"?', *Church Quarterly Review*, 161 (1960), 70–7.

Yates, Francis Amelia, *Giordano Bruno and the Hermetic Tradition* (Chicago: University of Chicago Press, 1964).

The Occult Philosophy in the Elizabethan Age (London: Routledge and Kegan Paul, 1979).

The Rosicrucian Enlightenment (London: Routledge and Kegan Paul, 1972).

Zagorin, Perez, (ed.), *Culture and Politics From Puritanism to the Enlightenment* (Berkeley: University of California Press, 1980).

Zeller, Eduard, *A History of Greek Philosophy*, tr. S. F. Alleyne, 2 vols. (London: Longmans, 1881).

Stoics, Epicureans and Sceptics, tr. Oswald Reichel (London: Longmans, 1892).

INDEX